MW00595291

BREAKING BABE RUTH

BREAKING BABE RUTH

Baseball's Campaign Against Its Biggest Star

Edmund F. Wehrle

UNIVERSITY OF MISSOURI PRESS

Columbia

Library of Congress Cataloging-in-Publication Data

Names: Wehrle, Edmund F., 1964- author.
Title: Breaking Babe Ruth : baseball's campaign against its biggest star / by
  Edmund F. Wehrle.
Description: Columbia : University of Missouri, 2018. | Series: Sports and
  American culture | Includes bibliographical references and index. |
  Identifiers: LCCN 2017052792 (print) | LCCN 2017060404 (ebook) | ISBN
  9780826274090 (e-book) | ISBN 9780826221605 (hardback : alk. paper)
Subjects: LCSH: Ruth, Babe, 1895-1948. | Baseball--United
  States--History--20th century. | Major League Baseball
  (Organization)--History--20th century. | Baseball players--United
  States--Biography. | BISAC: SPORTS & RECREATION / Baseball / History.
Classification: LCC GV865.R8 (ebook) | LCC GV865.R8 W38 2018 (print) | DDC
  796.357092 [B] --dc23
LC record available at https://lccn.loc.gov/2017052792

♾™ This paper meets the requirements of the
American National Standard for Permanence of Paper
for Printed Library Materials, Z39.48, 1984.

Typefaces: Frutiger and Minion

Chapter 2 contains a revised version of "Frenzy: Babe Ruth's Much Ballyhooed Premier
Season with the New York Yankees," *NINE: A Journal of Baseball History and Culture*
23, no. 2, (Spring 2015): 68–83, reprinted with permission of the University of Nebraska
Press.

Sports and American Culture

Adam Criblez, Series Editor

This series explores the cultural dynamic between competitive athletics and society, the many ways in which sports shape the lives of Americans, in the United States and Latin America, from a historical and contemporary perspective. While international in scope, the series includes titles of regional interest to Missouri and the Midwest. Topics in the series range from studies of a single game, event, or season to histories of teams and programs, as well as biographical narratives of athletes, coaches, owners, journalists, and broadcasters.

For my babes, Annabel and Josephina.

CONTENTS

ACKNOWLEDGMENTS

A PROJECT THIS SIZE and scope inescapably becomes something of a team effort, to use the inevitable sports metaphor. I owe much to the people and institutions that made up my team. Eastern Illinois University (EIU), where I have taught for nearly two decades, provided valuable institutional support, particularly in the form of a summer research grant and reassigned time. I relied heavily on the outstanding staff at EIU's Booth Library. Jana Aydt deserves special thanks for her resourcefulness in procuring materials for me from across the country. My colleagues in the History Department also provided valuable support. Special thanks to Lynne Curry, Martin Hardeman, and Debra Reid (now at the Henry Ford Museum), all of whom offered encouragement and trenchant insights.

This study also owes a debt to the fine librarians and staff at the National Baseball Library in Cooperstown, New York, at the Library of Congress's Manuscript Division and Newspaper Reading Room, and at the Milstein Microform Reading Room at the New York Public Library. As a scholar teaching a relatively heavy load at a rural state university in the Midwest, I am endlessly grateful for the growing collection of digitized newspapers and materials increasingly available online. The Brooklyn Public Library's digitized archive of the *Brooklyn Daily Eagle*, the Library of Congress's "Chronicling America" digitized newspaper collection, and Google News Archives (although more limited in its search capacities) were all godsends, allowing me to conduct research from my office between classes.

In the final stages of this project, Andrew J. Davidson, the editor in chief at the University of Missouri Press, proved a model of patience, wise counsel, and professionalism. He skillfully steered my manuscript to thoughtful readers and then expedited its publication. Mary Conley, assistant acquisitions editor at UMP, also provided prompt and valued help as this project neared completion. Dr. Adam Criblez, editor of the UMP's Sports and American Culture Series, carefully reviewed my manuscript and provided insightful commentary. My thanks as well to Amy Maddox, who patiently provided invaluable copyediting as the manuscript neared completion. Finally my wife, Jacqueline Wehrle, a professional editor, gave freely of her valuable time to review and comment on chapters, correct footnotes, and polish and proof the final manuscript. Words can never express my gratitude to her.

Suffice it to say, this book could not have been written without my winning team. Responsibility for its shortcomings and limitations, however, falls squarely on my own shoulders.

BREAKING BABE RUTH

INTRODUCTION

In 1959, THE eminent sports journalist Red Smith informed his readers how an entire class of young students rose up against a teacher who dared assert Babe Ruth had the "mentality of an eight-year-old." To the youngsters, Ruth was an inspiration and an icon. The very notion that he was anything less outraged the class. The teacher may have been "misinformed, though in that she isn't alone," explained Smith. Many, the columnist acknowledged, remember Ruth as something of a "dolt" off the baseball diamond. True, Ruth was "unschooled, unpolished, profane, widely uninformed, rowdy . . . but he was in no sense stupid." Smith aimed to defend Ruth, but a reader could hardly be blamed for finding the column something less than a vigorous defense of Ruth's intellect.[1]

Even today, more than a century after his birth, impressions of Babe Ruth, baseball's greatest hitter and biggest personality, remain perplexingly bifurcated. None doubt his prowess as an athlete, in particular his amazing capacity to hit home runs. Mention of Ruth immediately conjures up jumpy black-and-white film footage of a pudgy powerhouse launching stratospheric home runs, then clicking around the bases on spindly legs. His warm smile and memorable moon face remain instilled in American iconography. Yet we also have inherited other, less flattering impressions. Most recall a player who challenged authority, defied Prohibition, reveled with abandon, and womanized recklessly. If Americans went on a postwar bender during the 1920s, Ruth, in popular memory, hosted the festivities. The gluttonous side of Ruth persists very much as part of our public memory. The Babe might not quite have possessed a dark side, but, as his nickname suggests, his maturity remains an open question.

This study seeks to place Ruth's career in full context. It situates his story within the larger framework of baseball, sports, culture, and society during Ruth's reign. Popular impressions of the baseball hero, I argue, hardly emerged organically. Rather, they were consciously constructed and manipulated by the baseball establishment—in particular, club owners, league officials, and sportswriters—who viewed Ruth simultaneously as a savior and an existential threat. The Babe excited and inspired fans as no other baseball figure had, yet his independent streak and outspokenness gravely troubled elites at the helm of professional baseball. It was essential that the peril Ruth posed be checked, while his potential be exploited. Hence the split image of Ruth has passed down to us even today. For baseball writers, club owners, and league officials, the retort to the Ruthian dilemma was to contain, to infantilize, and ultimately to break the superstar player.

On one hand, Ruth became the saintly emissary to the nation's children, reflecting the innocence and joy of youth. As sportswriter Paul Gallico wrote, "They call him the Babe, and Babe he is."[2] Ruth's large, round visage and personal kindheartedness reinforced an aura of childlike virtue. This persona resonated deeply with the public. Ruth's undeniable charisma—that unquantifiable magnetic substance found in a select few—was unparalleled in his time. Sportswriters, the arbiters of a large chunk of popular culture in the 1920s, were quick to build on the magnetism and celebrate the hero's association with the hopeful innocence of youth.

On the other hand, when Ruth dared defy the authority of baseball's leadership, those same images of youthfulness quickly were turned against him. He became an unruly boy, unable or unwilling to control his impulses. He was a man-child, ruled by base passions and whims (a notion supported by his increasing girth over the course of his career). Rumors, sometimes spread by Yankee management, of Ruth's off-field escapades and vice reinforced the adolescent rebel image. Throughout his professional life, Ruth remained trapped by this infantilization.

This study approaches stories of Ruth's immoderation—whether it be eating, drinking, partying, or sex—with a skeptical eye. Concrete proof of malfeasance is scarce. Where it does exist, it is largely anecdotal and confined mostly to his early career. Of course, Ruth's "bad boy" reputation worked in favor of league and team officials. Rumors about the Babe's extravagant spending, for instance, clearly hurt him in contract negotiations. Resisting Ruth's demands for salary increases, Yankee management appeared less as cheapskates than as adults uneasy about enabling a profligate spender.

One wonders also how much stories of Ruthian excess simply played to audiences eager for sensationalism. Our sinners tend to be more engaging than our saints. One might also weigh such accounts against the more abundant and better documented stories about Ruth's personal warmth and generosity. Indeed, throughout his life, Ruth exhibited a consistent humanitarianism that went well beyond anything doctored up by public relations agents. His munificence is all the more remarkable considering the stark deprivation that defined his youth.

This is not to absolve Ruth of all culpability for poor choices, even if his foibles and troubles have been exaggerated. By his own acknowledgment, chaos ruled his early life into his twenties. Yet few would deny that he was, as he himself put it, "a victim of circumstances." Ruth grew up in poverty, essentially as an abandoned child. The challenge of severe privation followed abruptly by the temptations of great wealth bedeviled Ruth. "I had a rotten start and it took me a long time to get my bearings," he explained after his retirement from baseball, in words that perhaps sum up his life's journey.[3] Ruth was hardly alone, then or today, as a young man succumbing to the enticements associated with sudden enrichment. His stint as a playboy sounds remarkably familiar to anyone vaguely aware of the tribulations of the celebrity world. In Ruth's case, however, revelations of a bad Babe stirred (and still stir) a sense of hypocrisy, since they compete with the good and pure Babe, patron saint of children. Even allowing for a playboy period about which little evidence exists and which seems rather tame compared to present-day scandalous behavior, Ruth, by virtually all accounts, entered a period of real maturity later in his career. He married and transformed into something of a homebody. That he gained control of a life veering in so many dangerous directions seems a credit to his force of character.

Ruth's struggle to order his world remarkably parallels baseball's search for stability in the early twentieth century. As the first chapter of this study explores, a range of debilitating perils dogged America's pastime as it grew toward maturity and became institutionalized as a high-revenue sport with national appeal. In particular, "rowdyism" (violence on the field and in the stands), gambling, and labor tensions imperiled the plans of baseball entrepreneurs to stabilize and expand the game. During World War I and its immediate aftermath, baseball's liabilities multiplied, comingled, and almost derailed the game. When America went to war in 1917, key players left to join the military, while others defected to join shipbuilder leagues. Rowdyism increased, and joint player action protesting postseason bonuses almost upended the 1918 World Series. Immediately after the war, a group of players conspired with underworld figures to "throw" the 1919 World Series.

Babe Ruth, then an increasingly popular pitcher with the Boston Red Sox, had immediate ties to several of the unsettling developments. He openly supported efforts to unionize players, "held out" against contracts he deemed unfair, and brazenly challenged the authority of Red Sox management. His quick temper landed him in several confrontations with umpires. Ruth played in Boston, ground central of baseball's gambling problem, and in 1919 he joined a postseason barnstorming tour led by Buck Weaver, later revealed as one of the "Black Sox" conspirators. He was also no stranger to racetracks around the country. No evidence, however, exists that Ruth ever gambled on baseball, and his relationship with Weaver and the other Black Sox appears limited. All the same, he shared with his contemporaries the same general frustrations and grievances about a labor system that seemed hopelessly skewed against players.

To a group of reformers eager to rid the game of nefarious influences, Ruth glowed with promise, but he was also a problem child. A loose assemblage of reform-minded league officials, team owners, sportswriters, and others had worked since the early twentieth century to order what often appeared a game careening toward anarchy. Reformers envisioned a game appealing to middle-class standards of decorum: free of fighting, foul language, excessive drinking, gambling, or other questionable influences. Likewise, the reformers, many of them club owners, sought absolute control over their workforce. At a time when labor unrest and working-class radicalism stirred throughout the country, baseball magnates resisted unionization and strove to preserve an arcane and repressive labor system built around the "reserve clause." This contractual language essentially locked players to their teams, preventing them from pursuing better deals with other perspective clubs.

Chief among the reformers was Ban Johnson, who founded the American League (AL) with an eye toward curbing the umpire abuse and general rowdyism that so afflicted baseball. Johnson envisaged a game that might appeal as much to the refined tastes of women as to men. Other reformers included Colonel Jacob Ruppert and Colonel Tillinghast L'Hommedieu "T. L." Huston, wealthy co-owners of the New York Yankees, a team they purchased in 1917. The pair pictured a future of star players drawing huge crowds to New York sporting events. Briefly they allied with Johnson. Soon, however, they and other owners sought greater autonomy and broke ties with

Johnson. This and the Black Sox gambling scandal led to the installation of Judge Kenesaw Mountain Landis—a federal judge with a reputation for antiradicalism and middle-class moralism—as baseball's commissioner, with near complete powers. The intimidating and intense Edward Barrow, Ruth's manager in Boston and later the Yankees' business manager, also played an important supporting role for the reformers, especially in his determination to introduce more professional management of teams and to preserve managerial authority over players.

Sportswriters served as essential fieldworkers in the cause of reforming the national game. By the second decade of the twentieth century, baseball writing was attracting an increasingly professional and ambitious class of journalists. No longer were sportswriters viewed immediately as the dregs of the nation's newsrooms. Still, building broad interest in sports remained a priority. Writers relentlessly hyped big events and big personalities. Like baseball owners and league officials, sportswriters craved clean sports, above reproach and appealing to the widest possible audiences. Yet they also sought to infuse sports with drama and occasional controversy to maintain interest. More so than other journalists, they "made" their news by "puffing" favored events and sports figures. Additionally, in many ways sportswriters were beholden to the teams or events they covered. Not only did baseball clubs provide access to players and coaches (for interviews, etc.), but teams also covered travel expenses for writers (most often on luxury trains, in first-class hotels, and at top restaurants). Whatever dedication to "pure" journalism might have driven sportswriters of the 1920s and 1930s, they clearly served other masters as well.

Babe Ruth often bristled at the coverage he received. Invariably, newspaper accounts sided with baseball's ownership class, especially when Ruth challenged the authority of that class. Over time Ruth recognized that the press had essentially aligned itself with the powers that be, even when the public seemed to side with Ruth. In any test of wills, sportswriters, almost uniformly, would align against him.

Still, the press spent significant time building up Ruth, a player of unprecedented ability and popularity. Early on, the baseball establishment realized Ruth's power to take the game to a new level, to produce thrills, to draw millions of new fans to games, and—most importantly—to generate profits. To purists, Ruth's home-run bashing smacked of a coarse cheapening of the game, a sad surrendering of a more cerebral approach to baseball. Yet undeniably, most fans adored his power hitting and adored Ruth the man (even if it meant loving to hate him sometimes). Grasping his great potential, the reformers fanned the flames of the rise of Ruth.

While a new game built around power hitting might be tolerable, especially if offset by great profits, a fundamental challenge to baseball's leadership class could not be allowed. The national game, reformers believed, must progress and not return to the chaos of ascending rival leagues, wanton violence, and collective action by players. Ruth could not be allowed to become larger than the game itself. As the Babe rose to superstardom in the early 1920s, an undercurrent of nervousness pulsed through major league baseball. If a player so dominant and so alluring was to openly espouse unionization (and Ruth had supported such efforts) or break away and launch his own league, baseball might collapse into chaos. Likewise, Ruth, while essentially a good-hearted man, clearly had a temper and a love of parties and nightlife. With Ruth's ascent, the specter of scandal and rebellion hovered ominously over baseball's reformers.

Ruth's incredible promise became fully clear in his inaugural season with the New York Yankees in 1920, a year that had a definite best-of-times/worst-of-times feel. Hysteria surrounded Ruth throughout the season, and fans in greater numbers than ever flocked to ballparks. At the same time, baseball suffered the horror of Ray Chapman's killing when the Cleveland Indians shortstop was struck by a pitch. Then, at season's end, a nightmare story hit newspapers: eight Chicago White Sox players stood accused of conspiring to "throw" the 1919 World Series. Without the Babe as an alluring diversion, baseball might have been irreparably harmed. Instead, fans looked beyond the scandals and focused on the commanding Ruth. Interestingly, Ruth's public image remained remarkably fluid during his breakthrough year in 1920. Sportswriters experimented with depicting Ruth in numerous ways. He became a sort of "bridging figure," one transcending the great divides of the times.

In the years that followed, however, sportswriters increasingly emphasized Ruth's childlike nature and character. On one hand, this helped associate baseball with youth and innocence. On the other hand, the Babe remained infantilized and limited. In 1922, when Ruth defied the new commissioner of baseball and led an unauthorized postseason barnstorming tour, sportswriters and others branded him as an enfant terrible, determined to advance his own good above that of his sport. Subsequent clashes with umpires and authority figures that year threatened Ruth's career. With the help of a business agent, Ruth managed a high-profile comeback in 1923, but his career nearly derailed again in 1925. Ruth's timing that year could not have been worse. He launched an aggressive attack on Yankees manager Miller Huggins at the same time he suffered a serious intestinal illness, causing him to miss significant portions of the season. When he returned to active play, Huggins, with the support of sportswriters and the Yankees owner, sprang a surprise, coordinated attack on Ruth. To the press, the clash constituted a case of an out-of-control adolescent earning his comeuppance. By the end of the season, Ruth, as he did in 1922, assumed full blame for his and his team's struggles that year. Meanwhile, he planned for another comeback.

After 1925, Ruth managed to find a new equilibrium in both his professional and personal lives. On the playing field, he achieved impressive new heights. During the late 1920s and early 1930s, Ruth's salary clashes with Yankees owner Jacob Ruppert became the subject of much public attention and discussion. In his tense exchanges with Ruppert, Ruth often challenged the fairness of a labor system that treated players as chattel, literally selling them from one team to another and providing them no option of seeking employment on other teams. Even at the peak of his powers, the press dismissed Ruth as an intellectually limited man who never grew up. As his career wound down, Ruth increasingly aspired to manage in the major leagues. It was a role he hoped would keep him in the game he loved and belie the frequent assaults on his intellect. Yankees team administrators, however, were determined never to give him an opportunity. Further, Ruppert and Barrow moved to block managing prospects for Ruth on other teams. The Yankees hero drove baseball to new heights, but he remained too much of a rebel to be trusted.

Breaking Babe, in fact, seemed essential to the larger project of ordering baseball. By the time of Ruth's retirement, baseball had fundamentally transformed and stabilized itself. The "disorder" of labor disputes, rowdyism, and gambling appeared confined to the past. The future looked infinitely brighter, despite the challenges of the Great Depression in the 1930s. Ruth had paved the way for change, in many ways singlehandedly creating a prosperous wave that lifted all boats. The price he paid for his outspokenness and independence also set up the new era. After the Babe's ignominious departure from baseball following a painful half season with the Boston Braves in 1935, baseball banked increasingly on quieter, more cooperative stars such as, in the case of the Yankees, Lou Gehrig and Joe DiMaggio. Both players focused more on team play, and while both pushed at times for pay increases, neither tested the fundamentals of baseball's labor system.

Management essentially beat back the Ruthian challenge. Over and over again, Ruth challenged the baseball establishment only to capitulate when he found himself alone and facing overwhelming odds. The breaking of Babe Ruth sent an unmistakable message to the Gehrigs, DiMaggios, and Mantles who would follow.

Among the most appealing aspects of the Ruth myth is his rise from "orphan" to wealthy national hero. Ruth's real life rags-to-riches story bolsters the democratic ideals so cherished in America. Few would deny that Ruth's ascent affirms America as the land of opportunity. Still, a closer study of his career suggests the limits of such notions. Babe Ruth obtained great wealth, but he generated much greater wealth for others, and his personal fortune never competed with those in the top echelon of America's wealthy. His lack of education, refinement, and sophistication haunted him throughout his career. He remained always an outsider from the halls of baseball's power. In a nation that celebrates classlessness and mobility, class seemed to hobble Ruth. Rumors about his supposed mixed racial background—insinuations that frequently surfaced in the taunts of opposing players—added another layer to the mix. Later in his career, the issue of gender—in particular, Ruth's outspoken wife and advisor, Claire Ruth—also became an obstacle and may have helped spoil his ambitions to manage a major league team.

Returning to our opening story in which a teacher disparaged Ruth's intellect, sportswriter Red Smith suggested that contrary to popular opinion, the Babe possessed a certain earthy intelligence, "a blend of shrewdness and simplicity . . . and cheerful innocence."[4] Smith might have added that Ruth, despite his on-the-baseball-diamond heroics, faced a lifetime uphill battle to establish himself as a person to be taken seriously. Additionally, the Babe confronted a baseball establishment wary of his force of personality and popularity with fans. That establishment worked hard to break its biggest star—even as it worked to exploit his talents. Instead of dealing with Ruth as an adult, it infantilized and discredited him. This also needs to be part of the Babe Ruth story.

Invariably when friends or colleagues learned of my plans to write about Babe Ruth, the response amounted to a variation on "So much has been written already, can there be anything new?" Remarkably, despite voluminous books and articles treating the Babe's life and career, my initiatives to take Ruth seriously yielded much that is "new." Ruth, it turns out, was an early and lifelong advocate for ballplayer rights, from his membership in the Fraternity of Professional Baseball Players of America early in his career to his indignation in 1932 that the Chicago Cubs failed to evenly divide World Series bonuses among team members, outrage that inspired his famed "called shot" home run. While Ruth's clashes with baseball authorities are well known, the extent of baseball's campaign against Ruth remains largely untold. Indeed, sensing a threat, Yankees authorities dug into Ruth's personal life and peddled salacious rumors about the Babe to the press. While others, such as Leigh Montville, have developed the role of sportswriters in promoting Ruth, none have considered how the sporting press operated subserviently, essentially as the publicity arm of baseball's establishment. This study also considers very seriously the forces of race, class, and gender used against Ruth. Overall, framed in terms of baseball's struggle for stability, Ruth's story appears less a fabulous Jazz Age tale of fame and fortune and more the account of a talented and generous man's battle against larger forces determined to exploit the ballplayer and break the man.

ONE. BASEBALL'S SEARCH FOR ORDER

"Very Poor"

Destitution enough to break most men ruled the early life of George Herman Ruth. Born into a struggling working-class family in 1895, Ruth was essentially abandoned as a youth. His parents, overwhelmed evidently by illness and financial pressures, either could not or would not care for their firstborn child. Instead, almost from birth, the boy largely fended for himself on the dangerous and debasing streets of the southwest Baltimore neighborhood unaffectionately known as Pigtown.

Ruth's early life appears through a dense prism of legend created, shaped, and reshaped by sportswriters and promoters. Yet in some accounts, a stark truth breaks through. In a 1928 ghostwritten biography penned by baseball journalist and future commissioner of baseball Ford Frick, Ruth recalled his "earliest recollections" as centered "about the dirty, traffic-crowded streets of Baltimore's river front." There he remembered bustling thoroughfares and "heavy trucks whose drivers cursed and swore and aimed blows with their driving whips, at the legs of kids who made the streets their playground." Spiteful teamsters, "coppers patrolling their beats," and "shopkeepers who took bruising payment from our skins for the apples and fruit we 'snitched' from the stands and counters" hounded bands of semihomeless children. Frick undoubtedly sharpened the Dickensian imagery, but the grim scene rings true, as does Ruth's memories of family as "poor. Very poor. And there were times when we never knew where the next meal was coming from."[1]

Much remains in doubt about Ruth's youth, but the reality of poverty and delinquency seems irrefutable. Prospects for the young boy would not have been high. Few surviving such an upbringing could escape deep emotional scars and a base view of mankind. That Ruth emerged with not only a warm view of his fellow man but also a remarkable appetite for life defied all expectations.

Credit for Ruth's turnabout belongs largely to the intervention of the Xaverian brothers, a Roman Catholic religious order dedicated to education. Without question, the good brothers made the essential difference in the boy's life. At seven years of age, for reasons unknown, George Sr. and Katherine Ruth turned their incorrigible son over to St. Mary's Industrial School, a reformatory and orphanage operated by the Xaverians. On the surface the school, which featured many of the same rudiments as a prison, hardly appeared a vehicle for salvation. Some eight hundred boys in total lived in huge dormitories lined with neat beds. Privacy was nonexistent and conditions Spartan. Breakfast consisted of oatmeal with tea or coffee; lunch and dinner were hearty bread and soup. A slice or two of baloney decorated plates on Sunday.[2] Discipline was strict, and rule breakers could expect physical punishment. Days consisted of basic school instruction and long hours of industrial training. Ruth toiled as an apprentice tailor, making collars in a four-story shirt factory, which produced clothes for an independent contractor. Despite his austere surroundings, Ruth quickly settled into the structure of life at the industrial school, and he bonded with a number of the brothers who emerged as surrogates for his absentee parents. His real parents purportedly never visited him.[3]

Baseball proved essential in Ruth's acclimation to his new habitat. Inspired by the Victorian philosophy that organized sports promote good habits and hearts, not to mention the very real necessity of funneling energy from the throngs of adolescent males, St. Mary's kept residents occupied with a never-ending regiment of athletics, especially baseball—a game played nearly year-round at the school. Each dormitory had its own ballyard, where nonstop competition took place after work and on weekends. For boys and their caretaker brothers alike, baseball provided the major antidote to the monotony and austerity of life at St. Mary's. Competition was intense, and the Xaverians, many of whom played alongside their charges, were fine coaches. Early on, young Ruth's natural abilities caught all eyes. He excelled at every position, including pitching, and he was a feared hitter. Soon he was playing with older boys and honing talents that would take him far beyond the confines of St. Mary's. The experience prepared him well for his career as a ballplayer, although less so for the challenging world he would face as a modern sports hero.

By 1913, the teenage Ruth competed on weekends with local amateur teams. Word spread of his prodigious talents. That year, Jack Dunn, owner and manager of the minor league Baltimore Orioles, signed Ruth to his team. Since the Babe was under age twenty-one, Dunn became his official guardian, perhaps foreshadowing for Ruth the paternalism of the baseball world that he would face for the rest of his life. With little experience outside St. Mary's School, and probably never having traveled outside Baltimore proper, Ruth boarded a train for Fayetteville, North Carolina. Dunn well understood Ruth's potential. "This fellow Ruth," he informed St. Mary's administrators, "is the greatest player who ever reported to a training camp."[4]

By all accounts Ruth loved his new life, his newfound freedom, and his first taste of money. Yet he remained centered in his hometown and closely connected to St. Mary's, his only real home. Often he returned to his old stomping grounds to visit and play ball. Swarms of boys greeted him—his introduction to the hero-worshipping that followed him, for good and bad, the rest of his life.[5]

In midsummer 1914 came a sudden shock. Struggling with competition from the Baltimore Terrapins, a newly founded Federal League team, Dunn sold Ruth and several other players to the Boston Red Sox. Ruth's salary would grow, and he was now poised to play major league baseball. Still, the hometown boy bristled at the prospect of leaving Baltimore. Not for the last time in his career, Ruth learned he would have no choice in the matter: he was under contract to Dunn, and Dunn had sold him. If he wished to continue playing baseball, it would be in Boston.[6]

The "evil has grown to such proportions that the very life of the game is threatened"

Ruth's formative years in baseball, in fact, coincided with the most challenging times the national game has ever faced. Indeed, the period beginning around the time Ruth broke into professional baseball through to the end of the decade almost brought baseball to its knees. Longstanding threats—gambling, "rowdyism," and labor strife—resurfaced with vengeance. As reformers scrambled to contain the damage, Ruth, an emerging star, could not help but find himself caught up in the turmoil swirling around the game. This context is crucial to understanding why baseball later viewed Ruth both as a savior and a threat.

Those championing baseball in the late nineteenth and early twentieth centuries envisioned and promoted the game as a uniquely American, democratic sport embodying the best virtues of the young nation. In truth, gambling and the ancillary threat that players or umpires might be manipulated by gamblers afflicted professional baseball almost from its birth. In the 1870s, just as organized baseball emerged from its infancy, the first gambling scandal struck the game and the newly formed National League. "A mischievous and demoralizing element," according to sporting goods entrepreneur Albert Spalding, had infiltrated and corrupted the ranks of players.[7] Low salaries, scanty job security, and exhausting schedules fed temptations. When revelations surfaced in 1877 that members of the Louisville Grays had thrown games, the league acted quickly to expel four suspects and shore up rules against gambling in ballparks.[8]

Professional baseball worked to eradicate the problem. Reformers, in particular, pushed to rid ballparks of the ubiquitous presence of gamblers, some of whom had connections to the larger criminal world. Gambling, however, proved resilient. By the second decade of the twentieth century, it appeared more prevalent than ever. A Pittsburgh newspaper in 1912 charged that gamblers operated openly in major league ballparks around the country. Wagering represented an ongoing "nuisance and a menace to the integrity of the sport." So brazen were bettors, the newspaper reported, that on one notable occasion, two clergymen trying to enjoy an afternoon at a ballpark were forced to relocate themselves several times to escape exposure to "bookmakers and hustlers." Betting at New York's Polo Grounds was particularly omnipresent. The "example set by professionals became infectious," reported one paper, "and soon there was betting on a small scale all through the big stand." The small private security detail at the Polo Grounds focused much of its attention on pickpockets and drunks, leaving it no time to root out gamblers.[9] Blatant gambling at other parks rivaled that at the Polo Grounds. Exiting Boston's Braves Park around 1913, a sportswriter watched scores of "bookies . . . with bills spread through their fingers in real professional style to pay off after games."[10] With gambling increasingly part of baseball culture, fretted one sportswriter, "Umpires and players will be tempted."[11]

Indeed, reports of corruption swirled particularly around the annual World Series as the fall event became the nation's top sporting ritual. Rumors surfaced in 1913 when the Athletics and Braves played in that year's fall classic. Later, after losing the 1916 league championship to crosstown rival Brooklyn Dodgers, Giants manager John McGraw bitterly accused his players of "not doing their best," comments that "aroused more than just a breath of scandal to rest upon the heretofore carefully guarded virtuous sport."[12] As concerns mounted, sportswriter Hugh Fullerton warned, "There is more gambling to-day in the United States than ever before; the business is better organized, the earnings of the gamblers greater and the odds against the players much heavier."[13]

If the gambling amounted to a corrosive, shadowy menace potentially undermining the game, violence—rowdyism, as it was known—presented a more visible threat. Ballpark rowdyism—fights in the stands, attacks on umpires, assaults by players on fans, brawls between teams, scraps between players—like gambling, dated from the dawn of baseball. In fact the American League formed in 1901 in part out of an impulse by reformer Ban Johnson to curb rowdyism, especially violence against umpires. Still, the likes of Johnson made little headway stamping out the rowdyism that seemed woven into the game. "Brawling was common on the field and in the seats and baseball was regarded as a sport for low grade stags which no lady would be caught dead at," recalled sportswriter Westbrook Pegler of the game before the First World War.[14]

A brief survey of violent episodes flaring during the 1913 season, the year before Babe Ruth began his professional career, more than affirms Pegler's assessment. Trouble began in 1913 before regular season play even started. As often proved the case, umbrage at an umpire's ruling sparked passions. Playing on the West Coast against the Los Angeles Angels, Chicago White Sox players grew agitated by the officiating. Taunts and threats built until the umpire sought police protection.[15] It would hardly be the last time that season an umpire would feel physically threatened. At Ebbets Field on May 22, the visiting Pirates took a 1–0 lead over the Dodgers when it began to rain. Despite fan pressure to call the game, umpire Bill Klem resisted. Spectators then took the matter into their own hands: two thousand angry Brooklyn fans swarmed out of the bleachers and onto the field, refusing to vacate and effectively ending the game.[16] In July, Chicago saw a similar rebellion when an altercation between Cubs manager Johnny Evers and an umpire turned into an all-out riot. Stirred up, four thousand fans poured from the stands of the Cubs' stadium in support of Evers. Police struggled to restore order.[17]

Throughout his career, New York Giants manager John McGraw proved a particular magnet for violence, and 1913 was no exception. The pugnacious son of impoverished Irish immigrants, McGraw began his career in the 1890s with the Baltimore Orioles, a team renowned for rowdyism. As a player first and then manager, McGraw viewed intimidation and "judicious kicking" of umpires as legitimate tactics.[18] McGraw's methods, however, often spiraled out of control. June 30, 1913, found McGraw's Giants jousting on hostile grounds: playing the Philadelphia Phillies in the City of Brotherly Love—a city noted even then for fanatical and sometimes violent fans. Throughout the game, McGraw swapped vicious insults with opposing players. After the game, while attempting to exit the claustrophobic Baker Bowl (home of the Phillies), McGraw was violently attacked from behind. His trademark face badly cut, McGraw struggled to regain his footing as thousands of fans surged from the stands to join what a reporter described as a "melee and a scene of wild disorder." The Giants blamed a Phillies pitcher, whom they had "rode" mercilessly during the game, for launching the preliminary attack.[19]

When the Giants returned to Philadelphia later that summer, all parties anticipated trouble, and none were disappointed. During the game, Phillies' fans seated in a portion of the bleachers normally left unoccupied removed their jackets to create an all-white background, aimed at hindering visibility when Giants hitters came to bat. When the reigning umpire ordered spectators to put their jackets on, predictably, fans impolitely declined. In desperation, the umpire called the game a forfeit—essentially dousing the fire with gasoline, and "20,000 indignant fans swarmed the field." Giants players frantically fled, but several were caught in a gauntlet of rioters. Later, the battle reignited at the North Philadelphia Train Station as the Giants attempted to catch a train out of town.[20]

Not only did teams brawl with each other, with fans, and against umpires, but intra-team fights also broke out throughout 1913. Rivalries among McGraw's Giants resulted in "fisticuffs" between teammates after one game.[21] Members of the St. Louis Browns likewise came to blows over a missed fly ball at New York's Polo Grounds. As Browns players struggled to separate the two brawlers, New York fans bolted onto the field, some seeking a better look at the fight, others joining the melee.[22] Violence afflicted the minor leagues with even greater frequency than the majors.[23] The Negro League likewise suffered its share of near-riots, including a May 20 fight between Rube Foster's Chicago American Giants and the visiting Cuban All-Stars, which spiraled into a brawl involving armed fans. Police struggled to bring the riot under control.[24]

The rowdyism that plagued 1913 appears no worse than any other season in the early twentieth century. While no deaths were reported in the major leagues that year, fifteen young men reportedly died playing baseball in semipro and other leagues—ten struck fatally in the head by pitched balls.[25] Increasingly the baseball establishment worried that the game's reputation for vice and violence would be a barrier to attracting, or even drive away, middle-class customers and their sizable disposable incomes.

Violence on the field and the mounting temptation of gambling reflected the often-grueling life of ballplayers. Meager compensation, the constant threat of injury, endless travel, and the denial of basic workplace rights all ate at players. Mirroring the great labor struggles of the time, players strove to assert some semblance of control over working conditions and compensation.

From the inception of major league baseball until the Marvin Miller era of the late 1960s, professional baseball officials fervently resisted player organization and preserved labor regulations that gave team management unique control over its employees. Central to that power was the reserve clause. Written into every major league contract beginning in 1887, the clause essentially bound players to teams and prohibited free agency by allowing employers automatically to renew contracts every year. Short of receiving an unconditional release from a contract, players could not negotiate with another team. Conversely, teams could unconditionally release players with a mere ten days' notice. Club owners naturally relished the firm control over their workforce provided by the reserve clause and the stability it afforded their enterprises. Many fans likewise valued the mechanism that tethered popular players to hometown teams. Some players even saw utility in a system that maintained a certain stability.[26] Still, many seethed at the restraints a New York State Supreme Court judge in 1914 concluded amounted to a "species of quasi peonage unlawfully controlling and interfering with the personal freedom of the men employed."[27]

Labor-management tensions, especially surrounding the reserve clause, boiled over in 1889. That year a union of professional baseball players launched an ambitious protest. Instead of striking, union members struck out on their own and forged their own league that went head-to-head with the reigning National League. The initiative, christened the Players' League, lasted only a year before it collapsed.[28] Efforts to organize professional baseball, however, continued. In the early twentieth century, activists established the Players' Protective Association (PPA) to "fight the magnates in the matter of selling and farming players. The present obnoxious system of contracts will be bitterly fought."[29] Like the Players' League, the PPA quickly withered in the face of a merger of the American League (AL) and the National League (NL). Still, anxiety about player joint action, as well as rowdyism and gambling, continued to haunt baseball's leadership class. For a while, the AL-NL merger agreement seemed to calm stormy waters. Then in 1912, a particularly disturbing incident rekindled management's dread of disorder and joint player agitation.

"I don't care if he has no feet!"

On May 15, 1912, playing at New York's Hilltop Park, Ty Cobb, the hyper-competitive, perennial AL batting champion in his eighth year with the Detroit Tigers, began exchanging insults with a spectator. Cobb's nickname, the "Georgia Peach," appears most likely bestowed in jest; virtually everyone in baseball recognized the psychotic streak lingering barely concealed under the surface of Cobb's high-strung personality. His sparring partner that day, Claude Lueker, had lost one hand and part of another in an industrial accident. Taunting and heckling at sporting events, perhaps even more a tradition in the early twentieth century than today, allowed victims of modern, urban life—such as Lueker—an outlet for frustrations. But Lueker moved into dangerous territory when he loudly maligned Cobb as a "half-nigger." A native southerner with deep-set apprehensions about race mixing, Cobb immediately catapulted into the stands. There he mercilessly beat Lueker. Horrified bystanders protested that Lueker had no hands. Unrelenting, Cobb barked, "I don't care if he has no feet!" Brandishing their bats, Cobb's teammates followed him into the crowd. Armed, they surrounded the enraged Cobb to prevent interference. Finally an umpire managed to pull Cobb off his victim and ejected him from the game, but the Georgian remained on the Tigers' bench the rest of the game in defiance of the umpire.[30]

AL president Ban Johnson personally witnessed the brutal affair. As punishment, he slapped an indefinite suspension on the Tiger. The matter, however, was far from over. "When a spectator calls me a 'half-nigger' I think it's time to fight," protested Cobb.[31] His teammates, incensed at the lack of due process, announced a strike: they would not play until Johnson reinstated Cobb. "The assassin who shot President McKinley was given a trial. Cobb was suspended but he was given no opportunity for explanation," protested Jim Delahanty, a Tigers infielder.[32] Cobb, one of the great stars of the game despite his temperament, fed the fires. "We will stick together and win it out," he assured his teammates.[33] The Tigers essentially mounted a wildcat strike. In order to avoid a fine, Tigers owner Frank Navin fielded a crew of semi-professional players in Tigers uniforms for a game in Philadelphia. The Tigers replacement players lost 24–2. The walkout by baseball's top player and his teammates briefly threatened the game fundamentally. Johnson reached decisively for both a carrot and a stick to thwart Cobb's challenge. Johnson threatened the Tigers with expulsion from baseball, but then clarified Cobb's suspension at ten days and a meager fifty-dollar fine. With this the Tigers relented and called off the walkout.

Cobb, however, was no reformed citizen. Demanding a steep salary increase to $15,000 the next season, he refused to attend Tigers spring training in early 1913. Navin grew increasingly fed up with his recalcitrant star. "A player cannot be bigger than the game that creates him," insisted Navin (wielding a line later used against Babe Ruth). Any inference that "discipline and not money" were at the heart of the issue, retorted Cobb, "is enough to queer his whole vicious attack on me."[34] Defiantly Cobb slapped together a team he dubbed the Georgia Stars and mounted a barnstorming tour across his native South—a move implicitly threatening an even greater challenge to baseball. Meanwhile Senator Hoke Smith (D-GA) rose to Cobb's defense. Branding baseball's labor practices the equivalent of "slavery," the senator demanded a copy of Cobb's contract to admit as evidence in a planned investigation of baseball's antitrust exemption.[35] *Baseball Magazine* rejoined with an article ridiculing the slavery charge. The reserve clause, asserted the magazine, "enables baseball to grow to a magnitude that it can afford to pay Cobb a large salary."[36] Dutifully, the rest of the press fell in line, supporting Navin against Cobb. Several weeks into the season, Cobb finally signed a one-year contract for $12,000, but not before *Sporting News* assailed Cobb's holdout as "detrimental to baseball."[37]

"A Matter of Duress"

Both Cobb's wildcat strike and well-publicized holdout betrayed deep fault lines between players and baseball's ownership class. To owners, Cobb's actions portended the chaos and player empowerment feared by reformers eager to bring order to the game. To players, Cobb's defiance signaled opportunity. Attorney and retired major leaguer David Fultz moved to organize a new union of players in 1913. He christened his initiative the Fraternity of Professional Baseball Players of America. In blunt terms, Fultz railed against skewed baseball labor practices. "There can be no negotiation," he declared, "when one party is absolutely at the mercy of the other; it becomes a matter of duress."[38] Cobb served as a fraternity vice president and spoke enthusiastically in support of its agenda. A player with five years in baseball, Cobb insisted, should earn "clear title to his services" and then act as a free agent. To team owners, convinced the reserve clause remained the "foundation upon which baseball has been constructed," Fultz was "too radical," especially in his insistence that "the reserve clause wouldn't stand the test of the courts."[39] Cobb, in turn, decried "the harsh words directed at the fraternity . . . inspired by big league magnates and written by newspapermen in the pay of club owners." The rebellious Georgian even proposed a strike might be necessary to send the establishment a message.[40]

Fultz's timing, at least initially, proved propitious. In 1913, a group of wealthy entrepreneurs launched the Federal League, a combination of six teams aiming to establish a new minor league. The next year an ambitious Chicago manufacturer and Philippine-American War veteran, James A. Gilmore, took charge. He immediately moved to expand to eight teams and to compete directly with the established major leagues. Four Federal League teams set up shop in NL cities, and two in AL cities. Not only did the established American and National Leagues face Fultz's challenge on the labor front, but now a rival league also appeared ready to take on the monopoly controlling professional baseball. Elaborately planned opening day festivities for the 1914 Federal League season generated palpable excitement. In Pittsburgh, an "automobile parade" that included Gilmore presaged the first game at Expo Field. "Practically every section of the city and several booster organizations from outlying districts asked for places in the line of march," reported the local press. At the ballpark, despite wet weather, a "good sized crowd" enjoyed the premier game.[41] Excitement in Baltimore, which lost its last major league baseball franchise to New York in 1903, exceeded anything seen in other cities. Baltimore Federals games at newly constructed Terrapin Park dramatically outdrew those played across the street by the Baltimore Orioles, a minor league team for which Babe Ruth was making his professional baseball debut in 1914.

The promise of higher salaries and flexible contracts—including automatic free agency after ten years in the new league—lured several high-profile major league players, including Chicago Cubs player-manager Joe Tinker. AL president Johnson countered the challenge in shrill terms. "I will not take a single man back who steps over the line dividing the American and Federal league," he pronounced. "I hereby tell one and all of them that I will not even talk to them."[42] Still several prominent players defied Johnson and made the jump to the Federal League anyway.

Then Gilmore sent shockwaves through the established leagues with insinuations that he was negotiating with Ty Cobb. Speculation peaked in late June 1914 when Gilmore and Cobb huddled together at a Chicago hotel. "We just had a pleasant chat," Gilmore wryly explained.[43] Among the upstart league's conquests, at least temporarily, was legendary pitcher Walter Johnson, who negotiated a substantial pay increase to join the Chicago Feds but then pivoted back to the AL Senators for yet a higher salary—exposing as empty Johnson's blacklist threat.

For the first time since the Players' League in the late nineteenth century, professional baseball players enjoyed something akin to a free market. Salaries rose precipitously. Cobb had held out for $15,000 in 1913, then settled for $12,000. By 1915, he was earning $20,000 per annum. Cobb claimed baseball's highest income, but the rising tide lifted all boats from an average salary of $3,187 in 1913 to $7,327 in 1915.[44] These figures are substantial compared to the $687 earned by the average male worker in 1915, but very insubstantial compared to the earnings of the average major league baseball player today.[45] With rising labor costs, club owners struggled to stay afloat, especially as the country slid into recession. War in Europe in June 1914 forced the closure of the US stock market for four months and sent tremors through the US economy. Unable to compete, Connie Mack, owner of the Philadelphia Athletics, moved to sell off his top players.

With owner control weakening as the crisis deepened, their employees adopted new independent postures. The *Sporting News* described mounting "covert and overt insubordination" among players.[46] "This season players scorn discipline in many cases calmly informing their managers that if they do not like it they will jump to the Feds," reported sportswriter Hugh Fullerton.[47] Although the Federal League maintained baseball's strict color bar, the chaos enveloping the game prompted the *Chicago Defender* to speculate the new league might open its doors to black players.[48] At a time when race mixing signified the ultimate disorder, such speculation could not have been welcome among baseball's boosters. Professional baseball, where paternalism and absolute club-owner control once held sway, now seemed headed for the sort of labor strife so dogging industrial America in the early twentieth century.

Sportswriters by and large defended the besieged established leagues against the Federals. In print, many branded the Feds as "anarchists," "outlaws," or "traitors to the game."[49] Columnist Joe Vila assured his friend Yankees owner Frank Farrell that he would "roast the Federal League from hell to breakfast hereafter."[50] The *Sporting News* commenced with just such a roast: "Isn't it a crime to see baseball, once a prosperous institution providing high class sport for an army of fans, torn to shreds because the Lunch Room League still believes there is room for it?"[51] By early 1915, Fullerton, surveying wreckage from the baseball war, warned "Only a compromise and readjustment could save the entire fabric of baseball."[52]

Attendance and profits in all major leagues slid sharply in 1914 and 1915. Gate receipts in the American League dropped 30 percent; the National League tumbled by 41 percent.[53] In early 1915, AL and NL owners, launching "the biggest player raid since the beginning of the war," instructed their field agents to sign as many Federal League players as possible, regardless of need.[54] Meanwhile, "peace talks" failed to yield results. Hardest hit financially were the minor leagues, from which the Federals drew both players and fans. The International League, a minor league formed in 1886, became known as the "Belgium of baseball"—a potent analogy as war ravaged the lowlands of Europe.[55] Struggling Baltimore Orioles owner Jack Dunn started selling off his best players. Babe Ruth, all of nineteen years old, reluctantly went to the Boston Red Sox. Facing intense resistance and fiscal strains, the Federals began weakening by 1915. In desperation, the "outlaws" brought a lawsuit naming all sixteen major league ball clubs. Major league baseball, the Federals insisted, amounted to a monopoly in restraint of trade. In early 1915, prominent federal judge Kenesaw Mountain Landis, a known trust-buster, heard the case in his Chicago courtroom. He bristled at any notion of the national game as a mere business or that baseball "playing" equated to labor. Instead, the game, he proclaimed, was "a national institution" deserving of special status.[56]

By late 1915, all parties moved to end the baseball war. Half the Federal teams were essentially bought out. Some Federal League owners were allowed to purchase struggling franchises in the established league. Other teams folded. Regrets ran deepest in Baltimore, which again lost a major league team. Its minor league team, the Baltimore Orioles, now Ruth-less, fled briefly to Richmond. Amid the wreckage, the owners of the collapsed Baltimore Terrapins filed a lawsuit that slowly snaked through the court system, casting a shadow over the game while it struggled to recover from its war against the Federal League. As historian G. Edward White explained, at any point "the entire legal structure of the enterprise of major league baseball might be exposed, found to be unlawful or unconstitutional, and discarded."[57]

While the Federal League battle had raged, Fultz's Players' Fraternity made inroads. But with the collapse of the Federal League, owners struck back and began refusing to consider Players' Fraternity demands. Spurned, in late 1916 Fultz announced plans for a strike and moved to affiliate his Player's

Fraternity with the American Federation of Labor. Major leaguers, however, proved slow to support the threatened strike. Those under contract could not legally strike, and those negotiating contracts risked being blacklisted. Meanwhile, AL president Johnson and Ed Barrow, who was then president of the minor league known as the International League, threatened a lockout should players walk out. Johnson also cleverly declared he would welcome American Federation of Labor affiliation, which he claimed in the end would "standardize wage scales"—an implied threat to players with larger salaries.[58] Yankees owner T. L. Huston summed up management's reaction to Fultz's strike threat: "We cannot stand for the players taking such action as they contemplate. We must stabilize our business."[59]

Despite Fultz's claims that "star players" were lining up behind the strike, few big names moved to support the fraternity. One who did was Babe Ruth, whose Red Sox had shown significant support for the fraternity. Ruth's occasional roommate, first baseman Dick Hoblitzell, served as a "director at large" for the fraternity.[60] Fultz dropped Ruth's name to the press in early 1917 as tensions over his strike threat mounted.[61] On January 18, Ruth was among the roughly one dozen Braves, Red Sox, and minor league players called by Fultz for a special meeting at Boston's Hotel Touraine. The players emerged from the three-hour conference fully endorsing the fraternity.[62]

Elsewhere, however, support eroded, and Fultz walked back talk of a strike. Quickly his organization began crumbling. With war looming, management threatened roster cuts and reduced pay. Out of "self-preservation," players still holding out jumped to sign contracts.[63] Sensing opportunity to rid itself of the union, team owners, in one bold swipe, negated all past agreements with the fraternity and banned all future dealings. Decrying the "rank injustice" of the fraternity's agenda for baseball, NL president John Tener proclaimed, "Hereafter the clubs will have to deal with their players individually, and we can no longer deal with any outside body."[64] Joint action by players, as Tener suggested, now was unacceptable. Instead, professional baseball would proceed with a strictly paternalistic approach to labor relations.

"The game has been dying for two years"

Briefly, as the 1917 season opened, without threat from the Players' Fraternity or the Federal League, team owners dared dream they had put recent strife behind them. "Baseball will be played under more favorable conditions this year," prophesized NL president John K. Tener. "The players cannot run things to suit themselves."[65] Sportswriter Jack Veiock echoed Tener's sentiments. "With the Player's Fraternity crushed . . . club owners believe they can now give the public clean wholesome sport," he pronounced.[66] Only days after Tener's and Veiock's clear skies forecast, however, President Woodrow Wilson declared war on Germany. A real war now wreaked havoc for baseball and presented yet another existential threat.

Instead of renewed stability, baseball's 1917 season saw falling attendance, tumbling revenue, and a steady exodus of players to military service. Likewise, tension and rowdyism—no doubt fed by anxious times—spiked. John McGraw again found himself at the center of several high-profile fights. In late June, Babe Ruth punched umpire Brick Owens after an argument. Police rushed onto the scene to restrain Ruth.[67] Meanwhile, that same summer, a West Coast league game collapsed into chaos as players dueled with bats, and fans chased umpires from the ballpark.[68] Concurrently, an even more overt brand of gambling seemed on the rise, nowhere more so than at Boston's Fenway Park. At every game, gamblers conspicuously situated themselves in the right field pavilion. Their operations, reported a startled visiting Chicago sportswriter, resembled those of the "wheat pit of the Chicago Board of Trade."[69] On June 17, when the visiting White Sox jumped to an early lead, threatening the odds gamblers had set on the game, "A tall fan in a long rain coat took command." The ringleader dispatched hundreds of followers onto the field to delay the game, hoping a foggy drizzle might turn into rain and lead to a cancellation. When the initiative failed, a second wave of fans stormed the field, this time more violently. Fists and thrown bottles descended on the White Sox as they fled to escape the melee.[70] Increasingly, Ruth's Red Sox exemplified the disorders so threatening to baseball.

As the nation mobilized for war, questions also arose as to the draft status of ballplayers. Initially government officials accepted baseball's argument that spectator sports kept morale high. Baseball magnates generously donated to war-related charities, and, in the American League, military drill sergeants were appointed to each team. Players paraded before games with bats positioned like guns over their shoulders. Baseball hoped it could survive the patriotic climate in which men donning baseball rather than military uniforms seemed suspect.

Early the next season, however, the bottom threatened to fall completely out of the national game. Facing labor scarcity in key wartime industries, on May 23, 1918, Provost General Enoch Crowder issued a "work or fight" order: all draft-age men must either find work in an "essential" industry or face induction into the military services. Under threat from draft boards, players poured out of baseball into either the military or military industries, especially shipbuilding, where they were safe from the draft—and still able to play ball. Shipyard teams, now able to recruit some of the best talent in the country, coalesced into leagues. Among the major league stars enlisted were Joe Jackson of the Chicago White Sox and Yankees pitcher George Mogridge. Fans paid admission at shipyard games, and recruiters for the upstart leagues scoured the country in search of talent. A major leaguer could earn $500 a week working in a shipyard (rarely in a strenuous position) and playing baseball. In some cases, complained Yankees manager Miller Huggins, shipbuilder clubs offered players contracts in excess of what they would earn in the major leagues.[71] Major league baseball bitterly resented the competition. Defectors to the shipbuilding leagues "should be yanked into the army by the coat collar," snarled Johnson.[72] Rumors swirled of cushy jobs and high pay for minor and major leaguers recruited by the shipbuilders. *Baseball Magazine* branded the upstart leagues showcasing major league ballplayers as "a rising menace to the game."[73]

For disgruntled major leaguers, the shipbuilding leagues offered leverage, much like the recently evaporated Federal League. During the 1918 season, Babe Ruth began to come into his own as a hitter, but Red Sox manager Edward Barrow (having recently shifted jobs from presidency of the International League to Red Sox manager) insisted that he continue to pitch. Ruth protested, but Barrow kept pressure up. In early July, tensions boiled over. Barrow fined Ruth for insubordination, and the two exchanged angry words and threats of violence. In a fury, Ruth left the team and signed with the Chester Shipyard team in the Delaware River Shipbuilding League. Over the next several days, Barrow and Red Sox owner Harry Frazee managed to talk Ruth back to the Red Sox. The fine was negated, but the episode revealed yet again the star's independent streak.[74] Ruth's walkout also underscored the ongoing trials besetting major league ball.

As Ruth clashed with Red Sox management, dark clouds gathered over the future of the entire 1918 season. If fully enforced, the work-or-fight order would decimate baseball. By July, many expected the season to be canceled at any time. Baseball's hierarchy appealed urgently to government officials and made contingency plans to shutter the major and minor leagues. Finally Secretary of War Newton Baker consented to allow major league play to continue until Labor Day, followed by an early World Series.

On September 5, the fall classic between the Boston Red Sox and Chicago Cubs opened at Comiskey Park in Chicago, with Ruth pitching a shutout

game. Two days later, Charles Schwab, head of the Emergency Fleet Corporation, threw out the first pitch in the Atlantic Coast Shipbuilders championship series, played at Philadelphia's Baker Bowl and New York's Polo
Grounds, featuring several major leaguers, including "Shoeless" Joe Jackson.[75] Between competition from the shipbuilders and the ongoing drama of
one million Americans now fighting in Europe, interest in the World Series
wilted. Attendance lagged. Players and fans seemed distracted. Rumors of
gambling also haunted the series. The "evil has grown to such proportions
that the very life of the game is threatened," inveighed the *Pittsburgh Press*,
referencing the gossip.[76]

With World Series gate traffic down, inflation soaring, and baseball teams
expected to make large donations to war charities, the 1918 World Series
hardly promised to be a gainful affair. Normally a pool of "bonus" money
based on series profits would be divided between players on each team—
providing a handsome end-of-year windfall. Yet under the usual formula,
players in 1918 could expect little in the way of bonuses since profits would
be meager. Representatives of both the Cubs and Red Sox pressed baseball
authorities for a better deal. When no positive response came, members of
both teams began plotting joint action. On September 10, before game five, as
crowds waited in Boston's Fenway Park, both the Cubs and Red Sox refused to
take the field. Instead they demanded a meeting regarding their diminishing
bonuses. When news of the holdout spread, impatient fans grew edgy. Shouts
of "Bolsheviki" and "traitors" echoed through the park. During the delay,
ushers carried two invalid soldiers to their seats, sparking a massive ovation
by the crowd—the contrast between the wounded heroes and striking players
obvious to all. Fearing trouble, the Boston police sent mounted officers onto
the outfield, joined by patrolmen on foot.[77] Finally, a tipsy AL president Johnson arrived on the scene. Sternly warning players that public sentiment was
against them, Johnson persuaded the strikers to take the field. Still, a majority
of the players voted to maintain the holdout.[78] Catcalls greeted players as they
finally emerged. For all it was a disheartening experience. The next day, a
mere 15,874 fans arrived to watch the Red Sox win the series. "The game has
been dying for two years, killed by the greed of the owners and players . . .
the game just reeks of scandal after scandal," lamented Boston *Post* columnist
Arthur Duffey in the wake of the game five holdout.[79]

After the painful World Series wrapped up, players moved to secure their
futures, prospects that appeared centered on the shipbuilders leagues or the
military. "It is quite possible that the Yankees will be transplanted bodily to

the Tiejan and Lang drydock at Weehawken," reported one newspaper.[80] For his part, Babe Ruth moved his young wife to Lebanon, Pennsylvania, where he took up play for the Bethlehem Steel Corporation League. No one expected professional baseball the next season.

The armistice on November 11, 1918, saved the following year's season and put an end to the shipbuilders' league threat. Yet the game appeared maimed. Few among baseball's elite had much cause for optimism about the national game's future. Infighting, external threats, violence, gambling, labor strife, and legal challenges all seemed as insurmountable as ever. Anticipating another difficult season, team owners moved to shorten the 1919 season to 140 games and slash player salaries.[81]

By the end of the Great War, Babe Ruth had emerged as one of the most recognized players in major league baseball. The Red Sox pitcher turned hitter exemplified in many ways both the potential of baseball to grow and reach new heights of popularity and the demons that continued to dog the game. On a personal level, like the game he played, Ruth struggled to bring order to his life—with limited success. In 1914, nineteen-year-old Ruth married Helen Woodford, a sixteen-year-old waitress. The marriage, however, quickly grew strained under the pressure of their youth and Ruth's frequent absences and growing fame. Ruth also tried to reestablish a relationship with his bartender father (his mother had died), but circumstances abruptly turned tragic in 1918 when George Ruth Sr. was killed in a fight outside his bar. Increasingly Ruth found an outlet carousing with fair-weather friends attracted by his money and fame. His recreational habits became a major concern to the Red Sox, but Ruth clearly resented efforts to control him. In fact, as a ballplayer, Ruth sought more control over his career. He joined the Player's Fraternity and pushed back against the exhausting pitching schedule Red Sox manager Barrow laid out. With little family support and an antagonistic relationship with team management, Ruth's life remained disorderly even as his fame and wealth grew. This underlying turmoil would increase over the next several years as he transitioned from a pitching star to a home-run superstar.

Baseball's Reformers

Ruth's battle to stabilize his life and career mirrors the larger struggle to order America's national sport—a battle that, by the time of World War I, appeared all but lost. Baseball leaders, of course, well understood the growing challenges arrayed against the game. Within that leadership, a group of reformers emerged, determined to order the sport that so often seemed to veer toward chaos. In many ways, baseball's reformers paralleled the work of progressive activists operating during the same era, both seeking to impose middle-class orderliness—as opposed to the "coarse and vulgar" working-class and immigrant cultures—on a nation struggling with chaotic growth. These crusaders would not be wanting of challenges.[82] They would, however, have a powerful public relations arm in the nation's sportswriters, who consistently and forcefully supported the reform agenda. It is therefore worth taking a brief look at key figures among baseball's crusaders and their journalistic allies, many of whom would later both clash with and champion Babe Ruth.

Johnson's seminal role in creating the American League in 1901 has already been touched on. More than any other individual, Johnson led the drive to counter the chaos that seemed poised to overwhelm professional baseball. Born in 1864, into a distinctly middle-class Presbyterian family in small-town Ohio, the college-educated Johnson early on envisioned baseball as an orderly, commercial affair with strong appeal to families. He began as a sportswriter in Cincinnati for the *Commercial-Gazette*, where he attacked the Players' League as "treachery." Free enterprise, he proclaimed, offered a better deal for players. "The capitalists worked individually to better their condition and protect their interests," he argued.[83] He also decried rowdyism and sought to shield and defend umpires, who had few friends at the turn of the century.

In the final years of the nineteenth century, as president of the Western League, a minor league consisting of eight midwestern teams, Johnson imposed strict prohibitions against profanity and umpire "kicking." He introduced "Ladies' Days" to lure women to league games. "My determination," he explained, "was to pattern baseball in this new league along the lines of scholastic contests, to make ability and brains and clean honorable play, not the swinging of clenched fists, coarse oaths, riots or assaults upon the umpire decide the game."[84]

In 1901, Johnson fashioned his Western League into the American League and challenged the dominant National League. He then ferociously battled "outlaw" challenges to his American League. He also fought David Fultz's Players' Fraternity. When the fraternity threatened a strike, Johnson vowed to shutter ballparks, suspend salaries, and "heavily" fine all strikers.[85] Gambling, particularly reports of open wagering at Fenway Park, also came under fire from President Johnson.[86]

For a time, Johnson forged effective alliances with figures such as former major leaguer turned Pennsylvania governor turned NL president John K. Tener. "High class sport," Tener insisted, "is demanded by the public."[87] Alongside Johnson, Tener worked to maintain the reserve clause and waged war on rowdyism and gambling. In 1917, for instance, he arranged for Boston police to patrol Braves Field to dissuade gamblers.[88] That same year, when John McGraw appealed a suspension and fine to the NL Board of Directors, Tener quoted approvingly a letter from a Presbyterian minister in Ohio. "Do we go to the ballpark to watch a sportsmanlike contest . . . or to witness such an exhibition of rowdyism as characterizes the gatherings of toughs and thugs?"[89] The answer for the minister and Tener was clear.

As they battled the Federal League, struggled with the Players' Fraternity, and waged their war to clean up baseball, Tener and Johnson eagerly recruited new owners to shore up major league teams and bring stability to the game. Frank Farrell and "Big" Bill Devery, owners of the American League's New York Highlanders, hardly matched the reform ideal. Farrell owned several gambling establishments, and Devery, a former New York City chief of police closely tied to New York City's Tammany machine, had somehow survived numerous indictments on corruption charges. By 1915, Johnson was eager to ease Farrell and Devery out in favor of more respectable owners—preferably with pockets deep enough to survive the Federal League challenge.

Jacob Ruppert, a wealthy former congressman and millionaire brewer, drew Johnson's attention. Years before, Ruppert had attempted to buy the New York Giants, and James Gilmore, president of the Federal League, was known to have approached Ruppert about opportunities in the upstart "outlaw" league. Johnson moved quickly to interest Ruppert in the Highlanders (a team increasingly known by another nickname, the Yankees).[90] Unlike Farrell and Devery, Ruppert had a clean reputation and considerable resources. A fastidious lifelong bachelor who once declared "an aversion to women" but ended up leaving a portion of his estate to a chorus-girl "friend," Ruppert was the scion of a prosperous German-American family that made its fortune brewing beer. His tastes ran toward art collecting, racing horses, and raising champion Saint Bernards and Boston terriers. He occupied a twelve-room apartment on Fifth Avenue in the city when not on his aristocratic, 150-acre estate, the Eagle's Rest, in Garrison, New York. An affiliation with the New York National Guard earned Ruppert the title of colonel, which he proudly bore the rest of this life.[91]

Despite his wealth, Ruppert balked at the high price of entering baseball, a sport about which he knew little. Johnson then lobbied another interested party, "Colonel" Tillinghast L'Hommedieu Huston, to partner with Ruppert. The two colonels had never met and proved to be very different personalities. Huston hardly looked or acted like a millionaire. He wore rumpled clothes and enjoyed drinking and the night life. Notwithstanding his aristocratic surname, Huston had middle-class roots—born in Cincinnati, son of a railroad construction engineer. After fighting in the Spanish-American War (thus earning his colonel designation on the battlefield), Huston, an engineer like his father, remained in Cuba and won a concession to dredge and expand Havana's harbor. The enterprise, which allowed Huston to collect port duties for thirty years, enriched the Ohioan. He established an estate on Butler Island in Georgia and began investing his money.

Huston readily agreed to Johnson's proposal and put up half the $460,000 required to become co-owner of the New York AL club.[92] The team was a distinctly second-class operation, but the colonels had ambitious plans and deep pockets. "We are going to get a winner for New York in the American League," declared Huston. "We have instructed Bill Donovan, our new manager to go through this broad land and get a winner if he had to do it while the police aren't looking." The new Yankees owners, Huston promised, would not "pester" Donovan about salaries; there would be plenty of money to spread around.[93]

War, and disappointment with Donovan, who failed as "a team-builder," slowed progress. When the colonels went looking for a new manager, Johnson again offered his counsel. The AL president proposed Miller Huggins, a short (five feet, four inches), laconic, tense character, then managing the St. Louis Cardinals.[94] A strict Methodist from Cincinnati, Huggins had studied law at the University of Cincinnati under future president William Howard Taft. "You can become a pleader or a player but not both," Taft purportedly told Huggins. "Try baseball. You seem to like it better."[95] With Huston serving overseas in the US military, Ruppert made an executive decision to hire Huggins without consulting his partner (which resulted in Huston's lasting resentment).

In 1921, Ruppert hired another well-known and proven baseball executive, Edward Barrow. A close associate of Johnson, Barrow already had a storied and controversial career by the time he joined the Yankees.[96] In contrast to Johnson, Barrow's roots were humbler and his style grittier. After a youth on the plains of Nebraska and Iowa, like his friend Johnson, Barrow began as a newspaper reporter and editor before eventually finding a home on the business side of baseball. He never really played the game himself—a fact that distressed Babe Ruth. By 1911, Barrow was president of the International League. Although a fighter by nature and never opposed to using fists to settle an argument or revenge an affront, he set out to curb the violence that often plagued the minor leagues. Finding "a growing spirit of rowdyism" and umpire baiting in the International League, Barrow recalled being "determined to drive it out and re-establish the authority of the umpire."[97]

The International League president also earned the admiration of the baseball establishment with his unbending opposition to the Federal League and gambling. As Yankees team secretary in the 1920s, he spent thousands and dispatched a "secret police" squadron to combat betting at Yankee Stadium.[98] Not only was gaming to be thwarted at the stadium, but Barrow also instructed ushers to inforce a no-smoking policy for women. African Americans could and did attend games but often were made to feel unwelcome. Negro League games were barred from the stadium until 1930.[99]

Beefy and known for his "pugnacity," Barrow was intimidating. He maintained an active interest in boxing and promoted fights as a sideline. While opposed officially to rowdyism, Barrow was no stranger to brawling. In 1905, as manager of the Indianapolis Indians minor league club, he traded blows under the stands with an umpire known to carry a knife. The fight had to be broken up by police, as did other brawls involving Barrow.[100]

Throughout his career, from the minor to the major leagues, Barrow handled players so ruthlessly that he earned the moniker "Simon"—after Simon Legree, the cruel slave driver of *Uncle Tom's Cabin*. When he joined the Boston Red Sox in 1918, Barrow found the team willful and unfocused by his standards. Babe Ruth, he concluded, was "wild and fun loving and entirely without self-discipline or inhibitions."[101] Ruth and Barrow never got along. Sportswriter Westbrook Pegler later noted Barrow's "fixed opinion expressed a thousand different ways that the Babe is lucky not to have to plug along at some laborious working job, probably with a shovel."[102] Always eager to overcome his humble roots and establish himself among baseball's decision-making elites, Barrow remained burdened by a reputation as a tough-guy brawler. Sportswriters never warmed to Barrow, whom they often derided in print as "Cousin Egbert," or "Simon."[103] Yankees owner Jacob Ruppert always maintained a distance from his trusted aide, calling him "Barrows," with an *s* added to his name. When Ruppert penned a 1931 *Saturday Evening Post* piece on his success with the Yankees, he never mentioned Barrow, while heaping praise on Huggins (who had recently died).[104] Perhaps in Ruth, Barrow detected characteristics he despised in himself: a crudeness and sudden temper. Yet unlike Barrow, Ruth had stunning natural talent as a player and an equally notable warmth and charisma. Barrow never understood nor made much effort to understand Ruth. As Westbrook Pegler surmised, Barrow refused to acknowledge Ruth as "the artist who draws the customers who make him [Barrow] rich."[105]

Beyond Johnson, Ruppert, Huggins, and Barrow, a number of other key figures joined baseball's reformers. Philadelphia Athletics owner and manager Connie Mack insisted he would never tolerate a "rough neck" on his team. A teetotaler himself, Mack promoted temperance among his players and forbade umpire baiting. In 1916, he famously introduced a "code of conduct" to guide players. Prominent among his rules: "I will always conduct myself as a true sportsman—on and off the playing field."[106] In 1920, many reformers would cast their lot with Judge Kenesaw Mountain Landis, the first commissioner of baseball. They expected Landis to aggressively pursue their agenda.

"A Grotesque Argot Found Nowhere Else in Journalism": Sportswriters*

At the height of his bitter 1913 contract battle, Ty Cobb briefly flashed what one newspaper labeled "anarchistic tendencies" and directly took on the baseball establishment. Ballplayers, Cobb pronounced, should be prepared to walk off their jobs to challenge the reserve clause system. Standing in the way of much-needed reform were materialistic-minded club owners and "newspaper men in the pay of big league magnates."[107] In his antiestablishment rant, Cobb disclosed an awkward but important reality about sportswriters and the baseball establishment: sportswriters were hardly independent operators. For all practical purposes, they were on the payroll of teams and promoters. Enjoying subsidized travel and living expenses provided by major league teams, sports journalists embraced the reform agenda of battling vice and player agitation within the game.

Despite their indentured status, sports scribes of the 1920s were a remarkably talented lot. These "journalists" entertained millions of readers and generated unprecedented excitement and "ballyhoo." Rightfully, observers have labeled the era "the Golden Age of sportswriting."[108] By the early

---

* Silas Bent, Ballyhoo: *The Voice of the Press* (New York: Horace Liveright, 1927), 11.

1920s, sports writing had traveled far from its gritty beginnings. Modern sports writing essentially emerged out of the circulation wars of the late nineteenth century. Battling for readership, newspaper publishers such as William Randolph Hearst and Joseph Pulitzer introduced splashy headlines, illustrations, photographs, cartoons, and features stories. Sports coverage, all quickly realized, had great appeal, especially, but hardly exclusively, among urbanites. By 1896, Hearst launched the first separate sports page and greatly expanded coverage of baseball, boxing, football, biking, horseracing, and even yachting and polo. A newspaper "must have articles to suit different classes," counseled Hearst.[109]

Into the early twentieth century, fascination with college and professional sports soared. Rising newspaper readership, fed by increasing interest in sports, generated opportunity for the growing legion of sportswriters. Between 1910 and 1930, daily circulation rose from 22.4 million copies to 39.6 million, amounting to roughly two papers a day for every American family. Advertising revenue tripled over the same period, reaching $800 million by the eve of the Depression.[110] Newspaper technology likewise evolved as techniques developed for printing box scores and, of course, photographs increasingly illustrated sports stories. Evening papers remained the prime source of information for most readers; four times more afternoon dailies were published in the United States during the 1920s than morning papers.[111] Throughout the day, newspapers updated information in new editions. Breaking stories, which included sports events, warranted immediate special editions. With radio in its infancy, the printed word offered the only authoritative information available on sports until the late 1920s. Sportswriters essentially served as filters through which increasing numbers of Americans learned about sports and sports heroes.

By the second decade of the twentieth century, a number of sportswriters, centered primarily in the media hub of New York City, were becoming household names. In contrast to an earlier generation of writers, many were "college men," such as Grantland Rice, who made liberal use of his classics major at Vanderbilt in his syndicated "Sportlight" column. Politically minded Heywood Broun was a Harvard graduate, and John Kieran came out of Fordham University. Other figures emerged from grittier backgrounds: Westbrook Pegler started as a teenage reporter on the hard-knock streets of Chicago. W. O. McGeehan and Damon Runyon came to New York from the far reaches of the West.

Life for the nation's top sportswriters was glamorous. A post-World War I jump in circulation, which coincided with spiking interest in spectator sports, ushered in a prosperous era. Sportswriters often enjoyed the highest salaries among journalists. They dined at exclusive clubs and drank at speakeasies, such as Bleeck's, an establishment parked conveniently next to the *Herald-Tribune's* offices on West Fortieth Street. The Stork Club, opened in 1929 by bootlegger Sherman Billingsley, also proved popular with the bards of baseball. When in Philadelphia, scribes enjoyed sumptuous dinners hosted by ex-boxer turned underworld figure Max "Boo Boo" Hoff. As Westbrook Pegler biographer Oliver Pilat concluded, "Sportswriters . . . were presumed to be on terms of camaraderie with the underworld."[112]

On the road, sports reporters generally toured directly with the team at the team's expense. Baseball clubs covered dining, travel, and hotel costs, again invariably in posh accommodations. "Club road secretaries" made all arrangements, cared for baggage, and, as sportswriter Fred Lieb recalled, "often 'poured' a tipsy reporter into his Pullman berth."[113] Sportswriters had close access to players. They played endless card games with players aboard special Pullman railroad cars; they idled away the hours in conversation with team members and management in plush hotel lobbies; and they often accompanied players on extracurricular outings. During spring training in Arkansas, Marshall Hunt of the *Daily News* joined Babe Ruth on hikes, golf outings, and for excursions deep into the countryside in search of delicious "chicken dinners."[114]

Relations between sportswriters and club owners often were even more intimate. A country estate off the Georgia coast provided a particularly exclusive site for baseball's elite, including sportswriters. The Dover Hall Club was established in 1915 by Yankees owner Col. T. L. Huston, Johnson, and several others among baseball's leadership class. Members purchased shares and enjoyed hunting and vacationing privileges on the well-stocked "plantation" sprawling around an enormous Tudoresque mansion. Damon Runyon served on the board of directors, and several sportswriters counted themselves as members. Babe Ruth and Ty Cobb frequently joined outings. Women appear not to have been welcome, and drinking and heavy eating seemed the rule.[115]

Sportswriters remained among the most-read newspaper writers in America. Their styles varied from the "gee whiz" hero worshipping of Rice to the "aw shucks" debunking of Westbrook Pegler. All sought growth and advancement for their profession. This naturally meant promotion of spectator sports in general. The goal was mass appeal and profitability. Corruption, vi-olence, or any link to nefarious characters or influences detracted from that goal. At the same time, sports needed to be exciting, and sport stars would have to be dramatic and alluring figures whose athletic heroism could be marketed to the masses. Yet sports heroes would preferably be clean, ideally representing the best to the public—a tall order.

Sportswriters, without question, enjoyed halcyon days in the 1920s, but challenges abounded. In particular, questions rose within the profession about the quality of sports journalism and "entangling alliances" between sportswriters and the teams and promoters they covered. In general, critics complained of a growing frivolity in newspapers. "Some call it the Jazz Age, but we all know what it is," lamented Paul Bellamy, editor of the *Cleveland Plain Dealer*. "Most of us would admit that the reading public . . . cares less at the moment for the so-called serious and important concerns of society. . . . They want to be entertained."[116]

Sports coverage became a particular target of those concerned about news-paper sensationalism and lack of substance. In 1918, media critic Silas Bent pointed out that the *New York Times* devoted "four eight-column 'streamers headlines'" to announcing the armistice. The same paper used three eight-column streamers to trumpet Gene Tunney's defeat of Jack Dempsey in 1927. "This," protested Bent, "was not news perspective."[117] Publishers in search of circulation, complained M. W. Bingay, managing editor of the *Detroit News*, had created a "Frankenstein monster of public interest in sports and then worshipped their handiwork."[118] As coverage of the first Dempsey-Tunney fight reached a fever pitch in 1926, Ogden Reid, patrician publisher of the *New York Tribune*, confronted Grantland Rice. "Grant, you're making the *Tribune* more of a sports paper than anything else," he vented. "At this rate we're becoming all sports and damn the rest of the world."[119]

Frivolity in style ranked among the most repeated criticisms. Sports writ-ing as a journalistic art, lamented editor Stanley Walker, was "one of the finest and most abused in all newspaper work."[120] Observers decried "slang, hackneyed expressions, and faulty construction on the sport page."[121] *Louis-ville Times* editor Tom Wallace protested that "sporting departments . . . fall too largely in the hands of the incapable writers whose conception of writing is an abundance of slang . . . so quipped that the average newspaper reader doesn't really understand their reports."[122] Critics assailed lack of editori-al supervision. Sportswriters, noted Walker (in words Babe Ruth certainly would have endorsed), "are allowed more latitude, not only in their style of writing, but in the expression of opinion, than news writers. . . . They can puff or deflate any sports figure."[123] With the notable exception of the *Boston Globe* and a few other papers where all copy was read and reviewed at one desk, most sports departments edited their own materials, allowing them something of an independent existence.[124]

Apart from style, critics also found sports journalism lacking in sub-stance. John R. Tunis, then beginning a career writing fictional sports sto-ries for children, published a series of searing indictments of professional sports. Sportswriters, "sustained and built up by the large class of people now financially interested in sport," claimed Tunis in 1928, have elevated "our athletic heroes to peaks of prominence, by prying into their private lives, by following them incessantly in the columns of the daily press, by demand-ing of them victories and yet more victories, we force them to lose all sense of proportion."[125] *Milwaukee Journal* editor Marvin Creager echoed Tunis's assessment. Football hero Red Grange, Creager noted, "was raised to the tenth power by hero worshiping writers who then sold the very stuff that the newspapers had used to inflate his balloon right back to the editors to inflate it all the more."[126]

The strongest, most stinging criticism of sportswriters, however, was that they served less as journalists and more as corrupted, indentured publicists. As earlier noted, most depended on generous subsidies from teams to cover travel and other expenses. While the public may not have understood this relationship, sportswriters and those subsidizing them certainly did.

Understandably, sports reporters rarely challenged established team ver-sions of events, and when they did, it tended to be tentative and usually disguised with humor. Any other posture meant risking their livelihoods—possibly "finding themselves the next day writing obituaries."[127] Team offi-cials, likewise, were not above pressuring sportswriters. Outspoken Brooklyn Dodger manager Leo Durocher once berated a *New York Times* reporter for a negative story. "You're a part of this ball club. The club pays your expenses, doesn't it?"[128]

Within the newspaper industry, the "entangling alliances" between report-ers, ball clubs, and other promoters generated consternation.[129] "Probably the rottenest condition in American journalism is the sports departments," groused a prominent Detroit newspaperman in 1927.[130] The subsidies and favors provided to sportswriters by ball clubs, boxing promoters, and others seemed a fundamental violation of journalistic standards. Stories abounded of abuses. Eager to "make the Christmas season brighter," Chicago baseball teams presented local writers and editors with "merchandise checks" worth fifty dollars for editors and twenty-five dollars for sportswriters. Elsewhere, team "traveling secretaries" played Santa, distributing "handsome travel bags" to writers, containing cuff links, watches, and other goodies. Sportswriter Paul Gallico of the New York *Daily News* claimed that Madison Square Garden had sent "merchandise checks" to favored sportswriters as well. "Some of the checks, I know, were returned," explained Gallico, "many were not."[131]

Some newspapers even encouraged "sugaring" of their sportswriters. A story circulated among editors of a young reporter seeking a raise. "You don't want me to turn to graft, do you?" he asked his supervisor. "Don't bother me for raises," came the reply. "We are cutting down on expenses. Go outside and get all you can get."[132]

Despite apprehensions about "graft," newspaper management appeared largely helpless to halt the abuses. Few papers had resources to cover travel for their own writers, and with circulation dependent on sports, it was easier to disregard than address the issue. Nevertheless, in some newspaper circles, patience was wearing thin. "We could make a sickening list of bribery, improper influence, stupid betrayal of the public, venal participation in profits and overplaying of mediocre events," raged a Nebraska editor.[133] "It is just as important that sports editors be paid only by their newspapers as it is for the city editors and managing editors to have no employers except the newspapers they represent," concluded a report on sports coverage prepared by the American Society of News Editors in 1928.[134] Still, into the 1950s, roughly half of all newspapers continued to rely on baseball teams to cover travel expenses for correspondents.[135] As late as the early 1970s, sportscaster Howard Cosell grumbled about sportswriters who "go around purifying" their "profession" when "hell, they're the ones whose traveling expenses are being paid by the clubs they promote."[136]

In the early twentieth century, major league baseball teams did employ press agents and public relations. Businessmen like the Rockefellers, public figures such as William "Buffalo Bill" Cody, and opera sensation Jenny Lind already had blazed the trail and taken on press agents (in Lind's case the agent was showman B. T. Barnum). Impressed by these developments, the New York Giants hired "Charlie" Murphy, an ex-newspaper man, to precede the team on road trips to generate publicity. "I used to get up in the morning in those days and find from the newspapers I had done all sorts of things," recalled Giants pitching sensation Christy Mathewson. In truth, however, baseball needed little marketing help. The game, Mathewson boasted in 1913, "is its own press agent. Look at the attendance figures, and the proceeds of the world series."[137] Indeed, sportswriters themselves acted as promoters for the game.

If team owners and promoters ever doubted the crucial importance of sports scribes, they could consider the events of the fall of 1923. The Yankees were in the thick of a pennant race, and Babe Ruth was reaching the apex of a dramatic comeback, when New York City's pressmen (workers actually operating the presses) abruptly walked off their jobs. Newspapers, still the primary source for information, disappeared. Publishers of eleven daily papers linked forces to produce an abbreviated joint paper printed by the *New York Post,* whose pressmen did not join the strike. Nevertheless, attendance at Yankee Stadium, even as a pennant drama played out, fell 15 percent. "It would seem that the sports writers are largely responsible for the flocking of the customers to the professional sporting events themselves," concluded W. O. McGeehan. "The ballyhoo must be made continuous."[138]

The sports figure who consistently offered the best copy with the broadest appeal was Babe Ruth. Sportswriters sought a transcendent narrative or figure capable of galvanizing public opinion and delivering order and growth to the game of baseball and sports in general. Despite his occasional rowdiness, his obvious sympathy for player rights, and the association of his team with gambling, Ruth offered just the vehicle. If he did not come quite made to order, perhaps he could be made to fit the order. His deeds and heroism spurred unprecedented public fascination and popularity for the game. Never before or since had one figure so driven and so threatened the game.

TWO. FRENZY!

GRANTLAND RICE FIRST encountered Babe Ruth at the Red Sox spring training camp in April 1919. The most read sportswriter in the country, Rice was chatting baseball with Red Sox manager Ed Barrow while Ruth took batting practice in the west Florida humidity. In their conversation, Barrow aimed to convey two things about his rising young star: first, Ruth could be trouble. He was, Barrow explained, "our main holdout" that spring, signing a three-year deal worth a total of $30,000 only days earlier after the team had left for the South. More important, Barrow contended, "This kid can become the greatest thing that's ever happened to baseball." As if cued by Barrow, Ruth "blasted" a ball clear out of the practice stadium. Rice gaped as a Red Sox "publicity man" dutifully trudged out to measure the shot. It had gone some five hundred feet.[1]

Barrow proved prescient: Ruth became the "greatest thing" ever for the game. But the pugnacious manager also aimed to transmit to Rice something of equal concern: Ruth had an independent streak and was potential danger as baseball's establishment sought to rebuild after the tumult of World War I and the Federal League challenge. Ruth's strength and appeal grew ever clearer over the next two seasons. With his sale to the New York Yankees in 1920, Ruth emerged baseball's savior and its future. Sportswriters outdid each other championing the Babe as a superman, a hero capable of bridging the many chasms of American society at the dawn of the 1920s. They fashioned a persona with broad appeal, capable of opening the game to new realms of prosperity. Briefly Ruth's liabilities—particularly his temper, his sympathy for player rights, and his assertiveness in making salary demands—were lost in the ballyhoo, but they would later return. Both pro-moting and controlling Ruth became of equal importance.

Prelude: 1919

After briefly jumping to the shipyard league in 1918 and joining his team-mates later that year to demand a greater share of World Series profits, Ruth continued to chart his own independent career path. He began the 1919 sea-son by returning unsigned the contract sent him by Red Sox owner Harry Frazee. Pointing to the multiple positions he had played the previous season, Ruth demanded a hefty pay hike: $15,000 a year, or possibly $10,000 a year for three years. Frazee was unmoved, and Ruth joined other big names hold-ing out that season, including Tris Speaker and Ty Cobb. Alongside mone-tary disputes, Ruth also wanted greater control over where he would play. Early on Barrow announced that Ruth would pitch and pinch-hit in 1919, an exhausting and taxing directive. The Babe rejoined that he wanted to play in left field every day.[2]

A local Boston-area druggist and family friend, Johnny Igoe, had begun serving as Ruth's business manager. Since ball clubs refused to negotiate with anyone besides players, Igoe provided only amateur advice and han-dled press relations. To pressure Frazee, Igoe floated notions that Ruth might retire to his farm or possibly box professionally in lieu of returning to the Red Sox.[3] Few took the threats seriously, and the team left Boston by boat for spring training without Ruth. Still, Red Sox officials needed to sign a player of Ruth's popularity and talents. A few days after the team departed, Ruth and Frazee met in New York City and hammered out a three-year deal at $10,000 per annum. As some have suggested, by seemingly locking himself into a three-year contract, Ruth may have sold himself—"the most talked about name in major league circles last season"—short.[4] Ruth, however, was essentially negotiating on his own with Frazee, a veteran theatrical agent and producer with vast bargaining experience. Igoe appeared to have no qualifi-cations for his job other than a rapport with Ruth. His main function seemed to be making public statements and offering support. It is also possible that in the negotiations, Frazee extended verbal assurances that Ruth would be shifted away from pitching and become an everyday player. "I enjoy being in the game everyday" Ruth explained immediately after signing the new con-tract.[5] In fact, Ruth continued to pitch. He hurled seventeen games in 1919, but this was fewer than the twenty games he pitched in 1918, a shortened season.

Frazee clearly got a bargain. While the rest of the Red Sox team collapsed in 1919, Ruth held up his end of the deal, despite doing double duty both at bat and on the pitcher's mound. The Babe's value as a gate draw was obvious from opening day, when thirty thousand fans packed New York's Polo Grounds to see his Red Sox beat the Yankees. Ruth smacked his season's first home run that game, and, after a brief early-season slump, continued hitting them. By July he had equaled the American League's home-run record. In August, Ruth hammered "the longest hit ever at Chicago's Comiskey Park." *Chicago Tribune* sportswriter James Crusinberry recorded universal wonder at Ruth's home run: "All the Sox players stood in the tracks transfixed with the splendor of it."[6]

A month later at New York's Polo Grounds, Ruth slammed what *New York Tribune* columnist W. O. McGeehan called "the longest hit that was ever seen since the days when the goats roamed Coogan's Bluff [the upper Manhattan neighborhood that was home to the Polo Grounds] and even before that."[7] Throughout the game against the Yankees (the team he would soon join), Ruth "was hailed with cheers" by the New York crowd. His "great reception" and the pandemonium accorded his "glorious smash" undoubtedly planted seeds in the minds of the Yankees ownership, still struggling to chart a course for a floundering ball club.[8]

As Ruth charged through his record-breaking season, including the single season home-run record, his growing renown merited inclusion as a character, albeit a largely underdeveloped character, in Ring Lardner's popular "You Know Me Al" series of fictional stories. Lardner relayed his tales through the letters of a dim-witted major leaguer writing to a hometown friend. "Along Came Ruth" (a title borrowed from a 1914 Irving Berlin song) appeared in the July 26, 1919, *Saturday Evening Post.* As the yarn plays out, White Sox pitcher and correspondent Jack Keefe is promised a raise if he can beat the Red Sox. Things go well until Jack faces Ruth: "The next thing I seen of the ball it was sailing into the right field bleachers where the black birds sets." Later, the White Sox manager tells Keefe, "I would trade you to Boston in a minute only Babe Ruth wouldn't stand for it as he likes to have you on our club."[9]

By season's end, Ruth had obliterated the major league home-run record. Everywhere he played, attendance jumped. Fan mail, including "perfumed notes," piled up for the star.[10]

Ruth's independent streak, however, remained an annoyance for Red Sox authorities. Early in the season, Manager Barrow suspended Ruth for violation of team rules. Ruth biographers eagerly have retold Barrow's version of events, penned over thirty years after his confrontation with Ruth: Playing in Washington, Ruth had been slipping out of the team hotel after curfew, presumably for the purposes of enjoying the local nightlife. As Barrow recounted the story, he devised a clever trap and caught Ruth returning well after curfew, fully clothed in bed, underneath covers, smoking a pipe. The following day, Barrow suspended and verbally disparaged his delinquent star in front of the entire team. Enraged, Ruth threatened to punch the manager. Barrow, older but well-known for his fighting abilities, rose to take on his challenger. In Barrow's account, Ruth then backed down and slinked away. "If there ever was a big shamed-faced kid with a guilty conscience trying to get off the hook, that was the Babe," recalled Barrow. Later the two supposedly worked out an agreement whereby Ruth was to leave Barrow a note each evening verifying the hour he returned to the team's hotel.[11]

Barrow's version, published after Ruth's death, has the Babe playing the errant adolescent: a big kid with a big mouth and a cowardly streak. Barrow serves as the voice of authority ready to take on the threat to team order. Ruth and Barrow obviously clashed in Washington, but there is little reason to present the manager's self-serving story as the authoritative version of events. In fact, Barrow could be a brutal man, known for physical intimidation. In 1930, he punched sportswriter Bill Slocum for writing a piece critical of Barrow.[12] Undoubtedly his confrontation with Ruth was more complicated than Barrow suggested.

Ruth, to be certain, and by his own later accounts, had a temperamental streak typical of hypercompetitive athletes. Later in the 1919 season, he clashed again as he had in 1917 with umpire Brick Owens. This time, Ruth evidently threatened Owens over a call. Owens ejected Ruth, but the Babe continued to taunt the umpire until his teammates restrained their star player.[13] Few would mistake Ruth for anything other than an independent operator, chafing at rules, expectations, and regulations imposed upon him. But he also had incredible talent, charisma, and natural warmth. He drew fans in record droves to Fenway Park and baseball stadiums around the league, and he was dutifully pitching and batting for the Red Sox. Expectations and accompanying pressures were growing for the young man.

"You would have thought we were on trial in Russia"
As Ruth battled Red Sox authority in 1919, pressure mounted on major league baseball. Although attendance shot up compared to the 1918 wartime season

(some teams doubled or tripled their gate), shadows dogged the game.[14] Just as the season began, a federal court ruled in favor of the Baltimore Federal League team's suit, declaring baseball a monopoly in restraint of trade. Ban Johnson and other league officials immediately vowed to appeal. "You would have thought we were on trial in Russia," complained Johnson, who brazenly likened the Federal League's attorneys to Lenin and Trotsky. Should the ruling stand, Johnson and other officials warned, the reserve clause and other privileges enjoyed by baseball would evaporate.[15] Major league baseball filed its appeal, but legal costs grew (eventually running a million dollars), and no one could be certain how the appeals court would rule.

In August, Ruth's Red Sox presented two additional challenges to baseball's labor status quo. Joe Bush, a Red Sox pitcher, suddenly found himself suspended for the season for failing to remain in good physical condition. Bush loudly protested his ailments resulted from injury, not sloth. He demanded either his release or a full season's pay. Both sides eventually compromised, and Bush remained with the Red Sox.[16] A more serious challenge came in the person of Carl Mays. A brilliant pitcher but a surly, misanthropic man who intimidated batters with aggressive, submarine-style pitching, Mays was a bomb ready to explode. Early in the season, angered when rowdy Philadelphia Athletics fans began banging on top of the Red Sox dugout, Mays hurled a ball at full strength into the crowd. It barely missed a female spectator. Outraged fans gathered names of witnesses and called for the police. Athletics manager Connie Mack, however, mediated, and no criminal charges were filed.[17] Then, in early July, frustrated by what he perceived as his Red Sox teammates' poor play, Mays suddenly quit the team. Instead of suspending Mays, Frazee traded him to the New York Yankees. The move netted $40,000 for the cash-strapped Red Sox owner.

AL president Ban Johnson strenuously objected to the trade. A player had broken his contract and abandoned his team, but suffered no penalty. "Baseball cannot tolerate such a breach of discipline," Johnson declared.[18] With that, Johnson suspended Mays and invalidated the trade. Mays went to the Yankees and pitched anyway. Both sides raced to court, where ultimately Johnson lost. The Mays imbroglio exposed baseball's weak authority and the deep divisions among baseball's ownership. The Yankees, Red Sox, and White Sox owners lined up against Johnson. Other AL teams supported him, including the Indians (in which it was revealed Johnson had a substantial investment). So bitter was the fallout that veteran sportswriter Sam Crane warned that Johnson's critics might go rouge and form their own third major league.[19] Ever-present external threats now combined with pressing internal divides. Major league baseball remained a painfully volatile affair. Meanwhile, throughout the 1919 season, rumors persisted of gambling conspiracies.

"The Most Stupendous Deal in the History of the National Game"

Already in 1919 Ruth and his home-run hitting emerged as an antidote to baseball's troubles. Ruth had become "the game's greatest showman," according to Rice. "The fanatic . . . would rather watch a great home run hitter than a .400 hitter who depended more on science than on the wallop."[20] With the end of the official 1919 season, Ruth moved hurriedly to capitalize on his growing celebrity. He joined a barnstorming tour organized by Buck Weaver, the White Sox third baseman (revealed months later as a conspirator in the 1919 Black Sox scandal). The tour began in New England, then moved west, ending in California. With agent Johnny Igoe in tow, Ruth stayed on the West Coast for additional personal appearances. There was even talk of making a movie in Hollywood.

From California, Ruth—increasingly cognizant of the crowds he was drawing and perhaps regretting having settled for a compromise figure earlier in the year—returned his 1920 contract to the Red Sox unsigned.[21] Based on his talents and gate appeal, an increasingly outspoken Ruth opined that $20,000 yearly would be appropriate compensation. As the "best drawing card" in the game, superior even to Cobb (whose salary was $20,000), a raise doubling his salary only seemed fair, Ruth announced. Then Ruth went a step further and assailed baseball's contract system. His three-year deal with Frazee, he argued was "illegal," since it contained a ten-day release clause. "If I lost an arm or a leg, they could let me go and I couldn't get the rest of my salary," he told an interviewer. Ruth, it appeared, was prepared to challenge baseball's contractual system in court.[22] Again, the Babe threatened to abscond the game, "go independent," as Igoe suggested, or possibly take up boxing; perhaps he would fight Jack Dempsey or follow some other pursuit.[23]

The successful barnstorming tour undoubtedly fed the Babe's bravado and unnerved the baseball establishment. If Ruth banded with other popular players such as Buck Weaver, they could form a rival "outlaw" league with enormous appeal. After a successful 1919 season, few among the ownership relished prospects of another baseball war. Still, Ruth, brazenly threatening to "jump" his contract, was openly defying the system. The response from sportswriters was scathing. Syndicated columnist W. J. MacBeth took dead aim at Ruth. The Red Sox star player was bluffing, insisted MacBeth. West Coast newspapers, he added, report that Ruth "is beginning to pale as a 'seven day wonder' . . . [and] seems to have just about reached the end of his possibilities." Ultimatums for a new contract at $20,000, MacBeth bristled, were "ludicrous. . . . A sporting public has little use for contract breakers."[24] An equally unsympathetic Ring Lardner mocked Ruth as "stamping his spikes into the contract and yelping about the dreadful price of a barrel of flour." Accompanying Lardner's column, the *Chicago Tribune* ran a cartoon of a baby in a cradle wailing for "More!"[25] A Washington, DC, columnist added that Ruth's assault on baseball's labor system offered "insights into his particular brain process—if you will admit he possesses one."[26] Another columnist blasted, "The sooner such players as Ruth and Mays are handled without gloves, the better it will be for baseball."[27] Even Ty Cobb, his 1913 rebellion now long forgotten, weighed in, asserting Ruth had "no moral or legal right to be dissatisfied."[28] As tensions heated up, the *Sporting News* warned Ruth could "go independent" if "Boston does not come across."[29]

Despite the negative onslaught, Ruth correctly gauged his growing value to baseball. He had driven up attendance wherever he played in 1919. He was the future of the game. Red Sox owner Harry Frazee, however, found himself increasingly in debt and frustrated by the demands of the likes of Joe Bush, Carl Mays, and Ruth. Desperate for relief, he offered his star attraction, the Babe, to the New York Yankees, owned by the duo of Colonel T. L. Huston and Colonel Jacob Ruppert. The price of the sale: $100,000 (often erroneously reported as $125,000).[30] Huston, Ruppert, and Frazee, in fact, were all New York businessmen and recent allies against Ban Johnson's leadership of the American League. Despite the record price tag, the colonels jumped at the opportunity to acquire Ruth, already a renowned figure in New York. Still, they stewed over Ruth's reputation for independence so manifest most recently in his salary demands. Before inking the deal, Yankees owners dispatched their team manager, Miller Huggins, to Los Angeles to assess Ruth and ensure the star understood his subordinate status if the sale were to go through.

In California, Huggins tracked down Ruth at a golf course. After some awkward discussion, Huggins got to the point.

"Babe, how would you like to play for the Yankees?" he asked. Taken aback, Ruth insisted he was happy with the Red Sox, but if traded to New York, "I'd try to play as hard there as I ever did in Boston."

"We haven't put through the deal yet, but I want to know whether you will behave yourself if we do obtain your services for the New York ball club. I know you've been a pretty wild boy in Boston, Babe." By this time Huggins was "wagging" his finger at Ruth.

Ruth recalled "getting a little fed up with the sermon" and again responding positively: he vowed to commit himself to the Yankees just as he had in Boston.

Huggins had justifiable concerns with team discipline; still, his tone bordered on demeaning. The "wild boy" reference, in particular, belittled Ruth. Huggins had not arrived for an adult conversation. According to his account, Ruth took the high ground: he swallowed the indignities and pressed on to the financial side of the matter. Ruth, in his own fashion ("I want a lot more dough than the $10,000 Frazee paid me last year") reiterated his demand for a raise.

Huggins promised consideration but added condescendingly, "If you promise to behave yourself when you come to us the Yankees will tear up your old Red Sox contract and make it $20,000."[31] Huggins's tone was harsh but typical of the baseball establishment, which had significant leverage over its young employees. The encounter also bore more than just a passing element of class condescension. The highly educated, middle-class Huggins clearly did not view Ruth as his equal.

The next day, the Yankees essentially accepted Ruth's demand, keeping Ruth's 1919 contract intact but adding bonuses worth $21,000 over the next two years. Ruth was not quite done yet, however. He soon began demanding a share of the $100,000 price paid for his transfer to the Yankees. It was *his* services that had been sold, he argued. That demand, of course, would not be met, but it fully bared Ruth's rebellious take on baseball's labor relations.[32]

Infinitely richer between the sale price and promises of loans from the colonels, Frazee should have felt relieved. The Boston press and public, however, stunned by the loss of the slugger hero, lashed out at the Red Sox owner. One paper slammed the sale as a "tremendous blow," the loss of a champion player "in a class of ball payers that flashes across the firmament once in a great while, and who alone brings the crowds to the park, whether the team is winning or losing."[33] Initially, Frazee protested that he simply could not afford to keep Ruth, but as criticism mounted, he turned on Ruth to relieve the growing pressure on himself. The Babe's "attempt to flaunt the Red Sox . . . despite an unexpired contract," maintained Frazee, "called for a showdown as a matter of discipline." Hurling a line that would be used frequently against Ruth, Frazee charged that the Babe had come to "regard himself as . . . bigger than the game itself."[34] Elsewhere Frazee assailed Ruth as "one of the most selfish and inconsiderate men ever to put on a baseball uniform." A "smooth working machine" such as the Red Sox "could no longer put up with his eccentricities," insisted the embattled Red Sox owner. "Twice during the past two seasons Babe has jumped the club and revolted."[35]

Hardly one to back away, Ruth quickly issued a rejoinder. "Because I demanded a big increase in salary . . . he brands me as an ingrate and a trouble maker," the Babe slung back. "The time of a ball player is short and he must get his money in a few years or lose out," he explained.[36] At least on this occasion, Ruth basically won the argument. Frazee would go down in baseball lore as the shortsighted man who sacrificed a legend to finance forgettable Broadway musicals.

The grand sum paid for Ruth, however, and not his past conflicts with Frazee, in fact, became the favored topic of discussion that winter in the wake of the sale. Front-page news across the country, the hefty transaction appeared to some evidence of priorities seriously askew. At a time when American culture appeared increasingly divided between traditional and modern perspectives on a great range of issues, the sale hit a nerve. A stodgy *New York Times* editorial mockingly likened the "sale" of a ballplayer to the unlikely prospect of Columbia University paying the University of Chicago "for the release of an eminent professor."[37] Rice, perhaps the nation's premier sports columnist and something of a traditionalist, flipped an adage: the Yankees team slogan, he mused, should read, "If at first you don't succeed, buy, buy again."[38]

When Ruth once more challenged baseball's contractual system in February by asserting he was entitled to $15,000 of his $100,000 sale price, the response from sportswriters was dismissive. Rice again poked fun: "Babe Ruth would like to collect $15,000 more. In which case the Babe has practically nothing on 100,000 of his fellow citizens."[39] *South Bend Tribune* sports editor Eugene Kessler measured the flashy Ruth against the scrappy Ty Cobb: "Years from now you will hear about Babe Ruth dropping one. Not one home run, but just sliding from the majors to the minors, while Ty Cobb will still be the leading batter of the league."[40]

The sale and Ruth's robust raise also sparked apprehensions about what financial figures would mean to baseball's stability. Former pitcher Christy Mathewson, who had strong ties to baseball's establishment, warned Ruth's salary would end up "aggravating the tendency on the part of the other players to hold out for much higher salaries." Rumors in fact swirled "in some quarters" of a "general holdout" by players seeking a greater share of profits made the previous season, in particular the $800,000 raked in at the gates during the 1919 World Series, in which players shared very little.[41] No such "general holdout" occurred in 1920, but Mathewson's musings clearly spoke to the disquiet within the baseball establishment, anxieties heightened by Babe Ruth's growing fame and outspokenness.

Most sportswriters appreciated Ruth as great copy during the slow winter season, and they rallied around the big deal as infusing the game with new excitement. Hearst's star sportswriter Damon Runyon branded the sale "the most stupendous deal in the history of the national game." He reminded readers that merely "a few years ago George Ruth was a poor little orphan boy in Baltimore. Monday, as 'Babe' Ruth, the mightiest slugger in baseball, he brought $125,000."[42] Fred Lieb of the New York *Sun* echoed Runyon's enthusiasm: "Babe Ruth, balldom's premier mauler and greatest individual drawing card, is a Yankee, and don't be afraid to pinch yourselves either, New York fans, because it's the gospel truth."[43] Nor would Ruth's sale and the generous bonus he plied from the Yankees encourage others to demand higher salaries and threaten to destabilize the game. Less than a week before, William "Bunk" MacBeth had decried Ruth as a potential "contract breaker." Now he waxed that the Babe provoked no "professional jealousies" among his peers, who "do not enjoy his big salary." Ruth's stunning sale at a record price hardly portended "a general desire to hold out" among other baseball players, as Mathewson had feared. It served, MacBeth asserted, "rather to arouse even greater appreciation of the generosity of the owners."[44]

The Ruthian "Frenzy"

The lively conversation surrounding Ruth's sale clearly related to changing views of celebrity, capitalism, and the value of spectator sports. But the debate and the brash young slugger at the center of the issue provided welcome distraction above all else, particularly welcome during a record cold winter. Still, more than just weather fed the sensation surrounding the sale and the ongoing fascination during the 1920 season. A brief examination of the larger national context in which Ruth ascended to superstardom helps explain the frenzy that surrounded Ruth the entire season.

Clearly "frenzy" is the appropriate term: from beginning to end of the 1920 season, fans displayed intensely emotional reactions to Ruth. At a packed preseason exhibition game between the Yankees and Brooklyn Dodgers played at Ebbets Field, spectators enthusiastically "rode" Ruth when the hitter struck out, then celebrated wildly the triple he smacked in "revenge." By the ninth inning, the crowd "took things into its own hands [and] decided it could wait no longer for a close-up of Babe Ruth." Fans poured from the stands and encircled Ruth. The umpire briefly tried to corral the throngs off the field, but facing odds of "8,000 to 1," he relented and called the game.[45] At season's end, Ruth again found himself the object of a frenzied mob, this time in Chicago. After delivering a talk for charity, a crowd of both children and adults swarmed him. Future novelist, but then a sixteen-year-old fan, James T. Farrell watched in wonder as the mob "pushed, shoved, scrambled, and yelled so that Ruth could scarcely move. . . . There was an expression of bewilderment on his moon face."[46] Ruth fought for air and took refuge in a shoeshine stand to await a police escort.[47]

What accounts for this frenzy? Clearly sportswriters and publicity specialists fanned and directed the flames, but they did not create the phenomenon. To some extent, the social sciences help make comprehensible such intangibles as fame, collective hysteria, and idol worship. Sociologist Neil Smelser, for instance, suggests that a popular "craze" is indicative of deeper unstated social, economic, or political strains and tensions. Preconditions create "structural conductivity" that can lead to a craze or frenzy.[48]

Indeed, such conditions, seemingly insoluble domestic and international tensions, existed in overabundance in 1919 and 1920. Ruth's "mobbing" at Ebbets Field took place a mere sixteen months after the armistice ending the Great War. Americans lost over one hundred thousand (including death by disease), and well over two hundred thousand were injured. Although the United States was unlikely to reenter combat, wartime hostilities hardly appeared settled. Throughout the year, headlines celebrating Ruth shared space with grim news from the continent. As the baseball season opened, France prepared to reoccupy forcibly the disputed Ruhr region when Germany resisted heavy reparations. Elsewhere, the allies confronted with trepidation the emerging Bolshevik state in Russia. American troops remained in Siberia until April 1920. In the summer of 1920, a US naval officer was killed when US forces attempted to mediate between Jugo-Slavs and Italians in the Adriatic Sea. At the same time, the US Senate bitterly debated President Wilson's Versailles Treaty, eventually voting it down. Domestically, a wave of labor strikes followed the war. Race riots came as well, as did

America's first "Red Scare" and corresponding "raids" led by the attorney general against suspected radicals. To all of this, Ruth offered much-needed escapism. As sportswriter Bugs Baer joked of Ruth in 1920, "He made the Nation of Leagues forget about the League of Nations."[49] Compared to the day-to-day travails of most Americans, the topic of Ruth, his sale, and his salary was light and frivolous, rare welcome news.

If Americans needed a break from the gloomy intensity of national and international news, baseball also needed diversion. Its longstanding problems continued to fester. As the 1920 season approached, sportswriter Mc-Geehan reviewed the "hard knocks" recently besetting the game. Tensions between Ban Johnson and key owners, threats by players to "expose dishonest practices" in the major leagues, and "scandal rumors associated with several members of the White Sox in the last year's world series" all hung over the game. The future of baseball, warned McGeehan, "rests entirely with the players," who must show their "profession is kept above the breath of suspicion."[50]

Ruth offered the game of baseball what it desperately needed: a stunningly popular, marketable star capable of driving up attendance and profits. The Babe, as his name connoting innocence suggested, could also be marketed as an antidote to the specter of scandal hoovering over the game. After decades of instability and threats, such as gambling and antitrust suits, Ruth portended a brighter, more gainful tomorrow.

It was in the context of these draining "structural strains" and breakdowns that Babe Ruth mounted his blazing ascent into popular consciousness. By the end of the year, Ruth's name, claimed *Current Opinion* magazine, was "on the tips of more tongues than any living American."[51]

Rapidly changing cultural dynamics also made possible the Ruth phenomenon. More than ever, America had a national culture. Stories, images, and ideas increasingly could be broadcast across the nation. In 1920, radio had yet to emerge on a national basis, but it would within several years, further connecting the population to figures such as Babe Ruth. Still, between nationally circulated magazines and a plethora of daily newspapers featuring photo sections and syndicated columnists, Americans increasingly were exposed to one broad commercial culture. Within that culture, sports served more and more as escapist entertainment. Older notions of "athleticism" and "muscular Christianity" associated with moral uplift were cast aside.[52] Babe Ruth became a central element of that new culture.[53]

"Like a Circus"

Sensing a once-in-a-lifetime marketing opportunity brewing, interested parties mobilized to promote the Yankees and Ruth as the preseason neared. New York newspapers dispatched an unprecedented thirteen reporters to Florida to cover Ruth. The Tourist and Convention Bureau and local Rotary Club of Jacksonville, Florida, soon to host Yankees spring-training camp, joined forces to "launch an extensive advertising campaign" to foster tourism during the spring. "The Yankees with Babe Ruth as the headline attraction," announced the *New York Times*, "are going to be billed through Florida like a circus."[54] Following training camp, the Yankees planned to weave north slowly, playing exhibition games along the way aimed at building momentum and anticipation. Ruth personally got in on the marketing action. As throngs "anxious for a peep at the new home run sensation" mobbed him throughout the South, Ruth, "with a lavish hand," took to passing out sample cigars from a factory he co-owned.[55]

As the dark winter of Red Scares, Versailles Treaty debates, and Spanish Flu brightened with the first signs of spring, Americans, more than ever, turned to baseball for its regenerative powers. Nostalgically (and perhaps with Ruth in mind), Rice waxed, "Where the magnates yelp for lawyers / And the players howl for dough / Give us the breath of April / And the game we used to know."[56] Essayist Benjamin De Casseres celebrated baseball as "the greatest and cleanest sport the world has ever known . . . the sport of democracies." In particular De Casseres pined to see Babe Ruth, "the epical figure of baseball. . . . Like all honest-to-Allah heroes, the rise of the Babe has been mysterious and meteoric. He came trailing clouds of mystery . . . his origins are legendary."[57] Despite his association with the lamented business side of the game, Ruth now also epitomized the regenerative aspect of a game that began its season with the coming of spring. Anticipation crackled, but the question remained: Could Ruth meet mounting expectations?

Initially the answer was no. Always a slow starter, but also perhaps feeling pressure from the onslaught of attention, Ruth floundered. His emerging superhero status left him particularly vulnerable to comeuppances. As Ruth would later discover in spades, tearing down a hero, as much as building one up, seems an entrenched part of American democratic culture. For sportswriters, perennially seeking a story line, the story became what was *not* happening at the plate. When veteran yeoman pitcher George Mogridge twice fanned Ruth during a practice game, reporters pounced. A mere "revenue cutter," pronounced "Bunk" MacBeth, had crushed "battle cruiser"; in short "David slew Goliath."[58]

Even after Ruth's much-anticipated arrival north, his performance at bat remained anemic. Opening the season at Shibe Park in Philadelphia, Ruth "muffed" an easy fly ball, contributing to a Yankees loss. "The great Ruth, the King Ruth, the powerful Ruth, the puissant Ruth, the prodigious Ruth," wrote William Hennigan, "instead of being the hero was the player who obligingly presented [Philadelphia manager Connie] Mack with the victory on a silver platter."[59]

The next day, as the Yankees again took the field against the Athletics, a small boy seeking out Ruth suddenly appeared toting a large package. As several thousand Philadelphians gaped, Ruth opened the box to find a brown derby hat, the sort made famous in the comedic routines of vaudevillians Weber and Fields. If the intent was to mock the stumbling hero or goad him into revealing his much-discussed temper, it failed. He "took it like a regular guy," broke into a smile, and laughed with the crowd. Ruth then posed for cameras wearing the hat.[60] McGeehan took Ruth's response as a good sign, proving the "Babe has one asset, which is particularly valuable to a ball player, the ability to resist any attempts at goat-getting."[61] Days later, however, a rib injury further threatened Ruth's plans to start hitting. "Owners and Managers Bearing Up Bravely over Catastrophe," teased the New York *Tribune* in a subheadline lampooning the drama over Ruth's slump and injuries.[62]

Finally, on April 26, Ruth, "a pale and interesting invalid with his eleventh rib wrenched loose from its moorings," according to McGeehan, suddenly appeared as a pinch hitter late in a game against the Washington Senators. The Yankees had fallen behind, but Ruth's "presence, like that of a somewhat overfed Banquo's Ghost, so startled the Senators that they tossed the game right back to the Yankees." Ruth's hit helped win the game. "I thought hay ban a sick feller," mumbled a stunned senator in McGeehan's satiric depiction. "Hay don't look like hay ben sick feller," replied a teammate.[63]

Within days, Banquo's ghost appeared fully recovered. On May 1, Ruth clocked a mammoth home run out of the Polo Grounds. "What might be termed a monster celebration greeted the Babe," reported New York *Sun* correspondent William B. Hanna. "There was a spontaneous riot of enthusiasm to reward the big man."[64] Runyon described how "ladies and gents stood up and screamed at him. Small children cried for him. Ruth doffed his dices in recognition of the plaudits and sat down. From a box high up in the upper left field tier [Yankees Owner] Colonel Ruppert beamed effusively on the multitudes."[65] Days later Ruth "ran amuck with a heavy piece of timber at the Polo Grounds," blasting two home runs and a triple.[66] By mid-May 1920, Ruth was chasing down another home-run record, and hysterical crowds besieged ballparks around the country to see the spectacle. The first of many melodramatic Ruthian comebacks was complete.

"The Hardest Hitter of All Time"

As Ruth began his march toward a new home-run record and ever-greater prominence, sportswriters began to flesh out the hero's personality. The Ruth of 1920 bore little resemblance to the undisciplined, grown-boy-with-a-big-bat image that dominated later. Above all, writers stressed power and confidence, in marked contrast to pervasive postwar pessimism and exhaustion. Over was the "deadball" era when teams played conservative, low-scoring games. Now hitters aimed for the fences. Some claimed the league shifted to a livelier ball to accommodate more home runs. Most observers, sportswriter Hugh Fullerton explained, "seem to think that the greatest cause in the style of play is the fact that Ruth, because of great hitting and the terrific amount of press agenting he has received, has proven to owners and managers what the public likes to see."[67]

Sportswriters expended considerable exertion analyzing Ruth's power at the plate. "Paraphrasing the late lamented Mr. Shakespeare," wrote McGeehan, "Babe Ruth doth bestride the narrow baseball diamonds like a colossus . . . he is the hardest hitter of all time."[68] Sid Mercer of the *Evening Journal* depicted Ruth as a "Harveyized steel man . . . who can raise an automobile with a lame wrist."[69] Runyon insisted that the ancient "weapon which was the nearest approach to Babe's deadly drive was the catapult."[70] The Babe's preference for a weightier bat—fifty-four ounces over the thirty-six to forty-six ounces used by most players—also merited intensive scrutiny. Analysts devoted endless words in print to Ruth's dramatic batting style, which proved compelling even when the slugger struck out, which was often. Meanwhile, writers competed inventing elaborate, usually alliterative, nicknames for the hitter: Colossus of Clouters, Sultan of Swat, Son of Sock, Caliph of Crash, Goliath of Swat, Mastodonic Mauler, Knight of Swat, Master Mauler, Bazoo of Bang, Maryland Mauler, Rajah of Rap, Baron of Bam, Tarzan of the Diamond, and Batterin' Bambino.

Ruth promoter Runyon lent an additional wrinkle to the superman image. With his singular might, contended Runyon, "It is a blessing that Babe Ruth does not hit through the infield. He would kill or dangerously injure anyone who got in front of one of his powerful punches." In fact, despite his exceptional poise, Ruth held "a secret dread of smashing a ball back at a pitcher or infielder" and doing them serious harm.[71]

Still, self-assurance remained the key ingredient to Ruth's success, argued many writers. Anticipating the "autosuggestion" optimistic thinking fad soon to sweep America, courtesy of Frenchman Émile Coué, McGeehan credited Ruth's success to "that supreme confidence in himself that comes after certain achievement."[72] Focus and confidence characterized Ruth's ghostwritten weekly columns (syndicated in newspapers) as well. In marked contrast to the hyperbole of sportswriters, the ghosted Ruth approached his power in a matter-of-fact, mechanistic manner. "I wonder if I can't set my aim at 55 home runs for this season instead of only 50, and make good before this league schedule folds up on me," he informed readers in a September column. "Today's homer, my 49th, was my sixth in a couple of weeks and I'm clear out of the slump. . . . It doesn't seem impossible to get six more, for a total of 55 in the remaining games on tour and at home."[73] Ruth appeared almost as an accountant, dispassionately calibrating his assets. This focus on numbers and quantification, as several historians argue, represents a major component of modern sports.[74]

Of course fans were anything but dispassionate about Ruth's power and record-breaking hitting. Fanning the flames of the phenomenon, sportswriters helped sustain the hysteria so obvious in April at Ebbets Field. The public increasingly came to the ballpark largely for one reason: to see Ruth hit a home run. The atmosphere involved anticipation, then an explosion of excitement when the home run came. "The ovation that was accorded the great slugger," reported the *New York American* on the occasion of Ruth's thirty-first home run, "was in complete consonance with his mighty drive. Hats were thrown in the air. Men, women, and boys shrieked with delight and for almost five minutes, they howled their applause."[75] McGeehan described the same crowd as "packed with hysterical beings, screaming and waving hats."[76] By the end of the season, the Yankees, once an "orphan ball club, without a home of its own, without players of outstanding ability, without prestige," became the first team to draw over a million spectators.[77] Baseball and everything surrounding it, including sports writing, appeared suddenly on the brink of an unprecedented explosion in interest.

Ruth himself became a symbol of prosperity. Writers could not resist his rags-to-riches story. According to sportswriter Dan Daniel, Ruth landed at "St. Mary's Industrial Institution in Baltimore—a school for truants and incorrigibles—not because he was rowdy but because he needed a home. He was an orphan without friends or relatives."[78] For many writers, the irresistible comparison was to the still-popular dime novels of Horatio Alger, in which modest yet industrious boys end up rewarded for their thrift and goodness. McGeehan and Rice, however, both agreed that Ruth's astounding success went beyond anything Alger might have conceived. "The story of George Herman Ruth, the idol of the American male," explained McGeehan, "reads in life more like romance than any of the Horatio Alger stories of Ragged Dick and Tattered Tom or From Bootblack to Banker."[79] Rice concurred: "None of Mr. Alger's heroes was ever followed by vast mobs and acclaimed almost daily by striking headlines across the front page. Thus does Babe Ruth rise superior even to fiction—or what imagination twenty years ago could devise."[80]

Indeed, the deserving poor boy turned exceedingly wealthy sports hero intrigued the public. Throughout his career, Ruth's unprecedented salaries and general material prosperity generated intense fascination. As Runyon explained "If we seem to speak of Babe more than somewhat, we trust the reader will bear with us. All our life we have been poor, and Babe cost so much money that even to talk about it gives us a wealthy feeling."[81]

Capitalizing on public enthrallment with the heavy hitter, United News, the syndicate that handled Ruth's ghostwritten columns, produced a serialized, multipart "Autobiography of Babe Ruth," appearing in papers across the country. The series set the record straight: Ruth was no orphan but rather a street kid, "hard as a railroad doughnut," who landed in a Catholic reform school, where kindly Brother Matthias "soaked the doughnut in the milk of human kindness."[82] The autobiographical series allowed Ruth to combat lingering notions that he "suffered a case of ego." Recalling the derby episode in Philadelphia earlier in the season, "If they gave a conceited guy the brown derby in front of thousands, he'd never get over it." To Ruth, however, "It was just about the greatest joke ever put across on me."[83]

Ruth's altruism also drew media attention. As Sid Mercer explained, "Ruth is popular because he never refuses to aid worthy causes."[84] As might befit a man often labeled an "orphan," the hero took special interest in boys. Commenting on the mountain of fan mail he received, Ruth explained, "Letters come from people all over the country but the ones that I prize the most are from the boys. I'm strong for them, you know." Ruth added how he kept correspondence from boys as souvenirs.[85] Altruism, of course, generated positive public relations and could also translate into an effective marketing tool.

The Grand Central Palace Shoe Company, for instance, sought to capitalize on Ruth's renown by awarding him a pair of shoes each time he hit a home run. The company earned bonus public relations points when Ruth, then having smacked thirty-two home runs and having "no earthly use for 32 pairs of shoes all at once . . . found 32 orphan children" in need of footwear "for the coming winter." Shopping for the urchins, Ruth was reportedly so impressed by a product display that he vowed "to knock a few more home runs and get some shoes for himself and Mrs. Ruth."[86]

In 1920, the more flamboyant, intemperate side of Ruth's public image had yet to take hold. Instead, many writers painted the hero as modest, unassuming, and middle-class. Off the field, according to an interview with Ruth's wife, the baseball hero was a "homebody."[87] Veteran sportswriter Sam Crane insisted that Ruth was no "poser. . . . It is Babe's democratic ways that appeal. . . . Ruth is universally popular because of his forgetfulness of self." His "democratic ways," explained Crane, are "almost as big an attraction as his home-run ability."[88] In a magazine interview, Ruth supposedly explained that "as a class, baseball players are well read and take an interest in current affairs. Today there are scores of college graduates who select a career on the diamond in preference to in a bank or broker office."[89]

Along those lines, Ruth's temper, already a matter of public record, was played down. "Seldom," McGeehan wrote, does one hear of Ruth "quarreling with an umpire." The Yankees standout has the "native sense of fairness not to do this." No wonder, McGeehan explained, "all players and nearly all men like him."[90]

Rather unexpectedly, writers also linked Ruth to rural America. A product of urban Baltimore, living in a posh Manhattan hotel, the heavy hitter seemed the ultimate metropolitan. Yet a short 1920 biographical sketch written in Ruth's voice mused of a rural youth: "It does not take long for a boy to find out that the hills and creeks of Maryland are a wonderland, calling insistently to him to come bask in their secrets." As an adult, the piece explained, Ruth saw his "real home" as a working farm in Sudbury, Massachusetts.[91]

In the middle of the busy 1920 season, Ruth arranged to make a movie— *Headin' Home*, "a delightful photoplay of youth and happiness," that premiered in September at Madison Square Garden. The light comedy featured clever captions penned by sportswriter Bugs Baer. Ruth starred (naturally) as the "Babe," a simple country boy from Haverlock, "a hamlet in the sticks." Fashioning baseball bats from the trees he chops down, Babe proves a natural hitter. After some comic shenanigans, he arrives in the big city and makes good as a baseball hero. In the final scenes, hometown characters gather at the Polo Grounds to watch Babe—little surprise—smack a game-winning home run.[92] A reveling crowd then mobs the "Babe," but, viewers are informed, he remains at heart a "likeable country boy." The movie garnered positive reviews (several critics acknowledging initial low expectations).[93] It also reinforced Ruth's and baseball's mythic link to the America of small towns, even as big cities increasingly subsumed the nation. As the media would have it, Ruth, to paraphrase historian Richard Hofsteader, grew up in the country then moved to the city (but retained the innocence of simpler times and places).

In many ways, the Babe Ruth crafted in particular by sportswriters in 1920 was a malleable and all-encompassing figure. He bridged the gaping divides of an American society limping out of the war years. In a time of doubt, he offered brash power and confidence. In an era marked by corruption, he evinced, as the sobriquet "Babe" suggested, youthful innocence. Unashamedly wealthy and rarely self-reflective, Ruth appeared at times the quintessential modern urbanite. Yet through his farm and refuge in Massachusetts, and his association with baseball's mythic pastoral and democratic roots, Ruth harkened back to America's rural origins as well. He spanned, in a sense, the city-country gulf so evident in a nation evenly split, as revealed in the 1920 census, between rural and urban. His Maryland roots also bridged divides, seeming to suggest origins neither northern nor southern, but rather somewhere in between.

Ruth even managed in some senses to bridge the deepest chasm in American society—that of race. Rumors about his racial background swirled from his earliest days playing baseball at St. Mary's in Baltimore. Many African Americans suspected Babe was "passing" as white. Growing up in New York in the 1930s, Art Rust Jr., later one of the first African American sportscasters, recalled household debates about the "purity" of Ruth's racial makeup. "Maybe the Babe was just a 'high yallow' black guy. I didn't believe it, even though I wanted to," recalled Rust.[94] Ruth's rival, Ty Cobb, a fierce racist, shared those suspicions about Ruth. According to sportswriter Fred Lieb, Cobb viewed Ruth as racially suspect and refused at one point to stay in a hunting lodge with him.[95] Ruth's liberal approach to race, no doubt, fed such conjecture. While never an activist, Ruth appeared to relish the opportunity to play Negro League teams during barnstorming tours. He befriended black players and would conspicuously chat with them in dugouts.[96] Among the many charitable causes Ruth supported were black charities, such as when he arrived as the "honored guest" in 1923 at a fundraiser for Harlem's Mother AME Zion Church. Organizers of the event, held at the Renaissance Casino, Harlem's premier night spot, auctioned off baseballs signed by the Babe to support the construction of a large new church.[97]

Open insinuations about Ruth's racial makeup never appeared in print. Still, what appears coded language proliferated, such as when Bugs Baer, known for his colorful quips, celebrated the way "that gorilla glanded baby can wham that Spalding pebble."[98] Likewise, on the field, opposing players often taunted Ruth as "the big baboon," an insulting moniker that often found its way into print.[99] AL umpire Bill McGowan even used the degrading term to refer to Ruth in a 1930 guest newspaper column.[100]

As never before imagined, the combined impact of the Ruthian revolution of 1920 drove up attendance, and thus profits, throughout major league baseball. Turnout at Yankees games more than doubled to well over a million in 1920, making the Yankees the first team to draw over the million mark, and setting a baseball record for single-team turnout. The White Sox in Chicago saw an increase in attendance of over two hundred thousand. In Cleveland, over three hundred thousand more fans came to Indians games (helped by a fine team that won the pennant that year). Washington Senator attendance grew by over one hundred thousand, and the St. Louis Browns drew nearly seventy thousand more than the previous year. Even the last-place Athletics saw turnout grow by over sixty thousand. A major initiative launched by baseball to clean up gambling in ballparks created a more inviting environment for fans.[101] Still it was clearly Ruth driving the spectator boom.

In 1920, a Philadelphia reporter encountered a "grizzly scout" marveling at the changes in the game. "Babe Ruth is the biggest noise we have ever had," waxed the old scout. "The fans are crazy about him in New York and other American league cities, but it doesn't stop there. Down the bush leagues, where I spend most of my time, there is just as much excitement."[102] NL president John Heydler recounted how relatives previously indifferent to baseball had visited him in New York. They "got the Babe Ruth fever and wouldn't be content until they had gone out to the Polo Grounds and seen him play."[103] Yankees manager Miller Huggins concurred. Babe Ruth, he waxed, is "the greatest drawing card of all time. He pulls them in. He makes the turnstiles click. . . . He appeals to everybody. No matter how much of a novice."[104] Team owners around the league saw a healthy jump in revenue whenever Ruth and the Yankees arrived in town. Even the National League joined in the prosperity. Fans packed Pittsburgh's Forbes Field solid when Ruth played an exhibition game against the Pirates in September. Barney Dreyfuss, the Pittsburgh owner, enjoyed a "big financial day," reported one newspaper.[105]

A minor note of concern did surface. Some journalists began worrying about Ruth's skyrocketing popularity. Was he "being made to think he is greater than the game?" The *Sporting News* moved to assure its readership that Babe "seems to be pretty well balanced for such a super-star . . . not one whit spoiled by adulation and publicity." Should he develop other ideas, however, ample opportunity will exist "to read him a lecture reminding him that the game goes on, while stars, even as great as he rise and shine for a moment, then fade and are forgotten." In fact, many such lectures were to be delivered over the next several years.[106]

"The Valley of the Shadow of Death"

In late summer of 1920, cold reality suddenly intruded on baseball's to-that-point miraculous revival season, a year hitherto marked by renewed excitement, huge crowds, and Ruth's elevation to national hero status. First tragedy intruded. On August 16, at the Polo Grounds, troubled Yankees hurler Carl Mays delivered one of his trademark submarine-style pitches to Cleveland Indians shortstop Ray Chapman. A horrified crowd watched the pitch strike Chapman squarely on the head. Chapman was evacuated to St. Lawrence Hospital where he later died of a fractured skull. "Tragedy stalked the field at the Polo Grounds yesterday. Twenty thousand people saw a man go drifting into the valley of the shadow of death," wrote Runyon.[107]

Although Cleveland manager Tris Speaker immediately absolved Mays of blame, anger at the Yankees pitcher churned. Players around the league, including Ty Cobb, threatened to boycott Mays, and petitions circulated denouncing him. The Chapman incident built on others—in particular a spring training pitch that seriously injured Yankees "Chick" Fewster. Briefly, baseball reeled. If its future was not on the line, controversy undoubtedly threatened the wave of popularity that had recently boosted the game. Desperate to halt the hemorrhaging, a number of writers rose to defend Mays, including McGeehan. League officials also worked to get beyond the incident. Meanwhile, Ruth hit his forty-third home run the day before Chapman's funeral in Cleveland, providing much-needed diversion as baseball moved to squelch the boycott movement. Stories about Chapman shared space with news concerning "scientific" tests supposedly proving that ball manufacturing had not changed in 1920, as some had claimed. Ruth's popular power hitting resulted from his natural strength and prowess, not some conspiracy to manufacture a souped-up ball—hence headlines of "Babe's Swing Not Ball Is Guilty" (guilty of personally setting a new home-run record).[108]

A general pall, however, hung over baseball, and in September a still graver challenge surfaced. Rumors of gambling and underworld influence long had dogged the game. At the opening of the 1920 season, McGeehan warned of "scandal rumors associated with several members of the White Sox in last year's World Series. . . . It is up to the player to see that his profession is kept above the breath of suspicion," he concluded.[109] The innocence and purity ascribed to Ruth by sportswriters, in part, consciously aimed to counter shadows looming over the national game. In September, those shadows darkened. Early in the month, McGeehan again cautioned ominously of "an undercurrent of gossip going the rounds that is none too reassuring for the future of the game." Once more he directly referenced the recent World Series.[110]

Days after McGeehan's warning, Ruth found himself unwittingly at the center of a well-organized gambling conspiracy. On September 9, an alert arrived via tickertape at the Wall Street offices of E. F. Hutton. On their way to Cleveland, according to the report, Ruth and several Yankees suffered serious injury in some sort of automobile accident. Two prominent Yankees were killed, and both Ruth's legs were broken. The report turned out to be, as the New York *Times* put it, "a concerted effort by professional gamblers to increase the odds in the betting on the series which will be played in Cleveland."[111] As the *Daily News* added, the incident ironically backfired on the gamblers, since the Yankees, with a healthy Babe Ruth, still lost the game.[112]

The episode, despite the impressive level of underworld organization it suggested, could be dismissed as a comic interlude. Not so with revelations that exploded later in September: Chicago White Sox players had thrown the 1919 World Series in return for payoffs from underworld gamblers. The tainted team soon would be forever branded the Black Sox. For baseball, which had waged a long and apparently futile war to control gambling, the potential fallout was immense. "Thousands upon thousands of loyal fans . . . have been badly stunned," admonished Rice, who had initially dismissed rumors of scandal.[113] Days later he lamented that "no sport has ever known a greater tragedy."[114]

Again, Ruth, unassociated in any way with the scandal, provided welcome distraction. In the final weeks of the season, as the scandal unfolded before a grand jury, Ruth seemed to be hitting home runs at will. The day Arnold Rothstein, a notorious New York gangster, was named as a key figure in the Black Sox scandal, Ruth smacked his fiftieth and fifty-first home runs in front of big, enthusiastic crowds. Under a front page headline reading "Baseball's Dirty Laundry," the *Daily News* draped a huge photo of Ruth, seemingly contrasting directly the two phenomena.

As if to solidify all the elements of Ruth's 1920 heroism, the slugger began traveling with the St. Mary's Industrial School band in tow. The school, where Ruth had spent his youth and perfected his baseball skills, had suffered a devastating fire. The band tour aimed at raising money for the "orphanage." If Babe Ruth alone was not enough, the band reinforced the innocence and enthusiasm about baseball that seemed concurrently on trial in Chicago. The very week that ever-more-serious allegations bled from a Chicago grand jury, the Philadelphia *Ledger* ran a photograph of a beaming Ruth at Shibe Park, sporting a sailor's cap and cuddling an enormous horn. A caption explained that Ruth proceeded that day to smack his fifty-fourth home run, and youthful musicians serenaded him as he circled the bases.[115] In the evening, the band held concerts hosted by Ruth "with good grace, even with enthusiasm." Admiring the Babe's altruism, the *Sporting News* waxed that "all baseball would be the gainer" from such displays.[116] The boys, having the time of their lives on the tour, delivered a pitch perfect antidote to a looming public relations disaster.

Looking back on the Black Sox scandal several years later, McGeehan recalled "much public indignation." He remembered reading "through bales of letters denouncing the national pastime and all its works." Then Babe started "doing his stuff. . . . The swing of his bat was so sincere, whether it met the ball or not, that the customers started to renew their faith."[117] Contemporary assessments echo McGeehan. "The show [Ruth's 1920 season] was too exciting, too compelling, for a scandal to stop it," contended Leigh Montville in his Ruth biography.[118] The heroic image of Ruth constructed by sportswriters—innocent, powerful, charitable, modest, and confident—served the game well as it faced an unprecedented tempest.

"The Dawn of Hope"

On September 17, 1920, the New York *Daily News* ran a lead editorial titled "The Dawn of Hope." Despite recent hardships and challenges, "Things are not as gloomy as they might be." The economy was turning up after a postwar recession, "work is plentiful, and wages are high," the editorial contended. Endorsing an isolationist posture, the *Daily News* hailed "indications in politics that this country is going to mind its own business and be thoroughly

American." And of course Babe Ruth merited mention among the positive indicators for having "courted the Yankees into a pennant" (although ultimately the Yankees fell short of that achievement in 1920).[119]

Editors at the *Daily News* had every reason to feel personally pleased with recent developments. "New York's Picture Newspaper," as it billed itself, saw remarkable growth in 1920, roughly doubling circulation to three hundred thousand copies sold a day. Readers, it seemed, could not get enough of sensational stories like "Woman's Screams Save Her from Negro Intruder," "River Bares Girl's Sad Fate," or "Mutilated Torso Found off Jersey Shore." Babe Ruth, whose visage graced issue after issue, contributed mightily to the circulation boom.

Arriving on newsstands on September 17, the timing of the editorial could not have been less fortuitous. The previous day a bomb blast had ripped through the Wall Street offices of J. P. Morgan, killing thirty-eight and injuring over a hundred. News and pictures of the horrific bombing consumed the first several pages of the tabloid. Somehow in the shock of the moment, no one thought to pull the sunny editorial inviting New Yorkers to consider their improving lot. Yet despite the terror of the moment, the Wall Street bombings, like the Chapman killing and Black Sox scandal, faded quickly into the recesses of the public consciousness. Americans almost intentionally refused to engage the issues and moved on.

For the *Daily News* audience, the dawn of a better day, even if marred by paradoxes and tensions, perhaps had arrived. The residue of an exhausting war, recession, and disease, and the stain of postwar violence, remained and continued to fester. But, often willfully, the public searched for diversion and simpler pleasures. In 1920, Babe Ruth embodied those hopes. Ruth would continue to serve baseball's purposes, lifting the sport to ever-higher levels of popularity and profits. Concurrently, Ruth's successes stirred fears that the star was becoming "bigger than the game" and hence also represented a threat. Soon a campaign to break the superstar took its place beside the ballyhoo celebrating Ruth.

THREE. CHALLENGE TO AUTHORITY
PART I

Baseball owed much to Babe Ruth in the early 1920s. The Yankees powerhouse almost single-handedly revived and redefined the game. He drove
up attendance and profits around the league. As important, Ruth provided captivating distraction as tragedy and scandal threatened to envelop the
game. Never had an American athlete been so compelling, dominant, and
important to his sport.

Yet, as the Black Sox scandal revealed, baseball remained a troubled,
vulnerable affair. Ruth's ascent to superstardom, in fact, presented baseball
with yet another problem: his fame and popularity threatened the game's
lopsided power structure. An outspoken player, well aware of his value to
the game, Ruth as a free agent could set off an unprecedented bidding war
between teams. Worse, should the Babe defect to an "outlaw league," that
league would have instant credibility. Equally problematic, Ruth could start
his own league, again posing a monumental challenge to the game. Already
the Babe's off-season barnstorming tours had generated unmatched excitement. Could the tours become a springboard to a new challenge to major
league baseball?

Baseball's power brokers thus both venerated the Yankees star for the
profits he produced and feared him as a potential threat. Controlling the
outspoken Ruth became a priority after his stunning inaugural season in
New York. In late 1920, baseball leaders reinforced their ranks by appoint-
ing Judge Kenesaw Mountain Landis to the new position of commissioner
of baseball with supposed absolute authority. Likewise, at roughly the same
time, the Yankees hired Ruth's old Red Sox nemesis, Edward Barrow, as the
team's business manager. Barrow's charges included not only strengthening

the team around Ruth but also containing the star player, forcing him to adhere to the authority of the power brokers. The arrival of Barrow—the Babe's "particular *bete noir*," as Ruth's second wife described the intimidating figure with whom Ruth shared "enmity from the start with no quarter on either side over a quarter century"—was hardly reassuring news to the Yankees star.[1] Barrow made little effort to conceal his contempt for Ruth, at one point referring to him in a private letter as "the big poor simpleton."[2] Instead of hiring someone with a clean slate to manage a still-young athlete struggling with the temptations of sudden wealth and fame, the Yankees ownership turned to the aggressive Barrow, now known even to his friends as "Simon Legree," a relentless driver of players.

"Fleeced"

Attendance and profits soared at ballparks around the league in 1920. Yankees owners Huston and Ruppert incurred substantial risk bringing Babe Ruth to New York. Rarely has an investment paid off so quickly and so dramatically. Bolstered by their star player, the Yankees, once Gotham's stepchild team, surged to become a national conversation piece. All parties, from owners to players to sportswriters, basked in the glow of renewed enthusiasm and unprecedented profits.

Yet the Black Sox scandal cast a long shadow. A grand jury indicted eight White Sox players just as the 1920 season wrapped up. A trial with any number of potentially devastating revelations was slated for the next year during baseball season. On November 6, 1920, a Chicago special grand jury investigating gambling and baseball released findings that sought to paint the best face on recent events: players, it acknowledged, had thrown games, "but the practice was not general . . . a comparatively small number of players have been dishonest." Still, beyond immediate corruption on the ball field, thousands of people, the grand jury reported, had been "fleeced" of hundreds of thousands of dollars in "pools" operated by unscrupulous characters.[3] Gambling remained a serious millstone for the game.

As baseball struggled with the Black Sox scandal, the owners of three AL teams continued to make war on AL president Ban Johnson. As the stakes grew, the Yankees, Red Sox, and White Sox toyed with absconding to the National League. The move would have left just five teams in the American League and ballooned the National League to eleven teams. Creation of a "New National League," all parties understood, portended yet more chaos for baseball.[4]

Concurrently, the Federal Circuit Court of Appeals took up the case of *Federal Baseball Club v. the National League*, a challenge to the game's antitrust exemption with the potential of negating the reserve clauses and throwing organized baseball into turmoil. Over a year earlier, a federal court had ruled that baseball violated the Sherman Antitrust Act. Major league officials and owners had howled in protest and rushed to appeal the verdict. In the fall of 1920, amid disclosures about the Black Sox, the federal appeals court began deliberations. Perhaps anticipating a decision against the owners, some players again talked of reconstituting a players' union. Sportswriters, echoing the interests of the ownership class, dismissed such talk as the product of misbegotten notions the "game 'belongs' to the players." Such a perspective, argued the *Sporting News*, bore "hints of soviet tendencies."[5] Still, among baseball's leadership class, apprehensions grew.

Rowdyism also remained a concern. The implementation of double umpiring (two umpires working each game) lessened the number of disputed calls. Likewise, baseball authorities gave umpires more power to punish rowdy players. Still, problems persisted, especially among fans. Late in the 1920 season, the New York City chief magistrate warned of growing rowdyism among a "certain element." Throwing bottles at umpires and fans, in particular, was an "increasing" problem. "When the whole populace, as never before, is following with excited interest, the glorious contest at baseball fields," trouble, the magistrate warned, would be met with swift justice.[6] At roughly the same time, Giants manager John McGraw again found himself in the midst of controversy regarding his notoriously violent temper. McGraw emerged chief suspect in the violent beatings of two actors on separate occasions in August and September 1920. The incidents, clearly provoked by drinking, also prompted calls for McGraw's prosecution under the Volstead Act, which enforced Prohibition. In the end, the various cases against McGraw fell apart, but troubled and unseemly characters clearly lurked just under major league baseball's veneer of respectability.[7]

Between the gambling and violence crises, coupled with internal divisions and threats from players, baseball owners spiraled into full-scale panic. A new era of previously unheard-of profits and prosperity seemed threatened by old, unsettled demons. Desperate to create a sense of credibility and authority, and with the old National Commission system in profound disarray, baseball owners gambled on a new approach. They would cede authority over baseball to one figure, a commissioner with near-absolute power. Landis fit the bill flawlessly. A known national figure, the theatrical, ego-driven judge was to be baseball's "Puritan in Babylon," a figure of unquestionable integrity capable of reining in players, maintaining authority, and acting as a firewall to preserve and protect baseball's supposed purity.[8] Landis well understood his role as a symbol and respected the balance of power within the game. He focused on players, avoided interfering in the internal affairs of baseball teams, and maintained good relations with the game's owners.

Landis also forged strong relations with the press. "He always had the press on his side because he played up the press," recalled Philadelphia sportswriter Al Horwitz. "He was smart. . . . Landis knew that baseball could always use publicity."[9] When the judge's selection was announced at Chicago's Congress Hotel, assembled sportswriters "breathed sighs of relief" and threw parties in honor of Landis.[10]

Media support was essential. As the public face of baseball's establishment, Landis focused primarily on improving the game's image and bringing troublesome, potentially rebellious players publicly to heel. As a federal judge, Landis had acted against Standard Oil, Rockefeller's monopolistic oil enterprise; he thus had the reputation of something of a progressive. Still, presiding over early reviews of the Federal League case, Landis appeared sympathetic to the baseball establishment, and the judge was outspoken in his distaste for radicalism. He denounced World War I draft evaders (a category that might include Ruth) as "slackers" and oversaw the conviction of Big Bill Haywood of the radical Industrial Workers of the World on charges of violating the Espionage and Sedition Acts. Landis remained an establishment man, determined to maintain and fortify the status quo.

From a public relations standpoint, Landis proved a wild success. The self-assured and self-righteous commissioner took full aim at errant players while publicly ignoring the rivalries and tensions among baseball's ownership class. "If I catch any crook in baseball, the rest of his life is going to be a pretty hot one," he boasted as he took office.[11] Among his first directives, Landis ordered John McGraw to divest his holdings in a Havana casino. As 1921 spring training got underway, Landis expelled from baseball Philadelphia Phillies first baseman Eugene Paulette for accepting gifts from gamblers. Days later, he suspended New York Giant Benny Kauff, then under indictment for automobile theft. Landis never reinstated Kauff, despite his later acquittal.

The newly minted commissioner also took a strong stand against any player violating or compromising even in the most remote way the reserve clause. Six months into his term as commissioner, Landis vetoed the sale to the New York Giants of Heinie Groh, an outstanding third baseman for the Cincinnati Reds. Groh had held out at the beginning of the 1921 season, demanding that he be traded to McGraw's club, where he had begun his career. The Reds relented and agreed to the sale. Landis, however, saw an opportunity to curb any notion players might have about controlling their own destinies; he nullified the sale. "The decision handed down by Judge Landis compels me to play with a club I don't want to perform with and for a salary that is not agreeable to me," groused Groh before accepting the commissioner's mandate.[12] Baseball authorities meanwhile celebrated the move. Judge Landis, declared Cubs manager Johnny Evers, "has shown then that he will not stand for any foolishness and I think you will find a big improvement in the work of several men as a result of the decision."[13] Later that summer, Landis permanently suspended the eight Chicago White Sox involved in the 1919 World Series imbroglio. Clearly, the commissioner intended to enforce order in baseball as never before, and he sought high-profile cases to dramatize his control.

"Little which is new remains to be said"

On the surface, Ruth's 1921 season much resembled his 1920 season, only better. He hit fifty-nine home runs, breaking his own record, and batted a stunning .378 average. Even before the regular season, Ruth was the center attraction. His arrival at spring training camp in Shreveport, Louisiana, occasioned a near riot. "All of the Shreveport that knows of baseball and even those that don't thronged to the little railroad station and the street outside to get a glimpse of the great Yankees slugger," reported the *Daily News*, which tracked with dogged precision Ruth's every move throughout the 1920s.[14]

As Ruth set about again chasing down a new home-run record, writers turned to now-familiar staples. He remained baseball's "superman." "The superman has a subtle attraction. Napoleon said that impossible was a word found only in the vocabularies of fools. Babe Ruth doesn't say it, but what is more convincing he proves it," wrote F. C. Lane.[15] Hugh Fullerton attempted to ground Ruth's powers in science. The sportswriter persuaded the slugger to undergo a battery of tests at Columbia University, designed to determine, as Fullerton told Ruth, "just why *you* can slam the ball as nobody else in the world can." The investigation revealed that "brain not bone" lay at the core of Ruth's powers—"that the coordination of [Ruth's] eye, brain, nerve system, and muscle is practically perfect." In fact, "Ruth the Superman," as Fullerton hailed him, operated at 90 percent efficiency while the average person toiled at somewhere around 60 percent.[16]

Yet running alongside the superman theme, writers also increasingly played Ruth for laughs. The superstar did not help himself when in early June he landed in jail for speeding along Manhattan's Riverside Drive. A judge, noting Ruth had recently been nabbed for the same infraction, fined the star one hundred dollars and sentenced him to a day (six hours, in fact) in "traffic jail." Front-page news in the *New York Times* and other papers, the episode bore the potential of harming Ruth's image, especially as an idol to the young. Yet newspapers treated the hitter's incarceration as a joke. That Ruth's release from jail after several hours allowed him to race across town in time to play in that afternoon's game provided further grist for sportswriters. Covering the nine-mile journey to the Polo Grounds from prison in a mere nineteen minutes, newspapers noted, meant speeding again. "The outlook for the Yankees was most grim," reported the *New York Tribune*, "until the 'Babe' broke jail and suddenly appeared . . . at the Polo Ground, swinging his old war club."[17]

The arrest episode, soon forgotten, highlighted a problematic aspect of Ruth's persona: it reinforced a reputation for recklessness and borderline contempt for authority. "If I'm pinched again it won't be in this state," Ruth reportedly shot over his shoulder as he sped from jail.[18] In his ghostwritten column, Ruth later floated the claim that his speeding resulted from his commitment "to put every ounce of strength into everything that I do." The Babe's claim proved too much for the *New York Times* editorial desk. The comment "illustrates the amiable simplicity of his mind," fumed the editorial.[19] This new depiction of Ruth as reckless and simpleminded built on reports earlier that year of Ruth losing $35,000 in a few days betting on horse racing in Cuba, and having been "gypped out" of $37,500 for his work in the *Heading Home* film the previous year.[20]

That Ruth's speeding ticket would merit comment on the *New York Times* editorial page suggests the episode had some cultural resonance. Indeed, in the 1920s, many Americans saw traditional Victorian norms and authority as under fire. Traditionalists bemoaned a new generation with looser attitudes about morality and societal order. Observers often associated these new attitudes with the emergence of radio, movies, and automobiles. In this light, the fact that Ruth's clash with authority involved a car perhaps hit a particular sore point. His later collision with Commissioner Landis also might be read in terms of a society struggling to preserve tradition in the face of rapid change.

There appeared also a related but more basic challenge for Ruth: hero fatigue. Urban modern culture spurred the full-on arrival of mass culture, transmitted through newspapers, magazines, movies, and radio. The frenzy of fame and celebrity that enveloped Babe Ruth in 1920 owed everything to this mass culture. Basking in the adulation of celebrity, Ruth also ran up against a series of unpleasant realities connected to the fragile place of celebrity in the new mass culture. In particular, the media and public demanded news, a constant flow of fresh information. By its very nature, news requires novelty—things literally new. By the 1920s, the media's insatiable appetite seemed an ever-growing part of culture. Amory Blaine, the verbose protagonist of *This Side of Paradise*, F. Scott Fitzgerald's first novel, lamented that no sooner did a public figure establish himself than "the cross currents of criticism wash him away. My lord no man can stand prominence these days. It's the quickest path to obscurity. People get sick of hearing the same names over and over."[21]

That Ruth could hit a home run hardly passed for news in 1921. Writers struggled for a new angle on an old story as Ruth rounded off the 1921 season in strong form. On September 16, he broke his own home-run mark when he smashed his fifty-fifth in front of twenty-eight thousand fans at the Polo Grounds. During the season, he had hit the longest home runs ever at Navin Field in Detroit and Philadelphia's Shibe Park. Sportswriters obligatorily celebrated each milestone with the usual superlatives. Yet a note of resignation occasionally crept in. Ruth was such "a towering figure in contemporary sport," wrote F. C. Lane, "that seemingly little which is new remains to be said."[22] Heywood Broun concurred. "Ruth suffers a little from his infallibility," he explained. "It would be exciting to watch a man with a seven league boot run circles around the finest sprinters in the world, but it would not warm the heart."[23] Superman had grown predictable. The human interest side of the story was missing. "There is no contest left," fretted Grantland Rice. "The spectacle of Ruth batting against his own high mark has become extremely stale."[24] A cartoon sketched by sportswriter/cartoonist (and later broadcaster) Thorton Fisher of the *Evening World* underscored Ruth's dilemma. Fisher's first panel, labeled "When he hits a home run," presents two lively characters conversing: "Hey Harvey, Ruth knocked another one over the wall today," exclaims one. "Yeh, what's all the shooting for," answers his friend. The second panel, captioned "When he doesn't," features the same two friends: "Babe didn't sock a homer today, Harvey!" announces one. "Why the big bum, he must be on the skids!" Under the entire cartoon,

Fisher concluded in a caption: "The Fans Are Taking It for Granted."[25] As baseball authorities watched Ruth soar to new heights and wondered whether they could contain such a radiant star, both fans and media grew restless, ready for a new narrative.

"Home Run Hitters and Humorists"

There remained one place where Ruth could thrive with novelty as a Yankee: the World Series. Expectations entering the 1921 postseason soared. The Yankees, in their first series, would play crosstown rivals the Giants. Thousands of enthusiasts camped out all night in the rain to purchase bleacher seats. Once inside the Polo Grounds, fans raced to the left side bleachers to get close to Ruth. Venues across the city provided live updates for those unable to attend the game in person. For twenty-five cents, fans could watch the game "reproduced by wonderful little men" at the Sixty-Ninth Regiment Armory. Another option, at a cost of fifty cents, was the "Coleman Life-Like Board" at Madison Square Garden, essentially a giant screen of a baseball field behind which several workers manipulated lights to represent action telegraphed to them from the Polo Grounds.

Rice promised Ruth would be "the storm center of the program"; after all, he was the

> Mightiest mauler since the days
> When Cave men ruled the glen
> His arms leap out—his body sways
> The ball is lost in a distant haze
> And is not seen again
> And from afar the echoes run
> "Bambino hits another one"

Other players might be on the field, Rice allowed, but "there will be only one Mandarin of Maul. . . . And now the spotlight's voltage upon him has tripled—what's he going to do about it?"[26] One paper assigned Martha Coman, a pioneering journalist, to cover the series and Ruth "as a woman sees it." Like others, she celebrated the Babe's power, but she also contributed quite bluntly to the undercurrent of infantilizing Ruth. Coman noted his "kiddishness," adding, "You can't help wondering how he looked in pale blue rompers when he was an infant which he apparently has remained in some ways."[27] As if the hitter needed more attention, before one game, his wife,

Helen Ruth, boarded a plane and flew over the Polo Grounds. As movie cameras wound, she dropped several baseballs inscribed with encouraging messages onto the playing field.[28]

In the actual series, however, Ruth struggled to match soaring expectations. Over the course of a long baseball season requiring significant travel—152 games for Ruth in 1921 plus dozens of exhibition games—players inevitably suffer slumps, illness, and injuries. With fans going to ballparks exclusively to see the Babe, Ruth rarely skipped a game. Not surprisingly, he played more games than any other player in the league.[29] Perhaps due to the intensity and frequency of his play, more than most players, Ruth endured frequent setbacks. Despite his outward self-confidence, Ruth undoubtedly understood the high expectations under which he labored. He had played in World Series before, but never as a Yankee and never primarily as a hitter. Never before had he been the main attraction. Quite simply, the pressure was on.

Giants manager McGraw fully recognized Ruth's powers at the plate. He instructed Giants pitchers to approach Ruth with the utmost care, walking the slugger whenever necessary. In the second game of the series, Ruth walked three times. In effect, McGraw took Ruth out of the game, and there was little the Babe could do. Still, writers blamed Ruth, one proclaiming him "a disappointment to the many thousand fans who went to the Polo Grounds." Ruth had failed to entertain. "Home run hitters and humorists are subject to the experience which Babe suffered today," he continued. "Mark Twain was always expected to be funny and Babe Ruth is always expected to hit a home run. There is a lot of intolerance shown when humorists and home run hitters drop back to what is considered mediocrity."[30]

When fans started booing, Ruth offered a feeble defense in his column. "What did I say to them? Not a word," explained the Ruth ghostwriter. "All I did was raise my cap not in derision to the unjust few but in appreciation to the big majority of fair play enthusiasts who drowned them out with their applause."[31]

Besides the Giants' refusal to pitch to him, a severe arm injury limited Ruth's capacities at bat. But to veteran sportswriter and Ruth antagonist Joe Vila the injury appeared suspect. In print, Vila scoffed that "Ruth had possibly enjoyed the trick he played on the fans" of entering the game after news circulated of serious injury. Further reports of the Bambino's indisposition," Vila added, should be "taken with a grain of salt."[32] Fuming, Ruth confronted

Vila in the press box. "Take a picture of that and put it in your newspaper," he growled, rolling up his sleeve to reveal bandages.[33]

Among sportswriters, the Harvard-educated Joseph Spencer Vila remained something of an anomaly. In his midfifties, having covered sports since the turn of the century, Vila resented the slugger-style, home-run hitting orientation that rose with Ruth, despite its popularity with fans. He also resisted the hyperbolic style so common among other sportswriters, avoiding "jokes or newly-coined slang."[34] His charges of cowardice and duplicity against Ruth were serious in the age of the Black Sox scandal. In print, Ruth (through his ghostwriters) rebutted the allegations, but Vila, no doubt aware he was selling papers, held firm.

Meanwhile, pro-Ruth sportswriters worked to salvage some heroism from the series. In the fourth game, despite injury, Ruth flashed evidence of life at the plate. Ruth earned "one of the greatest ovations that ever thundered" when he powered his first World Series homer as a Yankee in front of forty thousand fans.[35] Still, the Giants won the game, and Ruth's wound worsened. Soon his arm "looked like an elephant's thigh," forcing Ruth to the sidelines.[36] In a last-ditch effort to save the series, an ailing Ruth pinch-hit in the ninth inning of the final game. "Here was his chance for fame beyond anything that even he had ever known," wrote Rice.[37] But Ruth managed only a weak groundout, and the series was lost.

"Who is bigger: base-ball or the individual Ruth?"

Following the World Series, Ruth prepared to mount, as he had in previous years, an extensive barnstorming tour of smaller cities in the Northeast and West. Financially, such tours were a boon to Ruth. He could gross more over several weeks of barnstorming than he earned in a full season with the Yankees. Barnstorming also promoted big league baseball, spreading its popularity beyond major eastern cities.

Ruth's harmless plans, however, drew the attention of a powerful interested party, one impatient to assert authority over baseball and its players. Commissioner Landis already had moved against the likes of lesser-known players for gambling and other nefarious acts. The judge now sought a new opportunity to solidify his power and rein in barnstorming. Ruth already had staked out a position as an independent and somewhat erratic force. His immense popularity might give him an unprecedented stage from which to challenge baseball's hierarchy. Ruth's weak World Series performance, during which fans booed him, offered Landis a rare opportunity to tame the Babe.

Citing a recently decreed regulation banning competitors from that year's World Series from participating in exhibition games (designed to prevent a restaging of the series), Landis commanded Ruth to cancel his barnstorming tour. The slugger flat refused. Contracts had been signed and games scheduled, and many parties depended on the tour for revenue. Undoubtedly Ruth sought financial gain, and he had little reason to expect anything other than a small fine for ignoring rules that seemed arbitrary.

After his first World Series in 1916, Ruth and his Red Sox teammates had similarly embarked on a series of exhibition games in defiance of the then-ruling National Commission. For their intransigence in violating anti-barnstorming language in contracts, Ruth and his teammates had paid paltry fines of one hundred dollars each. Even so, Player's Fraternity president David Fultz had protested vociferously the fines. The baseball season and player contracts had expired, insisted Fultz, hence players could do as they chose. The National Commission's actions smacked of "paternalism."[38] Later, with impunity, Ruth had barnstormed after both the 1919 and 1920 seasons, as had numerous others, including members of teams playing in the World Series. Baseball took no action.[39]

In 1921, however, Landis, hungry to uphold his power and baseball's institutional primacy over individual players, seized upon the heretofore ignored antibarnstorming regulations. A well-publicized standoff between star player and commissioner ensued. The issue, Landis sanctimoniously insisted, came down to "who is the biggest man in baseball, the Commissioner or the player who makes the most home runs. It may have to be decided whether one man is bigger than baseball."[40] Ruth countered that he only intended to make "an honest dollar" and entertain fans. Defying the commissioner, the Babe set off on his tour.[41] Preparing for an exhibition game in Elmira, New York, Ruth framed the issue squarely in terms of "principle" and player rights. "In no other business or sport is such an unfair, unjust, one-sided rule allowed," he proclaimed. In language sure to rile Landis and the establishment, Ruth branded the "baseball big guys" as nothing less than "un-American."[42] Reflecting later on his challenge to Landis, Ruth mused, "Maybe we were screwy. Maybe we were crusaders for the rights of ballplayers. But Landis gave us the full works."[43]

Before moving against Ruth, the commissioner judiciously lined up the support of baseball owners. Like Landis, owners sought reaffirmation of their hegemony over players and control over postseason barnstorming. Certainly Ruth had brought new levels of profits and excitement to the game, but his rise threatened, at the very least, to drive up player salaries. At worst, Ruth might spark another round of baseball wars. Before he got any bigger, Ruth must be brought to heel.

Management, of course, could expect support from sportswriters. The media-savvy Landis shrewdly "played up the press," as one sportswriter recalled, carefully cultivating reporters always looking for a story.[44] Writers, in turn, backed the commissioner and attacked Ruth. Their writings, however, often revealed the real issues at stake. W. J. MacBeth darkly warned that Ruth's recent actions represented an existential threat to baseball: "There seems to be a disposition on the part of players generally to set at defiance the government of the game. . . . Ruth's behavior may be only part of a general insurrection."[45] A Pittsburgh newspaper similarly reported speculation that "Ruth's action is not entirely individual, that perhaps there is something deeper behind it than the mere desire of the player himself to add to his financial returns." Perhaps, the story cautioned, the standoff with Landis related to "rumors . . . that another attempt is to be made to put across a player's union this winter." Initially, players had welcomed Landis's appointment as commissioner, but instead they got a "rude awakening." Now, the report continued, there appeared some talk of putting together an organization to replace the Player's Fraternity "of several years ago."[46] Indeed, within days of these reports, Ruth told a reporter that "ball players are strong for 'commercialized' baseball to the point of getting what they think is their fair share from the receipts at the gate, and the average baseball player is pretty much Bolshevik on that point."[47]

Hoping to head off the conflict, Yankees co-owner T. L. Huston dispatched several sportswriters, including MacBeth, to corner Ruth and "use all the arguments possible to induce him to abandon the trip." Huston then personally met with Ruth in Scranton to make an additional appeal. The colonel implored Ruth to recognize the danger posed by Landis. Facing the censure of writers and his Yankees employers, Ruth relented and called off the tour.[48] According to Ruth, Huston paid off promoters to cancel remaining barnstorming contracts.[49]

Ruth then tried to contact Landis by phone to make peace, but twice the commissioner hung up on Ruth. "I am a stickler for obedience in such cases," explained the commissioner.[50] From his offices in Chicago, Landis kept all parties in suspense for almost two months as he mulled Ruth's punishment. Rumors circulated of a possible banishment for the entire 1922 season.[51] Increasingly concerned, Ruth sent Landis an obsequious apology and worked to assure the commissioner his aborted barnstorming tour was not part of a broader conspiracy. The tour, Ruth swore, came about of "my own volition and above all I was not influenced by any one person or body of men as has been mentioned in the press."[52]

Finally, in early December 1921, the commissioner issued his decision: Ruth and Bob Meusel, a second Yankee involved in the barnstorming plan, would forfeit their World Series bonuses and would be suspended for thirty-nine days beginning opening day. Playing up the moment, Landis delivered another tongue-lashing: the aborted tour amounted to "a mutinous defiance intended by the players to present the question: who is bigger: base-ball or the individual Ruth."[53]

Fans reeled. Owners and league officials, however, backed Landis fully. "They apparently believe that Babe Ruth, the popular player in baseball to-day, made possible widespread rebellion among players by his flouting of the rule of Judge Landis," reported the *Washington Times*. Michael Sexton, president of the National Association of Baseball Leagues, echoed the sentiment: "It took some nerve for the baseball commissioner to soak up a player like Ruth, but the man who can go after Standard Oil . . . has courage enough to do the right thing."[54] Even the Yankees owners, facing serious financial losses from the suspension, stood behind Landis. Attending an annual convention of baseball officials when the commissioner announced the suspension, Colonels Huston and Ruppert immediately retired to a hotel suite to confer. After a time, they emerged and issued a statement: "We abide by the decision of Judge Landis."[55]

Few writers would stand up for Ruth. Most impugned the defiant slugger. Ruth, joked Westbrook Pegler, was "insured against fire, tornado and flood, mumps, dandruff, falling arches and falling gargoyles and almost every other ill or misfortune that human flesh is heir to—with the exception of 'willfulness.' One word from any constituted authority and Babe Ruth does as he jolly well pleases if convenient."[56] Dan Daniel of the *New York Herald* projected that the commissioner's decision would be "an influence for great good. The players now are served with notice that the greatest is only a cog in the machine—that orders are orders, and that what the Commissioner says, goes."[57] Sportswriter Oscar Reichow, who actively paved the way for Landis's selection as commissioner, likewise blasted Ruth.[58] The self-absorbed hero, Reichow insisted, should "thank his lucky star that he was not suspended for half the season." He had been profoundly disrespectful to the Yankees and Colonel Ruppert (Huston was not mentioned), "who made it possible for him to become the star he is."[59] Joe Vila predictably backed the commissioner: the "constituted authority in baseball must be respected and no player is bigger than the game itself."[60]

Under fire, Ruth wisely chose to remain silent, perhaps weighing his options and hoping that Landis might commute the stiff sentence. In fact, at the time of the announcement, Ruth was making his Broadway debut to mostly positive reviews (even his singing drew some praise). While the vaudeville act opening at New York's Palace Theatre relied heavily on gags exchanged between Ruth and a veteran actor, the topic of Landis was off-limits, except for a quick reference to the commissioner sending Ruth a telegram collect.[61] On New Year's Day, Ruth took to the airways to deliver his 1922 resolutions over a Pittsburgh radio station. "I shall barnstorm no more without the consent of Judge Landis and the other baseball authorities," he assured thousands of listeners over the new technology sweeping the country.[62]

Staking out such a hard line in an effort to tame Ruth and quell any threat of "insurrection," baseball authorities conversely ran the risk of sparking a rebellion (the very outcome they feared), especially given Ruth's propensity for independent action. At the very least, the Ruth suspension would cost baseball significant income. Fans not just in New York but also around the league paid to see Ruth. Absent the star attraction, attendance was sure to fall in the opening weeks of the season. That Landis could initiate such an extreme move with owner support reflects the extent to which Ruth unnerved the baseball establishment. Further, seemingly harmless on the surface, barnstorming also appeared a threat. The specter of players banding together for profit offseason outside the control of the major leagues was too much for some. Limited barnstorming might be tolerated, but baseball authorities needed control over it, lest exhibitions develop into outlaw leagues. The gains for the establishment in going after Ruth apparently outweighed the costs. Breaking the Babe on this issue, in a sense, would give the establishment control over players beyond the immediate baseball season.

Still, the powers that be made sure that Ruth was isolated and made well aware of the consequences of rash action such as going rogue. Sid Mercer of Hearst's *Evening Journal* fretted that "by outlawing the Babe entirely until late in May Judge Landis will probably drive him into an alliance with independent promoters and thus prematurely end a great career." In such a case, "Babe could undoubtedly make good money on independent bookings next year, but after that he may not do so well." Likewise, Ruth "might trade on his reputation in a third major league." This, warned Mercer, also entailed perils for Ruth. "The costly Federal League failure is still fresh in the memories of promoters," and hence few would take a risk on a Ruth-centered league.[63] Louis Dougher, a *Washington Times* sports scribe, issued a similar admonition. "One season with the bush league or an outlaw team and his record would begin fading," warned Dougher.[64] Veteran sportswriter Sam Crane added that outside the major leagues, Ruth's "baseball future would be spoiled, made nil."[65]

Belying his hothead reputation, Ruth remained penitent and resisted propositions such as that made by Bill Niesen, owner of a Chicago semi-pro team associated with the Midwest League. Niesen offered Ruth $25,000 for six months of play in Chicago.[66] Accepting the offer undoubtedly would have brought a permanent suspension from Landis and thrown the baseball world into chaos. Six years later, Niesen would again try to lure an "outlaw" player, this time Buck Weaver, Ruth's 1919 barnstorming partner and one of the eight "Black Sox" banished by Landis. Weaver ended up playing several seasons for a Niesen semipro team, but neither compensation nor playing conditions could compete with the major leagues.[67] Later, in the spring of 1922, another semipro "mogul" reportedly offered Ruth $100,000 to jump from the major leagues. Again the slugger wisely resisted.[68]

Meanwhile, Ruth and Yankees management continued to hope Landis might soften the penalty. Virtually no one viewed the barnstorming rule as fair or just, yet virtually all insisted that the edict had to be obeyed. Seeking some flexibility, Yankees owners Ruppert and Huston dispatched team business manager Ed Barrow to Chicago to meet with Landis. Barrow made little effort to disguise his antipathy for Ruth, and he and Landis were "warm friends." The Yankees business manager blamed Ruth and Meusel for the crisis—certainly not the judge, whom he deemed "a grand person." Meeting in the commissioner's Chicago offices, Landis branded Ruth and Meusel "two lawbreakers." In some accounts (although not Barrow's), Landis referred to Ruth as the "big baboon." If he was faced as commissioner with such intransigence, the judge demanded of Barrow, what would he do? "I would do the same as you've done," admitted Barrow. With that the meeting ended, and Barrow returned to New York.[69] Yankees support for Ruth appeared ankle deep.

The Flip of a Coin

While supporting Landis, at least one member of the Yankees inner circle worked to prevent Ruth from going rogue—Colonel Huston, Ruth ally and half owner of the team. From his start in New York, Ruth had gravitated toward Huston. Ruth's wife recalled her husband viewed Huston as "one of the good guys," as opposed to the "bad guys"—a group that included manager Miller Huggins, Barrow, and Huston's co-owner, Ruppert.[70] Fellow extroverts, Babe and Huston shared a love of parties and nightlife. Huston tried to protect Ruth in the face-off with Landis by paying off promoters to end Ruth's barnstorming tour.

As the 1922 season neared, Ruth and the Yankees prepared to negotiate a new contract. Huston hoped a pay hike would lock Ruth to the Yankees and block any thoughts the slugger might have of striking out on his own. Huston evidently agreed on terms with Ruppert in New York before traveling to Hot Springs, Arkansas, to bargain with Ruth. The Yankees star already had traveled south and had begun a regime of training and enjoying himself in the resort town before reporting for spring training, scheduled for March in New Orleans.

The friendship between Ruth and Huston allowed for the least contentious contract negotiations of Ruth's career. The pair met at one of Hot Springs' famous baths. From adjoining tubs, they began haggling. Quickly they agreed on something in the $50,000 range, although Ruth requested $52,000, ostensibly so he would be earning $1,000 per week. Huston and Ruth reportedly then agreed to flip a coin for the additional two thousand. Ruth won: the contract would be for $52,000 per annum for three years.[71] At that steep rate, few outside promoters could afford Ruth.

Huston, like Huggins in 1920, had concerns beside money. Ruth's continuing penchant for late nights and drinking troubled the Yankees ownership, which had much riding on its star. After settling on a dollar figure, Huston moved to less comfortable terrain. He had, as Ruth recalled, "a lecture to get off his chest." Huston reminded Ruth the Yankees had much invested in him and implored his star "to get away from those bright lights and settle down." Given Huston's own proclivities for late nights on the town, Ruth almost laughed, "for no one liked bright lights or hated settling down more than Huston." Nevertheless, Ruth "promised to do better."[72]

Anxieties about Ruth's extracurricular habits so burdened the Yankees that the ownership, probably Ruppert, inserted prohibitions directly into the 1922 contract: "The ballplayer shall during the training and playing term of this contract and any renewals thereof refrain entirely from the use of intoxicating liquors." Further, "He shall not during the playing and training season in each year stay up later than 1 o'clock AM."[73] The effort to contractually control Ruth largely failed. Given Huston's personal habits, the Yankees co-owner carried little moral authority, although Ruth obviously valued his friendship. On the other side, Barrow, Ruppert, and Huggins clearly viewed Ruth as a delinquent desperately in need of restraint.

Public interest in Ruth's 1922 contract, like all his contracts, was intense. Rumors circulated about contractual provisions. One report had Ruth earning a $500 bonus for each home run. Such an arrangement, fretted a New York *Evening World* editorial, would essentially "subordinate the gate to the star."[74] Newspapers as far away as London carried the fatuous home-run bonus story.[75] A more personally damaging rumor circulated as well: that a large portion of Ruth's salary was to be withheld and paid at the end of the season contingent upon "good conduct."[76] Ruth's 1922 contract contained no such provision. Still, while Yankees management eventually publicly disavowed the home-run bonus rumors, it never addressed gossip about behavior provisions in the contract. The effect, probably intended, left impressions of an impetuous star unable to control himself. While Ruth clearly struggled with the temptations of stardom and wealth, few in baseball appeared willing to help the star through the challenges of unprecedented fame.

The Exile of Babe Ruth

Fascination with Ruth's contract suggests that, despite his languid World Series performance and his clash with Landis, he remained a viable commodity. The marketing of Babe Ruth continued, in fact, unabated. One hundred percent leather "Babe Ruth Home Run Shoes," endorsed by Ruth, sold for four dollars a pair and included "a free History of Babe Ruth."[77] Smokers could purchase "Bambino Smoking Tobacco" for fifteen cents a pouch, "a full circuit clout when it comes to a buy for the money."[78] Ruth's arrival in New Orleans for spring training (hardly an optimum site for a player aiming to avoid temptations), only days after inking his new contract, again prompted overflow crowds. Yankees management, eager to capitalize on Ruth before his suspension kicked in, organized a preseason tour through Texas. "They are billing the Behemoth of Bust through the provinces like the latest acquisition from darkest Africa to the traveling circus," reported John Kieran, in words that hinted at persistent rumors regarding Ruth's racial lineage.[79]

Hope lingered that Landis, in the end, would ease the uniquely harsh sentence levied against Ruth. Fans inundated Landis with petitions urging a commutation. Some pointed out that several members of the New York Giants, the Yankees' World Series opponents, played without punishment during the off-season in the Pacific League.[80] In late March, Commissioner Landis visited Yankees training camp in New Orleans. A contrite Ruth, reported sportswriter John Kieran, spent his morning "dissecting a dandelion, murmuring softly 'He loves me, he loves me not.'" Ruth and Landis conferred for an hour in the commissioner's hotel room. Later, they posed for photographers. Obviously savoring the attention, Landis raised expectations by letting it be known he would make an announcement after the Yankees exhibition game. Lampooning the press frenzy and the commissioner's ego (and his manipulation of the press), Kieran depicted the scene when Landis summoned the media after the game:

> Newspaper correspondents rushed from all directions with paper and pencil at the "ready" position.
> "Are they all here?" queried the great megul of the national pastime?
> "We are" was the answering shout.
> The judge cleared his throat, gave a tug to the front of his coat amid a silence like that which reigns in the depths of the northern forests, he snapped out:
> "I have nothing whatever to add to my former statement."[81]

The commissioner's New Orleans shenanigans suggest a man making the most of his time in the limelight and his mounting power over Ruth. For his part, the Babe remained penitent and uncomplaining. Undoubtedly he resented the kowtowing ceremonies, seemingly designed to further cement Landis's power. Still, Ruth's record contract was on the line, a deal no outside promoter appeared ready to match. Meanwhile, baseball writers remained solidly in the commissioner's corner. "His logic is unanswerable, his fairness unquestioned, and his determination to administer his office without fear or favor is admirable," pronounced sportswriter Sid Mercer.[82] Facing this combined front, Ruth saw little option other than surrendering and thus affirming club owners' expanding control of their workforce.

The Texas tour, Ruth's first in the Lone Star State, attracted huge crowds from Galveston to San Antonio to Dallas. Yet Ruth, typical of his spring training form, struggled at the plate. MacBeth dismissed the tour as "one of the richest circus stunts ever perpetuated on the sticks," and added that Ruth "has been a gigantic bust."[83] References to circus acts seemed in fashion. At 240 pounds, Ruth, reported the New York *Evening World*, "looked like the fat man in the circus."[84]

Opening Day in New York with Ruth on suspension proved a grim affair. Landis prohibited Ruth and Meusel from even suiting up with their team for pregame workouts. Ruth, "crouched in a box" in the stands on opening day, presented "a picture of gloom," reported Bozeman Bulger. Bitter cold winds shot through the Polo Grounds, at one point tearing the Yankees pennant flag from its mast. A meager crowd braved the weather to see the Ruth-less AL team open its season.[85] (A few days earlier, when Landis had permitted Ruth to play an exhibition game in Baltimore, seventeen thousand enthusiasts besieged the hometown hero. Obligingly, Ruth had hit a home run for the crowd.)[86] Fans seemed to be "boycotting the Yankees," according to one report.[87]

Sidelined, Ruth personally appeared at loose ends. For the first time in his life, he was unable to participate in the one endeavor over which he had control: his on-field play. Spinning his wheels, Ruth seemed to cast aside conditioning. Instead, he delved deeper into a world of racetracks, parties, night clubs, and fair-weather friends. In Washington, DC, for the Yankees matchup with the city's Senators, Ruth skipped the game in favor of an excursion to the nearby Bowie (Maryland) track, "flanked by a bevy of United States Senators, Uncle Joe Cannon of their numbers."[88] Ruth had every reason to feel unfairly singled out in an initiative to shore up management's power over players and barnstorming. His newspaper column, although ghostwritten, most likely revealed real frustrations. The suspension, Ruth reported, was "preying on my mind," and his sense of helplessness grew as the season started without him. "No one who hasn't been through it can imagine the tortures of suspense I endure as I sit idly by." Increasingly, Ruth also struggled with his weight and worried about "having my spring training to do all over again."[89] Adding to Ruth's problems, doctors removed the slugger's tonsils in early May, further disrupting his conditioning.[90]

While the Yankees managed to win without their star player, sportswriters struggled to make copy. The *New York Tribune* ran a daily series titled "The Exile of Babe Ruth," describing the suspended star's nonbaseball activities. No amount of coverage of Ruth off the field, however, compensated for a Ruth on the field. As his suspension wound down in mid-May, attendance at Yankees games in New York and around the league plummeted to one half that of the previous year.[91] Fans felt frustration. On the road, the Yankees and Ruth had been a major draw, but increasingly tickets were going unsold. So began what proved a tense season, in which rowdiness both in the stands and on the field made an ominous return.

As the end of Ruth's suspension neared, sportswriters propelled expectations upward, the favored analogy being Napoleon's return from exile in Elba. In a poem entitled "The Return from Elba," Rice promised, "The long sleep is over / the Nation is waking / The Dead Epoch fades as the Live one is back / The old earth rebounds with a quiver and quaking."[92] Damon Runyon meanwhile depicted the suspension as worth any sacrifice because "law and order have won a tremendous victory in baseball. . . . Landis has finally put discipline above even the most temperamental star."[93] When tickets for Ruth's return game went on sale, fans swarmed Yankee Stadium, according to W. O. McGeehan, "hurling bales of bills through the windows and demanding reserved seat tickets." The game sold out in only a few hours even though Ruth's return was not guaranteed. As a final humiliation, Landis required Ruth and the two other suspended Yankees to apply formally for reinstatement, the last "legal formalities to be gone through before the terrible law of baseball release[d] him from its clutches."[94] Ruth's suspension had cost baseball financially, but now Ruth, the game's greatest attraction, seemed solidly under Commissioner Landis's jurisdiction.

"A Primitive Youth"

Landis's consent secured, Ruth resumed active play on May 20, 1922. Over forty thousand fans greeted him, as Heywood Broun put it, in the fashion of the prodigal son, with an overflow of "gifts by the truckload to symbolize the fatted calf."[95] Despite the warm welcome and presentation of a silver bat, silver cup, and floral wreath shaped like a baseball diamond, Ruth's ovation, the *New York Times* acknowledged, proved "not nearly as long as the several during the World Series last fall."[96] Likewise, understandably after several idle weeks, Ruth's performance in the game proved anemic. Noting the Babe appeared "a trifle portly," McGeehan wrote that, "like the return of the late N. Bonaparte from Elba, [Ruth's return] was followed by disaster in large chunks."[97] More succinctly, a *New York Tribune* headline the next day pronounced, "Babe Back Emulates Casey—Strikes Out."[98] Always a slow starter, Ruth now struggled to overcome weeks of inactivity and vexation.

Over the next several days, media criticism built. In one game, McGeehan jested that opportunity had knocked but "found nobody home but a young gentleman with a wide waist line."[99] Bleeding the Napoleon imagery, John Kieran conjectured as to whether Ruth had chosen "'The Retreat from Moscow' or 'The Return from Elba' with 'One Hundred Days of Conquest' as his story vehicle."[100] Quickly sportswriters chose the "retreat" story line. Five days after his debut, Ruth came to bat twice with the bases loaded, a situation "when even a single would have been worth its weight in Treasury notes"; both times he failed to produce.[101] Trying to sway coverage, Ruth dispatched a silver tray loaded with ice cream and chocolate in silver wrappings to the press box. "We tasted of his largesse," confessed one writer, "but even so duty compels us to record that for the day, the Bambino came mighty close to a plumb bust."[102]

From there circumstances turned decidedly worse. On May 25, determined to reverse his fortunes, Ruth tried to stretch an extra base out of a single. When called out, Ruth cursed and threw dirt at the umpire. Ejected from the game, as Ruth walked toward the Yankees dugout, every "step of the journey was a signal to the crowd to jeer and hoot."[103] As he neared the area where his spouse and other Yankees wives were seated, a fan, who by all accounts had been haranguing Ruth throughout the game, "let loose a remark that has no place in a family newspaper." Propelled by the dictates of masculinity and his own recent frustrations, Ruth "vaulted" into the stands after the perpetrator, who quickly fled the scene.[104] Ruth's nemesis, Yankees team secretary Ed Barrow, made a rare appearance on the playing field to lead the ousted Ruth to the locker room, no doubt adding to the humiliation.[105] Once again league officials moved to punish the star who only recently appeared to have saved the game from the disgrace of the Black Sox scandal.

Ruth's rowdyism put his ghostwriter in a knotty bind. The hitter's heroics centered on action at the plate, not introspection. Recent events belied the image of charity and balance cultivated the two previous years. Rather than mount some sort of explanation, the ghostwriter seemed confused. "Why have I fallen so far below in my former standards as a slugger that in a recent game at New York I was razzed beyond endurance and committed an act of reprisal which I shall never cease to regret?" the writer asked. "These and a hundred similar questions are hurled at me each day and my answer in every instance is the same—I do not know."[106]

Boos and taunts of "You bum!" now dogged the fallen star. Unsympathetic press accounts of his clash with Landis, it appears, turned many fans against Ruth. Yet while the May 25 episode stands out, Ruth, like many professional athletes (although to a greater extent), frequently faced jeering, booing, and fan hostility. At times, modern sports seems almost as much a forum for tearing down heroes as constructing them. Debunking perhaps offers odd reassurance that heroes—sports or otherwise—serve at the pleasure of the public. More basely, "razzing" or giving a player the "raspberry" provides an acceptable public outlet to express anger, a platform with particular appeal in changing and complex times. Yet the vehement anger suddenly aimed at Ruth unsettled some sportswriters, who long had sought to tame the more unruly side of the sport. "Baseball is a noble game," explained the *New York Times* in an editorial entitled "The Razzing of Ruth," "but the crowds who watch it average about as low in sportsmanship as any mass of human beings that can be found anywhere."[107]

Although he generally handled abuse better than most athletes, especially later in his career, Ruth understandably viewed the taunting as unfair and cruel. He was hardly the first player to have chased hecklers into the stands. Indeed, while playing in St. Louis in 1917, Yankees manager Miller Huggins "almost pulled a Ty Cobb" (as a St. Louis paper put it) and chased down an abusive fan. At the last minute, an umpire managed to restrain the diminutive Huggins.[108] Still, Ruth's actions in 1922 belied the baseball establishment's efforts to rechristen the game as an orderly, middle-class institution. Jumping into the stands—crossing over the divide between player and spectator—and pursuing a troublemaker harkened back to the violence and rowdyism of baseball's recent past. In particular, as the St. Louis newspaper describing Huggins's altercation suggested, such acts conjured up the ghosts of Ty Cobb's violent beating of Claude Lueker a decade earlier, an episode all parties wished to consign to the past.

It would fall to AL president Ban Johnson to punish Ruth. But Johnson, unlike Landis, faced deep-seated opposition from key team owners. Already the league suffered revenue decreases from Ruth's long suspension. Washington Senators owner Clark Griffith pleaded with Johnson not to suspend Ruth, who was slated to play soon in the nation's capital, where he was sure to drive up attendance.[109] In the end, Johnson fined Ruth $200, but more importantly stripped him of his position as Yankees team captain. Reviewing Ruth's sad recent history in his decision, Johnson reflected on the fallen hero's popularity, long suspension, and recent trials on the field. "Ruth plainly did not possess the mental strength and stability," Johnson condescendingly concluded, "to brave this sudden reversal of public adoration."[110]

Already trending critical, coverage of Ruth now went decidedly negative. Following Johnson's line, McGeehan branded Ruth as an errant youngster: "Sending the Babe to bed a few nights without supper would do the Babe good morally and physically." McGeehan, as did other writers, then moved to compare Ruth unfavorably to Christy Mathewson, the solidly middle-class, pious former pitcher for the New York Giants, who had been gassed while in service during the recent war. "Mathewson was a different type," McGeehan explained. "He was a wonderfully well balanced man, keenly intelligent. Babe Ruth is a primitive youth."[111]

It is difficult not to see McGeehan's coverage and Ruth's entire clash with Landis as emblematic of larger social and cultural tensions. Writers who dismissed Ruth as an errant child or "primitive youth" played on the exasperation of many adults in the face of what appeared youthful intransigence. Especially in urban areas, young people seemed increasingly contemptuous of tradition and authority. "In the great cities like New York, youth is out of hand," lamented etiquette guru Emily Post in the 1920s, summing up the frustrations of many.[112] Likewise, Commissioner Landis's insistence his dispute with Ruth boiled down to "the question: who is bigger: base-ball or the individual Ruth," also played to broader cultural anxieties. Extrapolated, the commissioner's line pitted selfish individualism against communal values. The acceleration of modern urban life in the 1920s brought such questions and tensions to the forefront. In some senses, the Ruth-Landis clash in 1922 and the Babe's continuing struggles during the regular season offered a drama through which to play out societal strains.

Indeed, the spectacle continued to unfold. In mid-June, Johnson again suspended Ruth for a verbal confrontation with Umpire Bill Dinneen. As the *New York Tribune*'s sports editors acknowledged, Ruth still produced crowds and emotion, but fans now "swarm out to jeer him. He has tasted the dregs of unpopularity with mighty poor grace."[113] That the Yankees of 1922 included a number of combustible personalities hardly helped Ruth, himself given to brief temperamental outbursts. Fights between Yankees teammates both on and off the field became commonplace, and Ruth often found himself in the middle of the strife. Playing in St. Louis, Yankees first baseman Wally Pipp physically attacked Ruth, who dared to criticize Pipp's fielding. Fellow players had to restrain the two.

Manager Huggins seemed incapable of controlling his team. Rumors swelled that he would soon be fired and replaced by either Ed Barrow or Brooklyn Dodgers manager Wilbert Robinson, a Baltimore native known to be sympathetic to Ruth.[114] Seeking leverage over players, Barrow took control and hired a private investigator to infiltrate the team and report on their after-hours pursuits. During a road trip, the "spy" lured the team to a "stag" party at a Joliet, Illinois, brewery. When prodded, the players unwisely sat for a group photograph. Although a majority, including Ruth, sat stone-faced and all had ties tightly knotted around their necks (hardly suggestive of a wild "roaring twenties" revelry), the evidence provided Barrow with precious leverage.[115] He shared the information with Landis; the commissioner then met with both Yankees and Red Sox teams for a closed-door session at which the commissioner threatened harsh reprisals against recalcitrant players. Landis promised to take a similar message to all ball clubs. The next penalty, he promised, would be "as a lumber yard to a toothpick on severity."[116] Barrow also shared news of his findings with select newspapermen, who obligingly reported "rumors and charges connected to the more or less wild doings of the Yankees off the field."[117]

Despite the ongoing tumult, by midseason Ruth emerged from his usual season-opening slump. He was soon hitting home runs at an impressive pace and challenging league leaders, who had an extra month to get their numbers up. By season's end, he had thirty-five home runs with a batting average of .315—respectable numbers, given his late start, team turmoil, fickle fans, and suspensions. Still, Ruth showed signs of strain. A third suspension came in early September in Chicago following yet another run-in with an umpire. Coverage of Ruth remained decidedly negative. Days later, after Ruth's return from his third suspension, McGeehan took aim at Ruth's increasing girth, describing the Yankee as rounding the bases with "the vehemence of a bull hippopotamus dashing though the jungle to keep a tryst with his mate."[118] Ruth critic Vila maintained his campaign against Ruth. In Vila's view, Ruth "had gotten away with murder and the privileges enjoyed by him soured some of the other players."[119]

While press criticism of Ruth abounded, one newspaper resisted the trend toward infantilizing and ridiculing Ruth. The New York *Daily News*, with a city-leading circulation of over a half million daily readers, continued to lure New Yorkers with sensational coverage of lurid murders and salacious fictional serials. Yet, perhaps because the tabloid covered travel expenses for its sportswriters, as opposed to virtually every other newspaper, *Daily News* correspondents felt less bound to the anti-Ruth line emanating from league officials and team owners. Focusing more on personality and human interest stories, the paper had established a strong working relationship with Ruth. "We recognized the Babe as a guy we could really do business with," recalled *Daily News* sportswriter Marshall Hunt. "So the Babe became sort of a *Daily News* man. . . . I don't think he was ever aware of his role as circulation builder."[120]

De-emphasizing Ruth's troubles, *Daily News* writers played up his 1922 successes. After Ruth drilled three home runs in a midsummer game against the Athletics, the tabloid ran a photo of a cocky-looking Ruth over a caption reading, "I Guess I'm Bad! Eh," highlighting Ruth's newfound bad-boy reputation. The next month, when Ruth pounded two home runs in one game, *Daily News* writer James Crusinberry raved, "All the wrong and past misdeeds of Mr. George Herman Ruth were righted in the eyes of New York's baseball public yesterday at the Polo Ground when his two tremendous four base socks won the game from the White Sox."[121]

Still, a tabloid remains a tabloid, and the *Daily News* could not forgo reporting an odd, gossipy episode as the season wound down. In late September, Helen Ruth, the hitter's demure wife who seemed every bit her effusive husband's opposite, appeared suddenly with a year-old baby named Dorothy in tow. The couple offered differing stories on the origins and age of their baby. Briefly Helen and Babe found themselves the subject of a series of sensational stories in the *Daily News* and other tabloids. Finally, the couple effectively shut down the story by refusing to discuss it. "People have been very mean about making all this mystery about Dorothy," explained Helen. "I won't give them the satisfaction of telling them anything."[122] For a brief moment, Ruth found some control over the media whirlwind surrounding him.

"The body was found near the pitcher's box just at sunset"

The 1922 regular season ended in a heated horse race between the Yankees and the St. Louis Browns. In September, the rivals met for a final tense series at Sportsman's Park in St. Louis. Fans jeered and razzed Ruth throughout. Toward the end of the first game, "wild scenes of riot and disorder never before seen on an American ball field" broke out, according to one source. A bottle thrown from the bleachers struck Yankees outfielder Whitey Witt. Armed with bats, Yankees players took the field and clashed with spectators. Mounted police finally cleared the playing area. Knocked unconscious, a limp Witt was carried from the field. Ban Johnson offered a $1,000 award to find the perpetrator of the bottle-throwing crime.[123] Officials meanwhile banned bottles from the St. Louis bleachers, and Witt recovered enough to play in the next game. Still, the ugly episode underscored a strained season. New York did manage to win two of the three games against the Browns, propelling the team to its second straight pennant.

The Yankees prepared to face the Giants in another "subway series." Again, Gotham braced for excitement. Sportswriters from around the country and the world (including correspondents from Japan) headquartered themselves at Manhattan's Commodore Hotel, which furnished large rooms with hundreds of typewriters to accommodate the assemblage. The New York *Evening World* erected a scoreboard near city hall in anticipation of crowds, as did other newspapers. For the first time, action would be cast over the air directly from the ballpark. Sportswriters McGeehan and Rice both broadcast their versions of the game, respectively, over General Electric's WGY out of Schenectady and WJZ from Newark. The broadcasts, despite on-air ineptness on the parts of Rice and McGeehan, appeared a success. Baseball owners, newspapers, and sportswriters would grow concerned about the new medium, which threatened to compromise the exclusive filter that sportswriters had over their field.

Like the previous year, Ruth figured substantially in the preseries hype. Ring Lardner promised readers that Ruth "will hit at least two out of the park."[124] Boxer Jack Dempsey's ghostwriter seconded the prediction, announcing the "big fellow will come into his own this fall."[125] Yankees manager Huggins added to the pressure on his top hitter. Ruth, he proclaimed, "will be the hero of the world series . . . [He is] the axis of the club. All the rest of the players revolve around him."[126]

Huggins, however, was hardly prescient. The 1922 World Series proved an edgy and raucous finale to a tense season. Ruth was a mere shadow of himself. As in 1921, Manager McGraw ordered his Giants pitchers assiduously to avoid throwing anything that Ruth might hit. Laboring under great pressure, and no doubt eager to turn a difficult season around, Ruth went after bad balls. The result, he admitted, was "the most unpleasant baseball week I have ever lived through."[127] After the third game, Rice described Ruth as "a marionette on the end of a string," dying a "death of slugging shame on easy grounders."[128] On the field, McGraw's Giants also aimed a nonstop barrage of verbal harassment at Ruth. Struggling at the plate, Ruth uncharacteristically allowed the attacks to eat at him. At one point he invaded the Giants locker room to demand an end to the insults. Despite flares of temper, Ruth was no brawler. As one sportswriter explained, the confrontation ended with "no fight, no argument, merely a little semi-friendly spoofing."[129]

Meanwhile fans seemed in a raw mood after a strange, unsatisfying season. When the second game of the series was called due to encroaching darkness, a near riot occurred. An estimated five thousand angry fans, believing the league was trying to profit by replaying the game the next day, and perhaps channeling rage over Commissioner Landis's early-season suspension of Ruth, surrounded the commissioner's box and "hurled threats, jeers and insults" at baseball's highest official. Police interceded and escorted Landis from the field as fans chanted "Fight, Fight!" "The reverence the baseball public is supposed to have for Commissioner Landis as a personage," noted the *Sporting News*, "is not so deep as we were told it would be."[130]

After heaping "jeers and insults" on the commissioner, the mob descended on the press box, where participants "informed newspaper men that they the fans had seen their last game of ball." Aroused by the commotion, a half-dressed Ruth emerged from the locker room. Told of the rebellion underway, Ruth sided with the crowd. "Well I don't blame them," he announced, finally getting a shot back at his season-long foe.[131]

To assuage public opinion, Landis announced that game two receipts, including the players' shares, would be donated to veterans' charities. Meanwhile, players spent the evening in "fraternity sessions," worrying that their share of series profits, originally to be based on the first four games, would be based on only three games. Some players proposed a game three walkout, akin to the aborted 1918 strike.[132] The next day Giants representative, shortstop Dave Bancroft, and Ruth (although no longer team captain), representing the Yankees, met with Landis. Eager to escape the game two controversy, Landis assured Ruth and Bancroft that as previously agreed, player shares would still be based on four games: now games one, three, four, and five. Ruth and Bancroft then insisted shares of game five must be equivalent to those of game two, now committed to charity. Landis readily agreed to the demand and then assured waiting reporters the "talk was friendly and pleasant."[133]

Players were now satisfied. Fans, however, remained disgruntled and agitated, and Ruth was next to draw their ire and anger. To *Tribune* correspondent MacBeth, game three "provides insights into mob psychology." After "rabid masses" had attacked Landis the previous day, fans turned on Ruth when the Yankee deliberately and aggressively bumped Giants third baseman Heinie Groh. Relentless "razzing" dogged Ruth the rest of the game. "All of this should make Ruth realize the fickleness of so-called public esteem and popularity," admonished MacBeth.[134]

To the distress of their fans, the Yankees lost the World Series in four games. With uncharacteristically grim imagery, Rice opened his report of the Giants series win: "The body was found near the pitcher's box just at sunset, with eyes gouged out, its throat cut and nine ribs crushed in—mutilated beyond all recognition."[135] A reader of Rice's account might easily be left the impression the body was that of Ruth, who managed only a meager .118

batting average and no home runs in the series. Accounts of his series performance had the air of obituaries. Vila eulogized Ruth as the former "monarch of all he surveyed," the former "idol of the fans and the most important player in baseball."[136] The Babe had only himself to blame, writers concurred. A New York *Sun* reporter attributed his poor season to eye trouble developed "by looking for the colors of horses on which he had wagered," and his refusal to practice during this period, "thinking that in his greatness the base hits would rain when he got back into the game."[137] Over and over, in accounts of the series, sportswriters ranked Ruth among the goats.

Ruth himself undoubtedly stood astounded and confused by his rapid fall from grace. Both the rhythms (slumps followed by streaks) and vagaries (injuries and other factors beyond a player's control) all natural to the game contributed mightily to Ruth's difficult season. Ego and arrogance also left the media hero vulnerable. Still in his twenties, the Babe's meteoric rise from poverty to wealth and fame left him with no shortage of confidence. Ruth's fall, however, correlated largely to a concerted effort by baseball's powerful to rein in the superstar and consolidate power.

"A strike was in the offing"

Toward the end of the grueling 1922 season, shadowy rumors that first surfaced earlier that year about union organizing and a challenge to baseball's establishment resurfaced—this time with substance behind them. In August, Raymond Cannon, a young, aggressive lawyer who had represented several of the disgraced Black Sox, went public with plans to forge a new union of major league baseball players. The new organization explicitly took aim at the controversial reserve clause.[138] Not since David Fultz's initiative collapsed several years before had anyone hazarded such a move. Throughout the 1922 season, Cannon worked "recruiting under cover."[139] He focused mainly on the National League and claimed by year's end to have enlisted 80 percent of the league. When the official season ended, Cannon christened his new organization the National Baseball Players' Association and publicized its constitution and member oath. Although the constitution made no mention of work stoppages, the "prevailing assumption seemed to be that a strike was in the offing," reported the *New York Times*.[140]

Cannon had exaggerated membership numbers, but baseball's leadership still fumed at the challenge. NL president John Heydler decried the need for a players' organization. With Landis, "Every player knows he can get a square deal," he claimed.[141] Charles Ebbets, proprietor of the Brooklyn Dodgers, maintained that players were "banding together merely to boost salaries. . . . This move, I am sure, will be bitterly resisted by every employer."[142] In the American League, Washington Senators owner Clark Griffith dismissed the initiative as an "effort to cover up a lot of crooked baseball players."[143] Colonel Huston of the Yankees echoed views that with Landis defending players, a union would be superfluous. "They don't need protection any more than I need a straw hat in December," fumed the colonel.[144]

Cannon clearly faced an uphill battle, but players were sympathetic. Only the most naïve among them could realistically believe the commissioner held concern for individual players. His harsh suspension of Ruth in 1922 belied that notion. One newspaper reported, "The movement is based on the dissatisfaction of some players" with Landis.[145] Few had more reason to be dissatisfied than Ruth.

The threat of an aggressive union representing player interests portended a return to the disorder the baseball establishment aspired to leave in the past. "Baseball players may be receiving more money than ever before but . . . their salaries are insignificant compared to the tremendous profits made by club owners," asserted Cannon. In the case of the Yankees, this remained true. Cannon promised to begin organizing the American League "in due time." There Babe Ruth would be his prize target. But thanks to Landis, sportswriters, and baseball's ownership class, Ruth's personal and professional reputation sank to a career low as the 1922 season ended. He would have to focus on a comeback. Step one would be signaling his capitulation, his acceptance of the power structure that had so tormented him in 1922.

FOUR. "A REMARKABLE CHANGE IN THE KING OF SWAT"
COMEBACK I

The most dramatic moments in sports are nearly always set up around "the comeback," the beaten champion who rises again, the prodigal who returns. There is something about beating back which appeals to the inner emotions of the multitude at large.

No one likes to feel that after being beaten there can be no return to winning days.[1]

—Grantland Rice, 1926

GRANTLAND RICE WELL understood the appeal and value of the "comeback" as a narrative device. A student of classical lore and mythology, he consciously aimed to construct his own mythologies, rife with classical allusions, celebrating contemporary sports heroes and epic athletic events. Instinctively, Rice saw what scholar Joseph Campbell later developed in detail as the structure of the heroic adventure, one with longstanding, universal appeal. The hero's journey, Campbell explained, is often cyclical, involving a "separation" followed by an initiation and a return. The separation brings serious trials, perhaps even a symbolic death, as in the descent of Aeneas into the underworld or Buddha's period of austere wandering. In some senses Rice followed this pattern when he all but killed off Ruth at the end of the 1922 World Series. The initiation, then, requires accessing a source of strength that revives the hero. Properly initiated, the hero returns to form, restoring a disordered world. In Hades, for instance, Aeneas encounters knowledge of the destiny of men. He harnesses this understanding to triumphantly return and to found the city of Rome.[2] This cycle, Rice correctly recognized, struck deep chords with the "multitude at large," and—marketed by

sportswriters, the baseball establishment, and Ruth's promoters—the comeback cycle provided the vehicle for Ruth's redemption.

Rice might have mentioned as well that for a columnist facing deadline
pressures, the comeback furnished an alluring story line. Like the earlier
Ruth-as-superman narrative, the hero-debunked story line had been played
out by the end of 1922. A new season called for a new narrative. Yankees
ownership and the baseball power brokers at large also desperately needed
a comeback. Ruth had been sent a pointed, unmistakable message in 1922:
power in baseball would remain in the hands of elites who had long controlled the game; players would remain in subordinate positions. By the
end of the 1922 season, the superstar's potential to make real trouble for
baseball's ownership class, by throwing his support behind unionization or
possibly defecting to a rival "outlaw" league, had been hobbled. But despite
the unrelenting campaign against Ruth in 1922, he remained essential to
baseball's long-term prosperity and hopes of conquering the ills still imper-
iling the game.

More immediately, Yankees owners Ruppert and Huston had staked their
fortunes on Ruth by constructing a massive new baseball stadium north of
Manhattan in the Bronx, a structure they hoped to pack with huge crowds
that would generate exceptional profits. It would truly be the "House that
Ruth Built," as sportswriter Fred Lieb dubbed the structure, and only a dominant Ruth drawing the masses to Yankees games could sustain the enormous investment.[3] Already some critics "stood aghast" when the colonels
revealed the sheer ambition of the classically inspired titanic ballpark. Without a prevailing Ruth, the stadium would be a "folly," a "white elephant."[4]
Clearly worried, Yankees business manager Ed Barrow maintained his goal
of cutting team salaries an average of $500 to $1,000 (Ruth, with a multiyear
contract, was exempt). The cuts, noted the *Sporting News*, were "unusual for
a championship team."[5]

"Tomorrow I'm going to my farm"

Despite his struggles in 1921 and 1922, Ruth had acquired one formida-
ble asset: Christy Walsh, his new business manager. Walsh, an enterprising
Californian, began as a cartoonist for the Los Angeles *Herald* before joining
the publicity department of automaker Maxwell Chalmers in Detroit. From
there he headed to New York in 1920 to work in the city's burgeoning advertising industry. A year later he decided to strike out on his own. While in Detroit, Walsh had created and marketed ghostwritten columns for World War

I aviator ace Eddie Rickenbacker. The experience had been lucrative, and Walsh imagined establishing a syndicate managing and selling ghostwritten columns. He decided to start with the biggest fish around: Babe Ruth.

Posing as a beer delivery man, Walsh talked his way into Ruth's Ansonia Hotel apartment, where he made his pitch to the slugger. Already the United Press syndicate published ghostwritten columns under Ruth's name. The Babe earned a very modest five dollars per ghostwritten column, which seemed a fine arrangement, given that it required virtually nothing on the Babe's part. Walsh, however, promised Ruth significantly more money if the slugging hero signed on with the nascent Christy Walsh syndicate. The Babe took an immediate liking to Walsh and agreed to try the new deal. On opening day 1921, Walsh presented his new client with a check for $1,000 supposedly representing Ruth's earnings. In reality, Walsh had borrowed the sum to impress his new client.[6] Real money, however, quickly began pouring in, and Walsh and Ruth bonded over their profits and their mutual affability. Ruth emerged the cornerstone figure of what quickly ripened into a syndicated ghost column empire.

Walsh also developed into a trusted ally, friend, and advisor to Ruth, taking the place of his former counselor Johnny Igoe, who remained in Boston. With his background in public relations and sports journalism, Walsh marketed Ruth to the public with dogged energy. In year one of their relationship, Walsh had Ruth endorsing "The Grafonola" record player, the "Whip Tie," Elcho Handmade cigars, and Dr. Reed's Cushion Shoes. Ruth also made dozens of personal appearances for businesses and served as the one-day guest sports editor for the *Boston Daily Advertiser*.[7] In 1922, newspapers urged readers to clip coupons printed in papers to present them for Babe Ruth "scorers," handy "little celluloid tabulators." Fans also could purchase Babe Ruth baseball mitts with the star's engraved autograph for $2.75, or a pair of Babe Ruth Home Run Shoes, which came with a chance to win $100,000 in gold.[8]

Despite his limited background in finance, Walsh also emerged as the star's trusted financial counselor. Ruth's impoverished background and natural extravagance worked against fiscal discipline. The slugger had on occasion failed to deposit important checks and admitted that he and his wife had waded alone through a dizzying number of endorsement offers, struggling to determine which "were sound or wildcat."[9] Walsh, while sharing some of Ruth's love of the high life, wisely channeled Ruth's earnings into conservative trusts and annuities, perhaps a reflection of Walsh's lack of expertise in the field. In any case, conventional investments served Ruth well when the economy collapsed in the 1930s.

While Walsh offered cogent advice and guidance for which Ruth remained eternally "grateful," he was distinctly not a sports agent in the modern sense of the term. Importantly, he did not negotiate the terms of Ruth's contracts with his Yankees employers. According to major league customs, Ruth alone could represent himself in such talks. As he did with Yankees part-owner Huston in 1922, Ruth fended for himself in salary talks. This amounted to an intimidating prospect for a man with limited education and experience. After 1923, Ruth faced off against Colonel Ruppert, a multimillionaire business owner and former US congressman. Often the intimidating Barrow accompanied Ruppert. The cards were always stacked against the slugger. Having Walsh at his side, as Ruth himself suggested, would have eased the process. Even so, Walsh had no more background in contract negotiations than financial planning. Additionally, he had conflicts of interest. In 1923, Yankees manager Miller Huggins joined the growing list of prominent sports figures on the Christy Walsh Syndicate payroll.[10]

The disadvantage at which baseball players operated appears in sharp relief compared to professional athletes in another sport: football. Sensing great opportunity, Champaign, Illinois, theater owner C. C. "Cash and Carry" Pyle approached University of Illinois halfback Harold "Red" Grange, promising college football's most dominant player a $100,000 payday if he went professional. Pyle then negotiated a deal with the Chicago Bears in which the team would split gate receipts with Grange, who made his professional debut on Thanksgiving Day, 1925, at Chicago's Cubs Park. Over the course of the next year, Grange earned an estimated $250,000 between playing for the Bears, endorsements, and other income.[11] The next season, when Pyle demanded Grange be awarded "an interest in the Bears," the team balked. Pyle attempted to push the NFL to grant him and Grange their own franchise in New York, but then the league balked, so Pyle slapped together his own rival league, starring Grange playing for the New York Yankees of the American Football League. During the whirlwind, rumors surfaced that Yankees owner Jacob Ruppert and Charles Stoneham of the New York Giants intended to launch a New York football team of their own, one starring Grange and Notre Dame's Four Horsemen.[12]

Had they moved into football, Ruppert and Stoneham would have faced a very different labor situation. While aggressive agents also handled all sports-related negotiations for top boxers—Ruth friend Jack Dempsey, for instance, enjoyed the services of agent Jack "Doc" Kearns, a veteran of the Klondike Gold Rush and a former prize fighter—professional baseball had no such aggressive advocates when negotiating their terms of service.

Still, as Ruth faced a career crisis at the end of the 1922 season, Walsh stood ready to help on the public relations front. He set about a plan to rehabilitate his client's reputation and mend fences with the powers that controlled the game. In fact, baseball authorities were more than ready to make up with Ruth. They had little choice. Financially, too much was riding on the superstar. Around the league, teams depended on visits from Ruth and the Yankees to drive up attendance. In New York, Yankee Stadium, designed to be "the most magnificent baseball stadium in the world in the heart of the greatest city in the world," at a cost of $2.5 million, was well under construction. Such an outlay was unprecedented, but, explained the *New York Times*, "the great expenditure probably has been off-set by the greater popularity of Ruth."[13] Still, Ruppert would owe money on the ballpark. Without Ruth or with a tarnished Ruth, the massive new facility would be a house of cards.

As fans turned their attention to Yankee Stadium's inaugural season, even Ed Barrow rose to defend the beleaguered Babe. "Ruth, whether he failed to deliver up to expectations or not, cannot be accused of giving other than his best efforts," pronounced Barrow after the 1922 World Series.[14] Perhaps in reference to Barrow's comments, the *Sporting News* concluded that Ruth's "predicament is so pitiful that even critics who used to pan him are speaking for him."[15] Barrow and the Yankees had reason to be concerned. A postseason Babe Ruth barnstorming tour (acceptable this time since Ruth sought and received Landis's permission) fell flat; crowds "didn't materialize," and the "jingle of coins wasn't heard."[16] In New Ulm, Minnesota, only five hundred fans braved poor weather to see Ruth hit two home runs. Promoters had expected at least two thousand.[17] Some sportswriters argued the Yankees should trade Ruth, if the team could find a club willing to take on Ruth's large salary. "The opening of the three-million dollars Yankee stadium in Harlem will be only a razz party if Babe Ruth and some of his kind are allowed to appear on the field, judging from present sentiments of the fans," predicted the *Sporting News*.[18] Such forecasts could hardly have been welcome as the Yankees prepared to open their new ballpark.

As the 1922 regular season wound down, Walsh pushed Ruth to send conciliatory signals. One ghostwritten column had Ruth coming "gallantly to the defense of the gents he once tossed sand at and cursed." League umpires, the Ruth column declared, "call 'em as they see 'em." Billy Evans, a game official and part-time sports columnist, was, according to Ruth, "the perfect umpire."[19] But Walsh realized he needed to make a grander statement.

Determined to halt the hemorrhaging, Walsh targeted New York sportswriters. Relations between Ruth and the media, never consistently good, strained to the breaking point in 1922. At the beginning of the season, Ruth had loudly and profanely complained to teammates about press coverage of his fielding. At least one reporter apparently overheard the comments, and as a result "he [Ruth] got in wrong with the newspapermen."[20] Whatever the circumstances of the rift, Walsh designed an occasion "with the hope that Ruth and the newspapermen might reach a clearer friendlier understanding."[21] He organized a lavish dinner for New York's prominent sportswriters at the posh Elks' Club, located just off Broadway in midtown Manhattan. Behind its impressive twelve-story, neoclassical façade, the Elks' Club catered to male sensibilities, with game rooms, a bowling alley, a grill room, and a grand lodge hall.

Walsh's November 13 banquet lacked all pretexts of subtlety. Hosted by theatrically minded state senator Jimmy Walker, the evening culminated with a personal mea culpa from Ruth. "I know just as well as anyone just what mistakes I made last season," he confessed to the assembled diners.

> But let me tell you something. I want to tell the New York newspapers and fans that I've had my last drink until the middle of next October. And that isn't any loose crack. Tomorrow I'm going to my farm. I'm going to work my head off and perhaps part of my stomach.

Ruth vowed to come back and break his own home-run record when he returned, rejuvenated from his Massachusetts farm. Standing before the press corps, Ruth was not averse to supplicating himself. "Fellows, I realize now what you have done for me and what you have tried to do. If I don't make good on my promises then I am a bum," he pleaded.[22]

Walker then rose to issue a mawkish coup de grace. "Here sit some 40 sportswriters. . . . They are sad and dejected. Why? I'll tell you. You have let them down! But worst of all," Walker continued,

> you have let down the kids of America. Everywhere in America, on every vacant lot where kids play baseball, and in the hospitals too, where crippled children dream of movement forever denied their thin and warped little bodies,

they think of you, their hero; they look up to you, worship you. . . . The kids have seen their idol shattered.

As Walker reached his crescendo, Ruth reportedly wept.[23]

So syrupy was Walsh's show that it nearly misfired. In a "hall filled with tough, hard-boiled, worldly baseball writers whose daily job it is to peddle treacle about baseball heroes and soft-pedal the sour stuff," recalled Paul Gallico of the *Daily News*, Walker's speech came off as "maudlin . . . cheap and tear-jerky." But, Gallico added, somehow in his sincerity and innocence, Ruth managed to rescue the evening: he "robbed it of all cheapness, of all sensationalism, or everything that was vulgarly maudlin, by getting to his feet and, with tears streaming down his big, ugly face, promising the dirty-faced kids of the nation to behave—for their sake."[24] Other writers seemed to concur. Davis Walsh of the *Washington Times* admitted he was "inclined to doubt his [Ruth's] strength of purpose," but the evening did kindle a "spirit of greater sympathy and understanding between Ruth and the press."[25] All parties appear to have left the dinner hoping a more symbiotic, profitable relationship might be rekindled.

The production choreographed by Christy Walsh aimed less at moving the hard hearts of sportswriters than at providing the assembled scribes a new plot line to pass to readers—a comeback narrative (one that would be very familiar to Joseph Campbell). Walsh wove his redemption story along classic themes, but also in the American tradition of celebrating outdoor toil and nature as soul sustaining and character building. Americans from the transcendentalists of the 1850s to the hippies of the 1960s counterculture viewed nature as holding redemptive powers. Walsh not so subtly reinforced the theme by placing a life-size papier-mâché cow in the dining room, lest anyone miss the message.[26] If the infantilization of Ruth in 1922 associated him with the chaos of urban youth in rebellion, Walsh's dinner proposed a new Babe grounded in the traditional, rural virtues of hard work and discipline.

At one point, after the speeches, two sportswriters complained of Ruth's oversensitivity to negative press reports. "When you guys write something about me, whether it's right or wrong, ten million people see it, but I have no way of replying except by cussing you out to my friends," Ruth explained.[27] But this remark appears the only opportunity Ruth had to defend himself; the rest of the evening amounted to a semipublic shaming. The Babe evidently understood the event as a necessary maneuver to regain positive press.

Still, if the Elks' Club dinner succeeded in wooing newspapermen and reclaiming the narrative, on the negative side, it further infantilized Ruth. Rather than presenting a case for mutual responsibility for a difficult, although not disastrous, season—responsibility that might be shared by Landis and others—Babe played the babe. He accepted a public chiding, took sole blame for all supposed sins, then vowed to better himself, to grow up, and become a positive role model. Headlines proclaiming "Babe's Gonna Be Good" naturally flowed from the spectacle.[28] Instead of displaying Ruth as an adult, he remained the errant youth.

The actual Elks dinner received limited coverage in the papers and not all of it positive. "Talk is cheap," sneered Ruth antagonist Joe Vila, "and so are dinners that get the desired publicity."[29] An editorial in the Ruth-friendly New York *Daily News* commended Ruth's vow to abstain from alcohol but noted the promise might have had more authority "had he not taken the 'little drink' at the dinner the other night."[30]

Nevertheless, the story of Ruth's retreat to the farm and updates detailing his rural life began regularly appearing in the press and soon became familiar features throughout the 1922–1923 off-season. Photo spreads in particular helped narrate the story. "Down on the Farm with Ruth," a pictorial essay in the *Sporting News*, depicted Ruth chopping wood, climbing a ladder, feeding wood into a stove, and seated by a fireplace with his wife and child. A caption read, "Photos prove Bambino has quit the Bright Lights." In December a reporter did manage to catch Ruth "playing hookey" at a New York City bike race, while "cows at Babe Ruth's farm are waiting impatiently to be milked."[31] But the fact that Ruth hardly seemed a mainstay in Massachusetts rarely interfered with the story line. "A gentleman farmer sowing the seeds of hard work, regular hours, and simple food," Ruth, an Associated Press story announced, is "seeking to lay a firm foundation for his comeback. If appearances may be taken at their face value, he's doing it."[32] The *New York Times* seconded the story, proclaiming, "The Babe has never looked so good in years."[33]

Ruth's self-imposed exile appealed in another way to the baseball establishment. It kept him safely removed from off-season efforts to unionize professional baseball. Even as Ruth made his confession and took off for his Massachusetts farm, attorney and labor organizer Raymond J. Cannon was ramping up recruitment for his National Baseball Players Association of America. Having made inroads in the National League, Cannon moved to the American League, where he claimed to have enlisted ninety-three players by year's end.[34] Rumors swirled of a strike in 1923 aimed at forcing management to recognize the new players' union.[35] Team owners and league officials pushed hard to discredit the union as, in the words of NL president John Heydler, the work of "a few disgruntled ones."[36] Only a smattering of players would openly support the nascent union in the face of a sustained campaign launched by management. Baseball writers joined in impugning the organization. John Kieran noted that Cannon's work as legal representative to the discredited Chicago "Black" Sox "created an unfavorable impression."[37] Vila worked to reinforce that impression. "Greed is the cornerstone of this new union," snarled Vila. "High salaried stars," he maintained, ruined the game and had caused the Black Sox scandal.[38]

Crucial court decisions also threw obstacles in Cannon's way. In 1922, the Supreme Court finally ruled on the specter that had haunted baseball's magnates for years: the Baltimore Federals charge that baseball was a monopoly in restraint of trade. Issuing a strong final victory for league owners, the court proclaimed baseball was not interstate commerce and thus not subject to the Sherman Antitrust Act.

Armed with the decision, owners doubled down on maligning Cannon's union. Toward the new year, the campaign against Cannon hit pay dirt when the aspiring labor leader was indicted for bribing a judge with a bottle of champagne. The charges were later dropped, but Cannon's union floundered under the bad publicity. The aspiring organization took another hit in February 1923 when veteran Cincinnati outfielder George Burns, who had been elected union president, declined the position.[39] By spring 1923, the National Baseball Players Association of America was dead.[40]

That Ruth, who had sided with earlier efforts to unionize players, had publicly sworn himself to solitude far from ground zero of the labor skirmishes undoubtedly comforted team owners. As Cannon's plans collapsed, Ruth adopted a more individualistic perspective on labor relations, although one no less critical of baseball's ownership class. "The only way a ball player can make sure of getting all that is coming to him is by keeping in condition, trying hard and making himself financially independent of the game," he told reporters from Yankees spring training in New Orleans. "He's got to lay up money, or he'll be at the mercy of the club owners."[41]

Ruth's highly publicized comeback hit several snags as spring arrived. No sooner did he exit the farm in Massachusetts and arrive at Hot Springs to begin his yearly training routine than he fell desperately ill with flu, almost contracting pneumonia. Ruth's weak immune system strained each spring with the sudden change of weather and the physical demands of getting back in shape. Professional physical training remained in its infancy, a fact borne out by the "reducing belt—a device with suction cups" that Ruth sported that spring around his waist in hopes of losing weight.[42] The steam rooms and public baths of the Arkansas resort wreaked havoc with Ruth's health (the saloons and casinos of Hot Springs contributed as well).

Following his recovery, Ruth struggled at the plate in preseason exhibition games. On an extended tour in Oklahoma, Ruth fanned out four times in front of a large Tulsa crowd. But this time, the press betrayed some sympathy for the struggling star. As the game in Tulsa ended, Hearst columnist Arthur Robinson, also a frequent Ruth ghostwriter, reported that "thousands" of young boys surrounded a dejected Ruth making his way off the field. "They looked up sad eyes at him. They stroked his back, they shook his hand, and little hero worshippers they followed their fallen idol in his slow funeral march across the field to the club house," Robinson wrote. Finally, Ruth spoke. "'I want to come back here next year,' he said quietly. 'I'd like to hit a home run for you kids—I'd like to hit a lot.'"[43]

More bad news came in early April with word that a young woman named Delores Dixon had hit Ruth with a paternity suit. For several days, the tabloids wallowed in the story. The *Pittsburgh Press* described the charges as an attack on Ruth's "morality, upon his decency as a man, a husband, and a father." Ruth hired detectives who disguised themselves as window washers to spy on Dixon. Eventually she retracted her story.[44]

Meanwhile, Walsh strove to counter the bad publicity. An exhibition game in Vicksburg, Mississippi, allowed Ruth to generate the positive public relations off field that were missing on the field. When told of a desperately ill young boy, "praying" to meet his baseball idol, Ruth borrowed a car and drove several miles outside town to spend an hour with the boy. "The home run king has often indulged in little kindnesses of this variety, but unfortunately they do not get the publicity that less favorable performances attain," reported the *New York Tribune*.[45] The story, in fact, did find its way into newspapers across the country. To the *Sporting News* it offered "a ray of hope that maybe the turn has come for Ruth, that maybe by accident he has been given the chance to comeback to himself. . . . Let Babe be 'natural' again and he'll do his stuff after a fashion that will make turnstiles click." By "natural" the *Sporting News* meant rediscovering an innocent love for the game rather than "brooding over the slams of the critics" and "trying to obey orders."[46] Months before, Ruth was maligned as an unruly youth; now he was too much a grown-up, too serious. Still, Ruth and Walsh could take some satisfaction that the press seemed to be siding with them after a difficult several months. Meanwhile, Ruth appeared on his way to redefining himself as an adult committed to altruism and traditional values.

"A Silver Flame through the Grey, Bleak April Shadows"

As Ruth endured his usual spring challenges of slumps and illnesses, the public's attention focused on the mammoth stadium rising in the Bronx on the east side of the Harlem River. Until Ruth's arrival in Gotham, the Yankees had existed as the neglected stepchildren of New York baseball. The Giants reigned as the premier New York team. The two clubs shared the Polo Grounds, a sunken field surrounded by grandstands in a part of upper Manhattan known as Coogan's Bluff. Following Ruth's arrival, however, the Giants grew resentful as the Yankees began outdrawing their NL rivals. Largely out of spite, the Giants evicted the Yankees, and Colonels Ruppert and Huston pooled resources to build their own ballpark, one that would leave no question about the dominance of the Yankees. Throughout 1922 and into 1923, the grand scale of the new stadium took form. The Polo Grounds, only a five-minute walk and visible from the new Yankees home, increasingly appeared outdated and paltry. Yankee Stadium's copper frieze along the roof, coupled with its striking concrete exterior and arches, lent it a classical feel. With two decks and a mezzanine, it could accommodate upward of seventy thousand spectators, far greater than any other baseball facility in the country. Unlike the Polo Grounds, explained sportswriter Fred Lieb, the new "stadium can be seen for miles, as its triple decks grand stand majestically rises from the banks of the Harlem."[47] In the new structure, marveled Heywood Broun, "Goliath could roll over twice."[48] It was, as the *New York Times* described it, "a skyscraper among baseball parks."[49]

The success or failure of Yankee Stadium fell largely on Ruth's shoulders. Not only was it the "House That Ruth Built," in the words of sportswriter Fred Lieb, but it would also have to be the house that Ruth would sustain. Yankees management envisaged spectator sports as a permanent, widely popular, and enormously lucrative feature of modern life. But as a business, baseball would have to be stable and profitable—and Ruth would have to be dominant. His comeback was now a critical issue.

Christy Walsh already had outlined a comeback narrative, and increasingly sportswriters were drawing on it. "Can he come back?" asked sportswriter F. C. Lane. "Overweight and not in particularly good health," Ruth had "retired to the farm which he had purchased in south Sudbury Massachusetts, where he had spent the winter far from bright lights, quietly, in the healthful environment of good hours and physical exercise." The fallen idol, Lane concluded, was primed for a comeback.[50] Ruth's ghostwriter harped continuously on the hitter's rural exile, promising readers that he would be aiming for a new home-run record: "I'll be swinging with all my might trying to get a homer. . . . I thought about it all winter while I worked on my farm up in Sudbury."[51]

The pressure on Ruth must have been nearly crushing by opening day 1923. The weather was cold and dreary, yet Lexington Avenue trains loaded with ecstatic fans began arriving at the stadium hours before game time. By midafternoon, a crowd, officially reported at 74,217 (more likely around 62,000), packed the stadium. It was baseball's largest audience to date. John Philip Sousa conducted the Seventh Regiment Band in the national anthem, and Governor Al Smith threw out the first ball as nearly four hundred ushers struggled to serve the overflow crowd. Meanwhile, some five hundred police officers and two hundred "special policemen" kept spectators under control.[52]

All eyes were on Ruth. After flying out in the first inning, he came to bat in the third. "In a scenario that couldn't have been any better if the members of the Baseball Writers Association of America had mapped it out in advance with a view for making the event good copy," recounted Damon Runyon, "Ruth hit a perfectly timed home run."[53] For Rice, Ruth's shot appeared "a silver flame through the grey, bleak April shadows."[54] Thunderous ovation burst from the crowd: "74,000 expanding throats in the greatest vocal cataclysm baseball had ever known," gushed Rice.[55] "Hats, canes, and umbrellas were thrown up and a tremendous volley of cheers greeted the smiling Bambino as he trotted around the circuit," reported Vila.[56] Even Commissioner Landis joined the exhilaration, tossing his hat in the air as "the crowd went hysterical, and the Babe almost wept."[57]

"During the winter we have never heard the name of Babe Ruth come up in any discussion without someone entering the conversation to remark, 'the big bum,'" reflected Broun. Yet after Ruth's home run, "There seemed to be not a representative of this misguided opinion. All stood and all shouted."[58] One swing of the bat reversed Ruth's fortunes and completed his comeback.

Off-season coverage, of course, well prepared fans for the return of Ruth. Following the home run, the slugger's Christy Walsh ghostwriter fastidiously reviewed the comeback narrative set out by Walsh months ago. "Looking back," reflected the writer portraying Ruth, "I feel that I have been rewarded in part already for all the hard work I put in. . . . I guess there must be something in that old gag about virtue brings its own reward."[59] Once the epitome of urban modern life and youthful rebellion, Ruth now was siding squarely with the traditionalists.

Only months before, W. O. McGeehan had branded Ruth a "primitive youth," raging out of control. Now, with a Ruthian comeback underway, Mc-Geehan celebrated the Babe as "a joyous and carefree youngster who walked to the plate with a laugh on his lips and a merry song in his heart and just batted the ball." McGeehan acknowledged a change in Ruth, but to him the Babe remained a child—only now an innocent child. Also, with much on the line financially, McGeehan acknowledged, Ruth's home run meant "much in relation to the prosperity of baseball."[60]

As Broun correctly noted, public perceptions of Ruth flipped completely. Days after his opening-day clout, Ruth hit a ninth-inning home run at a Paterson, New Jersey, exhibition game. Two thousand jubilant fans poured out of the grandstands and swarmed Ruth, who struggled to find his way to safety. Several of Ruth's teammates were "crushed against the dugout" as they tried to hold back the crowd. The mob trampled Ruth's friend Bob Meusel. Fifty policemen trying to fight back the crowd suffered similar fates. Finally, Ruth himself managed to calm the crowd, offering to say a few words. Then his teammates, armed with bats, ultimately escorted him safely from the ballpark. Even so, fans swarmed Ruth's car as he strove to make an exit.[61] The hysteria of 1920 also seemed to have made a comeback.

At the same time, press adoration returned in full force. Recounting a game-winning blast a few days after his opening-day home run, the *New York Times* reported, "Three and two, the bases full and one out, the next pitch was low. . . . As they say in boxing he swung from the floor. There was a crack, a whiz and a white streak. . . . That's all there was."[62] The "superman" imagery resumed as well. When the press arranged for a Dr. Frank J. Monaghan, commissioner of health for New York City, to examine Ruth, the doctor described a "body that I could honestly say from a medical and physical standpoint is close to perfect." Condescendingly, Monaghan added that "it is common for well-trained athletes or race horses to be high strung and extremely nervous, this is not so with Ruth."[63]

Soon Manager Huggins joined the chorus. "I cannot praise the big fellow enough for his conduct on and off the field. . . . For years Ruth reminded me of a kid out on a lark in his profession. But he has reached the age where he is getting serious," waxed the manager. Reviewing past concerns, Huggins added, "There have been a lot of wooly talk about Ruth. But don't believe half of what you hear . . . the public will gossip."[64]

With suspensions and misdeeds now months in the past, Ruth—at least in his ghostwritten column—returned as wise counselor to the nation's youth. In one column, Ruth offered fans nine rules (modeled on the nine innings of baseball) for success on the diamond:

> 1) No matter how terrible your slump—keep trying. 2) Don't forget cheer can quickly turn to jeer. 3) Don't play for a selfish batting average. 4) Don't forget one man can't win any games. 5) Don't lose your temper. 6) Don't reject advice or criticism. 7) Don't think about your past or kid yourself about your future. 8) Don't be a poor loser. 9) Don't quit until you win.[65]

Ruth's rules, of course, emphasized team play over individualism; rowdyism had no place in baseball. With his redemption cycle complete, Ruth now could offer with authority his experience as a guide for others—counsel that reinforced baseball's quest for order.

Ruth's ghostwritten columns also provided the occasional glimpse into his private life, all the while reinforcing the reformed sinner theme. In one column, Ruth described how "when I decided to get rid of a lot of ideas that got me in hot water last year, I decided to go without a chauffeur." This decision, Ruth explained, allowed him to view the world from "a fan's standpoint . . . from the angle of the boys and men who possibly find it hard to pay the price at the gate, but whose money makes it possible for me to own a car at all." This recalled for Ruth his modest past. "Here I was a ball player trying to pull banker stuff," concluded a populist-minded Ruth.[66] Again Ruth seemed at pains to identify himself with traditional America rather than the corrupt trappings of modern wealth and fame.

Yet under the surface, relations between Ruth and the baseball establishment remained strained. In late June, Ruth failed to appear at a Yankees exhibition game in New Haven. Alongside regularly scheduled games, the Yankees played dozens of exhibition games, greatly profiting the team but adding nothing extra to the paychecks of Yankees players. Ruth's absence left ten thousand fans ended up disappointed, and the Yankees were forced to offer refunds. Ruth claimed he was delayed in traffic, but some writers suggested missing the game was payback for the aborted 1921 postseason tour Landis had forced Ruth to cancel.[67] More likely Ruth was establishing a case that he be paid extra for spring-training and regular-season exhibition games. In fact, fans came largely to see Ruth, and the additional games put great physical pressure on the injury-prone star. By 1930, Ruth was earning a portion of the gate for exhibition games.[68]

"Like a Phoenix"

Despite positive press and renewed popularity, the Babe Ruth of 1923 was not the sole dominant figure in baseball. He had competition. Cy Williams of the Philadelphia Phillies led baseball in home runs for large portions of the year, although home runs came easier in Philadelphia's small Baker Bowl. At season's end, Ruth managed to tie Williams at forty-one home runs each, only six more than he had hit in his abbreviated 1922 season. (Still Ruth managed a stunning .393 batting average in 1923.) The tall, threadlike Williams had played football under Knute Rockne at Notre Dame. But he lacked Ruth's charisma and heartening comeback narrative. In late September, Ruth was the unanimous choice of sportswriters as Most Valuable Player, after failing to finish among the top eight players the previous year. The *Chicago Tribune* sports staff cited Ruth's comeback and character as the basis for the award. "At one time many fans questioned whether temperament or a sense of his own importance . . . might not seriously impair his usefulness and dim in part the luster of his name in baseball." But Ruth had grown and became a player who "devoted his talents to the best interests of the aggregation of which he is a member; that when occasion demanded he subordinated self to team play; that he observed club discipline."[69]

Still, Ruth's comeback remained incomplete. Two weak World Series performances, in 1921 and 1922, blighted his record. The 1922 series had been Ruth's nadir. In October 1923, the Yankees again prepared to meet their rivals, the Giants. As the series drew near, the pressure on Ruth was acute. Hearst's *Evening Journal* posed the question on all minds: "Babe Ruth—hero or goat? A million fans, scattered over a million square miles of territory, are waiting and watching—striving for the answer that the next ten days will bring."[70] Ruth, concluded McGeehan, would be the deciding factor in the competition, one way or another, and "Col. Ruppert expects the Babe to stand as a reason for a Yankees victory."[71] Rice turned to verse, casting Ruth as a hero, haunted by past failures, desperate for redemption:

> The scar is still upon my heart from nineteen twenty-two,
> The blight is still upon my soul for what I failed to do;

But now once more the battle cry comes sweeping down the plains
And so, I come with lifted mace to wipe away the stain
They buried me beneath the wreck a year ago to-day
They stopped me with two bitter hits Chough-out the bitter fray
But like a Phoenix, as they say, from ashes risen high,
I stalk again to face the lists with flaming batting eye.[72]

Ring Lardner mocked the media's emphasis on Ruth's performance. His first at bat, wrote Lardner, "will give us all a hunch one way or the other in regard to what to expect. If the Babe busts one, the Yankees still have a chance to lose. If he don't do nothing, the Giants may win."[73]

As the series began, Ruth bore the same burden he faced on opening day in April. It fell on his shoulders to furnish thrills and to complete the comeback narrative. Fortunately for Ruth, in 1923 all the pieces had fallen into place. Unlike 1921, he was healthy, and, unlike 1922, he was not in a slump. To the contrary, Ruth seemed to be peaking. As a result, Rice's prophecy crystallized and a revived Babe rose to the occasion. In the second game of the series, Ruth launched two home runs. Broun opened his front-page account of the game with one of the most famous lines written about the idol: "The Ruth is mighty and shall prevail. He did yesterday . . . Ruth crushed to earth shall rise again."[74] Rice likewise could fulfill his phoenix metaphor and resurrect the Ruth he murdered in print the previous season:

They hammered him into the dust and sat upon his neck. They tied him in true lovers' knots and rolled his vast withering body in the park. They fed him the juice of wild raspberry and threw dirt upon his gabardine. . . . But the ancient slogan still rides down the ages—Ruth crushed to earth shall rise again.[75]

(Presumably, Rice and Broun, close friends, jointly arrived at the play on American poet William Cullen Bryant's famous "Truth, crushed to earth, shall rise again" line.) Led by Ruth, the Yankees went on to win their first of many World Series.

A friend and frequent Ruth ghostwriter, Ford Frick avoided classical allusions and instead drew upon searing recent imagery in depicting Ruth's triumph. In 1920, as revelations about the Black Sox scandal surfaced, Hugh Fullerton poignantly had described a young boy approaching co-conspirator Shoeless Joe Jackson emerging from court. "Say it ain't so, Joe. Say it ain't so," the boy supposedly appealed to the fallen hero. Jackson could only turn away in silent shame. Frick replayed the scene in his column, beginning with Ruth's "deep and solemn pledge; a pledge witnessed by newspaper writers, cynics and unbelievers . . . a pledge of hope and loyalty to urchin friends who had themselves been loyal when others turned to scoff." With his comeback complete and pledge fulfilled, Ruth, like Jackson before him, is approached by a youth who with a "small voice shrilled" to his hero, "I knew you'd do it Babe. I knew you'd do it."[76] Ruth's triumph, in Frick's account, redeems not only him but also baseball.

Indeed, Ruth's conquering comeback of 1923 was really baseball's comeback. The shaky 1922 season, with the return of rowdyism, defiant stars, and threats of labor action, seemed a step back to the chaos of previous decades. For the major league baseball establishment, however, the clouds parted again in 1923. The menace of a players' union melted away. The Supreme Court preserved baseball's monopoly, and thus the reserve clause appeared unassailable. Fewer players held out on contracts, rowdyism seemed again abating, and a new obedient, adult version of Ruth appeared. The inaugural season of Yankee Stadium exceeded all hopeful expectations. Record regular-season attendance figures were topped by record World Series attendance. Some 62,817 fans witnessed game five of the series, and a grand total of over 300,000 fans attended the subway series. A new era of stratospheric profits was at hand, one in which athletes appeared willing to accept a subordinated role.

Ruth himself undoubtedly was relieved to be receiving better press and performing more consistently on the ball field. At the same time, he chafed at the lack of control he seemed to have over his career and life. He also felt increasingly isolated. His marriage had fallen apart, and in May his sole friend in the Yankees leadership, Colonel Huston, sold his portion of the team to fellow co-owner Jacob Ruppert for $1.25 million. The news came as "a crushing blow" to the Babe.[77] Ed Barrow, on whom Ruppert greatly relied, was quickly elevated to team secretary, given a seat on the Yankees Board of Directors, and extended the opportunity to buy 10 percent of the team. Manager Huggins would now surely continue with the team. In 1923, when Claire Hodgson, later Ruth's second wife, met her future husband, she found a "miserable" and "morose" figure who "hated himself." He lamented that "baseball writers were unanimous in taking the side of anybody with whom the Babe fought."[78] Ruth was clearly drawn to the strong-willed Hodgson, who quickly emerged his confidant. Despite his marriage to another woman, he moved in with Hodgson, into a household that included her daughter, her widowed mother, and her two brothers. In a sense, Ruth found the family and stability missing from his life to that point. Still, for religious reasons and fear of negative publicity, he resisted divorce and remarriage. His life, despite the fame and fortune (or perhaps because of it), remained unstable.

"If the Raspberries Should Come Again"

The glow of Ruth's comeback spilled over to the next season. In May 1924, Yankees ownership honored its franchise player with "Babe Ruth Day." Serenaded by the Marine Corps' concert band, Commissioner Landis awarded Ruth his "diploma" as 1923's Most Valuable Player.[79] In many ways 1924 eclipsed 1923. The Babe dominated the home-run race; no one else was even close. Coverage remained generally positive; however, a less deferential tone did slip back into columns and stories. Likewise, evidence began to mount that Ruth's reformation had not fully taken root. Traffic violations and speeding landed the Babe repeatedly in trouble with the law. During spring training in New Orleans, Ruth managed to lose a $1,000 bill on his way to the bank. The mishap was widely publicized, a comic example of a hero excessive in all things, including occasional stupidity. Weeks later, Commissioner Landis issued a stern private warning to Ruth against "wagering substantial sums on the races."[80] Ed Barrow, who maintained a close eye on Ruth, in fact, had brought the Babe's gambling to the commissioner's attention.[81] In mid-June, Ruth landed square in the middle of a full-scale riot in Detroit when a clash between Yankees and Tigers players inspired eighteen thousand fans to storm Navin Field to join the fight. Police struggled to shepherd Ruth and the Yankees to safety.[82] Later in the season, Ruth was ejected from a game after "a carload of oratory" directed at an umpire.[83]

As the gallant 1923 comeback faded into memory, the rawer version of baseball's top star returned in press accounts. In a *Sporting News* profile of the slugger, Arthur Robinson, who described himself as a sort of Boswell to Ruth's Johnson, portrayed the hero as "something of a clown . . . a good natured personification of brute force." Ruth was superstitious, never wore underwear, was "temperamental," but also "ever so gentle and tender."[84] The errant youngster of 1922 was slipping back into the coverage.

The writer who maligned Ruth as a "primitive youth" in 1922, McGeehan, used the occasion of the MVP award to reflect on the fickle nature of sports heroism: "Contrary to the general belief the national pastime in the US is not baseball. It is creating a national idol, lifting it to a high pedestal, then kicking it off to observe the effects of the crash," wrote McGeehan.

"They"—presumably baseball officials, sportswriters, and fans—"have patched the 'Old' Babe up and replaced him upon the pedestal, for how long, nobody knows." McGeehan obviously well understood the artificiality of Ruth's 1922 fall and 1923 comeback. The entire narrative aimed to contain a superstar player whose colossal popularity had become a threat to baseball's power structure.

Ruth, McGeehan suggested, would have little control over the process. "If the raspberries should come again—and that seems inevitable," he wrote, "the Babe can find some slight solace in looking at the framed diploma over the mantel piece at his Sudbury home and saying 'But life was not always raspberries.' He has it in writing."[85] In fact, Ruth would not have to wait long for the raspberries to return.

FIVE. CHALLENGE TO AUTHORITY
PART II

Since 1920, an ongoing tsunami of public fascination had swirled around Babe Ruth. Despite his wealth and fame, Ruth clearly felt confined by his role of celebrity athlete, known mainly for his on-field power and off-field colorful antics. In 1925, the Babe moved to assert greater control of his career, launching a series of attacks on Yankees manager Miller Huggins, whom Ruth sought to supplant. A star player of unprecedented skill and popularity, the Babe understood well the fortune he was generating for baseball, and he naturally felt a certain entitlement. Watching other star players, such as Rogers Hornsby and Ty Cobb, taking on player-manager roles rankled the Yankees power hitter, as did the condescending regard with which he was held by Yankees management.

Ruth's campaign against Huggins, however, proved ill-advised. The Yankees, under team secretary Ed Barrow and owner Jacob Ruppert, had staked its credibility on Huggins. Ruth's independent streak clearly unnerved the entire Yankees leadership, now solidly aligned against the Babe with the 1923 departure of Colonel T. L. Huston. Ruth's challenge to Huggins provoked a bitter backlash that stunned the star. Sportswriters from around the country predictably stood by the baseball establishment in impugning and infantilizing Ruth. At its height, the anti-Ruth campaign grew viciously personal, as the press revealed his frayed marriage and identified the "other" woman to whom Ruth turned for support.

By the end of the year, Ruth and any other player who dared defy baseball had been sent a very pointed message. Ruth himself found little alternative but to accept both full responsibility for his own personal failures and full culpability for the collapse of the Yankees team in 1925—the most brutal year of his career.

"Passed the Shadow Line of his Youth"

Ruth managed to lay much of the groundwork for his dramatic fall during the 1925 preseason. He had performed well in 1924, but the Yankees failed to win the pennant. Ruth clearly felt pressure to improve the team's performance. In February 1925, he journeyed to Hot Springs, Arkansas, for his customary regime of soaking in the city's famed baths and playing golf. Then in early March he moved south, to St. Petersburg, Florida, for Yankees spring training. Upon arrival, Ruth was greeted by mobs of admirers and a Scottish Highlander band playing "Hail to the Chief." He appeared as popular as ever.

Yet the assembled media focused primarily on Ruth's weight gain—ten pounds since the last season. To one newspaper, the Babe's waistline appeared "aldermanic."[1] Hardly oblivious to the problem, Ruth set out to get in shape. Wearing a heavy sweatshirt the first day of spring training, he thrust himself into a three-hour workout under a hot Florida sun. The display impressed all. Ruth even seemed to be outpacing rookies in exertion.[2] A chipped bone in his hand, however, interrupted his workouts. On the bench and unable to pursue his conditioning regime, Ruth continued to gain weight. Yankees management grew concerned.[3]

Meanwhile, as Ruth convalesced, rumors found their way into print that he was broke and in deep financial difficulties. In early March, a New York bookmaker sued Ruth in civil court for unpaid horse-racing debts.[4] Eventually Yankees owner Ruppert interceded to deny the gossip and proclaim Ruth fiscally sound. Such stories, however, along with Ruth's growing girth, reinforced impressions of a star athlete unable to control his base instincts. Likewise, any association with gambling, even if just on horse races, concerned baseball in the wake of the Black Sox scandal.

In truth, Ruth himself seemed in a dispirited and anxious mood. Frustrating injuries and illnesses prevented him from getting in condition. The Yankees' second place finish the previous season had left him brooding over the future of his team. As was his tendency, Ruth blamed Manager Huggins for the Yankees' shortcomings. Colonel Ruppert had hired Huggins in 1918 against the wishes of Yankees co-owner and Ruth friend T. L. Huston, serving in France at the time. Huston's candidate had been Brooklyn Dodgers manager Wilbert Robinson. A warm, corpulent man, Robinson was more likely to sympathize with Ruth than the undersized and introverted Huggins. Huston remained a sharp critic of Huggins, yet co-owner Ruppert refused to consider a change.[5] For Ruppert, the Huggins question clearly became a matter of personal pride rather than strict business. Ed Barrow recognized Ruppert's strong feelings and also emerged an entrenched defender of Huggins, a position that solidified Barrow and Ruppert's alliance.

Huston sold his share of the Yankees in 1923, but Ruth maintained Huston's campaign against Huggins. Robinson, who continued to be mentioned in the press as a potential Huggins replacement, remained a favorite of Ruth, and Ruth of Robinson. In 1925, the Dodgers held spring training only a few miles from the Yankees camp, and Robinson effusively praised the Babe in interviews that spring, calling him baseball's "greatest asset."[6] Increasingly, however, Ruth set his own eyes on the Yankees managerial position. Certainly there was precedent for a star player-manager. Since 1921, Ty Cobb had managed the Tigers while remaining an active player on their team. In May of 1925, the St. Louis Cardinals appointed star hitter Rogers Hornsby as player-manager. As part of the deal, arrangements were made to sell Hornsby a sizable portion of shares in the Cardinals team.

An excellent strategist who rarely made a fielding error, Ruth naturally began to think about a similar arrangement—and to talk openly about it. In a spring training interview, Ruth glibly tore into Yankees manager Huggins. While "not criticizing Huggins," Ruth pronounced the Yankees skipper out of touch with the contemporary ballplayer. Ruth, by contrast, had insights that could unite and turn the Yankees around. Betraying something of his own off-field predilections and habits, Ruth offered that if players "were stale and weren't doing so well, I'd take money out of my own pocket and tell every one of them to go out at night and cut a wide path, do a lotta clowning around and forget baseball." Tensions erased, players would be ready to win again. "That's the way to handle modern baseball players," asserted Ruth.[7] To some readers, Ruth's poorly articulated plan seemed an invitation to replace team discipline with anarchy. Yet Ruth well understood the pressures on "modern" athletes and their need to find outlets to offset the stress of a demanding profession.

Ruth's open jockeying for the managerial job undoubtedly alarmed Yankees officials, especially Barrow, who viewed Ruth essentially as a delinquent youth with the potential for unleashing significant disorder in baseball. Likewise, Huggins hardly welcomed Ruth's frontal assault on his management of the Yankees. In the wake of Ruth's attacks on Huggins, press coverage turned decidedly against Ruth. Joe Vila exposed Ruth's betting at racetracks and conjectured the Yankees star was on the verge of becoming "a gambler." Vila also dutifully passed along rumors about Yankees drinking at spring training. The team seemed more "interested in guzzling Scotch" than preparing for the upcoming baseball season, charged Vila.[8] The New York *Evening World* took direct aim at Ruth, who "has passed the shadow line of his youth" and was "growing fat and old." Moreover, added the report, debts to gamblers and generosity to charities had left Ruth broke. He had nothing to his name but the Sudbury farm.[9] In reality, Ruth was spending liberally, but his resources were hardly depleted.

Ruth's weight continued as a source of interest and amusement to reporters. *Daily News* correspondent Marshall Hunt reported that Ruth traveled with a bakery roller, which a trainer rolled over the slugger's "tummy" as some sort of antidote for excess flab. Meanwhile, noted the press with little sympathy, the minor injuries afflicting Ruth mounted. According to Hunt, Ruth was "anguished by no fewer than two charley horses, one in each vast limb, and his uprights bandaged up like a royal Egyptian cadaver."[10] Paul Gallico had Ruth struggling with "the grippe," numerous charley horses, and an ailing hand. "The fact is that the Babe has hollered wolf so much that a thermometer is about the only way of finding out how sick he is."[11]

By early April, in fact, Ruth had come down with a serious case of "the grippe," or influenza. An acute affliction of some sort was something of a seasonal ritual for Ruth. Like clockwork, he took ill every spring training. In an age before antibiotics and with limited understanding of the science of physical conditioning, Ruth was largely on his own. Sudden exposure to warm weather, sun, and physical exercise left him vulnerable. Prolonged steam baths used to control Ruth's weight dehydrated the slugger, making matters worse. Whether for food, alcohol, or partying, Ruth's prodigious appetite further weakened him. In the age of Prohibition, Ruth consumed more than his fair share of sketchy bathtub gin, moonshine, and other potentially perilous concoctions. The slugger's immune system remained the weakest part of his remarkable physique. Ruth, the *Sporting News* mocked, seemed susceptible to "the little ailments of life which a shoe clerk or other less robust person might shake off with a headache powder or a good night's sleep."[12] While Ruth's health cracked perennially every spring, 1925 brought a particularly serious rupture. In fact, a virulent strain of influenza had descended on the country that year. By mid-March, 279 had died in a Chicago "grippe epidemic" also afflicting numerous other cities.[13] Baseball players were hardly immune. As Ruth took ill, Ty Cobb was confined to bed with similar symptoms.[14]

Despite his malady and injuries, Ruth strove to resurrect his conditioning regime, and he played well in exhibition games, drawing huge crowds eager to see the hero. The Babe clearly felt "rotten," but neither the Yankees nor Ruth dared disappoint the large and lucrative throngs flocking to Yankees exhibition games, largely to get a glimpse of the biggest name in sports. In Birmingham, Alabama, on March 31, Ruth hit two home runs playing the Dodgers before a crowd of ten thousand.[15] Days later, Ruth again launched two homers, this time in Chattanooga, Tennessee, despite having spent the evening under a doctor's care due to a case of the chills.[16] Expectations began to rise. "If April Comes can Ruth be far Behind?" rhetorically asked Grantland Rice at the end of a poem.[17]

Ruth, however, remained ill, and no one seemed prepared to step in and order him to rest. A bumpy train ride over mountains drove him to the edge. On April 7, when the Yankees arrived in Ashville, North Carolina, their star player lay gravely ill. Just before a scheduled exhibition game, Ruth collapsed and begged to be taken directly back to New York. Will Wedge of *The Sun* painted a melodramatic scene with Ruth breaking down and crying upon learning he would be disappointing waiting Ashville fans. Ruth friend Bob Meusel stepped in. "Don't worry Babe, I'll show them how you hit 'em," Meusel offered, following through with a home run that afternoon.[18] A local doctor diagnosed Ruth as suffering the negative effects of "constant training and dieting in order to reduce weight."[19]

As Ruth's fever spiked, Yankees management came under scrutiny. At least one journalist, Thomas S. Rice of the *Brooklyn Daily Eagle*, assailed Yankees management for pushing Ruth to play through illness. Team leaders "should have been aware of Ruth's real condition," insisted Rice. He labeled Huggins "reckless" for his handling of the Yankees' key asset.[20]

Finally conceding the seriousness of the matter, Yankees officials decided to seek medical care in New York. When Ruth's train missed a connection to Washington, reports flew that he had died, and pandemonium broke out. Fans stood alongside the train route north to pay what they thought were last respects to their hero. The story went international. London's *Evening News* pronounced Ruth's passing "a national calamity."[21] Other British papers gave the bogus story "a prominence which the passing of a mere financier or politician would not have achieved."[22] Even after the record of Ruth's death was corrected, public interest remained elevated. Greater "general alarm beat in human breasts than if the President were equally ill," proclaimed one columnist.[23]

Briefly coverage took on a eulogistic air. "The early years of his life were spent at an orphanage in Baltimore," wrote Damon Runyon. "It was there that he received his baseball education. It was here that his boyish heart hoped someday to achieve one-tenth of what in later years came true. What dreams visited him in that orphanage never will be known. But they were all realized ten-fold."[24]

Ruth arrived at New York's Pennsylvania Station to a full-on media circus over which his handlers had little control. As his train pulled in, photographers, reporters, and the public surged forward, creating a dangerous, chaotic scene. Subsequent to his arrival, Ruth reportedly banged his head on a cabin washbasin and blacked out. He went into convulsions as attendants faced the daunting task of getting him from the train, through the crowd, and to a hospital. As the vulnerable Mrs. Ruth wept, porters passed her husband out through a train window on a gurney. Photographs captured the drama for newspapers around the country.

From Pennsylvania Station, ambulances rushed Ruth to St. Vincent's Hospital, where the media and crowds gathered on the street. A pall descended over the baseball world. At *Daily News* headquarters, Gallico observed that "the possibility of [Ruth] not recovering hangs like a cloud over the office and no one feels particularly like working or doing much of anything."[25]

Back at the hospital, Ruth's condition quickly stabilized, but the media carnival outside St. Vincent's only swelled, now including "several correspondents of European agencies." Melodrama flooded into news accounts. Ruth, reported Damon Runyon, "beat a long throw from Old Death, the outfielder in life's game. He slid in safe . . . but it was a close decision."[26] Several newspapers ran the story of two boys who arrived at Ruth's hospital saying "they spent their combined capital of fifty cents on the flowers . . . [and] hoped that when the Bambino smelled them he would get well and knock out some home runs."[27]

Some journalists resented the growing sentimentality and artificiality of the story. Gallico later rued a photograph his paper ran of "grimy street Arabs standing on the sidewalk beneath the hospital," clasping flowers in their hands. As a veteran reporter, Gallico acknowledged, "You come to regard such touching pictures with more than a faint tinge of suspicion." He imagined photographers cynically seeing the street kids on the street outside the hospital and saying, "Let's grab a couple and pose 'em."[28]

The overwrought coverage, however, quickly gave way to a new narrative, one that revived the mocking tone established after Ruth's attack on Huggins in March. Yankees team physician Dr. Edward King opened the door to the shift in tone. Explaining at a press conference that Ruth remained ill but was under no immediate threat, Dr. King added that the Yankees star did not take adequate care of himself, that he ate too much, played too hard, "becomes overheated, jumps into an automobile and cools off too quickly."[29] From Richmond, Virginia, Huggins also weighed in, blaming Ruth's condition on "indigestion . . . caused by overeating."[30] With fingers pointing yet again to Huggins's loose management style, the manager deftly maneuvered to deflect blame back onto his star player.

The press, no stranger to Ruth's mammoth appetite, ran with the story, playing up its comic dimensions. To Gallico, Ruth's emergency was "due as much as anything to his indefatigable drills with knife and fork."[31] Grantland Rice penned a poem called "One way to Stop Eating," beginning with the lines: "If Ruth finds his weight in a sheath / Where the flesh won't give way underneath."[32] Writers traded barbs about "Mrs. Ruth's heroic but overfed husband" and Ruth's "anguish of the alimentary canal." W. O. McGeehan famously dubbed the episode "the bellyache heard around the world."[33] Even Ruth's friend Ford Frick questioned the idol's common sense: "The whole world loves nerve and all things considered the man with nerve is very apt the public hero!" explained Frick. "But there is only a slight dividing line between 'nerve' and 'foolhardiness.'"[34] Ruth's immoderation increasingly took center stage. In an age of excess, excess had nearly killed the superstar athlete.

At the same time, Yankees team secretary Ed Barrow peddled stories of overindulgences of another kind to sportswriters. The true cause of Ruth's condition, he whispered to select reporters, was venereal disease—syphilis.[35] Barrow's antipathy toward Ruth was well-known, and the claim appears based on little more than malicious speculation. Ruth's symptoms seem more related to the flu than syphilis. Nevertheless, Barrow's accusations found their way into print. "Skeptics," McGeehan suggested, as Ruth lay in a hospital bed, "are inclined to believe that there is no stomach ache at all. . . . These suspicions are not entirely unfounded but are cruel."[36] Less concerned about "cruelty" was Joe Vila, who reported that "wild rumors concerning the nature and cause of Ruth's illness are in circulation. But the fact is that he is a victim of careless living."[37] Years later the "wild rumors" would surface again as charges that syphilis or another form of venereal disease had sidelined the idol. McGeehan and Vila seem to have been hinting at as much. Still, given the prevalence of the flu that spring, Ruth's prodigious appetite (the product of a youth spent in hunger and poverty), and the hitter's frequent ill health, speculation about other causes seem, as McGeehan suggested, "cruel." Additionally, within days of his admission to St. Vincent's, surgeons removed an "abscess" from Ruth's intestines. The surgery may have been a ruse to distract from other treatments, but the public explanation of severe intestinal illness seems most plausible.

Like the public debate around Ruth's clashes with authority, the "stomach ache heard around the world" episode also hit a cultural nerve. To cultural historian Warren Susman, Ruth was the "ideal hero for the world consumption."[38] From his large salary to his love of fast cars to his eating, Ruth seemed to epitomize the excesses of urban consumer culture. As traditional values about thrift competed with new attitudes, Ruth's collapse seemed a grand parable related to indulgence and excess. Since Ruth's personal gluttony appeared the source of his troubles, journalists felt free to lampoon the man whose lack of discipline led to his fall.

In the face of media mocking, Ruth's handlers strove to contain the damage. Christy Walsh organized a bedside news conference. There Ruth emphatically denied that overeating or other bad habits contributed to his collapse. "Hell no," Ruth told gathered reporters. "That's a lot of baloney. Why, I don't eat as much as two-thirds of the Yankee team." This, naturally, led one interviewer to ponder in jest whether Ruth had meant two-thirds of the Yankees collectively or individually.[39] Indeed, while Ruth had a prodigious appetite, tales of his dining feats clearly took on lives of their own. Ruth's denial in fact spurred numerous testimonies to his superhuman eating feats. One account had Ruth consuming, between the end of an exhibition game in Toronto and an early train for Detroit, seven large sandwiches and drinking "30–40 short beers," then worrying "about whether there would be dinner on that Detroit train."[40] As with stories about Ruth's spending and womanizing, his eating habits became the stuff of folklore. Lost was the reality of Ruth's dieting that spring, his injuries, exhaustion, and illness in the face of demands to keep fans entertained. That storyline could not compete with a tale of dozens of hots dogs consumed in gluttonous haste. Yankees management was more than willing to support the overeating narrative: it placed responsibility for Ruth's collapse entirely on Ruth and further humbled a star player the Yankees intended to keep on the team, playing at relatively bargain rates.

Without the Babe, opening day for the Yankees, as McGeehan explained, appeared "much like an opening of Hamlet with no Hamlet."[41] Absent their lead player, the Yankees stumbled and struggled. "It isn't too hard to discover just why our Yankees got away so badly," wrote Ford Frick. "The first and foremost reason is lying stretched out on a cot in St. Vincent's Hospital."[42] In late May, the *Cleveland Plain Dealer* mocked the visiting Yankees as "less than ruthless" for obvious reasons.[43] Ruth's physical illness seemed to spread spiritually to his team. The team that finished a close second in the American League the previous season now slumped severely. Attendance at Yankee Stadium correspondingly plummeted.

Following his operation, Ruth remained confined to St. Vincent's Hospital. His recovery, even walking again, proved painfully slow. The mental toll on Ruth undoubtedly grew when doctors admitted his wife to the same hospital. Mrs. Ruth was to be treated for a nervous breakdown. Under such circumstances, with the media keeping close watch, there was obviously little opportunity for Ruth to share time with his live-in girlfriend and confidant Mrs. Hodgson.

In early June, a still-weak Ruth rejoined a Yankees team desperate to put him back in uniform. Yet he remained a shadow of his former self. He appeared "slimmer and weaker, his face drawn"; he was "in no condition to play."[44] Westbrook Pegler likened Ruth to "a bag of oats on two toothpicks."[45] Still, in his first game, despite "legs so feeble they could hardly carry him," Ruth nearly hit a home run and managed somehow a diving catch at the right-field fence, one of the best plays of the season, according to one account. After the catch, however, the Babe crumbled to the ground in pain.[46]

Ruth himself was undoubtedly eager to return to play, and the Yankees organization needed a box office draw as attendance tumbled. By late May, Yankees profits had fallen by hundreds of thousands of dollars in the wake of Ruth's absence.[47] Still, the Babe was hardly ready to play, as several commentators noted. When Huggins pulled Ruth after the sixth inning of his first game back, sportswriter Thomas Holmes railed, "Ruth was not taken out soon enough . . . he should not be allowed to put on a uniform or pick up a bat for at least two weeks."[48] Even normally unsympathetic Joe Vila suggested economics were behind Ruth's premature return: "Really, the big fellow isn't in shape to play baseball . . . it seems that his presence in uniform is needed to attract the fans."[49] A week later, perhaps in response to pressure from Yankees management, Vila revised his stand to lay blame on Ruth. "Unkind persons said that greed for gate money made the club officials keep Ruth in harness," explained Vila. But, he continued, "Ruth took the matter into his own hands and resumed work," fearing his "further absence would prove injurious both to his health and reputation."[50] Vila was probably correct that Ruth was too eager to return from his convalescences. Yankees management, however, appeared to do little to stop their obviously ailing marquee star.

Throughout June, Ruth struggled. An extraordinary heat wave hobbled his rehabilitation. June temperatures soared to the 90s. New York public parks stayed open all night to accommodate "sleepers." The heat added to an unusually tense summer. In Dayton, Tennessee, proponents of evolution battled their evangelical foes led by Williams Jennings Bryan (McGeehan briefly traded his sports portfolio to join the gaggle of reporters in Dayton). In Washington, DC, a massive Ku Klux Klan rally sparked fears of a race war. Marine guards scrambled to protect government buildings from feared rioting. As for Ruth, he (or at least his ghostwriter) fretted that "Old Lady Bad Luck is camping right on my trail these days. If there is any sort of trouble that has passed me by this year, I can't remember what it was." Still he appealed to the fans: "I guess I never really appreciated the fans around the country before. Believe me, they certainly give a fellow new faith in human nature."[51]

By the end of June, Ruth's ankles grew so swollen that he was taken out of the lineup indefinitely. There was talk of a second operation. Stinging from criticism he brought Ruth back prematurely, Huggins vowed to let his star player heal. "I am not going to take the chance of ruining Ruth as a player simply because he is a great box office asset," insisted Huggins.[52] Yet when X-rays showed Ruth's ankle just bruised and not broken, Ruth returned to the lineup within days.

Slowly Ruth recovered some of his powers. The Yankees, however, continued to flail. Unlike 1922, when Ruth had struggled after missing the first part of the season, the entire Yankees team appeared afflicted alongside its star player. By mid-August, the Yankees sat firmly in seventh place, the second-worst record in the league. Pressure built on both Ruth and Huggins. John Kieran branded the team "the hilarious Hugsmen" (after Manager Huggins) who played "charity events," since the Yankees were gaining a reputation for "giving away" games to their opponents. The same rumors surrounding Ruth's collapse now swirled around the entire team—and found their way into print. Sportswriter Gallico openly exposed the Yankees team's dirty laundry. During spring trainings, "a nip or two was had," revealed Gallico. "In other words, they enjoyed themselves. . . . 'As ye sow' . . . etc."[53] Again the theme of overconsumption leading to comeuppance remained a favorite for journalists.

By midsummer, reports surfaced of a "mutiny" in progress, led by several Yankees veterans, "for the purpose of driving [Huggins] out of his position."[54] Key players reportedly were "laying down on" Huggins, who appeared incapable of controlling the team and would soon pay with his job.[55] Ruth, already outspokenly anti-Huggins, was obviously among the suspects. As rumors swirled that Huggins would soon be fired, Yankees owner Ruppert felt compelled to make a strong statement in support of his beleaguered employee. Huggins, Ruppert announced, would manage the Yankees "as long as he cares to."[56]

Meanwhile, Ruth sought to defend himself and his team. In his weekly column, he denied any and all rumors "certain papers" printed. "It's all wrong," he protested. "I don't say that the Yankees are angels or anything like that. . . . But they're just human and they're no better or worse than anyone else."[57] His defense, however, fell largely on deaf ears. Then, as if to acknowledge his shortcomings, Ruth put up for sale his Sudbury, Massachusetts, farm, site of his 1922–1923 winter rehabilitation. It had, wrote a Sporting News writer, "proven a failure so far as it concerns keeping a city born and city bred man actively employed and in good health."[58] Behind the scenes, Ruth's relationship with Huggins remained severely strained. Both blamed the other for the Yankees' collapse. Ruth made little effort to hide his contempt for his manager. The two squabbled constantly, and Huggins well understood Ruth represented an existential threat to his future with the Yankees.[59]

"An idol of America's boyhood has been shattered"

In the end, Ruth, especially in his enfeebled state, proved little match for Huggins, a trained lawyer nearly two decades older than his star player. More importantly, Huggins had the support of Yankees owner Ruppert, who had staked his credibility on his intense manager. In late August, Huggins began planning a surprise attack on Ruth. Before acting, Huggins carefully secured support from Yankees ownership and upper-level management. Barrow assured Huggins the organization completely backed its manager.[60] With Ruth mired in a season-long slump and sportswriters sharply critical of the struggling star, the timing seemed ideal. Ruth would be sent a strong message about who was in charge. Responsibility for the team's failings would be shifted from management to star employee.

Ruth, to be sure, had grown increasingly recalcitrant over the course of the difficult summer. He openly defied and disparaged Huggins. Frustrated by the team's poor showing and his ongoing physical ailments, Ruth apparently resumed his late-night carousing, although the extent and nature of his nocturnal habits remains the stuff of speculation. What is known is that Ruth refused to stay in the team hotel and disregarded team curfew. Likewise, his ongoing relationship with Claire Hodgson, a source of great support for Ruth, appeared unseemly to many, as he remained married to another woman whose fragility was obvious to all.

With no real warning, on August 29, Huggins struck against Ruth. The Babe arrived unsuspectingly an hour before game time at St. Louis's Sportsman's Park. The previous night he had been out until 2:30 am, violating the 1:00 am Yankees curfew. In the locker room, Huggins approached the Babe and curtly ordered him not to dress for the day's game. He was suspended indefinitely and fined a record $5,000. Huggins ordered his struggling star to return immediately to New York by himself. By all accounts, Ruth, a man of gargantuan temper, flew into a rage. He and Huggins exchanged harsh words, then Ruth bolted from the stadium.

With Walsh and Claire Hodgson back in New York, the Babe was on his own. His first instinct was to appeal his case to Commissioner Landis. This was an odd choice, given the personal history between the two. The commissioner, of course, was unlikely to support a ballplayer against management, and protocol required a ten-day waiting period before any matter could be appealed. In any case, Ruth shot to Chicago from St. Louis. There, at the Congress Hotel, an enraged Ruth held an ill-advised, impromptu news conference. Reviving his spring training attack on Huggins, Ruth labeled the manager "incompetent" and offered several examples of managerial mistakes. "Huggins only suspended me," Ruth railed, "because he wants the publicity. It's a grandstand play for the public so he can shift the blame on me for the team."[61] In fact, as Ruth complained, the Yankees dropped their eleventh game out of their last fifteen.

As the tirade continued, Ruth blamed his poor performance that season on his early return after his April collapse. Implying Yankees management had pushed him prematurely back into the game, he insisted he "needed a regular training trip to put me in trim." Huggins' fine, he inveighed, was "a joke.... Bootleggers and murders got off with fines of less than $5,000," raged Ruth. Finally furnishing a headline for the next day's newspapers, he blasted: "If Huggins stays, I quit."[62]

Back in St. Louis, Huggins told his side of the story to the media. After repeated infractions, he had run out of patience, he calmly explained. When a reporter asked the Yankees manager if Ruth's misconduct included drinking, Huggins responded in the affirmative but added, "It means a lot of other things besides."[63] The manager deftly left the door open to speculation about any number of additional wrongdoings, including gambling or other such licentious acts. For his part, Ruth denied the drinking charges. "If Huggins says I was drinking, he's a damn liar, and you can make that as strong as you like," he told the press.[64]

Ruth's intemperate remarks (and apparent lack of temperance) buried whatever case he hoped to make before the media. Predictably, sportswriters rallied around Huggins and sharply repudiated Ruth. "An idol of America's boyhood has been shattered," pronounced the *New York American* in the first line of its front-page coverage of the episode.[65] "With the fall from glory of Babe Ruth, a million young Americans are bereft," added the *New York Herald-Tribune*. "Being a boy isn't as certain fun as it used to be."[66] While disappointing the youth of the land, Ruth in turn was depicted repeatedly as an errant boy in the media: "Peck's bad boy of our national pastime."[67] Ruth, the *Sporting News* editorialized, had finally received "a dose of discipline. . . . He richly deserved it for betraying a ball club which had treated him so well." He had to learn yet again that he was "not bigger than baseball."[68]

As the media turned viciously on Ruth, an odd byproduct of the anti-Ruth narrative involved an unfavorable comparison with Ty Cobb, now rehabilitated as a gentleman of the game. Joe Vila, not unexpectedly, excoriated Ruth. Perhaps the stern "punishment" might "bring the big slugger to his senses," wrote Vila. Ruth "should realize by this time that his popularity is on the wane and that he must obey the orders of the Yankee's plucky little manager or take the consequences." Vila then launched an extended comparison of Ruth and Cobb, a player much more to the scribe's liking. As opposed to Ruth, Cobb's "wonderful record as a player has never been tarnished by fines or suspensions as a player for violating the rules against dissipation."[69] Vila, of course, brazenly omitted Cobb's history of psychotic violence, in particular the horrific 1912 beating of a handicapped man who evidently loudly questioned Cobb's racial purity.[70] Nor had Cobb dramatically matured in the years since. Only weeks before Ruth's clash with Huggins, AL president Ban Johnson had suspended Cobb over a confrontation with an umpire.[71] Vila's amnesia defies rationality. Ruth, despite his flaws and ego, simply did not possess Cobb's malice and capacity for violence (few did).

That Vila, deeply resentful of the long-ball game driven by Ruth's popularity, would lionize Cobb might be expected. That the *New York Times*, however, with its reputation for seriousness, would point in a similar direction was a surprise. Following Ruth's suspension, "the gray old lady" devoted a section of its editorial page to comparing "two heroes": Cobb, the "first citizen of Detroit," and Ruth, in disgrace. A baseball idol, the editorial concluded, "ought to have a strong character as well as strong eyes and perfectly coordinated muscles. That, however, as the run of them goes, would be asking too much."[72] *Literary Digest* also picked up the theme in its account of recent news: "The naughty boy and the good boy (of baseball the National Game)— Babe Ruth and Ty Cobb—jumped into the glare of publicity," recounted the news magazine in its review of Ruth's troubles.[73]

If lack of support in the media were not enough to unnerve Ruth, the Yankees rebel watched baseball authorities quickly close ranks against him. In Chicago, Ruth hoped to gain an audience with Commissioner Landis, but the judge was conveniently absent at his vacation home in Michigan, from where he signaled no intention of intervening in the matter. Worse, AL president Johnson weighed in with a vicious attack. Ruth, snarled Johnson, possessed "the mind of a 15 year-old boy and must be made to understand where he belongs."[74] Meanwhile from New York came word Colonel Ruppert was standing solidly behind Huggins. "Anything Miller Huggins says goes with me. . . . Huggins is running the club not Ruth." Regarding Ruth's threat to leave the team, Ruppert responded simply, "He can quit, if he wants to."[75]

Despite Ruppert's stated position, Ruth hoped to make his case, or at least save some face, in a one-on-one meeting with the Yankees owner. From Chicago's LaSalle Street Station, Ruth boarded the Twentieth Century Limited for the twenty-hour journey back to New York. As he moved across the country, his options appeared increasingly limited. "The Bambino has finally hanged himself. . . . He has been the Sultan of Swat and he has lived like a sultan. . . It looks as though the Babe had worked himself into a position where he has to surrender or to quit," opined John Kieran during a brief stint with Hearst's *New York American*.[76]

But Ruth's professional dilemmas were not all that appeared in newspapers. For the first time, accounts of Ruth's personal life, in particular his relationship with Claire Hodgson, filled papers. Photographs of Hodgson, labeled a showgirl and Ruth's "mistress," sprang up in New York newspapers, then spread to papers across the country. Reporters waylaid Helen Ruth with questions about Hodgson. Stories flew about "orgies," and a $100,000 divorce settlement demanded by Mrs. Ruth.[77] As one writer put it, "Shocking revelations of Babe Ruth's private life are being written by some who once held the Babe up as a little tin deity on roller skates."[78]

Whether acting on the explicit encouragement of Barrow or on their own, sportswriters communicated to Ruth a clear message about his vulnerability. The very relationship Ruth prized most suddenly was imperiled by his campaign against Huggins. Rumors of carousing and partying had long haunted Ruth, but now his private secrets were exposed to the world in a most brazen fashion. His only hope of regaining stability and protecting the woman he loved and her family (which had become his own) appeared capitulation.

A crowd of three thousand awaited Ruth as he disembarked at Grand Central Station. Photographers snapped pictures while reporters barked questions about Huggins, Ruppert, Mrs. Ruth, and Claire Hodgson. To shield Babe from charges swirling around his personal life, his handlers dispatched Father Edward Quinn, a Roman Catholic priest who evidently knew the slugger from his days at St. Mary's, to meet the Babe at the train station. Wisely, Ruth avoided any comment. He and Father Quinn silently fought their way through the gauntlet. Ruth waived off questions from reporters, promising to meet with them after talking with his wife. Quinn and Ruth then sped off to Ruth's apartment at the Concourse Plaza, where Helen Ruth lay bedridden, suffering anxiety and an infected finger (rumored the result of a botched attempted to remove her wedding ring). At the Concourse behind closed doors, Quinn evidently facilitated a reconciliation between the Ruths.

Newspapermen and photographers then were invited into the apartment. Ruth dutifully posed for a series of maudlin photographs seated over his wife's sickbed. At one point, Helen commenced sobbing. Ruth, leaning over the bed, covered his face, apparently weeping as well. Photographers snapped away. The next day the mawkish scene graced newspaper and tabloid front pages around the country.

Leaving his wife's bedside, Ruth then addressed the assemblage of newsmen. "When I was going strong," he protested, "Hug never bothered me." But Ruth was clearly in a conciliatory mood. He had been "rash" in threatening to quit the Yankees. Perhaps faults lay on both sides, Ruth suggested. He then shifted to the recent press coverage. Criticism of his weak play on the field was one thing. It was to be expected, Ruth acknowledged. But stories about women went beyond the pale. "Can't you lay off the women stuff?" Ruth begged. Immediately reporters shot back with questions about Hodgson.

She was only a friend, Ruth insisted. He then blamed the salacious coverage for putting his wife in her present condition. "I'd be obliged if you boys stuck to my baseball troubles and left my marital affairs alone," he pled.[79]

Leaving his apartment, Ruth, with reporters in close pursuit, traveled southward to the offices of Yankees owner Ruppert. By this time, Ruth fully comprehended the forces arrayed against him. He hoped full capitulation would suffice for reinstatement. Ruppert, however insisted the matter lay solely in the hands of manager Huggins. Ruth, it seemed, would endure a high-profile kowtow in order to win back his Yankees uniform. The first step was publicly accepting the position of adolescent in error seeking forgiveness. Emerging from Ruppert's offices, a submissive Ruth accepted a public tongue-lashing from Ruppert as correspondents gaped. "We have treated you very liberally in the past. We have several times accepted your regrets and your promises to turn over a new leaf," the colonel lectured. But now the colonel was drawing a strict line. He would insist that Ruth apologize to Huggins and acknowledge his subordination to the Yankees manager.[80]

All eyes shifted to Ruth. The colonel "has been very nice to me," Ruth began in an uncharacteristically muted voice. "I said a lot of things I shouldn't have."[81] It was a humiliating comedown. The entire spectacle, ending with a public scolding by the "Big Boss," was "eminently boyish," commented the *New York Times*, again devoting space on its editorial page to Ruth's ongoing drama. The *Times*' conclusion that Ruth had "the emotions of a boy of 15" proved only slightly more charitable than AL president Johnson's concurrent statement that Ruth had "the mind of a 15-year old."[82]

In a country grappling with the blossoming of modernity and new notions about youth, behavior, and consumption, Ruth's comeuppance seemed a victory for defenders of tradition and authority. Further, the concerted effort to demean and strip Ruth of his manhood sent a message not only to Ruth but to all professional ballplayers. Anyone who stepped outside their defined role as a player could expect overpowering retribution.

Examined in broader terms, Ruth's ill-fated clash with the Yankees fits the general pattern of labor-management relations in the 1920s. Following several decades of expansion, workplace rights and unionization lost ground during the more conservative 1920s. A probusiness climate reigned, and employers launched aggressive campaigns against labor.[83] During the earlier growth period, labor leaders and activists celebrated the ideal of "manly" producers, projecting "dignity, respectability, and defiant egalitarianism." Workers were to be true men, unafraid and unintimidated in the face of capital.[84] Ruth usually carried himself in just such a manner. His September 1 appearance in Ruppert's offices, however, seemed almost the antithesis of the manly ideal. Indeed, Ruth appeared "eminently boyish" in the presence of adults determining his future. His descent and humiliation were a fate familiar to many workers during an era of receding worker rights.

Following his session with Ruppert, Ruth, as instructed, attempted to apologize to Huggins. The Yankees manager, however, declined to even speak with his suspended star. Huggins dangled reinstatement over Ruth for several more days. While Ruth helplessly awaited forgiveness, he attended a Yankees game as Colonel Ruppert's guest. When fans recognized him during the seventh inning stretch, a roar went up through the stadium. Ruth took a bow, then a second bow as the cheering continued. Soon he was mobbed by autograph seekers. For the first time in several days, Ruth let loose a wide smile, relieved the fans remained sympathetic.[85]

The gratifying ovation no doubt signaled to Ruth and others that his popularity and career, contrary to the opinion of his detractors, had not derailed. After nine days of patience and further statements of contrition, Huggins reinstated Ruth. In the final month of the season, the Babe played the good citizen off field and the slugger on the baseball diamond, hitting ten home runs with a batting average of .345. The media made no further mention of Mrs. Hodgson. Instead, reports portrayed Ruth again as the contented husband of Mrs. Ruth and father of their young daughter, even as Helen Ruth and the daughter essentially disappeared from sight, and Ruth maintained his relationship with Hodgson.

With remarkable rapidity, might, and unity, the baseball establishment had joined forces late in the 1925 season to humble Ruth. "The ring of authority," concluded the *New York Times* as Ruth prepared to take the field again, "is growing tighter around the playboy of baseball."[86] Indeed it was, and constant references to "playboy," "naughty boy," and "bad boy" reinforced the infantilizing of Ruth. He had been served two clear messages by the end of September: first, that he had little power in the face of league officials and owners, and second, that he would have to become a more disciplined, conditioned athlete if he was to avoid further humiliation. It is a credit to Ruth, the supposed man-boy, that he recognized the forces aligned against him. In the end, he was willing to eat crow to preserve his career and protect the life he sought to build with Hodgson.

The 1925 season undoubtedly wore on Ruth. He remained the primary scapegoat for the collapse of his team. Viewed one way, Ruth had been a veracious competitor in 1925, pushing himself despite injury and serious illness. That the team could not win without a healthy Ruth should have made obvious his indispensability. The Babe's impolitic attacks on Yankees management, however, left him isolated and vulnerable.

While the vast majority of sportswriters joined in wholehearted support of Ruppert and Huggins, a few raised questions about the timing of attacks on Ruth. Sportswriter Gallico sided decisively with Huggins against Ruth. Still, he acknowledged, "Huggins's discipline smacks of opportunism. As long as the Yankees were winning, Ruth could get away with it."[87] During Ruth's apology tour, Damon Runyon also moved to introduce an air of realism. "The reader understands, of course, that what Mr. Ruth is really apologizing for is that .260 batting average of his." The fallen hero, Runyon advised, should "preserve his present humility of spirit toward Mr. M. Huggins and the world at large and craftily regain his .350 batting average."[88]

Runyon's advice became Ruth's strategy. He worked to regain his strength as an athlete, powers that he largely achieved by the end of the season. He also avoided future clashes with Huggins, whom he grew to grudgingly respect. As the 1926 season approached, Ruth better understood the power dynamics operating around him. Increasingly he accepted his subordinate role in the status quo. Given his relatively handsome income, this hardly amounted to a substantial sacrifice. At the same time, he retained hopes of one day managing, preferably with the Yankees. As his extended adolescence wound down, Ruth looked forward to a future free of the degrading and demeaning assaults that so dogged him in 1925.

Young Ruth as a left-handed pitcher for the Boston Red Sox. *Courtesy of Walter P. Reuther Library, Archives of Labor and Urban Affairs, Wayne State University.*

From left to right, Yankees owner Jacob Ruppert with New York Giants manager John McGraw and George Stallings, former Yankees manager. *Courtesy of Library of Congress, Prints & Photographs Division.*

Ruth, a natural with children. *Courtesy of the Boston Public Library, Leslie Jones Collection.*

The intimidating Ed Barrow, Yankees business manager. *Courtesy of National Baseball Hall of Fame and Museum.*

Yankees manager Miller Huggins, who trapped and humiliated Ruth in 1925. *Courtesy of Library of Congress, Prints & Photographs Division.*

Baseball Commissioner Kenesaw Mountain Landis and Yankees owner Jacob Ruppert. *Courtesy of Library of Congress, Prints & Photographs Division.*

Ruth with second wife, Claire, his "manager and secretary." Daughter Julia stands in between her mother and stepfather. *Courtesy of the Boston Public Library, Leslie Jones Collection.*

"Two Musketeers": Ruth and Gehrig. *Courtesy of Walter P. Reuther Library, Archives of Labor and Urban Affairs, Wayne State University.*

Ed Barrow mock strangling Manager Joe McCarthy. Neither held Ruth in high regard. *Courtesy of National Baseball Hall of Fame and Museum.*

(*Above*) April 15, 1935, newly minted Boston Brave Babe Ruth is awarded a key to Worcester, MA, by Mayor John Mahoney. *Courtesy of the Boston Public Library, Leslie Jones Collection.*

(*Above right*) Even at the end of his career with the Boston Braves, Ruth was "besieged and beset wherever he goes from dawn till dusk by autograph hunters." *Courtesy of the Boston Public Library, Leslie Jones Collection.*

(*Below right*) Ruth and Ty Cobb later in life. *Courtesy of Walter P. Reuther Library, Archives of Labor and Urban Affairs, Wayne State University.*

SIX. "IT WAS JUST A MATTER OF PHYSICAL CONDITION"
COMEBACK II

Surveying the upcoming 1926 Yankees season, team secretary Ed Barrow undoubtedly felt apprehension. The 1925 Yankees had finished seventh in the American League, second from last. Attendance at Yankees games collapsed from over a million in 1924 to 697,267 in 1925. His management team remained under attack for lack of discipline, poor personnel decisions, and slovenly game strategy. Yankees ownership was not pleased.

Toward the end of the 1925 season, Barrow and Yankees manager Miller Huggins had orchestrated a highly publicized and highly personalized assault on Ruth, designed both to force the star to adhere to team discipline and to transfer blame for the poor Yankees performance onto Ruth's considerable shoulders. When Ruth arrived at Colonel Ruppert's offices seeking a hearing after his August 29 suspension, Barrow was a conspicuous specter in the room. His presence, Ruth later recalled, took "the wind out of my sails."[1] From Barrow's perspective, the surprise attack on Ruth worked: the press wholeheartedly supported Huggins and vilified Ruth. Better yet, the Babe had completely capitulated; his shortcomings and indiscipline now solidified in the public mind. Seeking to move beyond the humiliation, Ruth focused on recovering from his many maladies and regaining his playing skills. The Babe's on-field play, in fact, was significantly better in the remaining weeks of the season (although even before the Huggins ambush, Ruth had been improving).

Still, few were picking the Yankees as winners in 1926, and there was no guarantee of Ruth's full reformation. Barrow and his management team set about shuffling Yankees players and finding new recruits to fill gaps.

Likewise, they kept a tight leash on their top attraction. But while Barrow had outmaneuvered his antagonist in 1925, the Babe's comeback in 1926—both Ruth's own physical reconstitution and the public relations campaign surrounding it—allowed the fallen hero to rebuild fully his reputation and career. Prosperity followed for the Yankees, in terms of both victories on the baseball diamond and profits pouring into Yankees coffers. At the same time, Ruth's efforts to project greater maturity, essentially to establish himself as an adult in his public persona, floundered. He remained depicted as an overgrown boy more than a man. This was exactly how Barrow saw Ruth, and where the Yankees team secretary sought to keep his star player.

"A Lot of Buncombe"

Following the doomed 1925 Yankees season, Ed Barrow announced some changes. For one, the team would no longer pay for a group of Yankees veterans, led by Ruth, to sojourn in Hot Springs, Arkansas, before the official start of spring training. The players were supposed to avail themselves of the healthful benefits of the Ouachita Mountains: hiking and strengthening themselves during the day, and then, after their workouts, relaxing in the resort town's famous baths. "Theoretically," the *New York Times* explained, that was the plan, but in practice "it was something different." Clearly Ruth and the other players also appreciated the casinos and nightlife abundantly available in Hot Springs. In an October 1925 interview, Barrow stamped "the whole Hot Springs idea a lot of buncombe and merely a waste of money." The Arkansas resort was now off-limits to the Yankees. As it turned out, Barrow's Hot Springs ban actually may have helped Ruth's recovery in the end. Not only did it remove him from some of the nefarious influences of the town, but the communal steamy baths probably wreaked annual havoc with Ruth's fragile immune system.

To Barrow, however, Ruth remained a problem. The star needed a wholesome regimen to prepare him for the next season. Barrow floated the idea of shipping Ruth to a "health camp." At such an establishment, trainers would "enforce discipline in dictatorial fashion." Ruth would be raised at the crack of dawn, and he would work all day, chopping trees and hiking. Bedtime would be 9:00 pm.[2] In a sense, this was the program Ruth was supposedly following at his Sudbury farm, a program that inspired Ruth's 1923 comeback. But after the Babe's 1925 season, the farm plan was discredited.

Barrow now suggested something more draconian: Ruth required adult supervision and strict oversight.

Barrow's plan certainly could not have been forced upon Ruth. But it did offer the Yankees team secretary one more opportunity to publicly humble Ruth and push him to get serious about conditioning. For his part, Ruth eschewed anything "so extreme" as the "health camp" plan. Already, he announced, he was down to 226 pounds, just from playing golf. Next, Ruth proclaimed he was looking for a workout gym in the city where he could keep in shape during the off-season.[3]

In fact, Ruth's physical comeback was well underway. By late summer 1925, he had recovered from his April surgery. Returning from suspension in early September, Ruth finally found the rhythm that had so eluded him throughout most of his annus horribilis. That month he smacked ten home runs and batted well over a .300 average. Sportswriters noted a new, more disciplined Ruth. "Babe Ruth's reformation is so complete," wrote Will Wedge, "that he is himself being a strict censor of conduct. Not of human conduct, but the conduct of dumb animals." Wedge then explained how the Babe, having found new respect for discipline, was now more demanding of his formerly pampered dog.[4]

Still, Ruth was a diminished commodity. Understanding this, he made a grand show of canceling a lucrative contract to tour Japan in the postseason. He had "voluntarily handed myself a penalty that tops Huggins' fine . . . to show my regrets for the past and my good intentions for the future," explained Ruth. Instead, he would remain at home, focusing on conditioning and preparing for his comeback season.[5] This was to be his first step toward establishing a fresh redemption narrative. The new plan would have to be different in detail from his 1923 comeback, but the outcome would be the same: a restored Babe.

In October, the Babe and several Yankees teammates traveled to northwest New Brunswick for a "moose hunt." According to his travel mates, "Life in the open made Ruth a new man." Upon arrival, the struggling slugger was in "pretty bad shape" and was forced to ride a horse to base camp while his teammates hiked. But after weeks of getting "up early in the morning and curled up in blankets early at night," Ruth regained his lost edge. At trip's end, he hiked forty miles out of the wilderness, rejecting the saddle horse that had carried him into the woods. The experience, penned sportswriter Harry Cross, "was a wonderful thing for Ruth."[6]

"A Babe and a Boob"

Given the rash of bad publicity in 1925, and what now appeared a discredited "back to the farm" reformation in 1923, the Babe's situation called for something beyond a moose hunt. It required a more demonstrable and sustainable narrative. As he had done in 1922 at the baseball writers' dinner, Christy Walsh had Ruth begin with a well-publicized confession of past sins and a public pledge to mend his errant ways. This time, Ruth gave an intimate interview to a journalist supposedly named Joe Winkworth, in actuality a cover for Walsh or a Walsh-employed ghostwriter. In the interview, published in October's *Collier's* magazine, the fallen hero poured out his heart: "I've been a Babe—and a Boob . . . the sappiest of saps." Parties, bad investments, and gambling, he admitted, had robbed him of hundreds of thousands of dollars, including a shocking $35,000 lost on one horse race. Friends and others had warned him not to follow the path of legendary boxer John L. Sullivan, whose taste for the high life maimed his career. Ruth had ignored the counsel. Now things were different, Ruth insisted. Now he was ready for reformation. "No more of this good-time-Charley business for me," he declared. "I'm going to start all over, and I hope they'll all be watching my smoke in 1926."

The Winkworth piece, while purporting to be a full confession, simultaneously furnished a defense of Ruth against the more egregious rumors surrounding the idol's off-the-field behavior, in particular his womanizing. Among his financial missteps, Ruth explained, was "money lost in fighting suits, attempted blackmail, 'hyjacking,' etc." Illustrating the point, he recounted how an "ultra-sophisticated young woman who had enjoyed a brief career in the Follies" had tried to take advantage of him. (Oddly, the showgirl, flapper description fit Claire Hodgson, exposed recently in newspapers as Ruth's love interest. Ruth, in fact, continued to cohabitate with Claire.) In the magazine account, after repeatedly phoning Ruth and traveling from New York to Philadelphia to watch him play, the woman's lawyer contacted Ruth, threatening to charge him under the Mann Act (illegally transferring a woman across state borders for "immoral purposes") unless he paid extortion money. "Better pay up or you'll be ruined," threatened the "legal hijacker." Ruth resolutely refused. Instead he initiated his own investigation, and the extorters supposedly backed off, concluding the hero "was not quite so sappy" as they anticipated. Ruth, in turn, recognized his own actions had contributed to his problems. "A fellow is defenseless unless he cuts out all good-timing," concluded Ruth. Subtly, while in the guise of a full confession, Walsh had Ruth minimizing the womanizing charges that so dogged the hitter toward the end of the 1925 season, even implicitly placing Hodgson among those seeking to use rumors and innuendo to harm Ruth.

Ruth's trademark innocence and generosity remained intact, insisted the "Babe and a Boob" piece—in fact they caused some of his troubles. He was too trusting, too innocent. "Winkworth" dusted off Ruth's reliable old ties to St. Mary's Industrial School, quoting friends that the Babe was "a boy at heart. . . . He has never forgotten St. Mary's." The piece ended by recounting the story of how Ruth lured his old mentor, Brother Mathias, to visit him in New York, where he presented the brother with a "beautiful car of expensive make" and a note reading, "For you, with many thanks for what you and St. Mary's have done for me."[7]

The Winkworth confessional, in fact, served up a model piece of carefully crafted public relations. While acknowledging the veracity of lesser charges, Ruth cast doubt on the most damaging of the 1925 allegations against him. At best, he pled to overexuberance and naiveté; in essence, he remained a good-hearted, generous man-child, deserving of a second chance—provided he made good on his vow to reform. For Ruth, the downside was that his depiction as an "over-grown boy," an effective alibi when charged with depravations, reinforced perceptions of simplicity and limited mental capacities.

At the end of November, Ruth—"looking stronger, healthier, and in better condition than he did at the end of last season," according to *New York Times* reporter Richards Vidmer—appeared at a dinner hosted by Christy Walsh celebrating standout football players from the 1925 season. The Babe starred in an opening skit that had waiters coming out of a football huddle at one end of the Commodore Hotel's ballroom. Ruth wore a red wig "masquerading as Harold Grange." When revealed, the Babe quipped to the crowd of sportswriters and sporting world luminaries that he was neither a quarterback, a fullback, nor a halfback; instead, he was "striving earnestly to be a 'comeback.'"[8]

Much was at stake. Huggins, eager to flash his authority, made clear that Ruth would be expected to get in shape and perform well. "Personally I have no feeling against Ruth," Huggins told sportswriter Joe Vila. "If he comes to Florida in shape for hard practice and makes good, nobody will feel more gratified than myself. But if Ruth has gone back and cannot play the game like he used to do, sentiments will cut no figure." Ruth's backup, Ben Paschal, a hard-hitting Alabaman, Huggins added, "already has proved an able substitute for Ruth in every way." The Yankees manager was clearly "wearing his spurs," noted Vila.[9]

CHAPTER SIX

"A Waist of Which Hercules
Would Not Have Been Ashamed"

In 1922, Walsh had chosen a backward-looking theme to undergird Ruth's comeback, sending Ruth back to the farm. For Ruth's 1926 comeback narrative, Walsh would tap into modern America's new obsession with fitness, health, and dieting. If Ruth had come to represent the excesses of the times, especially in his overindulgence, now, Walsh planned, he would epitomize the era's growing fixation with physical health. For both men and women, the nineteenth-century equation of heft with health and wealth had sputtered out. By the twenties, exercise, dieting, and a lean body type equated to well-being. Flappers, in particular, established a striking new model not only of sophistication but also of extreme slenderness. (Claire Hodgson, Ruth's companion and later second wife, typified the flapper look.) The goal of "slimming" or "reducing" intensely preoccupied many women. Magazines aimed at females offered nonstop counsel and endless diets designed to combat the "calorie," a battle made into a war by Lulu Hunt Peters, a doctor and bestselling author. Peters's own dramatic weight loss inspired her crusade against overconsumption. Diets such as the "Medical Millennium Diet" and the "Hollywood Eighteen Day Diet" developed into crazes.[10]

Men also aimed for a slimmer, more sporting look, although they operated under very different expectations than those placed on women. Still, an athletic, muscular but trim physique emerged the masculine ideal. Exercise programs, such as Walter Camp's "Daily Dozen," designed originally for US servicemen during the war, now were marketed across the country in book and phonograph record form. Similar workout regimes came from German immigrant Joseph Pilates, who successfully promoted a body building contraption based on his "contrology" approach. Meanwhile, the Battle Creek Sanitarium marketed a popular "health ladder" program through books and phonographic records. Celebrity athletes also got in on the act. Gene Tunney, the handsome and learned boxer, "peddled a 78-rpm record of 'Health Exercises' on Orthophonic Victor Records."[11]

Publisher Bernarr MacFadden was yet another prophet of the refined body. A body builder turned publishing magnate, MacFadden, mocked by some as "Body Love" MacFadden, trumpeted exercise and muscles in his many publications. By the 1920s, MacFadden had launched his own New York tabloid to compete with the *Daily News*. MacFadden's New York *Graphic* never turned a profit, but other publications, including his *Physical Culture*, did, and they helped reorient Americans' conception of their own bodies.

Along the way, MacFadden also pioneered the use of sensationalized "true" confessional stories in his magazines, first about physical transformation, then about any number of subjects, such as *True Story*, *True Detective Stories*, and *True Ghost Stories*. MacFadden's confessional genre, in fact, contributed mightily to the tone of Ruth's "Babe and Boob" piece.

Ruth frequently joined other noted athletes at MacFadden's celebrity dinners hosted by *Graphic* sportswriter Ed Sullivan (the first incarnation of a variety format that later became Sullivan's celebrated television show). In planning the Babe's 1926 comeback, Walsh borrowed liberally from both MacFadden's trademark emphasis on physical renewal and the publisher/body builder's belief in the power of a well-crafted confession.

Returning from his Canadian hunting trip, Ruth made a very public show of searching for a New York City gym. He opted for a facility owned by Artie McGovern, a colorful Manhattan trainer and long-time Ruth acquaintance. It proved an inspired choice. A fitness and health guru in the contemporary tradition of MacFadden, Camp, and Pilates, McGovern had made a fortune marketing to an upscale Manhattan clientele his own brand of dieting and training—replete with his own particular eccentricities. McGovern railed against drinking liquids with meals, warning the practice deluded the nutritional content of food. "No cold water," counseled McGovern. "Cold water often causes stomach distress, so hot water, which is a great aid in cleansing the system, was substituted." Around his faddish diet regime, McGovern organized intense exercise and training routines for his clients, supervised by his herd of personal trainers. In some cases, trainers actually roused clients from bed in the morning to begin prebreakfast training.[12]

A relentless self-promoter (in the grand tradition of the era's fitness/diet entrepreneurs), McGovern welcomed his new high-profile client, and the two quickly forged a symbiotic relationship. According to McGovern, Ruth showed up at the copious East Side gym in early December "a physical wreck," supposedly weighing 254 pounds, although contemporary newspaper reports have the Babe at least twenty pounds lighter, even before his supposed renewal in the Canadian wilderness. "He was as near to a total loss as any patient I have ever had under my care," recounted the trainer. Yet, McGovern concluded, applying his quasi-scientific theories to Ruth, the fallen hero remained an excellent specimen. In fact, the Babe was essentially "a digestive superman," gleaning "more nourishment out of a slice of bread than some men can get from a whole loaf." And so the training and "slimming" began. Under McGovern's immediate supervision, Ruth moderated his eating, cut out all sweets, ate only lean meats and salads, guzzled hot water, and partook in the trainer's unique regimen of calisthenics. The press appeared to enjoy open access to the Babe's sessions. Photographs, often inadvertently humorous, began populating magazines and newspapers, showing a red-faced Ruth tucked in a steam box or sucking his stomach in while engaging in a McGovern-sanctioned exercise routine or ingesting hot water.

By early 1926, none could deny Ruth's transformation: he had lost at least twenty-five pounds, and he continued to shed weight. The story made good copy in the slow days of winter before the baseball season officially opened. Sports pages continued to feature photographs of the lean and improved Ruth. Cartoonists got in on the story. A *New York American* cartoon pictured a lean Ruth, the caption lamenting "Gone! Gone! The Palmy Days when stuck for a subject I could always make a cartoon of the Babe's bay window."[13]

In mid-January, Ruth presented himself at Yankees headquarters to Barrow, who previously had pronounced skepticism about Ruth's metamorphosis. As if examining a race horse, Barrow launched an "impromptu inspection." He "prodded Ruth quite extensively," even digging his "knuckles into Ruth's abdomen." If Barrow doubted Ruth's self-discipline, he now had ample evidence to the contrary. The Babe was down to a reported 215 pounds, had "shoulders like Atlas, biceps like Thor, a chest like Hercules, and a waist of which Hercules would not have been ashamed," according to one sportswriter.[14]

"What a Ball Player"

In late February, the slimmed-down, reformed version of the Babe set off for St. Petersburg, Florida. There he planned to play golf and ease into spring training. In camp, the appearance of the newly buff baseball hero "astounded all," including Ruth's critics. Ruppert "gaped" and "rubbed his eyes" at the sight of the "new" Babe.[15] The Ruth redemption story appeared everywhere that spring. His weight loss visually affirmed tales of hard work and sacrifice in the McGovern gym.

Ruth himself plugged his reformation in his Christy Walsh syndicate column, reinforcing the "I was a babe and a boob" storyline from his Winkworth piece. "Lots of people think I'm an awful sucker," offered Ruth in his plainspoken style. "I guess I am in a lot of ways. But this winter I've learned a lot about taking care of myself. . . . I only wish I'd gotten wise a few years before."[16] The Walsh syndicate also provided subscribers a special handwritten note from the Babe, of which newspapers could reprint a facsimile:

> You noticed I made no fancy resolutions
> this winter. But just ask Artie McGovern
> if I'm in shape? I left 36 pounds in his
> gymnasium. My stomach is where it belongs
> and after two months of playing handball
> my legs are tough. I'm in the best shape
> since I started playing baseball. And
> I'm Just 32! That makes me young enough
> and strong enough and I'm going to have
> a big year or bust.
> Yours truly,
> "Babe" Ruth[17]

"The worst he deserves," counseled Grantland Rice, dean of sportswriters, "is a fair chance to get started again without the accompaniment of the Panvil Chorus in full blast."[18] Even skeptics like Westbrook Pegler conceded real change in Ruth, although not without the sportswriter's trademark acidity. Despite having "carried matches, played marbles for keeps, stayed out late, and sassed the manager," Pegler acknowledged Ruth had "trained down to the aggregate weight of the average infielder."[19] Hugh Fullerton added in a magazine profile that Ruth "has worked this winter as he never has worked before, with a determination to fight his way back to physical condition to play the 'game of his life' during the coming season." Yet to Fullerton, Ruth remained essentially a child: "loveable, big hearted, simple, careless, reckless, easily led, seldom thinking or caring of consequences, Ruth is just a big overgrown, naughty boy."[20] Sportswriter Arthur Robinson echoed Fullerton in a July profile of Ruth in the *New Yorker*. Ruth, concluded Robinson, "is a boy, alternatively good and bad—and will, I dare say, never grow up."[21] Ruth could shed weight but apparently not his reputation as a man-child.

Baseball, of course, had every reason to welcome a cooperative Ruth back into the fold. He remained tremendously popular, and team owners, responding to increased crowds, had invested heavily in expanding ballparks. Washington Senators owner Clark Griffith and the venerable Connie Mack of the Philadelphia Athletics both planned expansions of their ballparks. In

New York, Ruppert even moved to expand accommodations at Yankee Stadium, adding some twenty thousand seats.[22]

In 1923, Ruth's towering home run on Yankee Stadium's opening day had dramatically announced his comeback. The 1926 season started slower for Ruth, but on April 21, facing legendary Washington Senators pitcher Walter Johnson, Ruth began a tear that convinced all remaining doubters of his reformation. The Babe not only bashed his first home run, which one writer compared to "an army dirigible," but he also hit two doubles and two singles, leading the Yankees to an 18–5 victory. The morning before the game, a local Washington reporter had warned of the "grave danger that Babe Ruth will be just another ball player in the Yankees lineup this year." This suggestion, noted W. B. Hanna, "proved a trifle premature and ill-timed. There may be grave danger, but to the other club."[23]

By May, Ruth's comeback appeared undeniable. Again, public fascination centered on quantifying the towering home runs posted by the Babe, and writers celebrated each as a momentous event. On the occasion of Ruth's twelfth home run in mid-May, Marshall Hunt described "a tumult in the right field bleachers by souvenir hunters," during which "a youth fainted and had to be carried from the field and number 12 had been rung up on the Babe Ruth register."[24] Four days later, when Ruth launched his thirteenth and fourteenth home runs during the same game, Hunt declared, "Let the drums be pounded and flourishes ring from the bells of trumpets in honor of the Bambino, who was captain of the resolution industry last winter and who threatens to surpass his own home run total of 59."[25]

Around the league, the Yankees and Ruth again drove up attendance. During a June tour of "western" cities, gate receipts rose 25 to 100 percent over average. "Principally, because George Herman Ruth is one of baseball's greatest magnates," on June 20, a record-smashing forty-three thousand crammed Chicago's Comiskey Park, a facility with a capacity of thirty thousand, "meaning they packed them in the aisles and on the field."[26] The next season, White Sox ownership wisely added two decked stands to the park, raising capacity to over fifty thousand.

Even Joe Vila, Ruth's uber-critic in the press corps, bestowed faint praise on the redeemed slugger, although Vila attributed the comeback to Ruth's avarice, describing it as a "fight for renewal of his $52,000 contract."[27] Days later, eternally affirmative Rice countered Vila's contention. Ruth, he claimed, amounted to a child playing baseball solely for the love of the game. "If he had a million to spend," contended Rice, Ruth "could never buy half as much fun for himself off the baseball field."[28]

Ironically, Ruth's 1925 fall had made the Yankees a stronger team. Manager Huggins used Ruth's absences and the general Yankees slide to supplant older favorites with young, promising talent. Among others, he added power-hitting Lou Gehrig and Tony Lazzeri to the team, along with brilliant fielder but less than nice guy Leo Durocher. Huggins's recruiting efforts paid off: the seventh-place Yankees of 1925 became the first-place Yankees of 1926. Before the season was one month old, Paul Gallico proposed a musical play on Yankees' "murderer's row" (a term actually first applied to the pre-Ruth Yankees of 1918): "Sing a song of murderous sluggers, sing a song of faltering pitchers; sing of the whizzing ball, as it streaked o'er the far green outfield, but above all, sing a song of Babe Ruth, a lilting song from a full heart . . . Ruth is great . . . ain't he the cats."[29]

Ruth's Christy Walsh syndicate columns celebrated the redeemed Babe as humble team player, while also reviewing the comeback narrative at all opportunities. "I've had some tough breaks during the last two years. Most of them I brought on myself," he reminded readers in one column. Still, "being shot to pieces by illness and injury has taught me a lot of things about baseball. . . . I'm past the stage when I get any kick out of people saying, 'There goes Ruth, the home run hitter.' I'd rather hear 'em say, 'What a ball player.'"[30] Walsh cleverly positioned Ruth as a team player and team inspiration—in that sense taking some credit for the revamped Yankees.

Ruth's 1926 comeback proved infinitely more durable than his 1923 back-to-the-farm effort to right his life and career. The 1926 renewal seemed better suited to both the man personally and his times. Returning Ruth to the farm had smacked of artificiality. The notion of a social urbanite like Ruth in isolation on a farm communing with nature hardly seemed a recipe for genuine redemption. Likewise, a radical rejection of modern life for the simplicity and supposed purity of a largely passing rural existence hardly offered a model for society at large. In 1926, Ruth found discipline and focus in the city. He adopted a modern, somewhat scientific, approach to conditioning, and it seemed to work. In the process Ruth appeared to rediscover his commitment to both his teammates and children in need. For those struggling with the advent of modern America and its looser morality and dizzying pace of change, Ruth offered some direction. He found a balance whereby he could preserve and maintain a disciplined life in the midst of a modern city.

"Kids of the Street"

Only months before, of course, Ruth had been a fallen idol, a vivid illustration of excess and ego to be avoided. But with striking speed, he redeemed himself. His weight loss and strong performance at bat served up tangible proof that he had turned a new leaf. The only debate was Ruth's motivation. Some, Vila in particular, conjectured that Ruth's true impetus was financial. In the last year of his contract, Ruth wanted to negotiate from a position of strength. When debating Ruth's comeback, noted the *Chicago Tribune*'s "In the Wake of News" sports column, "It is customary to smile and say 'Why he's playing for a new contract.'"[31] At $52,000, Ruth already was the highest paid player in baseball, but given the crowds he drew and the excitement he generated, columnist James R. Harrison calculated Ruth the "most underpaid player in baseball."[32] By the end of the season, Ruth's handlers were floating the idea of a $150,000 per year contract, understanding it was highly unlikely Ruppert would pay such a sum.[33]

While the notion that Ruth somehow pulled himself together just for financial reasons lingered, his credibility, especially as a model for boys, recovered miraculously intact and in many ways stronger than ever in 1926. Fully redeemed (and now eminently marketable), he was again a paragon of virtue and a role model, especially for the poorer boys who made up much of Ruth's fan base. William Hennigan of the New York *Evening World* noted how the "kids of the street always give Babe Ruth a thrill . . . the big fellow is besieged each day as he comes out of the ballpark by an army of youngsters, some in rags, some in their bare feet, and some with dirty faces." Each child, Hennigan recounted, wanted an autograph. "Ruth seldom refuses to autograph a ball or a score card . . . for he does not forget when he was an orphan boy in Baltimore and the world was not so kind to him."[34]

Again Ruth became a much-in-demand speaker at fundraisers, boys' clubs, and youth leagues. His talks inevitably focused on baseball, although he also dispensed life advice. He counseled, for instance, three hundred thrilled members of the Fordham League at the Church of St. Nicholas of Tolentine that "no boy who aspires to be great in sports should smoke."[35] Ruth also associated himself with a more specific agenda to address the needs of impoverished youth. He joined Father E. J. Flanagan's campaign against "profiteering in homeless boys." Ruth also campaigned to halt the practice of adopting destitute boys during harvest or busy seasons, then abandoning them without compensation for their services. Ruth vowed to write "several articles on the issue."[36]

Throughout the latter part of his career, Ruth moved to become an ever-more vocal advocate for disadvantaged youth. Given his own background, it was a cause for which he could campaign with authority and passion. Yet the press and baseball establishment seemed reluctant to give Ruth a platform. Those leading the game still regarded Ruth as a risky proposition. Instead, the charitable episode for which Ruth became best known proved an odd affair, detracting from rather than contributing to the star's efforts to represent something more than just a home-run hitter.

Healing Johnny Sylvester

Perhaps the most famous legend associated with Ruth, alongside his "called shot" home run, is that of Johnny Sylvester, the "Babe Ruth kid." Sylvester's supposed "healing" has come to epitomize the sacred bond between Ruth and needy children. The connection, as often noted in the media, grew in part from perceptions of Ruth's own childishness, his image as an "overgrown boy," and his background as an underprivileged youth.

Eleven-year-old Johnny Sylvester, however, was anything but impoverished. His family, in fact, enjoyed the sort of opulent lifestyle increasingly celebrated in 1920s America. Period advertising promoted products by association with lavish, leisure-filled lifestyles and cosmopolitan sophistication. Such luxury became an ideal, especially to the social-climbing middle class aspiring to join the upper echelons of wealth.[37] The vast majority of Americans, however, toiled beneath the middle class in hand-to-mouth existences and no doubt realized images in magazines and newspapers would remain forever beyond their means.

The Sylvester family, however, enjoyed a rarified world well removed from the toilers. Sylvester ancestors arrived from Britain in the 1630s and quickly established themselves among the elites of the New World. The family occupied a sprawling mansion in an elite suburb of New York City, where patriarch Horace Sylvester worked in the banking field. By 1926, Horace rose to vice president of the National City Bank, managing the municipal department. Young Johnny Sylvester's youth was every bit the opposite of Babe Ruth's coming of age. Yet the two were thrown together in perhaps baseball's greatest media-driven legend.

Fashionable affluence, of course, proffers only illusory protection from the hazards of illness and injuries. In the summer of 1926, this reality became strikingly clear to the Sylvesters. While vacationing on the Jersey shore, young Johnny was thrown from a horse, which apparently then kicked him in the head. The injuries sustained led to a very serious infection. While the media never came to any consensus as to the exact malady afflicting Johnny (nor its immediate danger to him), fear clearly permeated the Sylvester home in Essex Fells, New Jersey, a prosperous bedroom community populated by businessmen commuters to nearby New York City. According to some newspaper accounts, Johnny suffered from septicemia, blood poisoning—the same condition that two years before suddenly had robbed the life of sixteen-year-old Calvin Coolidge Jr., son of the US president. The death of Coolidge's son had shocked the nation. Only days before, young Cal had been playing in tennis shoes without socks, from which he contracted a foot infection. As the most prominent family in the country watched helplessly, the boy spiraled downward. Newspaper stories about Sylvester's condition sometimes included mention of Coolidge's recent death.

Desperate to raise his ailing son's spirits, Horace Sylvester played on his connections. He contacted friends in St. Louis, soon-to-be site of the 1926 World Series between the Cardinals and Ruth's Yankees. He requested autographed balls for his son. Ruth's publicists sent a ball signed with the message "I'll knock a homer for you on Wednesday."[38] When, on October 6, Ruth smacked not one but three home runs that game, his publicity machine quickly shifted to overdrive: the show-stopping performance derived from Ruth's promise to a sick boy. The media could not resist the story. Around the country, photographs of the miracle ball (made available by Horace Sylvester) appeared next to the miracle storyline.

The *Daily News*, now thoroughly dominating New York City circulation, long had a close relationship with Ruth. The tabloid's editors understood instinctively Ruth's broad appeal, both in good times and bad. The paper also knew well how to capitalize on a good story, and it was in a financial position to aggressively pursue such stories. In August of 1926, for instance, the *Daily News* had gained exclusive rights to American Gertrude Ederle's second attempt to swim the English Channel. *Daily News* reporter Julia Harpman, wife of sportswriter Westbrook Pegler, rode on the boat ferrying Ederle's entourage, while the rest of the press tagged behind from a distance. From the flotilla, Harpman dispatched exclusives and ghostwritten stories to the *Daily News*. The entire event fascinated readers. Two million New Yorkers feted Ederle with a tickertape parade upon her return from her record-setting feat.

Heartwarming and straightforward, the Johnny Sylvester healing offered baseball the chance to appeal to new audiences, less intrigued by the day-to-day intricacies of the game. Women seemed the particular target, with the working assumption that females would be susceptible to the emotional draw of the story and the sophisticated and privileged world where the drama played out. Beyond this, the "Babe Ruth kid" story allowed baseball to associate itself more generally with the rarified world of the Sylvesters, part of a rebranding of the sport as more than the pastime of the urban masses.

As such, the *Daily News* assigned a well-known female journalist, Elenore Kellogg, as the lead reporter covering the Sylvester story. Despite gender barriers, Kellogg, Harpman, and other female reporters—including Sophie Treadwell, the wife of W. O. McGeehan—often covered crime and politics; still, editors generally expected females to present the "women's point of view."[39] Most often, they were restricted to the human interest side of stories. Kellogg, a graduate of the University of Wisconsin, began her career with the New York *Socialist Call*. She quickly emerged a "star reporter," who later wrote a political column for the New York *Evening World*, actually replacing sportswriter turned political columnist Heywood Broun.

The story that Sylvester somehow began a miraculous recovery following Ruth's triple clouts quickly spread. "Physicians thought Johnny Sylvester was dying a week ago," reported the *Daily News* in its syrupy coverage of the story. "'Gee, I wish I could see Babe Ruth wallop a home run before I die,' the lad gasped." But then "Doc Ruth Cured the Boy."[40] Even the serious-minded *New York Times* picked up the story, asserting that "the medical value of baseball was demonstrated today by the improvement reported in John D. Sylvester."[41] The following day, the paper went a step further, celebrating Ruth and the Sylvester story on its op-ed page. A year before, the same *Times* editorial page had maligned the fallen hero's failure in "remaining modest, in properly judging the fleeting nature of fame, in seeing the necessity of keeping in good bodily trim."[42] Now, in a complete reversal, the newspaper recounted the Sylvester story: "If there are any who protest the space given by newspapers to Ruth's prowess, let them consider how wholesome is the admiration he kindles." The piece concluded, "To make a hero out of a player like Ruth is well worthwhile."[43]

Paralleling the *New York Times* turnabout, universal and hyperbolic praise burst forth for Ruth's World Series heroism, especially his three home runs in game four. Ruth "went goofy, as they say, so did the nation as far as your correspondent can ascertain," marveled McGeehan.[44] "Babe Ruth fell upon the beleaguered city of St. Louis today and flattened it into a pulp of anguish," added Rice.[45] To Paul Gallico, Ruth was "a genius. . . . He walks alone, a huge, uncouth, graceful, startling person, whose glory is that he does what he does better than anybody else on earth doing the same thing."[46] Even Pegler, often eager to malign Ruth, wrote from nearby Chicago that "every time one of the Cardinal pitchers laid the baseball within a running board jump of where [Ruth] stood, the Babe just slapped that lively fruit clear out of the property."[47]

At one extraordinary point, hyperpartisan St. Louis fans shelved all bias and cheered Ruth as the slugger ascended to the summit of his career. To Heywood Broun, it was a defining moment. "From the beginning of time until the contest yesterday never has a St. Louis crowd cheered for a visiting athlete," wrote Broun. "But yesterday they cheered a stranger. They stood up for him and waved their hats. . . . After his performance yesterday it must be granted that he belongs to the Nation."[48] Ruth's ghostwriter offered the "wonderful reception they gave us" in St. Louis as proof of how far the game had come from its earlier chaotic days. "Baseball after all is a sportsman's game, and baseball fans I've found out are real sportsmen."[49]

Despite Ruth's Herculean feats, the Yankees fell short of winning the World Series. Still, after several disappointing series performances, Ruth more than eliminated one of the last remaining chinks in his armor. "Although the Yankees did not win, New York fans still have their Babe to talk about. From this we are forced to say that the Bambino is 'it,'" waxed the *Sporting News*.[50] Talk emerged that his next contract would be worth $150,000. After the World Series, Ruth embarked on a barnstorming tour that promised to bring him near the same sum.[51] Still, even as they began looking forward, Ruth's handlers were not done with the Johnny Sylvester storyline.

While "fourteen pennant-decked automobiles and the mayor of Bradley Beach, NJ waited at the railroad station" to escort Ruth; his agent, Christy Walsh; and his "All Star" postseason barnstormers to a game against the Negro League Brooklyn Colored Giants, Elenore Kellogg arranged for the hero to spend the morning of October 11 with a recovering Johnny Sylvester (whom she identified as suffering from a sinus condition) in Essex Fells. "The Mighty One," she explained to her readers, "was on a mission of his own, arranged by The News." Milking the meeting, Kellogg described Ruth as "towering over the bedside of the sick boy. The fist that had wracked so many home runs was holding a thin, white hand."[52] Sylvester appeared stunned and said little as he encountered his idol. The usually verbose Ruth, according to accounts, was also uncharacteristically quiet, perhaps unsettled by the odd mixture of public relations spectacle and supposedly life-threatening drama.[53] The next day, photographs of a somber Ruth at Johnny Sylvester's bedside appeared in newspapers throughout the country.

Later, stories surfaced suggesting that Ruth barely recalled the entire Sylvester episode. Sportswriters John Drebinger and Frank Graham remembered a man introducing himself to Ruth as Johnny Sylvester's uncle. After his departure, Ruth supposedly turned to the writers and asked, "Now who the hell is Johnny Sylvester."[54] To some this suggested the Sylvester story and Ruth's charity work in general were little more than well-crafted public relations.[55]

Certainly some of Ruth's "charitable" appearances appeared to be the work of publicists eager to sell newspapers and market an extraordinarily charismatic public figure. Conversely, enough stories exist of Ruth's bigheartedness to conclude that his generosity was more than an act. Ruth probably well understood the public relations value of appearing at the bedside of the likes of Sylvester; at the same time, there seemed an authenticity in his devotion to his work with children that few would deny. For every publicity photograph of Ruth visiting a hospital ward, claimed sportswriter Bill Slocum, "He visits fifty without publicity."[56]

Ruth obviously felt uncomfortable with the famed Sylvester story, a tale driven more by publicists and newspaper circulation wars than facts. Most likely Ruth had little recall of signing the famous ball that set the story in motion. In fact, he signed perhaps thousands of balls each season. Given his background and commitment to poor youth, his trip to the Sylvester mansion to comfort a boy so privileged must have seemed a departure. The entire manufactured melodrama, in fact, went beyond good publicity. A craven adolescent months before, Ruth was recast as a beatific hero, a healer. Neither the 1925 outlaw nor the 1926 saint seemed a sustainable, comfortable public role for Ruth, now in his early thirties and thinking about his future. Meanwhile the media melee around him continued unabated. In good and bad times, sensationalistic and simplistic depictions of Ruth dominated. Understandably, Ruth felt he had little control over the spectacle.

However he might personally have felt about the whole Sylvester episode, the legend proved enduring and difficult to escape—as much as Ruth might have wanted to put it behind him. In 1942, Ruth played himself in *Pride of the Yankees*, a biographical film depicting the life of his teammate Lou Gehrig. Not surprisingly, Ruth turned in a strong performance, one noted by many critics. In an odd scene reminiscent of the Sylvester story, Ruth, touring a hospital ward accompanied by a noisy horde of reporters and cameramen, promises to hit a home run for a sick boy. As Ruth and the media parade move on, Gehrig, played with saintly precision by the graceful Gary Cooper, approaches the ailing lad and makes a more sincere, private pledge to hit two home runs. Gehrig fulfills his private promise. The scene, of course, contrasts, rather unfavorably from Ruth's standpoint, the style and personality of the two icons (more about Gehrig in chapter 7). Perhaps Ruth, in that particular scene, may have sought to distance himself from the Sylvester story and the Saint Babe persona, which had taken on a life of its own. Later, a maudlin retelling of the Sylvester legend appeared in the 1948 film *The Babe Ruth Story*. The film, starring William Bendix, played the Babe as something of a childlike buffoon. At one point, the Ruth character shows up at Sylvester's bedside promising a home run. He then delivers it in the form of "a called shot" in the 1932 Chicago World Series.

The Sylvester episode stands out virtually by itself in baseball lore, fusing the game with purity, healing, youthful innocence, and positive thinking (a popular theme during the 1920s). Baseball boosters now had a powerful myth at hand to counteract the more sullied features of the game. Photographs of the weak, ailing Sylvester holding the autographed balls moved hearts. The story's appeal extended far beyond baseball diehards, in fact cleverly linking the aristocratic Sylvesters with the earthy national pastime. For his part, Ruth appeared more interested in committing himself to disadvantaged youth. The Sylvester narrative, set as it was among fashionable and wealthy elites, detracted from more than sustained Ruth's mission to aid boys sharing his deprived background. The demands of public relations and the climate of the times short-circuited Ruth's efforts to make something more of his unprecedented fame.

"I made my comeback! So can you!"

Still, from start to finish, Ruth's 1926 comeback season proved both a personal and a public relations triumph. It enshrined the comeback not only as a sports institution but also as a powerful cultural convention that would launch "second acts" for fallen and even disgraced public figures from all walks of life. The comeback also generated renewed fascination with baseball and Ruth, taking both to ever greater levels of prosperity. After Yankee Stadium attendance had fallen dramatically in 1925 (tumbling to under seven hundred thousand), it rebounded to over one million in 1926, and prosperity pulsed throughout major league baseball. Meanwhile, as Ruth's comeback climaxed, he negotiated extraordinarily lucrative barnstorming and promotional agreements. A single postseason exhibition game in Montreal played on October 16, 1926, netted Ruth over $3,000.[57] While the Yankees failed to win the World Series in 1926, losing to Rogers Hornsby's Cardinals, Ruth's performance in game four remained etched in memories. That Ruth's failed attempt to steal second base in game seven had ended the series in the Cardinals' favor was soon forgotten.

Just as the Johnny Sylvester story quickly became commodified to market baseball and build newspaper circulation, so too was Ruth's overall comeback packaged and sold to the public. During the 1926 World Series, newspapers around the country ran advertisements for "Babe Ruth's Health System." A personal testimonial from Babe explained how a mere "year ago I was all shot! You know what the papers said 'Babe Ruth is Through.' But I wasn't through, fellows. It was just a matter of physical condition." In fact, the ad continued, "When the season opened this year I was right back on my toes. The boys opened their eyes at the way I wholloped the old pill." Since then, Ruth explained, he had been besieged with requests "asking me the secret. There's no secret about it. I did it with a system that allows me to get back in shape and keeps me there." Those moved by Ruth's final appeal of "I Made My Comeback! So Can You!" were invited to invest $12 (over $150 in 2017 dollars) for the "system," which appeared to involve a signed bat and a leather-bound instruction booklet detailing exercises and offering batting tips.[58]

At the very least, "Babe Ruth's Health System" suggests that Ruth, to some extent, had taken control of what to that point had been a turbulent and often troubled career. The 1926 season, in fact, marked the arrival of a steadier period for Ruth. His reformed presence with the Yankees signaled a new stability both for himself and for major league baseball, which so strove to control and contain Ruth. Baseball had made major advances in cementing itself as the nation's pastime, with broad popularity and particular appeal to middle-class audiences. Ruth, too, certainly felt he had made progress in bringing order to his life and tumultuous career. In media depictions, however, he remained something of a man-child. As he pulled his life together, Ruth hoped to gain recognition for something beyond his ability to smack "the old pill" farther than anyone else. He hoped to advocate for children and manage a major league team. Baseball, however, remained leery of empowering Ruth. For Babe Ruth the player, the best was still to come. For Ruth the man, frustrations began to mount.

SEVEN. TRIUMPH

As the magical decade of the 1920s entered its final dizzying years, Ruth reached new heights of fame and public adoration. No longer did he portend immediate instability and menace to the baseball order. On the surface, he now appeared a good citizen, by and large accepting his subordinate position under Yankees and league management. As the turbulence that had defined his early career receded, Ruth increasingly realized his own personal potential. Spurred by its greatest star, baseball also realized new peaks of ever greater public interest and profits. Ruth's success on the playing diamond and his affluence off the field mirrored a nation basking in good fortune.

Still, despite his newly found positive attitude, Ruth's large salary demands and independent ways continued to concern the establishment. Sportswriters again toasted Ruth as a superman, dominating the game with his power; yet even as Ruth sought to project a more mature image, writers continued to treat him as a comical, juvenile figure. Ruth clearly desired to break out of this mold. He expanded his advocacy for disadvantaged children and talked increasingly of one day managing a major league team. In 1928, he campaigned with gusto for Democratic presidential candidate Al Smith. The media and baseball establishment, however, resisted allowing Ruth to move beyond the narrow confines of a colorful baseball hero.

Gone Hollywood?

By 1927, for large segments of American society, the economic uncertainties of the earlier part of the decade had faded into memory, replaced by a boom mentality. Rising wages (up 25 percent for industrial workers over the course of the decade), widely available credit, and mass manufacturing put

161

automobiles and durable goods, including radios and washing machines, easily within the grasp of an expanding middle class. Faith in the potency of technology and free-wheeling capitalism soared; both production and consumption correspondingly rocketed upward. Investment crazes, such as California and Florida real estate bubbles, generated the same frenzied response as other cultural vogues. Eclipsing all get-rich-quick schemes, the Great Bull Market drew millions of enthusiastic investors. As Ruth's professional career crested in the late 1920s, so too did the market. In 1927, 577 million shares changed hands on the New York Stock Exchange; a year later, traders exchanged some 920 million shares. While some economies, including farming and coal, lagged and wealth distribution remained skewed, vast numbers of Americans, especially those living in urban areas, could be forgiven for feeling they and their country were thriving as never before. At times, the celebration of materialism threatened good sense. The era, noted one prominent historian, bore a noticeable "hedonistic" tenor.[1]

As public fascination with wealth and celebrity peaked, so too did interest in Ruth's upcoming contract renegotiations. His 1922 contract, setting his salary at $52,000 per annum, expired at the end of the 1926 season. The 1922 negotiations had played out in comfortable environs for Ruth: a bathhouse in Hot Springs, Arkansas, alongside an amenable adversary, Colonel T. L. Huston, co-owner of the Yankees and a close Ruth comrade. The 1927 discussions promised no such reassuring surroundings. Huston had sold his portion of the team to Jacob Ruppert, who viewed Ruth more as a delinquent youth than an equal. Contract talks would take place inside a suite of offices at the Ruppert Brewery, etched in Ruth's memory as the site of his humiliating encounter with his employers in 1925, when he made a demeaning apology to Manager Miller Huggins and Yankees officials. At the talks, again, Ed Barrow would be at Ruppert's side. From Ruth's perspective, the setting was hardly reassuring.

In the wake of his 1926 World Series success, Ruth floated a "stupendous" opening bid for a new contract at $150,000 a year. He also announced he would "be represented by a personal manager," presumably Christy Walsh, when he met with Ruppert.[2] This was the arrangement practiced in other sports. Manager Jack Kearns directly handled negotiations for boxer Jack Dempsey, and C. C. Pyle had recently negotiated a $100,000 deal for football superstar Red Grange. Baseball owners, however, refused to negotiate with any party other than the immediate player (and maintained this policy until 1970). Owners, of course, held the upper hand, not only with the reserve clause essentially locking players into contracts but also by forcing young, inexperienced players, usually with scant business experience, to bargain with veteran businessmen.

Ruppert was a former congressman and a multimillionaire with considerable business background. His dealings with employees, whether at his brewery or his ball club, tended to be paternalistic. Although workers at the colonel's brewery were organized, the Ruppert family had clashed harshly with union leaders.[3] Baseball players, men who played a game for a living, deserved no such union protection, Ruppert believed, as did all the owners. Instead he viewed his players with patriarchal regard and bristled in contract negotiations whenever challenged. Additionally, he had the intimidating Barrow at his side. Holding to tradition, Yankees management barred Walsh from the proceedings. Ruppert and Barrow would only deal directly and solely with Ruth.

Following his postseason 1926 barnstorming tour, Ruth headed west to southern California, where he planned to make a movie. The highly publicized jaunt promised a sizeable paycheck. The trip and movie deal also signaled to Yankees ownership that other opportunities existed for Ruth beyond baseball. Unlikely as it was, given Ruth's love for the game, he might take a year off to pursue alternate interests. A season without Ruth portended financial disaster for the Yankees and general chaos for baseball. From the team's perspective, the trick was to raise Ruth's salary, but not to the point where it threatened the balance of power in the game. Ruth could not become a team shareholder, and his $150,000 trial balloon, likely the brain child of Christy Walsh, was quickly shot down by Ruppert. Walsh indeed may have angered the miserly Yankees owner with such a shocking opening offer.

In another gesture aimed at the Yankees, Ruth brought, at his own expense, trainer Artie McGovern with him to Hollywood. When not on a movie set, Ruth submitted himself to McGovern's routines and workouts. Journalists traveling with Ruth dutifully reported his training campaign and weight loss.[4] Ever devoted to hyperbole, McGovern attempted to make the case himself. "The world's super athlete, Babe Ruth," he wrote from the Hollywood Plaza Hotel, "has reached the height of physical perfection."[5] Hype aside, Ruth obviously remained committed to remaining in shape.

Meanwhile, although clearly an amateur, Ruth proved a remarkably engaging movie actor. In *Babe Comes Home*, Ruth, as in his 1920 debut, played a baseball player. Presented in a new technology that synchronized screen action with music and "shouts of crowds and comic noises," Ruth's movie garnered positive reviews when released later in the summer. To one critic, Ruth was "a pleasing screen figure" in a "fun and go" movie.[6] Again commodifying his comeback, Ruth appeared as "Babe Dugan," a baseball star with uncouth manners. The job of cleaning him up, literally, fell to a laundress played by Swedish actress Anna Q. Nilsson. Like his 1920 film, *Babe Comes Home* ended with a celebratory home run in front of an enthusiastic crowd.

As Ruth vamped for cameras and made the Hollywood rounds, the next volleys in his contract battle were exchanged. The slugger's handlers had already made clear they expected a substantial pay increase. Impressive salaries negotiated by Tris Speaker and Ty Cobb built pressure on Ruth to maintain his position as the highest-paid athlete in baseball. Typically, early in the new year, teams sent renewal offers in the form of new contracts. In California, Ruth received Barrow's opening offer: $52,000. It was the same rate for which he had been playing since 1922. Barrow insisted he meant no offense: preliminary contracts were just a legal formality to lock in players. All parties understood Ruth was free to ask for more pay. Still, the Babe fumed at the low-ball offer.[7] He returned the overture to Barrow unsigned.

Nursing annoyance, Ruth wrote a pointed letter to Ruppert echoing many long-standing labor grievances among baseball players. "If I were in any other business I would probably receive a new contract at a higher salary without request. Or rival employers could bid for my services," Ruth protested. Instead, the notorious reserve clause "forces me to work for the Yankees or remain idle." He would make no threats to quit the game, explained Ruth. After all, the unfair system, not he, would be forcing him out: "Unless I accept your figure I will be prohibited from playing with any other team and banned from baseball." Ruth further stressed his obvious drawing appeal at Yankee Stadium and around the league. He also explained that the Yankees played more exhibition games than any other team, generating sizable revenue for the franchise. Fans flocked, of course, to such games largely to see Ruth. Hoping to mobilize public support, Ruth released the letter to the media.[8]

Ruth's appeal to fairness echoed fifty years of professional ballplayer grievances, but few were listening in 1927. Sportswriters could hardly be expected to support Ruth against management. Instead, the media and fans focused on the seeming immensity of Ruth's counterproposal of $100,000 and the additional $7,750 he demanded to cover 1925 hospital fees and what Ruth saw as unfair fines levied against him in the past by the Yankees management (a "personal touch," according to John Kieran, that "only a ball player would think of inserting"). When Ruth unleashed his frustrations to Marshall Hunt, a *Daily News* reporter who followed the Babe to California, Hunt could not help but poke fun at Ruth. "My demands are not ex . . . what's the word?" asked Ruth, trying to sum up his argument, to which Hunt purportedly offered "exorbitant" to finish the hero's labored thoughts.[9]

In New York, Colonel Ruppert was displeased. The negotiations had gone public, and Ruth's letter raised issues baseball officials considered long closed. The brewery magnate insisted Ruth would "relent" and moderate demands that were both excessive and evidence of ingratitude. Ruppert condescendingly acknowledged that Ruth had written "a great letter," then he quickly added "even though Babe didn't write it. I feel that someone did the writing and Babe merely nodded."[10]

At an impasse, Ruth left California for New York. As always, mobs of media and fans trailed him. Ruth fought his way through a train station as "flashlights were exploding in the hands of the Los Angeles news photographers" and crowds pressed in.[11] As Ruth trekked across country (making use of a converted baggage car as a gym), throngs besieged the hero at every scheduled train stop. "The greatest one-man show on earth is progressing steadily eastward today," wrote Hunt, "but is making frequent stands in the western provinces to awe the yokelry with speeches." In Riverside, California, "a vast troop of boy scouts and their parents assembled at the station . . . to gaze in open mouthed wonder at this illustrious figure on route to one of the major business conferences of the winter."[12] In Chicago, Hunt recounted Ruth's conversation with a girl in a crowd that assembled to greet his train. "'Oh Mr. Ruth,' she trilled. 'I'm so glad to meet you. I have read a lot about your work in the movies. You're a baseball player too, aren't you?' The Bambino grinned and borrowing a Hollywood expression replied 'Well, I'm at liberty at present.'"[13] Asked directly about his contract, Ruth was less coy. "If we don't [come to terms,] I won't be playing since I can't go to any other team."[14]

Sensing public sympathy building for Ruth, Yankees management insisted the initial $52,000 contract was "offered only as a formality almost a jest." Contract renewal offers had to be submitted by a certain date or a player would become a free agent. Barrow, it was reported, "tactlessly" inserted the $52,000. Still, the Yankees promised to "take a cold blooded view of the situation" and suggested that Ruth's gate appeal in fact had declined over the years.[15] Ruth in turn hinted he might go as far as to quit baseball and focus on his performing career, where he was better compensated. Anticipation built as Ruth neared Manhattan.[16]

To sportswriter John Kieran, however, the chatter surrounding the contract dispute seemed premanufactured public relations. "The $100,000 salary demand is fine publicity for Mr. G. H. Ruth, the eminent Vaudeville performer; for Mr. G. H. Ruth, the movie star, for Mr. G. H. Ruth, the syndicated writer, and for Mr. G. H. Ruth, enthusiastic endorser of candy, suspenders, mouse traps, coat hangers or what have you?"[17] Given Ruth's many sources of income and obvious wealth, he hardly resembled exploited labor. Likewise, the intense interest surrounding the salary negotiations benefited Ruth, the commodity. But Ruth the man clearly aimed to make a statement about his worth to baseball. Compared to athletes in other sports, Ruth was underpaid. No one could reasonably argue that Ruth received a fair share of the income he generated for his sport. Ruppert, as team owner, and Barrow, as team secretary and owner of a share of the Yankees, profited immeasurably from Ruth. With some cause, Ruth carried a working-class view of the world and a strong impulse to defend the value of his labor and the value of baseball players in general. Further, he resented comments about his limited intelligence and uncouth manners. Yet, with little education or background in business (and living at the center of hysteria), Ruth was ill equipped to press his own agenda.

Still, it fell to Ruth alone to make his case. He arrived in New York on March 2 aboard the Twentieth Century Limited due to meet almost immediately with Ruppert (the same scenario that had taken place under much grimmer circumstances when he was suspended from the Yankees eighteen months earlier). As in 1925, excited crowds greeted him at Penn Station. To emphasize his ongoing commitment to conditioning, Ruth shot immediately to Art McGovern's gym, then visited his wife—again, as in 1925, hospitalized with a case of the nerves. By this time it was roughly noon, and Ruth journeyed, press in tow, uptown to Ruppert's red-bricked brewery. There was tension as Ruth arrived. The colonel "paced nervously up and down," waiting for his star employee. As the media assemblage waited outside, Barrow, Ruppert, and Ruth entered a conference room and began negotiating. It bears repeating that Ruppert, a sixty-year-old former congressman, had by his side Barrow, a veteran baseball executive with three decades of experience and a deserved reputation for toughness. Ruth, by contrast, was unaccompanied. His manager, Christy Walsh, remained several time zones away in California.[18] Despite his fame and acclaim, Ruth undoubtedly felt ill at ease.

The Babe also had more on his mind than pressing for the highest salary. An athlete in his thirties and a man prone to illness and injuries, he preferred a multiyear contract. Likewise, the distraction and tension of annually negotiating a new contract hardly appealed to Ruth. His goal was $100,000—given Red Grange's recent payday, not unreasonable. But he was ready to compromise for an extended contract.

The Yankees, conversely, wished to contain their risk, preferring a shorter contract as insurance against injury or a decline in Ruth's abilities. As discussions began at the brewery, Ruppert and Barrow pressed for a one-year contract. Ruth retorted that he, unlike most ballplayers, had other potential sources of income should he decide temporarily to leave baseball. Fully expecting Ruth's line of argument, Ruppert sternly lectured his employee on the risks involved in walking away from baseball. The Yankees very well might not be the only losers should Ruth leave the sport. Ruppert subtly seemed to suggest baseball might work to make Ruth's life very hard should he leave the game.

After some wrangling, management and labor came to an accord. Ruth would sign for $70,000 a year for three years, and a secret arrangement was brokered to address the question of past fines and hospital bills. Ruppert may have also inserted a provision allowing Ruth a share of profits from exhibition games. Such a provision showed up in later contracts. A very clearly relieved Ruth emerged from the conference room. "I'm glad that's off my mind," he blurted to the waiting media.[19] The next day, Ruth returned to Ruppert's offices to ink the contract. In a break from custom, Ruppert, delighted with the deal, passed the contract around to reporters. Ruth then spun off back to McGovern's gym.[20]

After insisting on $100,000 for months, Ruth settled for substantially less. The final contract, in fact, was less than half of Ruth's opening salvo, albeit he gained a multiyear contract in the process. Undoubtedly the negotiations wore on Ruth, just as they would on most players, let alone someone of Ruth's background. The constant commotion and hysteria that had followed Ruth from the time he left Hollywood was unnerving. "These last three days have been the busiest I can remember," Ruth told reporters as he prepared to leave New York for spring training after signing his contract. Again, as he departed, throngs jammed Penn Station to get a look at the hero.[21] Between his travel, movie work, conditioning program, and marital problems, Ruth was in little position to prepare for salary negotiations. His antagonists, Ruppert and Barrow, clearly held Ruth in low regard, adding to the overall tension.

Meanwhile, a sidelined Walsh bristled at the deal Ruth negotiated. He "would have liked to have been present at the negotiations, but no player has ever done business with the magnates through a manager," he complained to journalist Westbrook Pegler. Had he been at the brewery meeting, Walsh asserted, he "might have kicked Ruth in the shins under the table" to remind the slugger that in three years he would be thirty-six years old and probably past his prime earning years. Instead, the negotiations resulted in what Pegler branded an embarrassing "$6000 a minute retreat." Walsh's "disgust became more acute" when he learned the American League, spurred by Ruppert, had offered New York mayor Jimmy Walker $100,000 per annum to serve as AL president.[22]

"Tomorrow he'll get sixty"

The new Ruthian contract, signed at the height of his powers rather than during one of his downturns, essentially signaled the Babe's acceptance of (perhaps even capitulation to) baseball's power structure. No longer did he embody, consciously or unconsciously, the menace of violence, runaway salaries, rival leagues, or players making their own rules. When confronted by the powers that be, Ruth had affirmed their authority. A Babe Ruth column published in September drove home the point. "If I never do another thing in baseball, I want to set the record straight on one thing," announced Ruth. "Miller Huggins not only is the manager of the New York Yankees in name, but in reality. . . . We know he's square, we know he's fair."[23]

In fact, by the late 1920s, baseball had moved closer to the ideal set out by reformers in the early twentieth century: an orderly, stable affair with mass appeal and massive profits, free of the specter of outlaw rival leagues, nefarious ties to gambling, and the debilitating rowdyism of previous years, whether in the stands or on the field. When New York area boxing promoter Tom O'Rourke signaled interest in forming a rival "outlaw" league in late 1926, the major league establishment basically ignored the threat. As NL president John Heydler argued, the 1922 Federal League court decision meant court injunctions could be issued barring any player from jumping leagues. Organized baseball, Heydler crowed, is "better equipped at the present to meet the attack of an 'outlaw' major league than it ever was before."[24] And as for still-circulating murmurs about organizing a new players' union, players already had "jacked up salaries so high" there was little room for additional increases, asserted the *Sporting News*.[25] Concurrently, while gambling pools—"the lowest form of criminal existence," according to Commissioner Landis—persisted, aggressive action by baseball authorities curbed overt evidence of wagering.[26]

Commentators also frequently noted the decline of rowdyism at ballparks. Once a "live issue," noted the *Chicago Tribune's* "In the Wake of the News" column, "how comparatively seldom in these days do we read of diamond disturbances."[27] Ruth echoed these sentiments in a ghostwritten column praising Umpire Tommy Connolly's thirty-four years on the job. "I can remember where riots were common and when police had to be on hand a dozen times during the season to protect umpires and visiting players. Not anymore," he reflected. Over the past decade and a half, he continued, "rowdyism has been taken out of the game pretty much." In the past Connolly would eject two to three recalcitrant players a month. It had been four years since Connolly had tossed a player. The last ejected "was a fellow named Babe Ruth." He and Connolly, Ruth added, "were laughing about it the other day."[28] In the hands of his ghostwriters, Ruth's restoration intertwined with baseball's hard-won reordering. Essential to Ruth's reformation was his acknowledgement that baseball's authority reigned supreme, over himself and all players.

Ruth, as one sportswriter pointed out, was integral to another aspect of the modernization of the game. Mirroring the centralization of American culture, major league baseball became more of a national rather than merely a regional phenomenon. Fans turned out not only to cheer their own teams but also to see Babe Ruth, the national figure. Ruth, noted George Daley, who wrote under the moniker Monitor, "has changed the temper of baseball fans." Even die-hard St. Louis fans cheered Ruth and booed their own pitchers when they walked the Babe. "Fans don't care a whoop for local spirit. They want to see Babe Ruth," concluded Daley.[29]

Buoyed (and no doubt relieved) by his grand settlement with baseball, Ruth went on a hitting spree the likes of which baseball never experienced. Soon he was on pace to challenge his own home-run record of fifty-nine set in 1921. Among other 1927 feats, Ruth powered the first home run out of newly remodeled and expanded Comiskey Park in Chicago. For a while, young Lou Gehrig kept pace with Ruth's home-run production, lagging only a few home runs behind Ruth in mid-August. In the final weeks of the season, however, Ruth broke away. With the Yankees firmly entrenched in first place and little doubt the team would go on to win the pennant, Ruth's home-run fling continued to draw fans to ballparks. Of the competition between Ruth and Gehrig, Grantland Rice proclaimed, "Their home run records have made them a good story no matter what they do. It will be a good story if they are stopped, and it will be a good story if they keep up the blasting."[30]

Ruth's drive to overcome his own record climaxed as the season wound down. On September 29, he launched two home runs in one game to tie his 1921 home-run record; one game remained in the season. To some, Ruth seemed finally to be achieving his full potential. "The Big Hitter, George Herman Ruth stopped the sinking sands of time, turned back the calendar, peeled six disappointing years off his ball smashing career by swishing two mighty home runs into the bleachers in the Yankee stadium," enthused Monitor.[31] Whether or not Ruth's past six seasons could be dismissed as "disappointing," Ford Frick saw larger forces at work on September 29. After Ruth fired his second home run, "An unknown man in the right field bleacher rose to his feet," reported Frick. "And in a voice that echoed above the din strange and cheering, he sent his message hurtling out through the air: 'Tomorrow he'll get sixty,' the voice said. To your correspondent sitting up in the press box, it sounded like the voice of fate and destiny raised in exorable prophecy."[32]

Indeed, Frick was attuned to "the voice of fate," as were the thousands gathered at Yankee Stadium the next day "with no other purpose than to see Babe make home run history." The unusually strong crowd for a Friday afternoon after the pennant race had been decided was not disappointed. On September 30, 1927, as Ruth hit his sixtieth home run, ten thousand fans went "wild." The *New York Times* described a "Jovial Babe" who "entered into the carnival spirit and punctuated his Ringly strides with a succession of snappy salutes."[33] "The Babe is our most picturesque if not our most heroic figure and he can put more expression, more primal, yet sound, style and vitriol into a swing or crash of his bat than anybody else in any other line," enthused W. B. Hanna.[34] "A more determined athlete than Babe Ruth never lived," added Paul Gallico. "With a new record in sight he simply was bound to make it. Ruth is like that. He is one of the few utterly dependable news stories in sports. . . . Ruth lost no sleep over that 60th home run. He knew fate had it in the bag for him."[35] Even Joe Vila delivered Ruth a half-hearted tribute: "Ruth in return for his $70,000 salary, has played great ball this year. More power to him!"[36]

Ruth's timing remained impeccable. Not only had he broken his record on the final regularly scheduled game, but he also provided indispensable diversion from chaos in major league baseball.[37] As the season ended, a simmering conflict over gambling threatened to explode. Allegations surfaced against both Ty Cobb and Tris Speaker, two of the most prominent names in the game. Reluctant to take action against such high-profile players with immense popularity, baseball authorities tried to exonerate them quietly. Long-standing tensions, however, between Commissioner Landis and AL president Johnson upended efforts to negotiate a private settlement. Neither Johnson nor Landis wanted to punish the duo, but both maintained they held jurisdiction over the issue. Amid squabbling, the gambling allegations became public. On the day of Ruth's triumphant home run, the skirmish flared again, with Johnson branding Landis and Chicago White Sox owner Charles Comiskey "childish" for their refusal to work through his AL offices. The clash, warned the *Chicago Tribune*, promised a "winter of discontent," with threats of more allegations and tensions becoming public.[38]

As in 1920, Ruth cocooned baseball from unfolding scandal and corruption. The occasion of his record-breaking home run inspired W. O. McGeehan to review the Babe's contribution to rescuing baseball. Without explicitly drawing connections to dark clouds overhead related to the Cobb/Speaker affair, McGeehan recalled how in 1920 Ruth had revived baseball following the Black Sox scandal. "It has always been my contention that Babe Ruth pounded baseball back into popularity. There is no doubt as to the sincerity of Babe Ruth at bat."[39] And, once again, Ruth's "pounding" helped baseball move through the final stages of its struggle to establish new authority and tame chaos and corruption in its ranks.

Next stop for Ruth and the Yankees as they reached the peak of their combined powers was the World Series against the Pittsburgh Pirates. Mirroring the soaring US economy (with New York City sitting at its epicenter), the Yankees appeared invincible after a regular season of winning 110 and losing only 44 games. "The Yanks are entering the World Series as care free as a vegetable dinner," reported Ring Lardner covering his last World Series. "Whereas, on the other hand, the Pirates are nervous. If they ain't nervous, they ain't human."[40] Ruth's ghostwriter echoed Lardner's sentiment, although in Ruth's plainspoken language: "I believe we can beat the Pirates in the World Series. That, of course, is the natural thing for me to say—but I figure my opinion is backed up by the dope," he reported.[41]

The 1927 World Series proved a lopsided affair. The Yankees easily swept the Pirates. Ruth provided the only two home runs hit in the series. For the press, Yankees dominance was both a story line and a problem. "Unless something nerve tingling transpires pretty soon, several hundred inmates of the press section will be biting their telegraph operators in desperation," complained Damon Runyon.[42] Searching for the bright side, some journalists pointed to the series outcome as yet further proof that gambling, despite the upheaval over Speaker and Cobb, was on the wane in major league baseball. "The Yankees' sweep of the Pirates was welcomed by many as proof that, at least in this series both teams had played to win," concluded the *Literary Digest*.[43]

The newspaper media had another problem: a challenge to the dominance of their medium. By 1927 radio was no longer a novelty. A crowd of several thousand mobbed popular radio announcer Graham McNamee when he arrived in Pittsburgh.[44] Some fifty-three stations across the country carried McNamee's broadcast to an estimated twenty million listeners.[45] That week McNamee appeared on the cover of *Time* magazine. Again, print journalists registered annoyance at McNamee's lack of expertise (and no doubt his popularity). Sitting next to McNamee in the press box, Lardner complained, "was like attending a doubleheader. You saw one game and heard another."[46] Resistance to radio continued among both owners and sportswriters. No regular broadcasts of New York games were permitted until the 1930s; still, the future could not be denied. "Like Carl Sandberg's fog," acknowledged Ford Frick later, "radio slipped in on 'little cat's feet' before baseball and fans realized what was going on."[47] Concurrently, film also challenged newspapers. Footage from the opening games in Pittsburgh was airlifted 440 miles back to New York in time for evening viewing in Broadway theaters.

Earlier in the decade, newspapers had provided virtually the only conduit for information about sports. Closely tied financially to promoters and teams, sportswriters generally echoed the sentiments and positions of management. Individual athletes might be the focus of coverage, but they had limited ability to shape their public image. Even in the case of Babe Ruth this was true. Yet even as radio and film expanded, the new mediums offered few immediate opportunities for someone like Ruth to give an extended interview or present himself independently of the sports-writing establishment. Those developments were still decades away. What the public learned of Ruth and other athletes remained heavily filtered by the newspaper press.

"There are only two musketeers—Ruth and
Gehrig. And it ain't muskets, it's bats."

After the World Series, Ruth immediately launched another barnstorming tour. While the Babe ranked as the undeniable headliner, Lou Gehrig, Christy Walsh's new client, came aboard with much fanfare. The tour, beginning in Trenton, New Jersey, on October 12, covered almost the entire country from east to west. Some two hundred thousand fans witnessed the Ruth-Gehrig show over the course of the next month (major league baseball forbid any barnstorming after November 1). Fans could not get enough, and almost inevitably games ended prematurely with enthusiasts swarming fields. Keeping things simple (and profits in the pockets of Ruth and Gehrig), in each venue Walsh recruited amateur players to fill out teams headed by Ruth (the Bustin' Babes) and Gehrig (Larrupin' Lous). The tour climaxed in late October when thirty thousand fans gathered to see the pair in Los Angeles. Estimates had Ruth earning $100,000 on the tour.[48]

No sooner had Gehrig replaced Wally Pipp at first base on June 2, 1925, and become a Yankees starter for the next 2,130 consecutive games, than writers began celebrating the Ruth-Gehrig ("Babe and the Buster") partnership. For a time, at least, a real bond blossomed between the gregarious Ruth and his quiet star-struck sidekick. Yet the camaraderie was at least partly the creation of Walsh's public relations machine. Walsh aimed to capitalize on the relationship to build opportunities, such as the wildly successful barnstorming tour. The enterprising business agent no doubt sought to develop new talent as Ruth moved toward eventual retirement.

Sportswriters often emphasized the friendly competition between the two sluggers as inspiring Ruth to reach new highs as a hitter. In truth, batting in the lineup in front of a power hitter like Gehrig (who batted an average of .373 during the 1927 and 1928 seasons) forced pitchers to deal with rather than pitch around Ruth.

Most accounts also emphasized Ruth's role as mentor to and even protector of Gehrig. Writers took note of an incident in 1926 when Gehrig scuffled with Ty Cobb. Incensed, after the game Ruth marched into the Detroit Tigers locker room looking for a fight. He was ejected quickly, but the episode linked Ruth and Gehrig in the public's mind.[49] By 1928, a profile described Ruth as "proud of his young understudy and drags him before the public's eye as often as possible. Gehrig looks up to the Babe with all admiration that a boy might have for a champion."[50]

Still, in many descriptions of baseball's premier friendship, Ruth, although the seasoned veteran, appeared the less mature of the two. In ghostwritten columns for the Christy Walsh Syndicate, Gehrig credited his success to Ruth. He hailed the Babe as "a ball player's ball player," praising the slugger's generosity and talent.[51] In particular, however, Ruth provided an example of how not to conduct oneself. "The best advice I ever had in my life came from the Babe," confessed Lou to his readers. "'I've been pretty much of a sap in my day,' he said. 'I've played around a lot and I've wasted a lot of money . . . but I've learned something. I'm getting wise to myself at last.'"[52]

In contrast to Ruth, writers emphasized Gehrig's intellect. A 1927 *New York Times* profile celebrated "Columbia Lou's" Ivy League background. "Gehrig is the intelligent type of ballplayer, who knowing there must be some reason Babe Ruth is the home run king, sets out to find out what it is." While Ruth remained an influence, Gehrig "probably learns more from the Babe than the Babe, with the utmost painstaking, could ever teach him."[53] Educated, industrious, physically impressive, powerful at bat, Gehrig served up the precise mix major league baseball long had sought. Retiring AL president Ban Johnson, who once famously maligned Ruth as having the "mind of a 15-year-old," underscored this reality when he awarded "Columbia Lou" with the league's 1927 Most Valuable Player Award. Gehrig, Johnson pronounced, offered "a great example for the youth of today"; he respects umpires and "attends strictly to the business of baseball."[54] Risk averse to the point of meekness in his early playing years, Gehrig approached Yankees management with deference. After his brilliant 1927 season (forty-seven home runs with a batting average of .373), Gehrig assured Ruppert and Barrow he would not make "any unreasonable [contract] demands."[55] Indeed, in early 1928, Gehrig accepted Ruppert's first offer of $25,000 for three years. It was obvious that management preferred the cooperative Gehrig over Ruth. At one point after Gehrig obligingly accepted one of Ruppert's lowball contract offers, the colonel effusively praised his favorite player. "You are one of the few players who always does his work without a mummer. Since you've been with the club you've never given us a moment of worry. We always know who you are and what you will do."[56]

Still, Gehrig, despite his wholesomeness and power hitting, could not compete with the sheer charisma of Babe Ruth. As McGeehan acknowledged, Gehrig "never would be as colorful and as glamorous a figure in the game as the one and only Babe."[57] Together, however, the two nicely balanced each other, providing writers novel story lines and a bridge to a post-Ruth

future for baseball, a future without violence and rogue players. The reformed, tamed Ruth already had paved the way for Gehrig. "Iron Lou," in
his heroic steadiness and dependability, portended an orderly, stable future
for baseball.

In a sense, boxing, a sport plagued by even more disorder than baseball, had its own version of the Ruth-Gehrig dynamic. Boxer Jack Dempsey
shared similar physical features with Ruth (minus the Babe's natural warm
smile). A close friend of Ruth, Dempsey dominated boxing in the early 1920s. On September 23, 1926, however, upstart Gene Tunney defeated
champion Dempsey in Philadelphia before a record crowd of 120,000. A
year later, Tunney successfully defended his title at Chicago's Soldier Field in
the famed "Long Count" fight. Although the son of working-class Irish immigrants, Tunney had intellectual aspirations. He studied Shakespeare and
established a correspondence with Irish playwright George Bernard Shaw.
Like Gehrig, Tunney approached his sport from a "scientific" perspective.
He was no crude pugilist like his antagonist Dempsey, known as the "Manassa Mauler." Tunney's eagerness to establish his reputation as an intellectual,
such as when he appeared at Yale to deliver a guest lecture on Shakespeare,
drew ridicule from some sportswriters. Still, Tunney, like Gehrig, lent spectator sports a veneer of upper middle-class respectability and sophistication,
in contrast to the earthy, grassroots Ruth and Dempsey.[58] But unlike antago-
nists Dempsey and Tunney (who in actuality were friends), Ruth and Gehrig
were portrayed as pals, each complementing the other. Although the real
friendship between Gehrig and Ruth later unraveled, for a time Bugs Baer
appeared to have it right: "Dumas was all wrong about the 'Three Musketeers.' There are only two musketeers—Ruth and Gehrig. And it ain't mus-
kets, it's bats."[59]

"I'm no preacher"

As Ruth's career reached its pinnacle in the late 1920s, sportswriters more
than ever celebrated the slugger's altruism and dedication to youngsters. A
magazine profile told of how Ruth had disappeared suddenly in Chicago
during the 1927 barnstorming tour. From a "street address scribbled on a
pad," a concerned Lou Gehrig tracked down his partner. "He located Ruth
in a dingy bedroom of a Negro tenement telling a beaming little colored
cripple just how the Yankees won the last world series."[60] Ruth's ghostwriters
similarly played up his role as advocate for the nation's youth. He criticized
fans and players who argued with umpires for sending the wrong message

to children and women. "Occasionally," added the chivalrous Babe, "women like to sit in the bleachers too. But women don't dare go out there the way things are now. It's terrible."[61]

In his newspaper columns, Ruth increasingly fretted about the effect of urban street life on children, often citing his own gritty experiences growing up in Baltimore. The answer to such dilemmas—naturally—was baseball. "There's one thing about professional baseball," explained Ruth. "It's open to everyone. It doesn't take pull to get in, and it doesn't take money. All you've got to do is deliver the goods."[62] Protesting he was no "preacher" or "sermonizer," Ruth would then promote the national game as an antidote for troubled youth. "When a kid is playing baseball," Ruth explained, "he's getting good exercise and clean air and sunshine and he isn't batting around the street looking for trouble either."[63] Ruth proposed establishing a sandlot league to systematically address the problems facing urban youth. "I sort of wish there was some where we could take all the kids off the streets and say to them: 'Come on, kids, let's play a little baseball.'"[64]

Ruth's "I'm no preacher" columns and his later campaigning for Al Smith suggested aspirations to move beyond the confines of mere baseball celebrity. He now appeared interested in doing something with his celebrity. Undoubtedly, public relations drove some of those ambitions. Yet Ruth himself, described by one sportswriter as "besieged and beset wherever he goes from dawn till dusk by autograph hunters and those miscellaneous masses who rush in wherever crowds gather," unquestionably sought to forge a more durable public image for himself, especially as he realized his playing days would not continue in perpetuity.[65]

In moving toward the role of public advocate, Ruth struggled against lingering portrayals of him as an overgrown child, ruled by his passions rather than intellect. A *Collier's* magazine profile noted that Ruth "has long smarted under the imputations of light-worded sportswriters that he is not as bright as he might be."[66] Nor were sportswriters alone in casting such aspersions. At least two public intellectuals joined in. In 1926, Colgate University president George Barton Cutten, a prominent psychologist, published an influential book, *The Threat of Leisure*, sharply critiquing the increasing free time enjoyed by American workers. By any standards an elitist (and a eugenicist), Cutten condemned commercialized sports and other activities as "unproductive leisure."[67] Ruth, Cutten later complained, epitomized the problem with modern leisure and presented "a horrible example to the public." In response, sportswriter George Daley mounted a spirited defense of Ruth, but also noted the reformed hero's sordid past. "Ruth has learned his lesson by learning to control his impulses," concluded Daley. "He should be used as a good not a horrible example to college players."[68]

Sharing some of Cutten's chauvinisms, poet Carl Sandburg arrived in Florida for Yankees spring training in March 1928. His intent, according to Pegler, was to "write him a poem full of sarcasm about the Babe's intellect." Predictably, when Sandburg, writing for the Chicago *Daily News*, sat down with Ruth, things did not go well. Asked for five rules that might guide the youth of today, Ruth could only come up with three. Ruth balked when asked to identify his favorite verse from Shakespeare or the Bible. "A ball player doesn't have time to read. It isn't good for the eyes," protested Ruth. "The past doesn't interest the Babe. He is concentrated on the present hour," nor is he "strong on the classics," concluded the poet/journalist. Sandburg, announced one newspaper, "fanned Ruth in 750 words."[69]

Aroused, the populist-minded Pegler, writing for the rival *Chicago Tribune*, took on Sandburg. "What's the idea . . . of asking Mr. Ruth such questions? You know he will never get his bat off his shoulder against that kind of question," Pegler complained. The poet/journalist had a simplistic agenda of attacking "moron hero worship and dusting off an idol." Sandburg was little more than an "embittered" elitist "who wears suspenders and tried to be an outfielder but gave it up to write poems that don't rhyme."[70] Ruth, however, could take little comfort in Pegler's rebuttal, which left him still wearing the dunce cap. Meanwhile, lampooning Ruth's intellectual acumen remained a favorite device for some writers. A year after Sandburg's piece, Lardner published a short satire in *Collier's*, imaging fellow Baltimoreans Ruth and H. L. Mencken as boyhood friends who "used to take long walks in the woods together looking for odd flora."[71]

"The cripples came through"*

Debates about Ruth's intellect would persist. Yet in 1928, few could deny that Ruth was reaching novel career heights. That season represented Ruth's finest as a player and as a team leader. The Yankees began the season dominant. By July 1, the defending World Series champions led the American League by thirteen and a half games. Writers again faced the prospect of mining drama from a season whose outcome appeared predetermined. Richards Vidmer warned the Yankees were making a "joke out of the league."[72] The

* Ruth, "Babe Ruth Says," *Evening World* (New York), October 10, 1928.

previous year, the more competitive National League had outpaced that of the American League in attendance. The Yankees, complained one newspaper, "ruined the season financially for some clubs."[73] The new season threatened to see a repeat of a season absent of drama.

After July, however, things changed dramatically for the Yankees. Injuries plagued the defending World Series champions; then, in September, New York pitcher Urban Shocker died suddenly of heart failure. Ruth, struggling with a variety of ailments, slumped. As the Yankees slid, the Philadelphia Athletics surged. By September, the Yankees and Athletics ran neck and neck. Expectant Yankees fans desperately looked to Ruth. Tremendous pressure built on the ailing star. The *New York American* captioned a huge photograph of Ruth with an urgent appeal for action: "Please Mr. Ruth, do what you're thinking. If we ever needed that big stick, we need it now—every loyal citizen is looking to you to do your stuff. . . . Up and at 'em kid!"[74] Ruth himself promised action. "One of these days," he assured a reporter, "we're all going to snap out of it and when we do it's going to be a terrible thing for those other fellows."[75]

Mid-September saw a dramatic four-game series between the Yankees and Athletics. In a doubleheader in front of a record eighty-five thousand rabid spectators, New York reclaimed first place by taking both games. The next day, Ruth drove a home run to break a 3–3 tie and win the third game for his team. "It was the Ruth, the whole Ruth and nothing but the Ruth at Yankee stadium yesterday," penned Vidmer. "The Babe stepped out of a storybook and with one colossal clout broke a tie score . . . and the Athletics hearts."[76] Marshall Hunt echoed the acclaim. "George Herman Ruth, the most magnetic protagonist of them all, the illustrious, the incomparable Bambino, crashed a home run among the addicts in the right field terraces in the furious eighth inning, and single handed, crushed the Philadelphia Athletics again."[77]

Next stop was the World Series, pitting the Yankees against the St. Louis Cardinals. Commentary focused on Ruth's health and age. Pegler, for one, could not resist "the temptation to speculate gloomily on the nature and duration of [Ruth's] future."[78] A recurring knee injury surfaced. Ruth's status for the series was unclear. Hunt, however, assured readers Ruth would come through. "Crippled, ailing and worried, the incomparable Bambino still is the great dramatist, the flamboyant protagonist who incessantly makes suckers of skeptics and boobs of doubters," insisted

Hunt.[79] Yankees injuries thus provided writers a minicomeback story line for the series.

Clearly playing in discomfort, Ruth obligingly supported the back against the odds narrative. Appearing like a "decrepit turtle going uphill toward a soup cannery," wrote one writer, Ruth still managed to run out a series of hits in the first game "with the agility of eight starving antelopes on their way to an alfalfa patch."[80] Hunt fronted his column proclaiming, "Read how Babe Ruth, the sick, hobbling, washed-up Bambino (pardon a giggle), made only three hits, two of them doubles and scored two runs."[81] Reports that "the Sacbeth of Smack not only wasn't feeling any too sprightly," added Damon Runyon, proved premature. "Behold the Babe then walking up to his old saucer, or plate unassisted and knocking out two doubles and a single for himself."[82]

The series climax and perhaps the apex of Ruth's career came in game four in St. Louis when Ruth smashed three home runs, delivering the Yankees a series sweep. "That pale and trembling invalid, Mr. Babe Ruth, achieved something in the way of a convalescence out in the open air and summer sunglow this afternoon," reported Pegler in understated terms designed to contrast with the hyperbole pouring from other sportswriters.[83]

As Ruth crushed the Cardinals, anger among some St. Louis fans poured over into violence. Rowdyism in the stands, considered a thing of the past, suddenly reared its head. Disgruntled spectators began flinging bottles, wadded newspapers, and programs onto the field, some clearly aimed at Ruth. Rather than protesting or lashing out, Ruth "non-chalantly tossed the bottles to one side," then returned the ugliness with "his widest grin." So sportsmanlike was Ruth to his "attackers" that he finally "made them get up and give him a hand."[84] It was, recounted one sportswriter, a "great example of mob control." Frequent Ruth critic McGeehan waxed, "That man has amazing hidden resources and produces the proper solutions at what is familiarly known as the psychological moment."[85] Effusive praise for Ruth flowed from sportswriters. If there remained, wrote James R. Harrison of the *New York Times*, "anywhere in this broad land any misguided souls who believed that Babe Ruth was not the greatest living ball player, they should have seen him today." Ruth remained, in Harrison's account, "the play boy of baseball," but he had clearly achieved something exceptional.[86] An alleged source of disorder only a few seasons before, Ruth now, through the force of his personality, begot harmony and peace.

"Hurrah for the Yankees and Al Smith"

Sailing astride a tidal wave of accolades and fame enjoyed by no other athlete in American history, Ruth, surprisingly, embraced politics, injecting himself directly into the 1928 presidential campaign. In the public eye for over a decade, Ruth had befriended a number of politicians. In the early 1920s, he visited the White House several times as guest of Republican president Warren G. Harding. In 1924, Ruth "covered" the Democratic national convention as a special correspondent for the Christy Walsh syndicate. His ghostwriter found some amusement in the notion of a celebrity home-run hitter as a political reporter: "Here comes Will Rogers and Rube Goldberg. It looks like all us writers are on the job today." Still, Ruth and Washington Senators pitcher Nick Altrock, who also attended the convention, made their political preference very clear. Before arriving at Madison Square Garden for the convention, Ruth and Altrock met with New York governor Al Smith, then a contender for the Democratic nomination. Ruth already had met Smith several times and was a supporter. At the convention, he presented the governor with an autographed bat, instructing him to use it to "knock in" the Democratic nomination. "He's a human fellow alright," reported Ruth in the column, adding that Smith preferred to talk baseball over politics.[87]

Four years later, Smith's nomination as standard bearer for the Democratic Party drew Ruth further into the political arena. "Congratulations on the good judgment of the Democratic Party. Their selection assures us that public opinion demands a good president," Ruth telegrammed Smith after his fellow New Yorker's nomination at the Houston, Texas, convention.[88] From there the Babe led several other Yankees, including Lou Gehrig, in urging voters to support Smith.

Ruth's interest in politics, given his image as painted by sportswriters and others, seemed out of character. One might surmise he felt an affinity for a fellow Roman Catholic and New Yorker. As Ruth stressed, like himself, Smith emerged from a rough-and-tumble urban background to make good for himself. Never a teetotaler, Ruth also undoubtedly appreciated Smith's opposition to Prohibition, as did the Babe's boss, Ruppert, a prominent beer brewer. Whatever spurred Ruth, his support for Smith was no passing fancy. The Babe was outspoken. Given the deep cultural chasms surrounding the election, Ruth also brazenly jeopardized his marketability in diving headfirst into the divisive campaign of 1928, fraught with strong feelings on all sides. In a sense, Ruth's vocal support perhaps, consciously or unconsciously, presented a rejoinder to his frequent depiction as a man of limited interests and cerebral capacity, a way of striking back at the Carl Sandbergs of the world.

The complications of taking a political stand surfaced in early September 1928 when Republican presidential candidate Herbert Hoover arrived at Yankee Stadium to enjoy an afternoon of baseball and possibly get a picture with Babe Ruth. "Nothing doing; I'm for Al Smith," snapped Ruth when asked to pose with Hoover. The Babe's friendship with the late president Harding and his general affability perhaps led Hoover supporters to believe Ruth might be more amenable. But the Babe well understood the implications of posing with Hoover: a photograph of the candidate and the baseball hero, a prominent Catholic and New Yorker, would do Hoover no harm and perhaps some real good among urban ethnics, Smith's constituency. Ruth's refusal generated a brief media squall. Had he been disrespectful? Walsh immediately stepped in, eager to protect the Ruth brand. There had been a "misunderstanding," Ruth quickly explained. He would happily pose with the Republican nominee and looked forward to meeting him. Still, Ruth made clear he would be supporting Smith.[89] Later, Ruth patriotically vowed to do anything for Hoover—except vote for him.[90]

During the 1928 World Series, nine pro-Smith Yankees, led by Ruth, posed for a photograph. In uniform, joined by a batboy, each Yankee clutched a bat with a letter attached. Together the pinstripers spelled out "For Al Smith." A serious-looking Ruth stood in the foreground. The picture, featured in newspapers around the country, also appeared in a poster entitled "Champions of Al Smith," alongside photographs of other Smith supporters from the sports world, including Knute Rockne, Gene Tunney, and New York Giants manager John McGraw.

Immediately following his World Series triumph, Ruth turned more seriously to campaigning for Smith. As the Yankees departed St. Louis, sent off by a crowd of enthusiastic and forgiving Cardinals fans, a cry from the team's "special train" could be heard: "Hurrah for the Yankees and Al Smith!"[91] The train then chugged across the central Midwest, stopping at stations along the way. Hysterical crowds gathered even in the middle of the night to catch a glimpse of Ruth and the victorious Yankees. In towns like Mattoon, Illinois, and Terre Haute, Indiana, Ruth emerged in the dead of night to deliver spirited short orations for Smith. Later accounts claim Ruth appeared at several of the whistle-stops in his undershirt or hoisting a pitcher of beer or bottle of whiskey.[92] Contemporary reports include no such references, although the Yankees, having come back from near-collapse at the end of the regular season, were in a mood to celebrate. Ruth later claimed he received some seven thousand telegrams praising his vocal support for Smith, and only two hundred denouncing his foray into politics.[93]

Upon arrival in New York, Ruth, Gehrig, Yankees manager Miller Huggins (sometimes identified as a Hoover supporter), and team owner Colonel Ruppert made a beeline to Al Smith's Biltmore Hotel suite. Surrounded by throngs of photographers and reporters, Smith and Ruth made awkward conversation.

"By gosh, you're the champion of all," marveled Smith.

"No I ain't, you are," responded Ruth.

If only "kids would holler" for me "the way they holler for you," Smith advanced, he would be sure to be elected president.

"Everyone, young and old is hollering for you," Ruth assured Smith.[94] Cameras clicked, producing photographs that appeared in newspapers around the country.

Ruth and Gehrig then mobilized their barnstorming tour again, but this time politics barnstormed with them. At every opportunity, the two wore "Vote for Al Smith" buttons. Eager to capitalize on Ruth's popularity, the Smith campaign arranged for Ruth to deliver a nationwide radio address on behalf of their candidate on October 19. Sticking to familiar terrain, Ruth explained that as a boy he had admired Theodore Roosevelt, "a lover of sport." Smith, he continued, was today's Theodore Roosevelt. "The other day, I took a ride down to Oliver Street in New York City to look at the little two-by-four house that Governor Smith was born in," Ruth told listeners. "It reminded me of my own two-by-four home in Baltimore." He and Smith represented democracy in action: "There is a chance for everyone to get to the top in America—whether he wants to be president or a ball player." Ambassador John W. Davis, the 1924 Democratic candidate, then followed Ruth with a more substantive address stressing Smith as a "statesman."[95] Davis and Ruth later addressed an "uproarious" rally together in Louisville. When a "flimsy" chair in which he sat on stage collapsed, Ruth grabbed a railing to save himself from falling, much to the crowd's amusement. Ruth then waved a brown derby (symbol of the Smith campaign) to calm the assemblage. The New York governor, he told the southern crowd, resembled a ballplayer who "delivers the goods." As in the sporting world, "a clean fighter always wins public esteem regardless of petty prejudices," insisted Ruth, referencing popular reservations regarding Smith's Roman Catholicism.[96]

By 1928 Ruth had plenty of public speaking experience. Surviving film and audio clips reveal a deep, assertive voice matched by a familiar but impressive presence. He could "orate with the best of them," noted a 1928 magazine profile. "He is probably the best extemporaneous talker in sports, a fact that might surprise some people."[97] Indeed, Ruth's public image of a man-child power-hitter hardly meshed with the figure who showed up to speak before civic organizations and youth groups across the country. Few examples of Ruth's public talks were preserved. A star athlete born several decades later would have access to television, film, and much-expanded radio outlets. Without the filter of newspaper sportswriters, Ruth would have had greater control in shaping his own image and public profile.

Ruth's strong speaking voice and obvious charisma certainly aided the Smith campaign, yet stories later turned up depicting Ruth as a mixed blessing. A story that possibly surfaced during the campaign, but was retold repeatedly later, had Yankees second baseman Tony Lazzeri paired with Ruth for a radio broadcast supporting Smith. After his address, Ruth supposedly turned to Lazzeri and asked, "Now Tony, who are the Whops going to vote for?" Lazzeri appears to have been present for the broadcast, but contemporary accounts make no references to any such comments.[98] Another "legend" has a cheering Terre Haute, Indiana, crowd turning suddenly silent when Ruth mentioned Al Smith. "The hell with you then!" Ruth was supposed to have responded.[99] Like the Lazzeri tale, this story, too, appears apocryphal. Both fit well the vulgar Ruth image often seen in sports coverage. One could easily imagine Hoover supporters using such accounts to negate the impact of the strong pro-Smith stance taken by America's top sports hero.

Ruth's vigorous foray into politics in 1928 stands as unique among American sports stars. Never had or has a sports figure near Ruth's level (not that there have been many) taken such a strong and vocal stand for a political cause. Michael Jordan, for instance, whose basketball career matched many of the heights of Ruth's work with the Yankees, avoided politics assiduously, concerned with protecting his broad commercial appeal.[100] Why Ruth would risk alienating potential customers remains something of a wonder. That the Babe reportedly did not vote in the 1928 election, nor any election until 1944, deepens the mystery.

Ruth, by his own testimony, saw a kindred soul in Governor Smith. Certainly Ruth showed loyalty to his friends, and the Babe clearly considered the governor as among his friends, although their level of intimacy remains unclear. His campaign for Smith also allowed Ruth to paint himself as something more than a tremendous athlete with a tireless dedication to children's causes. Even when he denied knowing anything about this "tariff stuff," as he put it, his political activity suggested a depth rarely if ever seen in the media accounts of his highs and lows on and off the baseball diamond. The Smith campaign allowed Ruth an opportunity to counter lingering impressions, to which he himself had occasionally contributed, that "he is not as bright as he might be."[101]

Despite his on-field triumphs, the plague of injuries and woes suffered by Ruth in 1928 also served as a reminder that his career as a player had arced. Whenever asked, Ruth was clear that his future ambitions involved managing a baseball team, preferably the Yankees. His reputation as unruly, less than intellectual, and undisciplined, however, imperiled such hopes. Associating himself with statesmen, especially a statesman favored by Yankees owner Jacob Ruppert and millions of New Yorkers, seemed a good step toward projecting the image of a new, more mature Ruth. A decade's worth of work by American sportswriters, however, would prove difficult to overcome.

EIGHT. "FAIR ENOUGH IN TIMES LIKE THESE"

Even as he entered the twilight of his playing career, Ruth continued to captivate. His contract negotiations remained matters of public fascination and springboards for broader discussions of the nation's economic potency (or lack thereof). Likewise, although his athletic prowess waned, Ruth's mastery of the dramatic moment never left him, as he proved in the 1932 World Series with his "called shot" home run. Into the 1930s, he remained the most celebrated figure in the sports world. Still, despite an ever-growing list of heroic baseball feats, his public image remained essentially frozen. Reporters persisted in treating him as an eccentric figure: the talented, alluring, overgrown adolescent who never grew up.

Ruth's long-articulated, fondest hope was to transition into a team manager, preferably with his Yankees, but certainly somewhere in major league baseball. Yankees leadership, however, bore deep resentment toward Ruth, still viewing him as a source of potential disorder and a threat to its control. The 1930 contract negotiations left lingering bitterness on both sides: Ruth felt yet again that he had failed to get his due, while Barrow and Ruppert fumed at Ruth's pointed jabs about baseball's exploitative labor system. When the Yankees managerial job opened in 1929 and 1930, Ruth was deemed far too independent-minded and unreliable to be trusted as a member of the establishment.

"Let her stay dead. That's all I've got to ask."

After the Yankee's crushing of the Cardinals and Herbert Hoover's crushing of Al Smith in 1928, Ruth returned to his off-season routine, centered on his home life with girlfriend Claire Hodgson and workouts at Artie McGovern's

Manhattan gym. Now in his midthirties, Ruth found it increasingly difficult to keep off weight and remain in condition, although he continued to throw himself with gusto into his workouts. In early January 1929, a *Daily News* reporter visiting the gym commented on the "unknown and probably occult power" McGovern held over Ruth, appearing like a "hippopotamus" who "roars and grunts as several drivers or beaters [presumably McGovern's gym attendants] went at him."[1]

Days later, the odd merriment at the gym came to a sudden end. On January 14, 1929, startling headlines blared: "Love Nest Fire Kills Mrs Babe Ruth," "Mrs Ruth Dies in Fire, Her Secret Romance Bared," "The 'Perfect' Romance That Ended in Lost Love and Tragic Death," "Mrs. Ruth's Brother Blames Her Death on Opium." Helen Woodford Ruth, married to the Babe at the tender age of sixteen when the ballplayer himself was but nineteen, had succumbed in a house fire in the Boston area. She had been living with (and sometimes presenting herself as the wife of) a local dentist named Edward Kinder. When revealed as the wife of baseball's greatest hero, the sensationalistic media of the day pounced. Questions whirled: Had Kinder been involved in the death? Was it possible the Babe had some connection? Where was the young Ruth daughter? What exactly had become of the home-run hero's marriage? More so than any previous scandal, the death of Helen bore the potential to thoroughly derail Ruth. For the burgeoning tabloid press, Helen's death had everything: celebrity, inferences of drug use, illicit sex— even the possibility of murder. Almost immediately the story exploded and spiraled beyond control.

From New York, Ruth and Christy Walsh scrambled to contain the damage. "Regardless of the terrible circumstances I am deeply grieved at the death of Mrs. Ruth," explained Walsh. "She was a grand little woman and her devotion to Babe especially in some of his past difficulties was a beautiful example of loyalty."[2] Ruth immediately distanced himself from the evolving scandal. He and Helen had been separated for three years, he confessed to the press. "During that time I have seldom met her and I have done all that I can to comply with her wishes."[3] Ruth's timeline, in fact, placed his separation with Helen at right about the time in 1925 that the press published revelations about Claire Hodgson and the Babe. Initially, Ruth's assurances failed to quell the story. Reporters descended on Boston to sift through evidence; rumors bred more rumors. One report had Helen as an opium addict. Her grieving sisters meanwhile pointed fingers at Claire Hodgson, with whom Ruth in fact was cohabitating.[4] Other stories had Helen Ruth demanding

$100,000 in return for a divorce. Meanwhile, Helen's brothers and mother inferred the death was no accident: it was foul play. That Dr. Kinder, the dentist who posed as Helen's husband, disappeared following the fatal fire cast a dark twist on events.[5]

As the story took over the headlines, a clearly shaken Ruth arrived in the Boston area for the funeral. He appeared inconsolable, stunned by grief and shock. Reporters may have wanted a story, but there was little interest in indicting Ruth, the popular symbol of the national sport. New York reporters certainly understood that Ruth's marriage was over and that he had little contact with Helen. For all practical matters, he was married to Hodgson. Reports thus focused on Ruth's grief and innocence. Arriving in Boston, one account explained, Ruth immediately made his way to St. Cecilia's Church in the Back Bay area for 9:00 am mass. "Head bowed" throughout the service, Ruth could be seen visibly "fingering his big brown rosary which has numerous relics from the Shrine of St. Ann de Beaupre enclosed on cross."[6]

The following day, Ruth called a press conference. Reporters, "sympathetic . . . but inquisitive, professionally, seeking to search beyond the arc of the spotlight into the personal life of the man and in doing so causing the broad-shouldered fellow to lay bare his very heart," circled Ruth. "With red-rimmed eyes and quivering chin," Ruth struggled with his emotions. "Please let my wife alone!" he pleaded. "Let her stay dead. That's all I've got to ask." Then Ruth's "jaw squared, the head came up. Words sharp and decisive as though each syl'able had been clipped off short came from his lips" in "firm decisive tones." Taking command of the conference, Ruth proceeded calmly and lucidly to address questions about the circumstances of his marriage and separation.[7]

Ruth clearly had the backing of the assembled reporters. Quickly the story deflated, aided by the appearance of Dr. Kinder with a solid alibi and official reports that the fire in which Helen perished resulted from improper electrical wiring. Likewise, the Ruth daughter surfaced, safe and sound, at a nearby boarding school. Helen's family pulled back, after initially casting aspersions everywhere. They offered their support for Ruth, whom Helen's brother asserted was "always friendly and so far as I know, he has always done the right thing."[8]

Reports from Helen's funeral and snowy burial fell back on the old Ruth-as-overwhelmed-youth trope. Accounts emphasized Ruth's near unrestrained grief. He sobbed openly several times during Helen's funeral and internment. Photographs of the burial in subfreezing temperatures revealed

Ruth's enormous face furrowed in grief. Virtually every report depicted Ruth as an emotionally devastated youth. "The big fellow whom Boston knows so well, resembled a grief shattered school boy who had lost everything for which he had to live," explained one account.[9] Another writer described Ruth collapsing on Helen's casket: "Babe Ruth, the swaggering, smiling, baseball idol, became a crushed and broken child of sorrow at midnight tonight, collapsing with a low moan at the bier of the woman who once shared his triumphs and his disappointments."[10]

The combined effect absolved Ruth, whose extramarital relations, both casual and sincere, were well-known to the journalists covering him. Ruth, a childlike innocent, shattered by sadness, stood apart from the scandal. Within days, the story completely dropped from newspapers. The distressing aspects of the story fell more on the shoulders of Helen. The Babe emerged largely unscathed from the episode, although it reinforced impressions he was more of a boy than a man in control of his fate. His personal life appeared seriously disordered, but Ruth, a well-meaning, emotional man-child, could hardly be blamed. At the end of January, the Babe left early for spring training in Florida.

Three months after Helen's death, Ruth married Claire, a widow with a young daughter. That Ruth had essentially lived with Ms. Hodgson and her family for several years was well understood and silently accepted within the sports world. Only when Ruth brazenly took on Yankees management in 1925 did their relationship briefly become public. Once Ruth capitulated to Huggins and Barrow, Hodgson immediately regained her anonymity. Now she could safely emerge as the new Mrs. Ruth.

To avoid publicity, the two wedded at 6:30 am mass at St. Gregory the Great in Manhattan on opening day of the 1929 season (crowds in the thousands still gathered when word got out about the ceremony). Afterward, the newlyweds enjoyed a simple breakfast wedding reception. The next day (the previous day's game canceled due to rain) Ruth shot off to Yankee Stadium, where he hit an opening day home run for Claire. "Only to the Mr. Ruths of this life do the Gods give the gift of keeping promises to blushing brides," marveled Damon Runyon.[11] If Ruth slumps in July, suggested Yankees owner Ruppert, somewhat flippantly, "I know what he can do then—have him get married again."[12]

The sad events of January were absent from all press accounts of the wedding. Helen and her unhappy life and death were all forgotten. "I'm happy to-day and I guess I should be—a new wife, a nice home run to start the season and the Yankees winning their opener. You can't beat that, can you?" waxed Ruth's ghostwriter.[13]

Since their first meeting in 1924, Claire had provided a stabilizing force in Ruth's life. In an age before star athletes had staffs to meet their every need and aggressively promote their interests, Claire and Christy Walsh (who was not strictly a sports agent) provided Ruth some basic support. On the surface a glitzy showgirl, Claire, in fact, managed a household that included two brothers, a widowed mother, and her daughter, supporting them all on her modeling and stage career. Once married, Claire became an ever-greater and ever-more public force in Ruth's life. Intensely protective of her husband, the new Mrs. Ruth afforded him essential professional counsel alongside much-needed emotional support.

Operating in the almost exclusively male domain of professional base-ball, however, Claire's aggressive promotion and her outspokenness about her role (that of her husband's self-proclaimed "manager and secretary") alienated many in baseball. Claire stridently opined that when it came to the national game, she knew "about as much about it as anyone off the dia-mond. . . . Sometimes by the way they perform, I think I know as much as the players." Her main job, Claire Ruth vociferously explained, was to safe-guard the Babe from both others and himself. Her frank and insistent sup-port and willingness to challenge gender norms well solidified in the male sports world reinforced impressions of Ruth's immaturity. "He takes orders beautifully," she told an interviewer.[14] The Babe appeared the bear cub, now protected by an aggressive mother bear.

Two months into the marriage, Ruth fell seriously ill. Claire immediately confined him to their apartment and handled the press. She told reporters how she personally had to prevent Ruth from risking his health and going to Yankee Stadium. He "would have all his friends here, too, if I hadn't set my foot down. Rest and keeping away from excitement are all he needs," she ex-plained.[15] Seeking some privacy in which to recover, the Ruths then slipped out of the city by automobile to a secret location. Days later, to Mrs. Ruth's chagrin, reporters found the two vacationing in Maryland, where Ruth was greatly improved to the point that he was fishing in Chesapeake Bay.[16]

Opinionated and candid, Claire Ruth rarely shied from defending her hus-band or taking credit for his supposed reformation. The Babe's turnaround, of course, was never as dramatic as portrayed and was long underway be-fore Hodgson's marriage to Ruth. But the effect of such an aggressive part-ner, especially given Ruth's more accommodating nature, served to further infantilize the Babe. Walsh, Ruth's business partner and the other essential Ruth insider, also frequently took credit for Ruth's successes in such a manner as to diminish his client. Ruth, Walsh explained in a 1929 interview, had essentially gone broke some five years earlier. The impulsive slugger supposedly recklessly tore through $100,000, much of it at the racetrack. Seizing control of the situation, Walsh insisted Ruth establish a trust fund. He had to explain the whole concept twice before Ruth understood it. "Grumbling," the Babe signed on and saved himself financially. But Ruth remained economically reckless. "There is a side to Ruth that businessmen will have difficulty understanding," Walsh told the interviewer. "He is not a businessman, not in any sense of the word." Instead, understanding Ruth's propensities, Walsh permitted the Babe to spend the profits on his considerable savings, or "there would be no fun in saving." Gehrig, a more balanced, educated sort, invested his earnings in New York real estate, Walsh added.[17] Emphasizing Ruth's profligate spending and lack of financial acumen, of course, well served those such as Ruppert and Barrow, who saw as wasteful the supposedly large salaries demanded by reckless star athletes such as Ruth.

"You can't manage yourself, Ruth"

After his June illness, Ruth managed to return to the Yankees, but he and the team struggled through the remainder of the 1929 season. The world champion Yankees, Ed Barrow later explained, "began to wear out."[18] Manager Miller Huggins, a small, wiry, intense man, seemed to internalize the team's struggles. In September, he fell seriously ill, and quickly his condition turned grave. Since their clash in 1925, Huggins and Ruth had developed a strong working relationship. Ruth and the entire team were shaken by the grave illness. News of Huggins's death arrived on September 25, 1929, in the middle of a game against the Boston Red Sox. The team reeled. Barrow himself fell ill under the strain of losing Huggins.

Coach Art Fletcher took over the dispirited team for its remaining few games. When offered the permanent manager's job, however, Fletcher demurred, fearing its impact on his own dubious health. Barrow and Ruppert pursued other options, but each fell through. Meanwhile Ruth, long interested in the job, began jockeying for the position. To observers, Ruth seemed the moral center of the Yankees. "Despite the presence of three coaches," reported Arthur Mann of the New York *Evening World*, "Babe Ruth is leading the Yankees." The shattered team looked to "Ruth as wandering sheep harken to the bell carrier. Ruth is a man today awakened to the responsibilities which the passing years thrust upon us," wrote Mann.[19] The Babe "appeared the logical successor" to Huggins, wrote *New York Times* columnist John Drebinger.[20]

Yet Yankees upper management resisted with all its might. Despite his recent cooperative conduct, memories of Ruth's defiance remained fresh. The deluge of eulogies to Huggins rarely failed to cite the manger's 1925 disciplining of Ruth for "misconduct off the field" as a high point of Huggins's career. Memories of Ruth's existential threat to the team and to baseball lingered. Neither Barrow nor Ruppert would consider Ruth for the manager's post, either in 1929 or at any other point.[21]

The Yankees administration, however, hardly wished to convey those sentiments outright to Ruth, who remained a fan favorite and a unifying force on the team. Seeking to make his case, Ruth again traveled to the Ruppert brewery, this time to petition for the job of player-manager. In Ruppert's eleventh-floor office suite, Ruth explained how he knew the game inside and out. Having played from each vantage point, he could easily relate to both pitchers and hitters. He was, he insisted, ready for the manager's job. Ruppert, however, remained unmoved. Looking rather sadly at his star player, he issued a cutting line that no doubt originated with Barrow (who often used it in reference to Ruth): "You can't manage yourself, Ruth. How do you expect to manage others?" The Babe absorbed the slight and protested that he had changed; if not he would never have survived in the game. His triumph over obstacles was not a liability; rather it was an asset that could be shared with young players. Faced with Ruth's passion, Ruppert pretended to relent and asked for time to consider Ruth's candidacy. Ruth left the brewery hopeful. After several days of hearing nothing from Ruppert, however, Ruth picked up the newspaper to find his team had named Bob Shawkey, a former Yankees pitcher, as the new manager.[22]

Humiliated by management, Ruth yet again pledged loyalty to the team and sought to salvage future opportunities to manage the Yankees. "Frankly I have the ambition to manage a big league ball club someday and I hope it doesn't sound conceited to say I think I have the ability and experience to and sufficient knowledge to qualify as a manager," Ruth announced in a public statement issued by Walsh. But he and Ruppert mutually "agreed that as long as I can deliver the goods as a player it would not be wise to take on the troubles and worries of a managership." He vowed allegiance to Bob Shawkey, the new Yankees manager, and promised to get back in shape—"no vaudeville, no movies, no monkey business" off season (a considerable financial sacrifice). Still, he made clear his ultimate ambition: "But don't forget someday I hope to realize a great ambition by having my name listed in a manager's column along with one of the greatest in baseball history—Miller Huggins."[23] The graceful and diplomatic statement allowed Ruth to save face. It also aimed to signal patience, maturity, and determination to Yankees management. Ruppert and Barrow, however, had no intention of tapping Ruth for the top Yankees job. Instead they strung their superstar along, continuing to profit from his skills and remarkable popularity while determined that the team's future would not include Ruth. No matter how much Ruth might act like an adult, management continued to view him as a child.

"I have lost every salary argument I ever had"

In public, Ruth played along with the line that he had "eliminated himself" for the managerial slot.[24] In private, he seethed. Although the highest-paid player in baseball, Ruth always nursed a sense he was not paid his real worth. He fully understood fans came to ballparks largely to see him. When injured or unable to play, attendance fell, sometimes dramatically. Likewise, the Yankees played more exhibition games than any other team. Ruth's presence at these thirty games or so drew throngs to ballparks. Yet he appears to have been paid no extra for the exhibitions.[25] Unlike in 1927, when many including his agent felt he settled for too little, Ruth determined to challenge Ruppert and Barrow in 1930. Even before Ruth was passed over for the Yankees manager job, he and the Yankees began exchanging jabs. In Florida during 1929 spring training, Ruth declared himself "underpaid." The Yankees, he claimed, had made enough in the 1928 series with the Athletics to pay his salary for several years. Next time around, he would insist on $100,000. For his part, Ruppert swore he would never pay such a sum and vowed to offer only a one-year contract next time around.[26]

By early 1930, Ruth was more resolute than ever. In January he sat down with Barrow and Ruppert. The atmosphere was tense. The Yankees had offered to renew Ruth's contract at $70,000, the rate from his 1927 contract.

"You don't like your contract?" began Ruppert in a stern manner perhaps designed to intimidate Ruth.

"No I do not," Ruth responded flatly. He acknowledged that $70,000 might be a lot of money, but it did not represent what he was worth. He simply "wasn't being paid in proportion to the number of people [he] was drawing." He reminded Ruppert of the Yankee's extensive exhibition schedule for which he received no added compensation.

Growing impatient, the brewery mogul asked what Ruth considered a fair contract. Ruth's response: $100,000, the figure Ruth had quoted repeatedly in public. Surprisingly, Ruppert appeared stunned. Ruth, he blurted out, must be crazy. Shaken by the ingratitude, Ruppert abruptly ended the conference, saying he would not discuss the matter further that day. The two met again several times in January. Ruppert eventually countered with a two-year offer totaling $150,000. Ruth insisted on three years at $85,000 per annum.[27] They remained deadlocked.

While dropping his demands from $100,000, Ruth vocally rejected the Yankees counteroffer. Now in his midthirties and suffering frequent injuries, Ruth understood this would be the last contract negotiations where he held the upper hand. "I have lost every salary argument I ever had. I was always the one to back up," he insisted. "Now it's the club's turn to give some ground. I'm standing pat." As Ruth took his stand, other "ambitious players" watched carefully. At a time when $20,000 was considered an excellent salary (other than Ruth, in 1929 only one Yankee, Lou Gehrig, earned over $20,000), many hoped a rising tide, despite increasingly ominous economic times, might lift all boats.[28]

For the first time in his career as a Yankee, Ruth was now a holdout. Desperate for leverage, he worked to mobilize public opinion. As in 1927, he dispatched a "fac-simile" of a letter affixed with his signature to newspapers all over the country (although this time pointedly not to Yankees headquarters). Short of an equitable settlement, Ruth threatened, he would retire. Baseball's contractual system left him with no other choice (a point he also had made during the 1927 negotiations). In fact, he was unique in having a choice. Most players, Ruth explained, are "obliged to sign at any terms" for a simple reason: "bread and butter." But, having put aside large amounts of his earnings, Ruth had "enough bread and butter in our home" to assure $25,000 a year income. "A few years ago I could not take this attitude," he asserted, for like 95 percent of players, he needed the money. Baseball's discriminatory system essentially coerced him into taking what he was offered. No longer was that the case, at least for Ruth.[29]

Indicting baseball in general for coercive labor practices hardly endeared Ruth to his employers. "We are not interested and we have nothing to say," bristled Barrow when asked about Ruth's missive. "Everyone in baseball has told us we have been most fair. . . . It is my opinion that Ruth has been badly advised," added Ruppert.[30] The entire organization, insisted the Yankees front office, had assumed substantial risk purchasing Ruth at such steep rates. Indeed, the team "should be examined" for having invested so heavily in such a risky prospect, he continued. Ruppert and the Yankees had taken a chance when they secured Ruth (and other high-profile players they acquired). Yet the Yankees had profited spectacularly from their investment.[31]

Sportswriters largely dismissed Ruth's letter and his campaign for higher compensation. John Kieran found the "ultimatum" to be "humorous."[32] Few took Ruth's threat to retire seriously. "Deep down in this boy's heart," wrote columnist Herold C. Burr, "he knows he would play for nothing." Claire Ruth, that "slip of a girl," would never sacrifice $75,000, claimed Burr. "That little sum can buy a lot of linoleum for the kitchen."[33] Nor did Ruth's assault on baseball's iniquitous labor system move hearts. With the nation's economic system collapsing, Ruth's protests suggested a materialism associated with a rapidly passing time. In present circumstances, wrote Westbrook Pegler, it seemed a stretch to apply the lessons of "the teachings of the Tarbells and Lewises" to Ruth's circumstances.[34] As Ruth sought a raise, in fact, many sportswriters faced pay reductions and uncertain futures in the face of the economic collapse.[35]

While officially a holdout, Ruth traveled to Florida to join the Yankees at spring training. He worked out with the team and played in exhibition games. Ruppert and Barrow followed later that month, arriving in the St. Petersburg area still proclaiming they had made their best and final offer to Ruth. Both sides maintained an icy distance. Finally in early March, the contract crisis moved to a head. The Yankees had scheduled in thirty-two exhibition games over the next several weeks. "They've got my name plastered all over the South as appearing," complained Ruth. He had willingly played in several games, but he grew concerned that a serious injury could short-circuit the negotiations. "Suppose I pull up with a broken arm or leg in one of these exhibition games?" Ruth fretted. "Ruppert is cashing in while our conferences are going on." Ruth was done with the exhibition games and appeared ready to return to New York.[36] The prospect of a season without Ruth suddenly appeared very real, and unnerving to the baseball establishment.

A group of concerned sportswriters, including the *Evening Telegram's* Dan Daniel, Allen Gould of the Associated Press, and Ford Frick of the *Evening Journal*, took action and began to seriously press Ruth to settle with Ruppert. Holding out longer, the group warned the slugger, would severely undercut Bob Shawkey, the new manager who was also Ruth's friend and former teammate. Likewise, the ongoing battle over $10,000 appeared unseemly at a time when so many faced unemployment. Idle workers were protesting for bread around the country. To underscore his point, Daniel fetched Ruth a newspaper baring headlines reading "Riot in Union Square."[37] The sportwriters' persistent pressure, alongside Ruth's understandable reluctance to sacrifice one of his remaining playing years, swayed him. Daniel, Gould, and Frick no doubt felt they were saving Ruth from a mistake. Yet as members of the team for all intents and purposes on the payroll, especially during spring training, they were also doing management's bidding. Barrow, for one, rarely shied from making clear to sportswriters their subservient role. When one writer dared publish a player's side in a contract dispute, Barrow lashed back. "Stories like that are subversive," he told the writer. "Any story which backs the players against the club on salary is against the best interests of baseball."[38] From the perspective of sportswriters, a Ruthian capitulation or compromise would preserve stability as baseball and the country faced difficult times.

Suddenly in a hurry, Ruth flew to Ruppert's temporary residence at the luxurious Princess Martha Hotel. Dan Daniel then tracked down Ruppert out for a walk. "Ruth was ready to give in," he told the colonel.[39] Barrow and Ruppert quickly gathered at the hotel and settled with Ruth on $80,000 for two seasons. Seeking some face-saving measure, Ruth inquired again about the $5,000 fine levied against him in 1925. Two years before, repayment of the fine and hospital expenses had been part of Ruth's initial demands. Now he raised the issue again. Ruppert looked uncomfortably to Barrow. "If it's up to me, the fine will have to remain," Barrow predictably pronounced. Ruppert then took Barrow aside. When they returned, Ruppert conceded the $5,000 to Ruth. "So long as Huggins was alive," Ruppert explained, "I'd never have given it back. . . . But he's dead now and he'll never know about this, and if it will please you we will give you back that five thousand."[40] Likewise, an addendum to the contract did provide Ruth some compensation for participation in exhibition games.[41]

Emerging from the session, Ruth appeared drained, missing his usual smile and bravado. He looked "like a man who had been made to swallow a dose he didn't exactly relish," noted sportswriter Marshall Hunt.[42] "I'm glad I don't have to talk or think about money for a while," Ruth offered. He settled in the end, he claimed, to help the new Yankees manager, Bob Shawkey. He was "a great believer in Shawkey."[43] Most press accounts avoided mention of the sportswriters' role and instead played up the unpopular Mrs. Ruth, who supposedly issued "a command from the 'head of household'" that Ruppert's offer be accepted.[44] Beneath headlines of "Wife Ordered Bambino to Take Offer," readers learned how Claire Ruth had dispatched her husband to the Princess Martha Hotel with a pen and orders to "get it over with."[45]

Enter Joe McCarthy

The Yankees investment paid off: in 1930, Ruth improved on his 1929 performance, hitting forty-nine home runs and averaging .359. Under Shawkey, however, the team struggled to meet the high standards of the late 1920s. A third-place finish in the American League displeased Ruppert. Pressure built on Shawkey and the entire team. When sportswriter and Ruth friend Bill Slocum published a piece criticizing Barrow, the pugnacious Yankees secretary flew into a rage and struck Slocum, knocking him to the ground. The episode exposed Barrow's temperament and brought a rebuke of sorts from owner Ruppert, who expressed "profound regret" over the assault. Ruppert announced that henceforth his private secretary, not Barrow, would handle Yankees relations with the press. Still, Barrow continued as the main guiding force behind the Yankees.[46]

Understanding Shawkey's days were numbered, Ruth again approached Ruppert about the manager's job. This time the brewmaster was ready for him. Ruppert rattled off a long list of Ruth's past failings and indiscretions. "Under those circumstances . . . how can I turn the team over to you?" asked Ruppert pointedly. Ruppert seemed definitive.[47]

His treatment of Shawkey proved even more ignominious. Shawkey dropped by Yankees headquarters unsuspectingly one day in October only to find reporters gathered around Joe McCarthy, the newly appointed Yankees manager. Barrow had not even bothered to tell Shawkey of his firing.[48] Ruth shared Shawkey's shock; he also had not been consulted about the change.

McCarthy was Barrow's sort of guy: "pugnacious," but a serious professional with a reputation as a disciplinarian.[49] He had never played major league baseball and viewed himself as part of management, not a middle-man. Unlike Huggins, McCarthy was no compromiser. He could be counted on to establish a hard line and stick to it. Players and sportswriters dubbed McCarthy as "Marse Joe,"—"Marse" being a variation on "master." Barrow now had a dependable overseer to keep recalcitrant players in line.

McCarthy wasted little time in asserting his authority. Uniforms were only to be worn when clean and crisp. The old "gas house" style of dirty, gritty dress was unacceptable for champions like the Yankees. McCarthy summarily banned card playing, shaving, and radios from the Yankees locker room.

It was, the new manager announced, "a clubhouse not a club room."[50] The hyperdisciplined Gehrig appreciated the manager's structured, no-nonsense style. Ruth, however, was accustomed to doing things his way. Attracting crowds wherever he went, Ruth tended to dine alone in his hotel room when on the road. The practice annoyed McCarthy, who felt the Babe was getting special treatment.[51] For his part, Ruth naturally resented the rule changes and privately dismissed McCarthy as a "weak hitting busher."[52] The two, however, avoided direct conflict, much to their credit. Still, the team divided quickly into Ruth and McCarthy factions. Claire Ruth and McCarthy's wife stopped speaking to each other. Ruth, meanwhile, defiantly continued to harbor hopes that he might one day manage the Yankees.[53] Barrow and Ruppert, in turn, looked forward to the day when they would be free of Ruth's huge salary and overbearing personality. A team led by the likes of Gehrig and McCarthy seemed infinitely preferable and considerably more orderly (in addition to being far cheaper).

Sportswriters dutifully supported McCarthy's hiring, but Pegler, ever a contrarian, warned that McCarthy might step aside after a year in favor of Ruth. The Babe had a reputation for "baseball instinct . . . so strong that he has rarely if ever been seen to commit an error of judgment," Pegler insisted.[54] Elsewhere, however, Ruth found it difficult to escape his past reputation. A *Sporting News* profile from early 1931 titled "Babe Ruth Wants to Forget 'Bad Boy' Days" reviewed Huggins's clash with the "big overgrown boy." Asked about his "past," Ruth was quick to respond, "I don't want to talk about that."[55] Despite repeated compromises and capitulations to authority, Ruth continued to be depicted as something less than an adult. The media, in fact, was echoing Barrow and Ruppert's perspective. The two resolutely opposed trusting their team's fate to a player whom they believed remained an independent operator.

Under McCarthy, the Yankees steadily improved in 1931. Disgruntled as he might be, Ruth hit forty-six home runs with a batting average of .375. His team finished second to the Philadelphia Athletics. Expectations were high for the next season. Nonetheless, Ruth was aging and remained injury prone. Early in 1931, a leg injury landed him in the hospital. He would often sit out the later innings of games.

As McCarthy and Ruth maneuvered awkwardly around each other, the US economy plummeted deep into depression. Baseball, at least initially, appeared immune from the downturn. It offered, as John Kieran suggested, "cheap amusement." Both attendance and profits were solid in 1930.[56]

Yet besides the Yankees and select other franchises, few teams enjoyed great prosperity even in the roaring 1920s. Player compensation long had been an issue of contention among owners, who, despite their control, resented even the modest remuneration they paid out. When the economy continued to contract, owners saw an opportunity to trim payrolls. "Slashing salaries is the new slogan," warned sportswriter F. C. Lane.[57] Layoffs and pay cuts were announced. Even Judge Landis took a cut of $15,000 in 1933.[58]

As front offices began hacking salaries and pruning rosters, Babe Ruth slapped back. "They're carrying this cutting business too far and making a joke of it," he complained to reporters.[59] Ruth, of course, enjoyed baseball's largest salary by far. Ruppert's fellow owners began pressing him to act against Ruth. As *Sporting News* editor J. G. Spink explained, "Ruth is the bellwether of the salary rolls; if he takes a cut, other players must do likewise."[60] Conversely, should Ruppert reward Ruth with a raise or even maintain his substantial salary, "The squawking of Babe Herman, Mell Ott and the rest of the slashed athletes," warned one sportswriter, "would have been practically continuous."[61]

In late 1931, as Barrow prepared to send out new contracts, Ruppert made clear that Ruth would face a pay cut. "Never again will a player get that much in a year, and that means the Babe," announced the Yankees owner referencing Ruth's $80,000 per year recent contract. Gehrig and McCarthy now, not just Ruth, were also drawing crowds, claimed Ruppert. While the Yankees continued to prosper, the times were bad. Ruppert and Barrow offered Ruth $70,000 for one year, a cut of $10,000. At an initial conference with Ruppert, Ruth agreed to $70,000 but requested a two-year contract. Given Ruth's age and health, Ruppert rejected any multiyear arrangement. The only way he would agree to a contract spanning more than a year was if it was for $25,000 a year, Ruppert bristled. Again, Ruth headed to Florida spring training without a deal.

Public interest in Ruth's salary talks as always remained high. But by 1932, after two years of severe economic retraction, the public's mood had changed. As Marshall Hunt explained, the contract negotiations took place "at a time when the almighty dollar is as elusive as a pea on a plate."[62] Holdouts such as Ruth's do "not get much of a rise out of the J. Q. Public who is glad to have a job at all, if he's got one," opined the *Chicago Tribune*.[63] Pegler added that Ruth was "so far out of touch with the realities of the world that he not only declines an offer of $70,000," but he also failed to meet Ruppert at the St. Petersburg train station when the Yankees owner arrived in Florida.[64] Trying to pressure the Yankees, Ruth refused to participate in exhibition games. Mc-Carthy, his manager, found out about the refusal in the newspaper, no doubt feeding tensions between the two.[65]

With waning leverage and little public support, Ruth was lucky Ruppert raised his offer to $75,000 for one year. The two hammered out the agreement in the Moorish-style grand lobby of the Rolyat Hotel in St. Petersburg while newspapermen stood nearby trying to read their lips and gestures. In the end, Ruth acknowledged the "cut is fair enough in times like these."[66]

"Clown and Hero"

Ruth continued to struggle with injuries through the 1932 season. His overall performance slipped from the previous year but still remained impressive: a batting average of .342 with forty-one home runs. Still, Ruth was eclipsed statistically by teammate Lou Gehrig and Jimmy Foxx of Connie Mack's Athletics. Foxx managed to better Ruth by seventeen home runs, coming within three of breaking Ruth's record.

With Ruth contributing mightily, McCarthy's Yankees came on strong that year, winning the pennant and heading to their first World Series since 1928. Their opponents were to be the Chicago Cubs, the team that had fired McCarthy in 1930. Cubs players had voted not to grant a share of World Series profits to Manager Rogers Hornsby (a Ruth friend), and shortstop Mark Koenig, a former Yankee, was granted only a half share since he had joined the team in August (after a showgirl shot Cubs' starter Billy Jurges in the hand). To the Yankees, and Ruth in particular, Cubs stinginess equaled a moral failing. Teammates stuck together, and money should not impede team unity. Now in its third year, the Depression and the salary cuts facing players probably reinforced those collectivist sentiments.

When the series opened in New York, hard times cast a long shadow. Only 41,450 fans attended the first game in Yankee Stadium. Reserve seat packages costing over fifteen dollars went unsold. The tense national mood spilled over onto the field. Both teams mercilessly rode each other. The Yankees bench, led by Ruth, shot charges of "cheapskates," "tightwads," and "nickel nursers" at their opponents. The Cubs returned fire, focusing on Ruth's supposedly dubious racial heritage.[67] When the venue switched to Chicago, Wrigley Field fans showered the Yankees with lemons. Ruth was a favorite target.

Game three of the series, the first in Chicago, provided the setting for one of baseball's most enduring myths. As Mayor Anton Cermak and

Democratic presidential candidate Governor Franklin D. Roosevelt looked on, Ruth came to bat in the fifth inning. With the score tied at 5–5, jeering from the crowd grew louder and cruder. Ruth entered into a lively exchange with Chicago pitcher Charlie Root. Ruth held up one finger after the first strike and two fingers after the second. Most likely, he then pointed to the far fence, indicating the direction in which he would send the next ball. Ruth then indeed poled a home run. Exactly what transpired during the most famous at-bat in baseball history remains the source of debate. Clearly, Ruth was issuing signals with his arms (as recovered films later clearly reveal). Perhaps Red Smith, "dean of sportswriters" and witness to the "called shot," came closest to the truth when he admitted that he was still confused by what went on: "I was there but I've never been sure of what I saw."[68]

In reports the day after, only Joe Williams of the New York *World Telegram* described the "called shot" home run, although a significant number of eyewitnesses claim Ruth, in fact, called his shot. Other writers only picked up the story later. Like much written about Ruth in the 1932 series, the Williams account of Ruth in game three was not entirely celebratory. In his write-up, Williams predicted a pay cut for the Yankees star and declared Ruth no longer the best player in baseball. "Old Man Time has finally caught up with him. He can still swing that big bat with magnificent effect but that is all. You might say that that is enough, but the critics seem to think otherwise. And, what's more important so does the management."[69]

After writing nothing about the called-shot immediately following the game, Paul Gallico of the *Daily News* picked up the story two days later. To Gallico, like Williams, Ruth's heroics were a mixed bag. In game three, he was "a divine comedian at work, a man who is both clown and hero in the same breath, the same being George Herman Ruth, who . . . pointed like a dualist to the spot where he expected to send his rapier home and then sent it there." It was, Gallico concluded, "probably the most daring gesture ever made in any game."[70]

It is tempting to associate the myth of the called shot with a nation locked in economic depression searching for a shot of confidence. Indeed, the bravado shown by Ruth (and witnessed firsthand by Franklin D. Roosevelt) stands in marked contrast to the degradation experienced by many Americans at that hour. That sportswriters quickly adopted and retold the story speaks to its power. For Ruth, however, the episode marked a career capstone rather than a career renewal. He returned to New York from Chicago triumphant yet injured and exhausted. Likewise, reports of his "razzing" the

Cubs and thumbing his nose at his opponents after his victorious home runs did little to convince the public he had matured. To Yankees management, Ruth remained ever problematic, still a potential threat to authority and still an independent force capable of mobilizing other players to challenge the establishment. Increasingly, easing Ruth out of baseball became a priority.

NINE. REMOVING RUTH

Ruth's 1932 world Series "called shot" may have captured the public imagination, but Jacob Ruppert and Ed Barrow were imagining something very different for their star player. Both wanted him gone. Ruth's high salary and seemingly constant demands were something the baseball establishment wished to relegate to a bygone era. The Yankees front office envisioned a future defined by the quiet, efficient, and loyal Lou Gehrig and the disciplinarian Joe "Marse" McCarthy. Ruth, however, had his eyes set on the Yankees managerial job; he would not make it easy for his employers. Nor could the team painlessly oust the legendary player. The Babe remained a crowd favorite and an effective force on the field. Team leaders thus sought an opportunity to ease Ruth out with as little collateral damage as possible.

Barrow, in particular, continued to nurse deep resentment against Ruth. He had spent a decade and a half trying to break Ruth, with decidedly mixed results. By the 1930s, Ruth was more acquiescent. He accepted pay cuts and worked cooperatively under McCarthy, despite the Babe's personal dislike of "Marse Joe." Yet Yankees management was hardly ready to trust Ruth. Early on, Barrow convinced Ruppert that Ruth was unacceptable as a Yankees manager. While Ruppert never directly conveyed this to his star player, over time Ruth recognized his managerial prospects with the Yankees were limited. Beyond the Yankees, however, Barrow worked to dissuade others from hiring Ruth. In the end, the Babe paid a significant price for challenging baseball authority.

"Plenty Burned Up"

Between the Yankees' victory in the 1932 World Series and the commencement of spring training the next year, America's economy sank even deeper into the Depression. The nation's banking system essentially shut down, awaiting the arrival of the new president, Franklin D. Roosevelt. Baseball, too, felt the tough times. Team revenues fell precipitously, although smaller city franchises suffered most. Club owners, led by Ruppert, approached the Depression individualistically and conservatively. Profit-sharing schemes to help struggling clubs were off the table. "Every club owner must make his own fight for existence," pronounced Ruppert.[1] For the most part, team owners responded by cutting salaries and expenses rather than embracing novel notions like night games or broadcasting games on radio to build interest. There was to be no New Deal for baseball. Between 1930 and 1933, payrolls dropped from $4 million to $3 million.[2]

Shrinking the payroll, of course, was a program Ruppert and Barrow could back. Both long had felt players were taking advantage of the team's generosity, especially Ruth. Conventional wisdom within the baseball world was that Ruth had driven up all salaries. "Every other ball player is a friend of Ruth's," explained sportswriter Herald C. Burr. He "knows that Ruth has probably doubled his salary in the past 10 years."[3] Rogers Hornsby, one of the few power hitters capable of occasionally challenging Ruth's dominance, seconded Burr's appraisal. "Every ball player, if he has any sense, knows that because Babe was able to command such a tremendous amount, it helped raise salaries in general."[4] Owners conversely resented Ruth's inflationary impact. As they moved to slash salaries, baseball magnates looked to the Yankees to set the pace. "It's pretty hard convincing a player that conditions demand his salary being cut from $12,000 to $10,000 while the Babe is pulling down $75,000," complained one owner.[5] Sports editors at the *Chicago Tribune* reiterated the concern. Cutting Ruth's pay "would be a moral influence in bringing about lower salaries for other players," something "which club owners seem to think necessary."[6]

Ruppert and Barrow needed little convincing. Hard times provided them cover to cut what they already considered inflated compensation. In truth, Ruppert's team was hardly struggling. Yankees attendance in 1932 was under a million, but not dramatically so, and 1932 attendance exceeded that of 1931. The team remained profitable.[7] Meanwhile Ruppert took advantage of plummeting real estate prices to gobble up choice properties in New York City. In January of 1932, for instance, he paid $3.5 million in cash to acquire the thirty-five-story Commerce Building in Manhattan.[8] Additionally, the election of Roosevelt promised the end of Prohibition—welcome news for Ruppert, owner of a major beer brewery. Ruth himself professed optimism about upcoming salary negotiations, assuring reporters that the return of legal beer would fill Ruppert's pockets and in turn sustain Ruth's salary.[9] So confident was Ruth that he dismissed entreaties from Boston Red Sox owner Bob Quinn, interested in a celebrity manager to compete with the increasing popularity of Boston's NL team, the Braves. Knowing the Red Sox could hardly match any salary offered by the Yankees, Ruth chose to play another season, assuming there would be other opportunities to manage.[10]

The Babe unquestionably expected a pay cut for the 1933 season, but the contract that arrived in early January left him "stunned," "indignant," and "plenty burned up." The Yankees offered him $50,000 for one year—a $25,000 cut. Other members of the world champion team, including Lou Gehrig, also received contracts with pay cuts. Ruth immediately cast blame on Barrow. The team secretary already vocally advocated a pay cut of at least $25,000 for his longtime antagonist.[11] Ruppert, the Babe surmised, probably was not even informed of the proposed pay cut. Fuming, Ruth complained to reporters that he was being singled out "to lead players back to lower pay checks." Even with the cut, he would be well-off, but he did not "relish being used as a 'come-on guy' who might induce fellow players to accept lower wages." He had taken previous salary disputes lightly, but, according to reports, "This time he feels he's being shoved into an unsportsmanlike role." Despite the Depression, the Yankees, Ruth insisted, had made money in 1932. Calls for economy by the Yankees management, he pled, were self-serving.[12]

As Ruth ranted, Lou Gehrig took a more diplomatic approach when his contract reached him at his New Rochelle home. Refusing to divulge the amount Barrow proposed shaving from the Iron Horse's 1932 salary of $27,500, Gehrig explained he would "drop around the office and see if I can get it adjusted." In early March Gehrig signed with little fanfare, accepting a cut of several thousand dollars. Ruth at least had asked Barrow's permission to make public the $25,000 cut he faced. But when Barrow requested the Babe hold off exposing the sum, Ruth defiantly went to the press anyway.[13] The Babe yet again would be a holdout.

As in previous years, Ruth, accompanied by Claire, journeyed to Florida to join Yankees training camp despite the absence of a signed contract. When the couple arrived in St. Petersburg, eager reporters pounced, asking if Ruth would settle for Ruppert's $50,000 offer. The Babe replied with an emphatic no, echoed by Mrs. Ruth's no "that lacked nothing in emphasis." By this time, President Roosevelt had taken office and shut down the nation's banking system as part of his emergency program. But none of this was relevant to his situation, Ruth insisted. Ruppert still had substantial financial resources and could still sign checks.[14]

If doubt existed regarding Ruth's continuing esteem among fans, they were dispelled by the swarms yet again descending on Yankees training camp to get a look at Ruth. As other Yankees worked out on the first day of camp, Ruth, sporting a heavy woolen sweatshirt, posed for pictures and signed autographs, "not only without complaint, but with a smile for everyone." Purposefully or not, Ruth's display communicated to the Yankees just why he remained a valuable commodity and "from the viewpoint of popularity, he is as great now as ever."[15]

After retaining a resolute silence, however, Colonel Ruppert arrived in Florida in mid-March determined to hold to his initial offer to Ruth. A contract worth $25,000 less than the president earned, Ruppert maintained, represented a fair deal for Ruth, especially since this president "is taking one of the toughest jobs in history." For his part, Ruth remained unwavering. "If they want me to quit over a matter of $10,000, it's okay with me," asserted Ruth, although he clearly hoped the Yankees would rise to meet his concessions.[16]

Ruth and Ruppert conferred briefly in Joe McCarthy's office at the Yankees training camp. Ruppert held fast to the initial offer. Ruth insisted on $60,000, still a substantial cut. Leaving the failed conference, Ruppert complained bitterly to the waiting press. His "auditors" recently had reviewed the Yankees' financial books, he bristled. Contrary to published reports and Ruth's assertions, the team had lost money in 1932. "We are passing through a depressing business situation which is unparalleled. Do you think I would go through this situation if it was not necessary?"[17]

The Yankees soon would embark on an eleven-game exhibition tour on their way north. Ruth, naturally, would be the main attraction. In the past, the specter of empty seats and disappointed fans had moved Yankees management to settle. This time, however, Ruppert flipped the formulation on Ruth. Without his star player on the tour, the team would lose money, he conceded. Therefore, he would begin cutting his $50,000 offer to Ruth commensurate with the number of exhibition games missed. Ruppert was playing hardball. The threat evidently shook Ruth, who asked for another meeting at his apartment in St. Petersburg. By this time, Ruth had dropped his demands again, to $55,000, but Ruppert remained unmoved. "Ruth must mean business. I am getting tired of these conferences," fumed Ruppert as he made his way to Ruth's Florida abode. "This thing is getting childish."[18]

With Ruth adjusting ever downward the amount he would accept, Ruppert was obviously tempted not to compromise. Forcing the Bambino to settle on $50,000 would send a strong message to other players and make up for a lingering sense that the Yankees hitter had abused Ruppert's liberality over the years. Ruth, however, had publicly and repeatedly insisted he would not settle for $50,000. To "save his pride" and close the deal, Ruppert raised his offer $2,000 to $52,000, the same amount as Ruth's famous $1,000 a week deal with Colonel Huston during happier negotiations in 1922. An exhausted Ruth emerged to announce the deal. To waiting reporters, he issued the concession the baseball establishment wanted to hear: "I also know there is a depression and I am satisfied to get a pay cut."[19] Ruppert appeared more energized. "With Ruth's name on a new contract and the president's name on a new beer bill, everything will be fine," he waxed. After having added considerably, at rock-bottom prices, to his real estate holdings, Ruppert was in the process of planning a massive expansion and modernization of his brewery to prepare for the end of Prohibition.[20] The brewer anticipated a bright future.

Watching from the sidelines, Barrow also felt a sense of triumph. In the past, Barrow had participated in the Ruth-Ruppert negotiations, but in 1933, Ruth had insisted Barrow, whom he blamed for the dramatic pay cut, not be involved. Behind the scenes Barrow told reporters that neither Ruth nor any player was worth the sort of money he believed the Babe had extorted. When news arrived that Ruppert and Ruth had agreed on $52,000, Barrow took the settlement as signaling a restoration of managerial control. "There will never be another $80,000 ball player," he prophesized.[21] Ruth's capitulation, to Barrow, signaled the dawn of a new era of absolute managerial dominance.

"Fat and Forty He May Be"*

Ruth remained an intimidating presence at bat in 1933. Opposing teams well understood his power. Babe could still change the trajectory of a game instantly with one of his titanic swings. A Ruth home run won the first ever All Star game played in July in Chicago. Yet his powers were declining. He hit thirty-four home runs in 1933, two more than Gehrig, but off Ruth's pace of forty-one the previous year. But injuries and illness dogged him. Ruth ended the season with a batting average just over .300. All understood another salary cut lay on the horizon. Not only did the Yankees fail to win the 1933 AL pennant, but the team watched crosstown rivals, the Giants, win the World Series. Bill Terry, a youthful player-manager, led the team in its post–John McGraw turnaround.

Ruth watched as Terry, his contemporary, moved from player to player-manager. He hoped to make a similar shift. Moving into management would keep Ruth in the spotlight in the game he loved and stave off the pain of decline. Proving himself as a team leader also promised to counter longstanding impressions that Ruth was little more than an intellectually limited power hitter, charges he deeply resented. Ruth never shied from declaring his desire to manage the Yankees. As the 1933 season wound down, a lively debate surfaced as to his qualifications and suitability for such a post. It came down to one question: Had Ruth changed?

Several key analysts responded with a yes: Ruth had changed and deserved a chance to manage. "Many competent critics believe he is admirably endowed" to be a manager, offered sportswriter Ed Hughes.[22] John Kieran, the erudite sportswriter for the *New York Times*, devoted a full column to "the debate . . . as to whether the Big Bambino would make a good manager." Despite Ruth's past as "the careless, boisterous, swaggering, and unruly Playboy of the Western World," Kieran concluded, baseball's biggest personality had reformed. "Though no one would have expected it years ago, the fellow is naturally smart . . . clubs in search of a manager should not overlook one worthy candidate, G. Herman Ruth."[23]

While debate over Ruth ensued, a comedy (or tragedy) of errors took place within the baseball world. Halfheartedly, both Ruth and the Yankees searched for a managerial job for the declining Babe. Ruth, of course, desired the Yankees post. Under no circumstances would that be acceptable to Barrow or Ruppert, despite persistent rumors to the contrary. As

---

* "Bambino to Take Huge Pay Cut in 1934," *Florence Times*, January 15, 1934.

speculation bubbled at the end of the 1933 season, team owner Ruppert attempted to clarify his position. "I think Babe Ruth will make a splendid manager. He's settled down and is very serious. . . . I'd like to keep Ruth with the Yankees, but I'll not interfere if he gets a chance to better himself." Ruppert certainly intended to signal Ruth's availability to other clubs. Barrow in particular was eager to be rid of his well-paid nemesis of nearly two decades. Yet to some, Ruppert's words signaled support for Ruth as future Yankees manager. The *Chicago Tribune* ran the Yankees owner's comments under the headline "Babe Ruth May Manage Yanks after McCarthy."[24]

Sensing opportunity in New York, Ruth was in no hurry to explore job openings elsewhere. When Frank Navin, owner of the Detroit Tigers, requested an interview, Ruth, on his way to a barnstorming tour of Hawaii, delayed. Ed Barrow later claimed to have warned Ruth to move quickly, "but the big fellow wouldn't listen and went on his merry way."[25] Meeting with Navin, Ruth claimed, would have required breaking barnstorming contracts. The two could confer, Ruth had assured Navin, after the Hawaiian trip. The delay, however, appeared to convince Tigers management that Ruth was not ready to manage, a position Barrow long had taken. Yet given Navin's reputation as a "tightfisted" owner, determined to keep player salaries low, and the shaky financial state of the Tigers, it is difficult to imagine Navin would have hired Ruth or that the two would have gotten along had the Babe been given the chance.

Better prospects for Ruth appeared to exist in Boston, where Tom Yawkey, a young wealthy industrialist, recently had purchased the Boston Red Sox from Bob Quinn with the intent of returning the team to its Ruthian glory days. In the depth of the Depression, Yawkey prepared to spend vast sums of money and aimed to be a players' owner. He hired retired star second baseman Eddie Collins as his business manager. The two planned to establish the sort of working relationship that had brought success to Barrow and Ruppert. Prospects of Ruth making a royal return to Boston excited Yawkey. His Red Sox struggled to compete with crosstown rivals, the Braves, in a small-market town. Ruth's return could jump-start Yawkey's planned Red Sox revival.[26] While in New York for the Giants-Senators World Series, Yawkey and Collins took the topic of Ruth up with Barrow. According to reports, Barrow "labeled Ruth risky management material"—an opinion he almost certainly also shared with Frank Navin in Detroit. Yawkey remained infatuated with Ruth, but his right-hand man, Collins, vehemently opposed the move.[27] Stories surfaced later that Yawkey went as far as interviewing Ruth, but the young owner was put off when "Mrs. Ruth supplied all the answers."[28]

Not only did Barrow undercut Ruth's job search, but Ruppert also appeared reluctant to release Ruth. When colorful and aggressive Cincinnati Reds general manager Larry MacPhail approached Ruppert about purchasing Ruth to manage the Reds, the Yankees owner responded with "a voracious 'no.'" Details of the exchange are unclear. Perhaps MacPhail refused to meet Ruppert's price or perhaps there was reluctance to send Ruth to the rival National League.[29] The result, again, was lost opportunity and a further signal to Ruth that he might still someday get a shot at piloting the Yankees.

In fact, Yankees management continued to struggle with ambivalence regarding Ruth. At reduced rates, Ruth more than paid for himself as a player. Most observers felt he had one to two more seasons left. Still, Ruth was insistent on managing. In later times, professional agents would have weighed options and handled negotiations. Christy Walsh clearly offered advice, but he focused on his ghostwriting operations and had moved on to other clients, including Lou Gehrig. Ruth and wife Claire, by themselves, almost exclusively handled planning and negotiations. Over and over, Ruth made clear his desire to manage. At times he appeared desperate. Supposedly to placate their star and keep him in the organization, Ruppert and Barrow offered Ruth the manager slot with the Newark Bears, the Yankees' International League minor league affiliate. It would be, they asserted, a chance for Ruth to prove himself. Walter Johnson had managed at Newark in the 1920s and later moved to the major leagues.

Ruth, however, resented the offer. Other star players, including Ty Cobb and Bill Terry, had stepped directly into major league manager positions. To accept the Newark job essentially would mean affirming those enduring disparagements that the orphan from the streets of Baltimore lacked the acumen to pilot a major league team. Ruth brazenly turned down the offer. After twenty years, he refused to return to the minor leagues. "It's like learning all over again. They play a different game in the minors," he complained. Indeed, Ruth may well have suspected a setup. If he failed in Newark, his prospects would be all but over. Barrow, whom Ruth rightly did not trust, urged the Babe to take the Newark job. The Yankees secretary went as far as calling Claire Ruth to urge that she influence her spouse to go to Newark (Claire stood by her husband and also rejected the minor league job).[30] That Barrow, fiercely determined Ruth would never manage the Yankees, was pushing the Newark job, hardly was reassuring.

To the surprise of many, by year's end, no managerial position surfaced for Ruth. "Everyone in the official Yankees family, including Bam himself, was astonished," commented one sportswriter.[31] Another noted it was "a weird business item that club owners aren't falling all over themselves for Ruth." The scribe could only conclude owners were "either extremely poor or amazingly dumb . . . probably both."[32] In fact, Ruth had signaled a willingness to manage at a rate of $35,000 per annum, too rich for many clubs during the Depression. Additionally, an interested club would have to purchase Ruth from the Yankees, presumably at a hefty cost.[33] Still, no one even got to the point of negotiating. In the end, the comedy (or tragedy, from the Babe's perspective) of errors, miscues, and misunderstandings worked against Ruth. Neither he nor Ruppert appeared fully ready for Ruth to leave the Yankees nest. Meanwhile, Barrow labored overtime to undermine Ruth. The Yankees' secretary believed the game better off without its greatest star. While others were caught amidst cross signals and ambivalence, Barrow ruled the day.

Options exhausted, Ruth decided in early 1934 to lock in a position with the Yankees. To embarrass Ruth and possibly force him from the team, Barrow leaked his initial offer of $25,000 (a $27,000 cut) to the press. Sensing the odds stacked against him, Ruth moved quickly and early to negotiate a new contract with Ruppert: a one-year deal worth $35,000, a $17,000 cut (in Ruth's words "a helluva bump") from 1933.[34] The next business day, Ruth, decked out in a coonskin coat, returned to Ruppert's brewery to sign his contract. An exuberant Ruppert did most of the talking, assuring assembled reporters the topic of the Yankees manager post never came up and boasting of his friendship with Ruth. Still rumors floated that Ruppert and Ruth, especially given their tranquil contract negotiations, had arrived at some sort of "tacit" agreement Ruth would soon take over for McCarthy.[35] They had not.

As his knees and ankles grew weaker supporting his 235-pound frame, Ruth was relegated during the 1934 season essentially to the status of "part-time outfielder and extraordinary pinch hitter."[36] For the first time in a long while, fans began to boo and razz Ruth.[37] Fully cognizant of his decline, Ruth promised 1934 would be his last as a regular player. "I'm not fooling myself and I don't want to fool the public. I'm through as a regular player," he told a Knights of Columbus luncheon in Cleveland in September.[38]

Ruth remained hopeful his recent pay cuts and acquiescent contract discussions with Ruppert might help land him a managerial job in 1935. For the second year in a row, the Yankees failed to win the pennant in 1934. Ruth assumed that Ruppert, always emphatic that the Yankees win, would look to replace McCarthy. Ruppert, in fact, had made clear to McCarthy his disdain for anything less than a first-place team. "I warn you, McCarthy, I don't like to finish second," he told his manager at one point.[39] Days after the final game of the season, Ruth approached Ruppert about the Yankees pilot job.

"Are you satisfied with McCarthy as your manager?" he asked Ruppert bluntly.

"Why, yes. Of course I am. Aren't you?" responded the colonel, no doubt fully aware Ruth wanted McCarthy's job.

"No, I'm not. I know I can do better than he can."

"McCarthy is the manager," responded Ruppert sternly, obviously un-nerved by Ruth's candor, "and he will continue as manager."

"That suits me. That's all I wanted to know," Ruth responded quickly, and the meeting ended.[40]

Both men left annoyed. The paternalistic Ruppert resented being put on the spot by a man he believed he had generously patronized over the years. The question of what to do about Ruth, no doubt much discussed between Ruppert and Barrow, could no longer be temporized. Ruth, for his part, naively believed the Yankees job might still be open to him. He never fully realized his team had essentially blackballed him. The chaos of Ruth's early career and his continuing outspokenness remained fresh in the minds of baseball's elites.

Ruth had planned to join other AL stars on a large-scale tour of Japan during the 1934–1935 off-season. The entourage was to leave in late October. That would give Ruth little time to land a managing post. Again the possibility of the Red Sox position arose, but Yawkey and Collins moved in a different direction and purchased Senators manager Joe Cronin for a stunning $250,000 (when Boston most likely could have had Ruth for nothing or very little). A door closing in Boston seemed to open one in Washington. But Senators owner Clark Griffith quickly settled on another candidate, insisting Ruth was never in consideration.[41]

Watching opportunities fade and bearing no small sense of entitlement, Ruth reeled. In Detroit, covering the World Series for the Christy
Walsh syndicate, he opened up to sportswriter Joe Williams as the two
took a short walk around Tiger Stadium. Ruth vowed he would not hang
around the game as a fading pinch hitter. He intended to be a manager,
but he did not want to take a job away from a manager "under contract,"
presumably a reference to McCarthy. Ruth claimed to have job offers from
NL teams, including one for $45,000 a year (possibly the Cincinnati Reds
job). But Ruppert, he complained, refused to release him to pursue such
opportunities. "The reasoning is," Williams speculated, "we have spent a
million dollars exploiting Ruth. Wouldn't we be foolish to hand him over
to the NL now and help their business?"[42] Rivalries and confusion seemed
to be thwarting Ruth's ambitions. Another possibility, of course, was that
Ruppert and Barrow felt Ruth remained too much a rebel to trust with any
major league team; they would rather have him outside the game.

The Williams "scoop" irked Yankees management. Ruppert responded
with a public statement on October 8 explaining that he was "well satisfied" with McCarthy as manager. "And I'm not going to have two managers. Then too, How [sic] do I know Ruth would make a good manager?"[43]
Now Ruppert seemed to be impugning Ruth's abilities. Other owners
anonymously piled on. "It is doubtful whether [Ruth] would take the time
and exhibit the patience necessary to building up a second division club,"
warned one owner.[44]

Flailing, Ruth turned to baseball commissioner Landis. It was an odd
choice. Landis had suspended Ruth in 1922 and refused to help him in
1925 during Ruth's showdown with Huggins. Whatever Ruth's reasoning, he met with Landis in Detroit. The Babe complained bitterly that he
deserved "better treatment" from the media and the baseball establishment. "I'm practically on strike. I want to manage a club in the American League but the league will neither give me a job nor let me go to the
National League, where I have a chance to manage." Wielding the word
"strike" clearly was as ill-advised as turning to Landis. Nothing came of
the conference other than more bad publicity.[45]

Without a job, Ruth left in October for Asia. So "we find [Ruth]," wrote
Tommy Holmes of the *Brooklyn Daily Eagle*, "at the most critical point of
his career on his way to Japan or just about as far away from the locality
in which he might reasonably get a 1935 contract."[46] In fact, a prospec-
tive employer was aboard the ship: Connie Mack, longtime manager and

owner of the Philadelphia Athletics. From New York, Ruppert, desperate to be rid of his Ruth problem and sensitive to the accusation he was holding Ruth back, signaled willingness to release Ruth at no cost to any takers. This was a great incentive to the cash-strapped Mack. The septuagenarian, who had managed the Athletics since 1901, was loath to give up his job. Still, the prospect of Ruth and his gate appeal clearly tempted the aging Mack. Ruth was slated to manage the American touring team, and exhibition games in Japan would give Mack a chance to assess Ruth's skills up close. By all accounts Ruth handled the exhibition team well, but whatever chances Ruth had to pilot the A's quickly evaporated. Mack professed to be dismayed by the assertive Claire Ruth. If he hired Babe, he fretted, "She would be managing the team in a month."[47]

The matter of Claire Ruth remained a stumbling point for many in the baseball establishment. Opinionated and enthralled by the business of baseball, she was no silent partner. Claire operated outspokenly in an almost exclusively male world; it was noticed and resented. "One thing in baseball that club secretaries and business managers object to is wifely interference—as they call it—around the ballpark," recalled John Kieran. The "angry opinion of baseball officials," he later wrote, "was that Mrs. Ruth was dictating to the Babe what to say and do at all times and they didn't like it a bit." According to Kieran, this explained some of the resistance to hiring Ruth for a management position. Of course, according to the dictates of the times, a strong woman advocating for Ruth also served to debase Ruth and reinforce notions "he couldn't manage himself."[48] More recently some have suggested that Ruth's social progressivism, in particular his sympathy for players of color, may have alarmed the baseball establishment, who feared a strong advocate for integration of the sport. Members of Ruth's family have made this case.[49] There is, however, virtually no historical evidence that Ruth held strong views regarding the desegregation of baseball.

"They'll have to force me out of the game, I like it too much"

In Japan and throughout the world, Ruth commanded massive crowds, the sort of reception "reserved for the Lindberghs, and presidents and kings."[50] "Banzai Babe" proved a remarkably skilled goodwill ambassador. Upon his return, Connie Mack crowed (erroneously, as it turned out) that Ruth's Japanese triumph would ensure peace between America and

Japan "for at least ten years."[51] Ruth's baseball future, however, remained cloudy. Had he not been traveling, Ruth might have been in a better position to line up a managerial job. Even so, the baseball world appeared aligned against him. Ruth later recognized the Yankees were also "in a spot."[52] They could ill afford to forcibly retire a player of Ruth's unprecedented fame and popularity. Still, the team had no real place for an aging Ruth in its lineup. His very presence also undermined Manager McCarthy, and Ruth was a liability in the field. As the 1935 season approached, Barrow, in particular, was desperate to be rid of Ruth.

When Babe, Claire, and daughter Julia (Ruth's adopted daughter from Claire's first marriage) finally pulled into New York Harbor on February 20 following an around-the-world tour, Ruth wasted little time telling the gathered media he remained intent on managing. "They owe me a chance as manager, don't they? Twenty-one years in the game, you know," he contended. "They'll have to force me out of the game, I like it too much." Ruth acknowledged, however, that he had few prospects. He also made clear that he remained a rebel. When reporters raised the issue of one-dollar "provisional" contracts sent out by Barrow to Ruth and four other "convalescents," contracts designed to keep players locked to the Yankees until the status of their injuries could be determined, the Babe's demeanor noticeably changed. His back "stiffened" and "eyes flashed." "Why'd they send one to Combs," he bristled, referring to Earle Combs, an ailing Yankees outfielder, "just because he didn't kill himself last season running into that wall after a fly ball."[53]

Ruth's combination of bravado and desperation hardly endeared him to those still considering the fading star either as a player or manager. Yet during his travels, one team had expressed some interest: the financially struggling Boston Braves. By 1935, Braves owner Judge Emil Fuchs barely had control of his team. Other stockholders, including grocer Charles E. Adams, openly conspired against him, and his team struggled. Desperate for additional income in the midst of the Great Depression, Fuchs attempted to introduce dog racing to Braves Field, a move that sent the National League into turmoil. Since gambling and baseball could not be mixed, Fuchs proposed moving Braves games to the Red Sox's Fenway Park. Sox owner Tom Yawkey immediately rejected the idea. Fuchs backed away from the dog-racing scheme but continued to look for a quick fix for his and the Braves' financial woes.

In December 1934, Adams, the New England grocery magnate, contacted Ruppert, the beer magnate, regarding Ruth. The two had had dealings before and quickly hatched a plan. Ruth would go to the National League to serve as assistant manager (a novel position in baseball) and pinch hitter for the struggling Braves.[54] By this time, both Ruppert and Barrow were willing to do almost anything to free themselves of Ruth. Still, sending Ruth to an insolvent, dysfunctional operation like the Braves hardly was in the Babe's best interest, although Ruth retained final say over the Braves job.

Whirlwind negotiations began almost immediately upon Ruth's return. Judge Fuchs, convinced Ruth could be a rainmaker, moved quickly to make a deal. Behind the scenes, however, there was no consensus among the warring ownership of the Braves on removing the team's current manager, Bill McKechnie, who had operated effectively under trying circumstances. Fuchs promised Ruth the ill-defined positions of assistant manager and team vice president. Supposedly, Ruth would apprentice under the skilled McKechnie. If things went well, then Ruth would be promoted to team manager, possibly in 1936; McKechnie would move to general manager.

Eager to stay in baseball and with no other options, Ruth jumped at the Braves offer. Five days after returning from his world tour, Ruth sat with Fuchs, Barrow, and Ruppert in the offices of Ruppert's brewery. If Ruth had hoped Ruppert would make a last-minute play to keep him with the Yankees, he was quickly disabused of the notion. Explaining that he had shopped Ruth around at the last minute to AL teams and found no takers, Ruppert offered his star player an unconditional release. To further facilitate matters, he tendered Ruth to the Braves at no cost. As one newspaper noted, the arrangement cost the Braves $47.50—all in long distance phone charges. From Ruth's point of view, it was all rather humbling. Ruppert, however, insisted his accommodating actions represented yet another example of his munificence. "They've said I've been rough on [Ruth] and haven't given him a chance," protested the defensive brewer, "but I'm doing this . . . just so he could get a chance."[55]

Almost immediately the "chance" proffered to Ruth proved a cruel chimera. Like Joe McCarthy before him, Braves manager Bill McKechnie hardly appreciated being saddled with a presumed successor. In interviews, McKechnie claimed he welcomed Ruth and was involved in the talks leading to Ruth's hire, but the manager "quickly dissipated any idea that might be lingering around that Babe is to replace him as manager."[56]

On February 28, Boston celebrated its returned hero when Ruth made a quick trip north before heading to Florida for spring training. An effusive Fuchs announced publicly that if Ruth so desired, he would be Braves manager in 1936. Fuchs's rival, Charles Adams, however, delivered a pointed speech at a dinner honoring Ruth. "Babe will have to show he merits the post if he receives the job. No one is fit to give orders until he can take them himself. Judging from Ruth's past career, we can hardly consider him of management caliber now."[57]

From Boston, Ruth traveled to Braves training camp in St. Petersburg, also the longtime site of the Yankees' training camp. Living up to his role as rainmaker, Ruth drew swarms to Braves workouts and exhibition games throughout the South. In Florida, seven thousand fans witnessed the Babe duel pitching ace Dizzy Dean of the St. Louis Cardinals. On the way north, one third of the population of Fayetteville, North Carolina, gathered to see Ruth with his Boston Braves. His presence at the Polo Grounds in late April for the Giants opening game generated the largest opening day crowd in Giants history. Braves manager McKechnie feigned acceptance of his "assistant," trying the slugger at first base, a position that would be easier on his aching knees. But, McKechnie insisted, Ruth's real place would be in the outfield, where his legs would see significant wear and tear. As for the position of assistant manager, McKechnie confessed it meant "nothing particularly."[58]

As the scene played out, Ruth rival Rogers Hornsby, now the manager of the AL St. Louis Browns, seethed at Ruth's treatment. The Babe had been "railroaded" by AL team business managers, claimed Hornsby. Ruth "would make a great manager . . . and would be the boss." But under Ruth, general managers or business managers "would play second fiddle." That was the reason Eddie Collins of the Red Sox refused to employ the Babe. Hornsby himself claimed to have tried to hire Ruth as his St. Louis assistant manager, but the Browns, always struggling financially, could not afford Ruth, and the American League refused to subsidize the hire.[59] Indeed, a skilled agent might have been able to arrange an "apprenticeship" for Ruth under either Hornsby or, better yet, Connie Mack. In essence, however, the Yankees engineered Ruth's deal with the Braves. Instead of a loyal agent, Ruth essentially was represented by his antagonist, Ed Barrow.

Within a couple of weeks of the opening of the new season, Ruth began to share Hornsby's sense he was being "railroaded." Every spring, Ruth seemed to take ill. An unusually frigid spring in 1935 made it difficult for Ruth to shake his annual cold. His legs and, particularly, his ankles ached. Meanwhile, McKechnie showed no signs of expanding Ruth's authority. Sensitive to the manager's awkward position, Ruth tried to be supportive. "You wouldn't see me taking someone's job away from him," insisted Ruth to reporters.[60] Meanwhile, it became ever clearer that front office dissension, rivalries, and financial woes raged within the Braves organization. With Ruth as a drawing card, Judge Fuchs managed to make initial payments to his creditors. The judge, however, pushed Ruth hard to make promotional appearances for the team. At one point he required that Ruth report to a clothing store to sign five hundred tickets the business apparently had purchased to boost sales. In bed with yet another severe cold, Ruth cancelled the appearance, the store returned the tickets, and the relationship between Fuchs and Ruth took a permanent turn for the worse.[61]

As the novelty of Ruth wore off, crowds slackened. Meanwhile, Fuchs had bills to pay. Fearing bankruptcy, the good judge tried to get Ruth to invest in the team. Wisely, the Babe refused and began talking about retirement.[62] "I hate to think of the Babe stepping out when he is low in temperament," said Fuchs, who labeled Ruth "a person of moods."[63] Indeed, by all accounts, Ruth was struggling with his declining abilities and his transition from active playing. The realization that he had made a bad choice in joining the Braves added to his depression.

Ruth reluctantly agreed to join the Braves for a "western" tour in late May. He worried about disappointing fans and alienating teams anticipating big crowds for the tour. Playing in Pittsburgh on May 25, Ruth suddenly came alive and launched three home runs. Forbes Field fans cheered wildly for the fading hero. In subsequent games in Cincinnati and Philadelphia, however, Ruth reinjured his chronically battered knees. By the time he returned to Boston, the Babe was sitting on the bench, frustrated and fed up.

As Ruth stewed, the French superliner *Normandie* was making its maiden voyage across the Atlantic, headed to New York harbor. The $60 million ship was the largest on the sea and aimed to break the transatlantic speed record. The anticipated arrival of the luxury liner and a new speed record excited the US media. Planners invited Ruth to join the official celebration welcoming the ship. Sitting idly on the Boston bench, Ruth saw no reason not to attend the ceremonies. Fuchs disagreed and refused the Babe's request for time off. To forty-one-year-old Ruth, already contemplating retirement, it was the last straw. Fuchs, he believed, was acting vindictively. Ruth's famous temper kicked into motion.

On June 2, Ruth called "New York" writers into the Braves locker room and announced he was placing himself on the voluntary disabled list. Working himself up, Ruth turned on the Braves ownership. Fuchs had "crossed me so many times, and double crossed me," he steamed. Ruth offered to play in a scheduled exhibition game the next day, but after that he was done. "I don't want to drop out entirely. I can't quit this game," he lamented, but no longer would he play for Fuchs.[64]

As Ruth issued his farewell, Bill McKechnie, the Braves manager, approached. "[Ruth's] the finest guy I ever met. I hate to see it end this way," McKechnie told the reporters. Ruth and McKechnie shared an emotional handshake for photographers. McKechnie later saw Ruth off at his hotel. Roughly two hours later, a worked-up Fuchs announced Ruth's firing. In comments "laced with assertions of his own loyalty to dear old New England and grand old Boston," Fuchs maligned Ruth for having "disorganized the whole team." True, Ruth had generated some crowds early on, but "later absences and his failure to show up balanced the ledgers the wrong way." Ruth, Fuchs continued, acted like "an imbecile." Manager McKechnie had asked repeatedly that Fuchs release Ruth, who had proved a constant source of "dissension" on the last-place Braves (and McKechnie might have also mentioned a threat to his job as Braves manager).[65]

The next day, Fuchs called a press conference to pile on Ruth. An uncomfortable McKechnie stood beside his employer, then stepped forward to speak. His "hand still stinging from Babe Ruth's hearty farewell handshake," as one newspaper explained, McKechnie, now rid of Ruth's threat to his job, backed Fuchs entirely. The "main problem with the ball club was that it was not able to function properly with Ruth in the outfield." The Babe's presence resulted in a severe "lack of discipline on the club," he explained. Blame for the Braves' last-place standing rested squarely with Ruth. To his credit, the Babe, now in New York, chose not to engage McKechnie nor respond further to Fuchs.[66] The damage, however, was done.

While commentary focused on the abundant pettiness on all sides, Ruth was the one who lost his job. Ruth also seemed the most compromised party. The dustup, in effect, buttressed every negative impression about Ruth. "Irked Because He Can't Greet French Liner," read one subhead line.[67] Paul Gallico, columnist for the New York *Daily News* with a circulation of over 1.5 million by the 1930s, penned a brutal portrait of Ruth's departure from the Braves, one that exhumed all the ancient damaging images. The break with the Braves derived from a "little boy's fit of pique and disappointment because Judge Fuchs wouldn't let him go to what looked like a pretty swell party." Ruth, Gallico concluded, remained very much a child who never grew up. "They call him the Babe, and Babe he is. Life to him is very often the life of a child and bosses are not bosses at all, but grownups who interfere with his fun," wrote Gallico.[68]

Even Ruth's old friends seemed to turn on him. Ford Frick, a former Ruth ghostwriter and now president of the National League with a reputation as "a compromiser who lived in fear of the club owners who had knighted him,"[69] lamented that he did "not know of any further opportunities in the National League" for his old friend. "[Ruth] failed to take advantage of the chance given him in Boston. There was every reason for him to buckle down, keep himself in shape, obey orders and make a real future for himself there," claimed Frick, "but he didn't do it."[70] The Boston club's insolvency and Fuchs' empty promises to Ruth, however, hardly proved conducive to any "buckling down." Indeed, Fuchs lost control of the Braves weeks after releasing Ruth. Baseball officials, such as Frick, worked primarily to protect baseball's ownership class. As such, Ruth was expendable.

On July 14, 1935, Ruth attended a Sunday double-header at Yankee Stadium. As he took his seat in a box just above the Yankees dugout, the crowd of thirty-eight thousand burst into "a tremendous ovation." The demonstration reminded all parties of Ruth's continuing standing among fans. Two days later Ruppert signed Yankees manager Joe McCarthy to a two-year contract. Once again, the Yankees officials made abundantly clear to Ruth he would never manage their team.[71] Ruppert's and Barrow's message also radiated to the rest of baseball. As one writer put it, "Obviously they do not think much of Babe's dormant qualities of leadership. Otherwise Ruth would be in there as field marshal of the Yankees."[72]

After the regular season, Ruth played in a series of exhibition games. He clearly enjoyed himself and drew large crowds. On October 21, fifteen thousand fans packed Dexter Park in Queens to see the Babe. After the first game of a double header, Ruth addressed the crowd. Struggling still with injuries and soreness, he announced this would be his last game. He no longer had the ability to play even in exhibition games.[73] Ruth continued to hope a managerial slot might open for him in the major leagues. It never did.

As time passed, Ruth betrayed some bitterness alongside an optimism that he might one day get a break. Speaking to a crowd of over nine hundred at the annual baseball writers' dinner in 1937, Ruth complained of having dedicated twenty-two years of his life to baseball, "But just when it seemed to me I was on top I was dumped out." The Babe then pivoted to insist "baseball has always been fair to me . . . Col. Ruppert in particular." Heywood Broun, a sportswriter turned political columnist, known for his leftist politics, rose to defend Ruth. "It's silly for the club owners not to find a place for Ruth somewhere. Things haven't been the same since he was forced out."[74]

Baseball's elite no doubt chafed at the notion Ruth had been "forced out," but the next season, one struggling franchise saw opportunity in the Babe's eagerness to return to baseball. Larry MacPhail, the executive vice president of the Brooklyn Dodgers, who, while working earlier in Cincinnati, had tried to hire Ruth for the Reds, made a move halfway through the 1938 season. MacPhail hired Ruth as a coach. Many speculated Ruth would be in line to manage the Dodgers the next season. But in Brooklyn, Leo Durocher, a rival for the manager position, worked hard to discredit Ruth. At a particularly crucial juncture, Durocher accused Ruth of missing signals and scuffled with him in the clubhouse. Years later Durocher titled his memoirs *Nice Guys Finish Last*. Ruth, he recalled uncharitably, "was the dumbest man I had ever known."[75]

Ruth faced the ruthless likes of Durocher, Barrow, Ban Johnson, Ruppert, and Fuchs largely on his own. Athletes of the later twentieth century had staffs, agents, spokesmen, and representatives who sorted out opportunities and handled negotiations. At the height of his powers, Ruth occasionally could hold his own against the powers that be, although quite often he found himself manipulated and forced to make concessions despite his immense popularity. Baseball's reformers early on set out to hold Ruth in check, to limit and channel his power within the game. By the 1930s, both the US economy and Ruth's playing skills spiraled downward. A player of Ruth's intuitive intelligence and charisma deserved an opportunity to manage. To baseball authorities, however, he remained a threat to a longstanding cherished project. The baseball establishment was happy to see Ruth shunted aside.

TEN. "A WELL-PAID SLAVE IS NONETHELESS A SLAVE"

Baseball transformed significantly as an institution over the twenty years marking Ruth's career. Despite the costly Depression, the game had stabilized by 1935. Large crowds flocked to baseball games while millions of others followed on radio and newsreels and in newspapers. Compared to earlier in the century, baseball had extended its appeal across the country, uniting Americans of different classes, races, genders, ethnicities, and cultures.

The network of ambitious, reform-minded owners and baseball officials who formed a loose coalition before World War I could be pleased with these developments. The forces that had so worried these activists—gambling, rowdyism, and labor strife—appeared well in check by the 1930s. Baseball's ownership class now rested firmly in control; increasingly, club owners enjoyed the stability and prosperity that seemed so elusive in the early twentieth century.

Gambling, once an existential threat and a visible presence in most American ballparks, persisted, but was thoroughly contained. Baseball's well-publicized campaign against betting convinced fans that gambling and the national game were incompatible. Likewise, the violence or rowdyism so prevalent in ballparks in earlier years now was a rare occurrence. Families could venture out for Sunday games with little fear of what they might see or hear. The nation's court system had made it all but impossible for rival leagues to challenge major league baseball. The reserve clause—as restrictive a labor system as existed in America—also now bore the explicit imprimatur of the US court system. Salaries accordingly remained in check. It would not be until 1949 that another player (Joe DiMaggio) reached Ruth's high-water mark of $80,000 a year. Ruth may have led baseball to a new era of prosperity, but his fellow ballplayers remained underpaid.

All in all, the highest aspirations of the likes of Jacob Ruppert, Ban Johnson, and Ed Barrow were realized: major league baseball had become a stable, orderly, and often very profitable institution, with a distinct hierarchical and steadfast power structure.

The transformation owed much to Babe Ruth. His charisma, skill, charm, sense of drama, and wondrous persona generated unprecedented goodwill and fascination. His seeming innocence and pure love of the game inspired legions of new baseball devotees. Like never before, and arguably never since, Ruth drew fans to ballparks; he revived the sport and sustained it through scandal and tumult. Most importantly, from the point of view of baseball magnates, he produced tremendous income for the game. Even at what seemed at the time a gigantic salary, Ruth offered fabulous return on baseball's investment. Having successfully untethered itself from Ruth in 1935, the Yankees team found (after a difficult spring with Ruth still playing for the Braves) that it could sustain fan interest without the Babe. Lou Gehrig, a player who modeled propriety and stability, succeeded Ruth as fan favorite at significantly less cost. The next season, a young rookie named Joe DiMaggio joined the lineup. Barrow, it turns out, was right: the Yankees no longer needed Ruth. The team could build on what Ruth had done. Yankees management kept its distance from Ruth. Barrow made no effort to retire Ruth's team number. When he left the Yankees, Ruth's signature "3" simply passed to his successor in right field, a Canadian named George Selkirk.[1] Only Ruth's desperate illness in the late 1940s prompted the team move to honor its greatest player.

None of this was an accident. As this book has argued, Ruth always presented a dilemma for both the Yankees and baseball in general. The brazenly outspoken star threatened order in the sport as much as he drove its popularity and profitability. While largely harmless, Ruth's infrequent bursts of temper troubled baseball reformers, eager to put rowdyism and disorder behind them. His occasional gambling (never on baseball) and rumors of carousing also worried officials, who always viewed employees from a paternalistic perspective. The baseball establishment needed Ruth to project the wholesome innocence of a child playing a thrilling game; it feared, however, that Ruth might become "bigger than the game" and compromise the order owners and league officials so coveted. Most vexing was Ruth's readiness to challenge baseball authority. He had obvious sympathies for the various movements to unionize ballplayers, although he never took a leadership position in any of the organizations. His outspoken insistence that he be paid his fair due drove up salaries around the league and rattled owners. The impressive postseason exhibition tours he undertook, from which Ruth regularly profited more than his regular season earnings, also unnerved the establishment. Under the right circumstances, Ruth imaginably could organize his own rival league or join an outlaw one. A competing Ruth-led league might have provoked the most fundamental challenge ever facing major league ball. Players, frustrated by restrictive work contracts and inspired by the rebellion of a player of Ruth's unprecedented stature, might flock to such a new league.

For all of these reasons, baseball needed to break Babe Ruth, even as it aggressively strove to exploit him. Ruth's batting heroics and immense charm contributed mightily to the soaring popularity and profitability of baseball. But for the reformers, breaking Ruth was equally important to furthering the game. Owners and league officials, not players, needed to be in control. From their first meetings, Ed Barrow instinctively understood both the potential and challenge of Ruth. As his manager in Boston, Barrow violently confronted Ruth, thus initiating a power struggle that would last nearly two decades. Yankees management brought Barrow to New York largely to continue his campaign against Ruth. There, he and the Babe engaged in an ongoing tug-o'-war. Joining with Judge Kenesaw Mountain Landis, the new commissioner of baseball; Yankees owner Jacob Ruppert; and Yankees managers Miller Huggins and, later, Joe McCarthy, Barrow helped engineer a series of confrontations designed to humble and break Ruth. At every point Ruth resisted. The Babe, however, fought largely alone, and eventually he capitulated in the face of the combined, overwhelming weight of his opposition. Sportswriters, the major shapers of information about the game and its players, provided invaluable support to the reformers as they worked to contain Ruth.

In the face of sustained attacks, the Babe hung on and maintained hope that one day he would join the baseball establishment as a manager recognized for his intelligence and cunning, not just his power at bat. With record-breaking achievements both at the mound and behind the plate, to many his qualifications seemed obvious. Ruth, however—who grew up an impoverished, castaway child in Baltimore and never enjoyed much education or refinement—remained forever an outsider to baseball's halls of power. The establishment essentially blackballed him for lack of sophistication and a supposed dearth of intelligence. In truth, to baseball's ownership class, Ruth always represented the specter of player empowerment. Even as he drove the game to new heights of popularity and profits, he remained suspect. In an age when class and ethnic divisions remained sharp, Ruth's swagger, his self-confidence, his independence, and his demands all made him appear a dangerous apparition of a baseball world upside down.

"The Greatest Single Influence on Sports of the Century"

In the years following Ruth's retirement, the innocent man-child image that often surfaced during his career became increasingly cemented in popular culture. For the most part, Ruth proved a willing partner in mythologizing himself. Ruth, wrote Red Smith in a 1973 portrait, "recognized his role as public entertainer and understood it."[2] A naturally effusive personality, he enjoyed people and enjoyed giving them what they wanted. It is hard not to suspect Ruth, at times, was playing a character he had perfected over the years.

What the public seemed to want in the early years was an uncomplicated vision of youthful virtue. The year after Ruth's retirement, Rand McNally Company published *Babe Ruth's Baseball Advice*, the first of several baseball advice books written under the Babe's name. Dedicated to "American boys," the book featured instructional photographs of Ruth tutoring boys on the fine points of the game. He proffered philosophic advice such as, "Be a good loser if you have to lose." In the late 1930s, Ruth also starred in several entertaining instructional films, cementing his playful and charitable image.

In 1941, Ruth journeyed to Hollywood to film *Pride of the Yankees*, a biographical film based on the life of Lou Gehrig. Ruth played himself. As in his other movies, Ruth's charisma easily translated to celluloid. The film explicitly plays the serious, purposeful "iron man" Gehrig against the fun-loving, showboating Ruth, a contrast first constructed by sportswriters over a decade and a half before.

By the time of the film, the Babe already was ill with the cancer that eventually took his life. As his health declined, Ruth prepared his memoirs with the aid of sportswriter Bob Considine. The not-surprising result was a sentimentalized version of his life, with some useful insights. Controversial episodes received light treatment, comic stories were played up. Of his troubles in the 1920s, Ruth passed the blame to bad luck and bad associates. "The 1920's seemed to be full of fair-weather friends," he wrote, "and I wound up with most of them."[3] Ruth did offer an extensive retelling of the Johnny

Sylvester story, with added mention of Johnny's later service on a submarine during World War II. As the Babe's health faded, the New York *Daily News*, which had expended so much ink covering Ruth over the years, brought Johnny Sylvester to his idol's hospital bed. With the Babe now fighting for his life and a healthy Johnny Sylvester bringing cheer, the role reversal provided the *Daily News* its final Ruthian exclusive.[4]

Recognizing time was running out, Yankees officials finally organized a tribute, a Babe Ruth Day, reminiscent of the Lou Gehrig Day held several years earlier for another struggling pinstriped star. Appearing worn and barely able to speak, Ruth managed a couple of words to the crowd. A year later, clinging to life, he returned to Yankee Stadium and donned his old uniform for Old-Timers' Day. On both occasions, crowds showered him with sustained ovations.

With Ruth's end near, Hollywood, the success of *Pride of the Yankees* in mind, moved to produce a film version of Ruth's life. Finding an actor capable of capturing Ruth's charisma and personality proved challenging. Producers settled on character actor William Bendix, who sported a rubber nose that made him appear more daft than Ruth-like. *The Babe Ruth Story* proved a saccharine bore, playing Ruth largely as a good-hearted comedic simpleton. The film glossed over all controversy to the point of ridiculousness. Bendix-as-Ruth at one point enters a bar and orders milk. Ruth's infamous clash with Huggins in 1925, as portrayed in the film, grew out of a Ruthian line drive that hit a dog. Persuaded by the young owner of the pet dog to rush it to a hospital, Ruth ends up missing team curfew—hence the clash with Manager Huggins.

As the film debuted, Ruth neared death. With great effort, he managed to leave his hospital bed to attend the film premiere. Whether driven from the theater by the pain of illness or—equally likely—the sight of himself depicted as an on-screen clown, Ruth, accompanied by Claire, left the movie well before its end. Days later, he died.

Ruth's passing triggered a massive outpouring of public grief and sentimentalizing. Grantland Rice's eulogistic column ended, "Game called by darkness—let the curtain fall / No more remembered thunder sweeps the field. . . . The Big Guy's gone—by land or sea or foam. May the Great Umpire call him 'safe at home.'" An estimated eighty-two thousand mourners wound around Yankee Stadium, where Ruth's body lay in state. An overflow crowd of six thousand later stood outside St. Patrick's Cathedral during Ruth's funeral mass.

The stunning public response in turn inspired numerous glowing pro-files and sentimental biographical treatments. Sportswriters Dan Daniel and Tom Meany each penned popular portraits. Despite his chosen title *The Real Babe Ruth*, Daniel's book avoided reality and controversy. Tom Meany dis-avowed his book as a work of biography; rather it was, he explained, "one man's impression of the greatest baseball figure who ever lived."[5] Christy Walsh supplied the introduction to Meany's work, concluding that "Babe Ruth was the greatest single influence on sports of the century."[6] Meany at-tributed Ruth's famed stomachache, the source of so much debate, to a rocky train ride over the mountains from Knoxville, Tennessee. "Babe loved living and felt that he was as much above ordinary rules as he was above ordinary, or even extraordinary pitching," claimed Meany. This in turn explained "the big fellow's more turbulent moments" and penchant for "extra-curricular activities."[7]

Waite Hoyt, a Ruth teammate on the Yankees, weighed in with his own memories of playing with Ruth. The Babe, Hoyt acknowledged, had been something of a "Peck's bad boy" at certain points, and often "nobody knew where he went at night." But Hoyt dismissed the "usual crowd of hero snipers [who] say Babe Ruth was a good-time-Charlie, a nightclub denizen. Nothing could be further from the truth."[8]

Dozens of children's books championing Ruth played up the Horatio Al-ger, rags-to-riches angle. Guernsey van Riper Jr.'s *Babe Ruth: Baseball Boy* (1959) stands out in the genre.[9] Weaving fiction and fact and focusing on Ruth's early life at St. Mary's, Riper created a warm story of obstacles over-come with the aid of baseball. Formation of the Babe Ruth Foundation in 1947 also built Ruth's legacy as an advocate for children. The foundation promoting youth baseball boasted an awards program that distributed six thousand "Babe Ruth Sportsmanship Awards" in 1952 alone. It also provid-ed grants for cancer research and for programs encouraging recreation and the prevention of juvenile delinquency.

"Not a Boy Scout Piece"

As the 1960s, a decade that would see the rise of historical revisionism and the "new journalism," neared, Ruth's place in public memory would be turned upside down. The process began in 1959 when Clay Felker, an ambi-tious editor at *Esquire* magazine, approached sportswriter Roger Kahn with a proposal. Felker wanted a serious exposé revealing Babe Ruth as he really was, "not a boy scout piece." Kahn was too young to ever have seen Ruth play.

Offered "an attractive price" for the article, he jumped at the opportunity. He prepared a survey, sent to Ruth's surviving teammates, that became the basis of the article.[10]

Kahn aimed at nothing short of overturning a "tradition which distorts and remolded Babe Ruth almost as extensively in a decade as it remolded Abraham Lincoln in a century." The Babe, Kahn concluded in his published piece, was "a holy sinner," a man of almost "measureless lust, selfishness and appetites," a man driven by "women, money, and liquor." Kahn suppressed his conclusion that Ruth's 1925 "bellyache" was actually gonorrhea (an insinuation made by Ruth's teammate Joe Dugan), but he withheld little else. Royally debunking Ruth amounted to a public service, according to Kahn. "Just as good money drives out bad in economics, so heroic fantasy drives out historic fact and, in the case of heroes, we are often left standing in a forest of chopped down cherry trees," he postulated.[11]

Months later, sportswriter Gerald Holland followed up with an exposé in *Sports Illustrated* titled "The Babe Ruth Papers." Citing copies of Ruth's contracts and a smattering of correspondence, Holland argued that Ruth lived "a sort of double life—hero in public, a rake and a hell raiser in private."[12] In particular, Holland exposed the "no drinking" clause in Ruth's 1923 contract and the photograph of Ruth and teammates at a brewery, a photograph commissioned by Ed Barrow.[13]

The demythologized Ruth made his television debut in 1962 in a documentary, "Babe Ruth: A Look Behind the Legend," written by Kahn and produced by Howard Cosell. The program sought to offer something of a balanced view by interviewing Ruth's wife and friends, such as Waite Hoyt. But Ruth detractors, including Leo Durocher, were also featured prominently. Like Kahn's article, the television version sought to clear away the inaccuracies and reveal an individual who hardly fit the public model.

By the 1960s, an era of questioning national institutions, hero debunking, and disillusion, Ruth's public image already had swung sharply away from saintly man-child. To the public, Ruth became an adolescent on an extended binge. Concurrently, baseball itself, the supposed ideal American sport, also underwent revisionism and reappraisal. In 1970, major league pitcher Jim Bouton shocked the baseball world when he published *Ball Four: My Life and Hard Times Throwing the Knuckleball In the Big Leagues*. Bouton mercilessly mocked major league baseball with an unvarnished depiction of tightfisted management and jaded players not immune from the temptations of alcohol and drugs. To the chagrin of mainstream sportswriters and the baseball establishment, the book became a best seller. Bouton's editor, Leonard Shecter, a former sportswriter for the *New York Post*, followed up with his own sports exposé, *The Jocks*. The public, complained Shecter, persists in regarding Ruth as "a sweet soul who spent all the time he wasn't hitting home runs in hospitals making happy the last hours of children with terminal cancer." In truth, he "was a gross man of gargantuan, undisciplined appetites for food, whisky and women." Unlike Kahn a decade earlier, Shecter eagerly traded in rumors claiming Ruth's famed bellyache in reality resulted from a case of venereal disease, a story first peddled by Ed Barrow nearly fifty years earlier.[14]

In Shecter's book, Ruth does find himself in good company. Joe DiMaggio, Shecter grumbles, is "a vain, lonely man, who is a tyrant to the sycophants who surround him"; Yogi Berra, "a narrow, suspicious man, jealous of the man other people suppose him to be"; Mickey Mantle in truth was "a country boy, ill-educated, frightened, convinced by a series of deaths in his family that he was doomed to live only a short life."[15]

In 1975, as Henry Aaron approached Ruth's career home-run record, a number of high-quality biographies came out offering balanced, sophisticated treatments of Ruth's life and times. "Hank took the record, but the Babe is getting the ink," noted Roger Angell, commenting on the onslaught of Ruth books in the mid-1970s.[16] Chief among the works was Robert Creamer's *Babe: The Legend Comes to Life*. "Like all legends, Ruth's had a strong vein of truth in it—and an equally strong vein of baloney," concluded Creamer. "Researching this book was an exploration into a curious world of misleading fact, perceptive misstatement, contradictory truth, substantiating myth."[17] University of Notre Dame history professor Marshall Smelser's biography *The Life That Ruth Built* approached the story from a more scholarly but equally sensitive and substantive standpoint.

The good labors of Smelser, Creamer, and others, including Ken Sobol (*Babe Ruth & The American Dream*) and Kal Wagenheim (*Babe Ruth: His Life & Legend*), however, hardly held back the tide of Ruthian revisionism. *The Baseball Hall of Shame*, produced by Bruce Nash and Allan Zullo in the mid-1980s, for instance, brazenly rehashed gossip about Ruth. Titling their chapter on Ruth "The Most Disgusting Role Models for America's Youth," the duo painted an unrelenting negative portrait. "Thank goodness children will never know the real Babe Ruth," a man obsessed with "booze, buffets, and bimbos." Like Shecter, with little evidence beyond rumors, Nash and Zullo link Ruth's 1925 collapse to venereal disease.[18]

The Zullo and Nash book paved the way for a successful "Hall of Shame" series and a second, equally dreadful Ruth film biopic. Despite the development of color film, Hollywood still prefers some issues in black and white. If William Bendix's *The Babe Ruth Story* played Ruth as a good-hearted man-child, *The Babe* (1992), starring an obese John Goodman, fully explored the unruly, insatiable adolescent version of Ruth, glossing over any and all redeeming qualities. *The Babe*, wrote film critic Roger Ebert, depicts "a human pig who wenched and cheated on those who loved him, who was drunk during many of his games, who was small-minded and jealous." Ruth in the film appears as "a man almost completely lacking in the ability to have, or to provide, happiness."[19]

Dennis Lehane's 2008 historical novel *The Given Day* offers a more artful and thoughtful experience than the Goodman movie. Lehane's story, in which family, race, and radical politics intersect in 1919 America, features a fictional version of Ruth then playing with the Red Sox. Still, Lehane's Babe is not far from the "Hall of Shame" version. Talk of money or politics makes his head hurt. Another character describes Ruth as a "hippo-size, jiggling child with thighs so big you'd expect them to sprout branches, but a child all the same." On a train, a wound up Ruth suddenly bursts loose, tearing up and down the aisles, loudly bellowing, "I am the ape man! I am Babe F---ing Ruth. I will eat you!" Lehane's Ruth then "slapped his hands together like a wop's monkey and he scratched his ass and went 'hoo hoo, hoo' and they loved it, they loved it."[20]

Leigh Montville's *Big Bam: The Life and Times of Babe Ruth*, a best-selling biography of Ruth, appeared in 2006. A veteran sportswriter and skilled biographer, Montville penned a wonderfully entertaining and well-crafted portrait of Ruth and the sports world in which he so thrived. Montville's Babe, however, for all his talents and charity, appears largely as ringleader of a circus. At one point, Montville quotes Ban Johnson's ugly comment that Ruth bore the mind of a fifteen-year-old. It was, concluded Montville, "probably the best appraisal of the man in all of the words spoken or written."[21]

A century after he began playing professional baseball, the worst impressions of Ruth not only linger today, but they also seem to dominate contemporary representations of the baseball hero. Perhaps Americans bear a deep-seated need for a clown/hero/prince of excess. Perhaps such a figure speaks to buried desires to escape the trappings of civilized behavior. Such speculation, however, might best be left to cultural anthropologists.

Today, in fact, Ruth is remembered very much as Edward Barrow would have him remembered: a great baseball player with a crude adolescent mind-set. Barrow and others, in fact, worked diligently to undermine Ruth. The intent, of course, was to champion the Babe as an accessible and alluring popular hero while crushing the threat that "the individual Ruth" posed to the business of baseball.

Clearly, Ruth often proved a willing party in his own marginalization. Yet much of what we negatively remember about Ruth is based on impressions that often can be traced back to Ruth critics—Barrow most obviously, but others as well. Rarely do the tall tales about Ruthian excess and bad behavior stand up to close scrutiny. True, in his younger playing years Ruth openly violated Prohibition (although he was hardly alone in doing so). Yet sportswriter Red Smith, who knew the Babe well, remembered Ruth as "no boozer . . . three drinks left him fuzzy."[22] Given Ruth's size, six foot two and over two hundred pounds, Smith's comment is notable.

Emerging from abject poverty, young Ruth certainly indulged excessively in any number of vices. There is ample reason, however, to question tales of his gluttonous exploits. For one, they make good stories. Ruth's former teammates, sportswriters, and others who knew the Babe spent their lives spinning tales about the "big feller." Comical yarns of excesses and over-the-top incidents amused audiences and sold books. No one really wanted stories about a nice guy who lived cleanly and did his job well. Likewise, tales of Ruth's reckless spending abounded during his career. Many bore elements of truth: a poor boy with virtually no education suddenly enriched beyond his imagination is a recipe for disaster. But the Babe, at a relatively young age, managed to right his financial ship and secure his savings for his and his family's future, an accomplishment that has alluded many on whom fame has bestowed sudden riches. Legends of Ruth the spendthrift, it might be added, worked against him in heated contract negotiations. Casting themselves as sensible adults, Ruppert and Barrow could be seen as refusing to enable an improvident spender.

Likewise, legends regarding Ruth's sexual adventurism should give us pause. From his youth, whispers about his racial background trailed the Babe. Tales of his supposed voluptuous deeds and sexual appetite parallel all the negative racial stereotypes of the times. Peddling such gossip, those seeking to discredit Ruth, consciously or not, traded in the bigotry so very much a part of America in the 1920s, an age in which immigration restriction, eugenics, Jim Crow, and harsh discrimination of all sorts thrived largely unchallenged.

If questions hoovered in the background about Ruth and race, there was no doubt about his class background: Ruth emerged directly from "the other half," his grim early life conjuring up images from Jacob Riis's classic study of tenement life in New York City, published only five years before Ruth's birth in Baltimore. Baseball's reformers aimed to remake the game into a solid, orderly, middle-class institution. Ruth's unabashed, unapologetic, earthy persona hardly fit the model. Baseball's reformers would prefer to have championed the likes of college-educated, devout Christy Mathewson, the New York Giants ace of the prewar years. But it was Ruth—not Mathewson, Cobb, or other heroes of early baseball—who truly stirred fans as never before seen and in ways never really understood. Baseball authorities were stuck with the fan-favorite Ruth, but they never accepted him and never stopped their efforts to break him.

A New Game

While not a transformative figure like the Babe, the modern-era player who came closest to matching Ruth's style and appeal is perhaps Reggie Jackson, whose most notable feats came during his years playing for the New York Yankees. Early on in his career, Jackson experienced some of the same challenges as Ruth, in particular playing under the restrictive reserve clause. But Reggie's peak as a player coincided with a period of great change for baseball. He played the latter part of his career in what was essentially a new game, in which players had significantly more power and protection. Jackson's later experiences are worth briefly comparing to those of Ruth.

Born fifty years after Ruth, Jackson began his major league career in the late 1960s. The old reserve clause system remained intact, and Jim Crow was a very recent memory. Jackson's father, in fact, had played second base for the Newark Eagles of the Negro League. Young Reggie faced discrimination, but opportunities closed to his father were open to him. He attended and played baseball for Arizona State University and was drafted by the Kansas City Athletics in 1966. His major league debut came in 1967.

Early on, Jackson encountered the same one-sided labor system as had Ruth a half century before. The Athletics owner, the colorful Charlie O. Finley, Jackson recalled, had a simple "my way or the highway" approach to handling his players. In 1970, Reggie managed to talk Finley into a substantial raise, but the next year when Jackson struggled at bat, he suffered a corresponding pay cut. Change, however, was at hand. Inspired by the civil rights movement, Curt Flood, a St. Louis Cardinal, brazenly challenged the game's labor practices. Proclaiming that a "well-paid slave is nonetheless a slave," Flood risked his career in 1970 taking on the reserve clause system.[23] Club owners managed to beat back Flood's challenge, but early in 1975 an arbitrator's decision essentially ended the reserve clause and ushered in the era of free agency. Jackson well remembered the excitement the decision unleashed. "For the first time in 80 years, ballplayers had the same right that every other American citizen enjoys," recalled Jackson.[24]

Already, Jackson had the benefit of having a player-agent represent him in negotiations (a hard-fought right won by players in 1970). Jackson and his agent, Greg Walker, grew particularly close. In tense times, the two prayed and read Bible scriptures together.[25] Walker represented Jackson aggressively, and he, rather than Jackson, often took the heat when negotiations went sour. In 1976, under the new free-agency system, Walker negotiated a five-year, $2.96 million contract with the Yankees (his 1973 salary was $75,000). Jackson's outspoken bravado—such as pronouncing himself "the straw that stirs the drink" for the Yankees—angered some teammates and earned bad press.[26] During a June 17, 1977, game at Fenway Park, an argument between Jackson and his manager, Billy Martin, devolved into open fisticuffs in the Yankees dugout. Television cameras broadcast the confrontation live. In the combustible "Bronx Zoo" atmosphere, Jackson could count on support not only from Walker but also from Yankees team owner George Steinbrenner, who formed a close bond with his star acquisition.

The Jackson-Steinbrenner relationship later soured, and Reggie's relations with the New York press corps remained forever frayed. As a result, in 1982, again a free agent, Jackson signed with the California Angels for a salary of nearly a million a season plus a piece of the Angels gate, adding substantially to his overall yearly compensation. Among the appeals of California was owner Gene Autry, the aging film cowboy with whom Reggie forged a strong connection. Toward the end of Jackson's career, he served largely as a designated hitter, another option not open to Ruth. Retiring at forty-one (the same age as Ruth at retirement), Jackson, having reconciled with Steinbrenner, became a special assistant and consultant to the Yankees. He also has become involved in attempts to buy major league teams, although without success.

Jackson's career was both memorable and tumultuous. Yet he always benefited from strong support networks, including an aggressive players' union and an agent who handled complex dealings, allowing Jackson, to some extent, to focus on baseball. Likewise, with the era of free agency, when dissatisfied with a manager, owner, or his compensation, Jackson could simply shift teams. That his final years as a player were less turbulent than Ruth's (although never turbulent free) undoubtedly related to Jackson's return to the more peaceful confines of Southern California.

By contrast, Ruth faced the challenge of career management largely by himself—in the glaring spotlight of New York City. Sports agents were not unheard of in the 1920s and 1930s, but baseball club owners simply refused to negotiate contracts with anyone other than the players themselves. A player of unprecedented talent and popularity, Ruth managed to secure extraordinarily lucrative contracts, largely the result of fears he might go "outlaw." Still, the sums Ruth negotiated remained negligible compared to salaries in the later free-agency era (and smaller than those negotiated by contemporaries in other sports).

The idea that Ruth in any way operated under a handicap struck observers at the time as absurd. By and large, the public in the 1920s and 1930s accepted the narrative of owners as paternalistic figures looking out for the best interest of the youthful employees. Even to modern ears, the notion of Babe as a victim strikes a sour note. Curt Flood was not the first to compare the lot of ballplayers to slaves, but he was the first to be taken seriously (by some, at least). During Ruth's era, activist players and others often made the analogy, but a compliant press always summarily dismissed the notion. In the 1930 baseball season, a New York State assemblyman proposed doing away with the reserve clause. In doing so, he linked, as others had done before and have since, the reserve clause to slavery. The comparison drew immediate rebuke and ridicule from sportswriters. "Everyone knows," mocked John Kieran, that baseball players "are held in cruel bondage by the reserve clause. From time to time, they are shipped here and there by some Simon Legree. They are purchased and bartered like cattle at a country fair." For instance, "That famous slave G. H. Ruth . . . was offered a miserable pittance of $70,000 to play in the hot sun at Yankee Stadium next summer." Appalled at the sum, "The Yankees slave fled the plantation and made his way to Florida."[27] Adding his two cents, Grantland Rice weighed in that "the ball player is in no part of a slave."[28] Nearly a half century later, Flood also encountered sharp criticism for the slavery analogy, but he also generated defenders. His defiance led to the collapse of the reserve clause and a new era of player empowerment.

Certainly, the injustices facing Ruth in the 1920s and 1930s, and Flood in the 1960s and 1970s, hardly rival the most egregious wrongs of the times. In Ruth's case, he amassed a tremendous fortune and enjoyed the adulation of millions. Yet in many ways, Ruth succumbed to the power of baseball, which generally mirrored the larger culture and priorities of the times.

This story is really about broader power structure and an outsider's efforts to carve out a place within. As Curt Flood would find in the early 1970s, defiance exacted a heavy price. By the late 1970s and 1980s, an unjust system collapsed. The likes of Reggie Jackson still encountered obstacles—both those fashioned by themselves and those associated with the baseball establishment. Jackson, however, unlike Ruth, was afforded the dignity of taking his talents and moving on if he found circumstances not to his liking. Ruth, for all the luxuries in which he rejoiced, never enjoyed that freedom.

In many ways, the Babe's life amounted to a study in contrasts. Harsh material and emotional deprivation marked his early years. At St. Mary's Industrial School, he received structure, regular meals, and baseball. Still, the school bore an unmistakable resemblance to a prison. Beginning in 1914, when he left St. Mary's to play professional baseball, his life utterly transformed. Few have experienced such a swift and complete turnabout. Suddenly Ruth enjoyed more wealth and adulation than he ever imagined existed. Most of all, he seemed to revel in freedom, an ingredient so absent from his early years. Ruth milked that freedom with reckless joy. His abandon left victims, his first wife in particular. But he also indulged a generous streak, borne no doubt from vivid memories of his own poverty. His outspokenness seemed a product of his newfound freedom. Ruth supported joint-player action, criticized baseball's unfair labor practices, pressed for his fair share in contract disputes, and supported other players against management. He even dared attack his own team's management.

None of this was well received by the baseball establishment. Owners and league officials welcomed the wave of prosperity that Ruth brought, but fretted over his willingness to challenge their control. The Babe arrived on the baseball scene amid an ongoing, often futile battle to rid the sport of nefarious influences. Ruth presented a real threat to their plans. His freewheeling ways needed to be curbed. Baseball officials thus launched an offensive against Ruth that lasted several decades. Dramatic moves such as suspensions combined with a low-level campaign to infantilize the Babe. Quickly that campaign forced Ruth into a corner.

Initially, Ruth failed to recognize the forces assembled against him. In fact, he was never as free as he thought. By the late 1920s, Ruth had caught on and recognized baseball's supreme power. Increasingly, he played the good citizen and talked of carving out a place for himself as a manager and advocate for disadvantaged children. As he entered the last years of his career, he regularly signaled his support for baseball's establishment and the reform agenda. Yet memories of Ruth's early intransigence proved too much for baseball's leadership class to overcome. The Babe was essentially forced out of the game and blackballed from future management positions.

In the last years of his life, he no longer seemed to revel in freedom. Certainly he had matured, and the carousing had gotten old. Yet he also had grown cautious of baseball's iron fist. As late as 1945, Ruth still was fruitlessly offering his services to manage either the Yankees or another team. "I am entitled to at least one chance," he pleaded.[29]

As Ruth strove to get back into the game, African Americans grew increasingly vocal, demanding the integration of baseball. Activists pointed to the large number of blacks serving in World War II. A pamphlet distributed in New York City bore the photograph of a dead African American soldier with the caption, "good enough to die for his country but not good enough to play baseball."[30] As pressure built, a reporter from the *Pittsburgh Courier*, the nation's leading African American newspaper, contacted Ruth for his position on desegregating baseball. Ruth's willingness to play against black teams and his befriending of black players had drawn notice over the years. Clearly activists hoped a word from the Babe, once so outspoken, might have made a fundamental difference. Ruth, however, offered only a "no comment"; he remained "silent" on the issue.[31] Perhaps he harbored unspoken biases; more likely he feared offending the baseball establishment. Despite all he had done to mend and address the challenges plaguing baseball, in the end, the forces combined against him were stronger than the powerhouse hero. More than any other individual, Babe Ruth forged modern professional baseball, but the business of baseball, in return, broke the man.

NOTES

Introduction

1. Red Smith, "Did Babe Ruth Have the Mind of an Eight-Year Old, Writer Has His Doubts," *Milwaukee Sentinel*, January 27, 1959.

2. Paul Gallico, "Exciting Truth," *Daily News* (New York), June 4, 1935.

3. George H. (Babe) Ruth and Bob Considine, *The Babe Ruth Story*, 12.

4. Smith, "Did Babe Ruth Have the Mind of an Eight-Year-Old."

Chapter One

1. George Herman Ruth, *Babe Ruth's Own Book of Baseball*, 3–4.

2. Brother Gilbert, CFX, *Young Babe Ruth: His Early Life and Baseball Career, from the Memoirs of a Xaverian Brother*, ed. Harry Rothgerber, ix.

3. Leigh Montville, *The Big Bam: The Life and Times of Babe Ruth*, 22.

4. Ibid., 37.

5. Ibid., 38.

6. Ibid., 41.

7. Albert G. Spalding, *America's National Game*, 219.

8. William Cook, *The Louisville Grays Scandal of 1877*.

9. "Open Gambling at Polo Grounds," *Pittsburgh Press*, June 20, 1912.

10. Thomas Rice, "Giants Beginning to Prep for World Series Games," *Brooklyn Daily Eagle*, September 9, 1917.

11. "Open Gambling at Polo Grounds."

12. "M'Graw Angry at Giants; Accuses Them in Defeat," *The Day* (New London, CT), October 4, 1916. Earlier, McGraw himself had been the object of some suspicion. See Charles Alexander, *John McGraw*, 72–73, 224–15. In 1909, an NL inquiry into what amounted to an end-of-season playoff game between the Chicago Cubs and New York Giants revealed attempts to bribe an umpire. Evidence pointed to a Giants team doctor or possibly even Giants manager John McGraw (an iconic but troubled figure around whom allegations of gambling constantly swirled) as the source of the bribe.

13. Hugh Fullerton, "American Gamblers and Gambling," *American Magazine,* February 1914, 33.

14. Westbrook Pegler, "A Look at Baseball Fans," *News-Tribune* (Rome, GA), August 6, 1951.

15. Sam Weller, "White Sox Down Coast Team 5–2," *Chicago Daily Tribune,* March 24, 1913.

16. "Umpire's Action Arouses Fans' Ire," *New York Times,* May 23, 1913.

17. Sam Weller, "Averting Defeat by Unfair Tactics Is Not Worth the Price Paid," *Chicago Daily Tribune,* July 7, 1913.

18. Alexander, *John McGraw,* 5.

19. "Attack M'Graw after Giants Win," *New York Times,* July 1, 1913; "To Investigate Fight," *New York Times,* July 2, 1913. Ad Brennan was the Phillies pitcher in question.

20. "White Shirts of Ball Fans Caused Riot at Philadelphia," *Pittsburgh Press,* August 31, 1913; Alexander, *John McGraw,* 170.

21. "Giants in Fisticuffs: Manager and Players Exchange Blows in Cincinnati," *New York Times,* August 10, 1913.

22. "Fight on Bench," *The Day* (New London, CT), July 19, 1913.

23. "League Umpire Knocked Out," *Chicago Daily Tribune,* July 4, 1913. An early July Kentucky-Illinois-Tennessee League (or KITTY League) matchup turned very ugly when the manager of the Cairo, Illinois, team struck and knocked unconscious a league umpire over a disputed call.

24. "Near Riot Marks Diamond Battle," *Chicago Daily Tribune,* July 21, 1913. Also see "Walter Johnson Loses," *New York Times,* October 6, 1913. An end-of-season barnstorming game in New York between the Schenectady Mohawk Colored Giants and the Walter Johnson All-Stars also brought angry fans onto the field. A crowd of six thousand became restless when the Giants refused to take the field until paid six weeks of back wages owed by their manager. The standoff became unbearable for fans who "surged upon the field, and it was with difficulty that the squad of police" quelled the riot. Remarkably, peace was reestablished, and the Giants went on to beat Johnson's assembled stars.

25. "Baseball Claims 15 Victims," *Chicago Daily Tribune,* December 15, 1913.

26. G. Edward White, *Creating the National Pastime: Baseball Transforms Itself 1903–1953,* 62–64; Lesley Humphreys, "Diamond Mines: Players Organize the Major Leagues Exhibit at the National Baseball Hall of Fame," *Labor's Heritage* 10 (Fall 1998): 7, insists most players resented the reserve clause.

27. Harold Seymour, *Baseball: The Golden Age,* 210.

28. Seymour, *Baseball,* 221–39; on Ward, also see Bryan Di Salvatore, *A Clever Base-Ballist: The Life and Times of John Montgomery Ward.*

29. "Baseball Players," *Lewiston Daily Sun,* July 30, 1900.

30. Amber Roessner, *Inventing Baseball Heroes: Ty Cobb, Christy Mathewson, and the Sporting Press in America,* 85–86; Charles Leerhsen, *Ty Cobb: A Terrible Beauty,* 255–61.

31. Charles C. Alexander, *Ty* Cobb, 105–6.

32. Dan Holmes, *Ty Cobb: A Biography*, 60.

33. Alexander, *Ty Cobb*, 106.

34. "Cobb Answers Navin," *Pittsburgh Gazette-Times*, April 14, 1913.

35. "President Navin Tells of Some of His Troubles with Star Baseball Player, Ty Cobb," *Lewiston Evening Journal* (Lewiston, ME), April 16, 1914; "Baseball Is to Be Probed," *The Day* (New London, CT), April 23, 1913.

36. "Baseball Player Enviable Slave," *The Day* (New London, CT), July 19, 1913.

37. Roessner, *Inventing Baseball Heroes*, 99.

38. "Fultz Demands Better Treatment of Players," *Pittsburgh Gazette-Times*, June 5, 1913.

39. "Magnates Sour on Fultz," *Pittsburgh Press*, May 7, 1914.

40. "Driving Rain Storm Prevents Game at Augusta Today," *Brooklyn Daily Eagle*, March 19, 1913.

41. "Local Feds Open Season," *Pittsburgh Press*, April 14, 1914.

42. Seymour, *Baseball*, 202.

43. "Denies Fed Offer to Cobb," *Reading Eagle*, June 30, 1914.

44. Benjamin Rader, *Baseball: A History of America's Game*, 3rd ed., 112.

45. Carol Leon, "The Life of American Workers in 1915," *Monthly Labor Review*, US Bureau of Labor Statistics, February 2016, accessed August 29, 2017, https://www.bls.gov/opub/mlr/2016/article/the-life-of-american-workers-in-1915.htm. The average MLB salary exceeded $4 million in 2015.

46. Seymour, *Baseball*, 208.

47. Hugh Fullerton, "Discipline Disappears in Baseball," *Pittsburgh Press*, April 27, 1914.

48. Seymour, *Baseball*, 208.

49. Seymour, *Baseball*, 216.

50. Daniel R. Levitt, *The Battle That Forged Modern Baseball: The Federal League Challenge and Its Legacy*, 111.

51. Seymour, *Baseball*, 219.

52. Hugh Fullerton, "When Will This Cruel War End," *Milwaukee Journal*, April 27, 1915.

53. Levitt, *Battle That Forged Modern Baseball*, 145.

54. "Sign Everyone Is Order Sent Out," *Pittsburgh Press*, January 10, 1915.

55. "Barrow Circuit Is Opening Today," *The Day* (New London, CT), April 26, 1916.

56. Seymour, *Baseball*, 212–15. Landis, however, made no ruling in the case. He held off, expecting an out-of-court settlement between the parties.

57. White, *Creating the National Pastime*, 70.

58. H. C. Hamilton, "Fultz Says He Is Sure of Support," *Pittsburgh Press*, January 17, 1917.

59. Robert F. Burk, *Never Just a Game: Players, Owners, and American Baseball to 1920*, 214.

60. "Hoblitzel Will Back Fraternity," *Pittsburgh Gazette-Times*, January 21, 1917. Tom Simon, "Dick Hoblitzel," Society for American Baseball Research (SABR) biography project, accessed July 9, 2016, https://sabr.org/bioproj/person/cb3838ec.

61. "Fultz Dictation Irksome to Minors," *Boston Evening Globe*, January 18, 1917.

62. "Boston Players to Support Fultz," *Boston Evening Globe*, January 19, 1917.

63. Thomas Rice, "Few Hold Outs Anticipated," *Brooklyn Daily Eagle*, February 15, 1917.

64. "Break with the Players' Body," *Boston Evening Globe*, January 18, 1917.

65. "Tener Proposes to Prevent Rowdyism," *The Day* (New London, CT), March 29, 1917.

66. Jack Veiock, "In the World of Sports," *Evening Independent* (St. Petersburg, FL), March 27, 1917.

67. "Pitcher Babe Ruth Punches Umpire Owens on the Jaw," *Pittsburgh Press*, June 24, 1917.

68. "Baseball's Rowdy Era Has Returned," *The Day* (New London, CT), July 25, 1917.

69. James Crusinberry, "Riot at Sox Game Started by Gamblers of Boston," *Chicago Daily Tribune*, June 18, 1917.

70. James Crusinberry, "Fans in Boston Riot on Field, as White Sox Win 7–2," *Chicago Daily Tribune*, June 17, 1917; Roger Abrams, *The Dark Side of the Diamond: Gambling, Violence, Drugs, and Alcoholism in the National Pastime*, 58; Daniel E. Ginsburg, *The Fix Is In: A History of Baseball Gambling and Game Fixing Scandals*, 85.

71. Jim Leeke, "Delaware Shipbuilding League, 1918," SABR, accessed August 27, 2015, http://sabr.org/research/delaware-river-shipbuilding-league-1918.

72. "Slacking Baseball Players," *Reading Eagle*, May 17, 1918.

73. F. C. Lane, "A Rising Menace to the National Game," *Baseball Magazine*, August 1918, 345.

74. Robert Creamer, *Babe: The Legend Comes to Life*, 161–64.

75. "Shipbuilders in Baseball Series," *The Day* (New London, CT), August 30, 1918.

76. "Gambling in Baseball Must Be Wiped Out, *Pittsburgh Press*, November 26, 1918.

77. "Jangle over Money Retards Game an Hour," *Chicago Daily Tribune*, September 11, 1918.

78. Allan Wood, *Babe Ruth and the 1918 Red Sox*, 324–26.

79. Wood, *Babe Ruth and the 1918 Red Sox*, 327.

80. "Most League Ball Players Will Become Ship Builders," *Milwaukee Journal*, August 29, 1918.

81. James Crusinberry, "Holdouts Start Worrying Baseball Magnates," *Chicago Daily Tribune*, December 27, 1919.

82. John Kasson, *Amusing the Million: Coney Island at the Turn of the Century*, 4–5; also see Robert Wiebe, *The Search for Order: 1877–1920*.

83. Eugene C. Murdock, *Ban Johnson: Czar of Baseball*, 23.

84. Ibid., 39.

85. "Ball Players May Strike," *Star and Sentinel* (Gettysburg, PA), July 22, 1914.

86. "Ban Johnson Hears of Gambling at Boston," *Milwaukee Sentinel*, August 31, 1915; Michael T. Lynch, *Harry Frazee, Ban Johnson, and the Feud That Nearly Destroyed the American League*, 56.

87. "Tener Proposes to Prevent Rowdyism."

88. Thomas Rice, "Giants Beginning to Prep for World Series Games," *Brooklyn Daily Eagle*, September 9, 1917.

89. "A Bit of Testimony," *Brooklyn Daily Eagle*, June 16, 1917.

90. Jacob Ruppert, "The Ten-Million Dollar Toy," *Saturday Evening Post*, March 28, 1931, 18, 116.

91. "Ruppert, a Bachelor, Left All to 3 Women," *Brooklyn Daily Eagle*, January 20, 1939.

92. Michael Haupert and Kenneth Winter, "Pay Ball: Estimating Profitability of the New York Yankees, 1915–1937," *Essays in Economics and Business History* 21 (2003): 92.

93. "Yankees Are Sold after Many Delays," *Brooklyn Daily Eagle*, January 31, 1915.

94. Ruppert, "Ten-Million Dollar Toy," 119.

95. Harry Grayson, "Huggins Excelled as Lead-Off Man," *Pittsburgh Press*, June 5, 1943.

96. Thomas Rice, "Lit'ry Feller Fail to Shine at Covering World Series," *Brooklyn Daily Eagle*, October 17, 1917.

97. Edward Barrow and James Kahn, *My Fifty Years in Baseball*, 65.

98. "Yankees Favor Move to Fight Diamond Polls," *Evening Independent* (St. Petersburg, FL), December 3, 1926.

99. David Halberstam, *The Summer of '49*, 198; Neil Lanctot, "A General Understanding: Organized Baseball and Black Professional Baseball, 1900–1930," in *Sport and the Color Line: Black Athletes and Race Relations in Twentieth Century America*, ed. Patrick B. Miller and David K. Wiggins, 85.

100. Barrow and Kahn, *Fifty Years in Baseball*, 60.

101. Barrow and Kahn, *Fifty Years in Baseball*, 91.

102. Westbrook Pegler, "Meet Ed Barrow, Philanthropist, Friend of Ruth," *Chicago Daily Tribune*, March 20, 1933.

103. Levitt, *Battle That Forged Modern Baseball*, 226.

104. Ruppert, "Ten-Million Dollar Toy," 18, 116, 119.

105. Pegler, "Meet Ed Barrow."

106. Connie Mack, *Connie Mack's Baseball Book*, 34.

107. "Driving Rain."

108. William Harper, *How You Played the Game: The Life of Grantland Rice*, 523.

109. David Nasaw, *The Chief: The Life of William Randolph Hearst*, 76.

110. Michael Emery, Edwin Emery, and Nancy L. Roberts, *The Press and America: An Interpretive History of the Mass Media*, 9th ed., 289; Ivy Lee, *The Press Today: How the News Reaches the Public*, 5.

111. William Maulsby, *Getting the News*, 11.

112. Oliver Pilat*, Pegler: Angry Man of the Press*, 103–4.

NOTES TO PAGES 36–42

113. Ibid., 218.

114. "Marshall Hunt," in *No Cheering in the Press Box*, ed. Jerome Holtzman, 18; Roessner, *Inventing Baseball Heroes*, 76–77.

115. Ruth and Considine, *Babe Ruth Story*, 126.

116. *Problems of Journalism: Proceedings of the 5th Annual Meeting of the ASNE*, Washington DC, January 14 and 15th, 1927, 153.

117. Silas Bent, *Ballyhoo: The Voice of the Press*, 31.

118. Ibid., 44.

119. Grantland Rice, *The Tumult and the Shouting: My Life in Sport*, 147.

120. Stanley Walker, *City Editor*, 111.

121. Lawrence W. Murphy, ed., *Sport Writing of Today and Selections from the Best Sport Stories*, 8.

122. American Society of Newspaper Editors, *Problems of Journalism: Proceedings of the 6th Annual Meeting of the ASNE*, Washington, DC, April 20–21, 1928, 17.

123. Walker, *City Editor*, 125.

124. ASNE, *Problems of Journalism: Proceedings of the 4th Annual Meeting of the ASNE*, Washington, DC, January 15–16, 1926, 98.

125. John R. Tunis, "The Great Myth," in *A Literature of Sports*, ed. Tom Dodge, 208, 214.

126. ASNE, *Proceedings of the 4th Annual Meeting*, 27.

127. Maury Allen, *Where Have You Gone Joe DiMaggio? The Story of America's Last Hero*, 55.

128. Dick Young, "Being a Baseball Writer," *Baseball Digest*, January 1953, 86–88.

129. ASNE, *Proceedings of the 4th Annual Meeting*, 108.

130. ASNE, *Problems of Journalism: Proceedings of the 5th Annual Meeting*, 103.

131. ASNE, *Problems of Journalism: Proceedings of the 8th Annual Meeting of the ASNE*, Washington, DC, April 17–19, 1930, 177.

132. ASNE, *Proceedings of the 8th Annual Meeting*, 177.

133. ASNE, *Proceedings of the 5th Annual Meeting*, 96.

134. ASNE, *Proceedings of the 6th Annual Meeting*, 16.

135. Young, "Being a Baseball Writer," 86–88.

136. Marian Christy, "Controversial Howard Cosell Tells It Like It Is," *Reading Eagle*, July 2, 1973.

137. Christy Mathewson, "Just Baseball," *Pearson's Magazine*, June 29, 1913, 730.

138. "Scribbled by Scribes," *Sporting News*, October 4, 1923.

Chapter Two

1. Rice, *Tumult and the Shouting*, 101.

2. "Pipp and Lewis Sends in Contracts," *New York Times*, February 25, 1919; Creamer, *Babe*, 187.

3. Creamer, *Babe*, 187.

4. Creamer, *Babe*, 188; Billy Evans, "Ruth Sensation of 1918 Season," *Chicago Sunday Tribune*, November 17, 1918.

5. "Babe Ruth Finally Signs with Boston," *New York Times*, March 22, 1919.

6. James Crusinberry, "Ruth Cracks Record Home Run," *Chicago Sunday Tribune*, August 17, 1919.

7. W. O. McGeehan, "Longest Drive Ever Seen under Shadow of Coogan's Bluff . . .," *New York Tribune*, September 25, 1919.

8. "Ruth Wallops Out His 28th Home Run," *New York Times*, September 25, 1919.

9. Ring Lardner, *Selected Stories*, ed. Jonathan Yardley, 140–41.

10. "Perfumed Notes for Ruth," *New York Times*, September 21, 1919.

11. Barrow and Kahn, *Fifty Years in Baseball*, 103–6; Creamer, *Babe*, 194–95; Montville, *Big Bam*, 87–88; "Ruth Is Suspended," *Boston Globe*, May 1, 1919. In his "as told to" autobiography, Ruth acknowledges the clash with Barrow but portrays himself as taking the high ground. Had the two fought, Ruth concluded, "I had sense enough to realize I couldn't win, even if I beat him." Ruth and Considine, *Babe Ruth Story*, 76.

12. Daniel Levitt, *Ed Barrow: The Bulldog Who Built the Yankees' First Dynasty*, 73, 215; "Barrow Is Sorry for Attack on Slocum," *Schenectady Gazette*, June 24, 1930.

13. Creamer, *Babe*, 202.

14. Mark Inabinett, *Grantland Rice and His Heroes: The Sportswriter as Mythmaker in the 1920s*, 40.

15. "Baseball Moguls See Dire Changes," *New York Times*, April 14, 1919.

16. "Bush Demands Release or Season's Pay from Boston," *Chicago Daily Tribune*, August 15, 1919.

17. Norman Macht, *Connie Mack: The Turbulent and Triumphant Years, 1915–1931*, 193.

18. Lynch, *Harry Frazee*, 78.

19. "Scribbled by Scribes," *Sporting News*, December 4, 1919.

20. Grantland Rice, "The Sportlight," *New York Tribune*, December 19, 1919.

21. "Ruth's Contract Is Turned Back," *Chicago Daily Tribune*, December 25, 1919.

22. Louis Dougher, "Looking 'Em Over," *Washington Times*, November 1, 1919.

23. "Ruth Signs for Movie Stunt," *Chicago Daily Tribune*, October 23, 1919; "Ruth's Liking for Boston Is Pathetic," *Sporting News*, January 1, 1920.

24. W. J. MacBeth, "Home Run King Bound to Club by a Contract," *New York Tribune*, January 3, 1920.

25. "In the Wake of the News," *Chicago Daily Tribune*, December 31, 1919.

26. Dougher, "Looking 'Em Over."

27. George Moreland, "Ruth Now Pulling Hold-up on Frazee's Red Sox," *Washington Herald*, December 26, 1919.

28. Dougher, "Looking 'Em Over."

29. "Ruth's Liking for Boston Is Pathetic."

30. Haupert and Winter, "Pay Ball," 96.

31. Ruth and Considine, *Babe Ruth Story*, 81–82.

32. "Transfer of Contract Does Not End Story of Ruth Deal," *Sporting News*, January 15, 1920.

33. "Editorial," *Boston Post*, January 6, 1920.

34. "Mightiest Slugger Reaches Agreement with Manager," *New York Tribune*, January 7, 1920; "Frazee Finds Defender in His Release of BR," *Sporting News*, January 15, 1920.

35. "Ruth Accepts Terms of Yankees," *New York Times*, January 7, 1920; Creamer, *Babe*, 212.

36. "Ruth Puts Frazee on His In-Bad List," *Sporting News*, January 15, 1920.

37. "The High Cost of Home Runs," *New York Times*, January 7, 1920.

38. Rice, "Sportlight," *New York Tribune*, February 7, 1920.

39. Rice, "Sportlight," *New York Tribune*, February 26, 1920.

40. Eugene Kessler, "Short Sport," *South Bend Tribune*, February 27, 1920.

41. Christy Mathewson, "Matty Supports Work of Umpires," *New York Times,* January 16, 1920.

42. Damon Runyon, "Th' Mornin's Mornin'," *New York American*, January 7, 1920.

43. Fred Lieb, "Ruth Brings Joy to Yankee Fandom," *The Sun* (New York), January 6, 1920.

44. W. J. MacBeth, "Huggins Faces an Easier Task Than Last Year," *New York Tribune*, January 8, 1920.

45. "Yanks Pound Ball and Blank Robins," *New York Times*, April 12, 1920. Also see Richard Freyer, "Frantic Fans Breakup the Yankee-Dodger Game to Lionize Babe," *Evening World* (New York), April 12, 1920.

46. James T. Farrell, *My Baseball Diary*, 191.

47. "Babe Ruth Mobbed by Admiring Crowd," *Daily News* (New York), September 18, 1920.

48. Neil Smelser, *Theory of Collective Behavior*, 170–76. On collective behavior and sports, also see Jerry Lewis, *Sports Fan Violence in North America*; and Leon Mann, "Sports Crowds and the Collective Behavior Perspectives," in *Sports, Games, and Play: Social and Psychological Viewpoints*, ed. Jeffrey Goldstein.

49. *Headin' Home*, directed by Lawrence Windom, (New York: Kessel and Baumann, 1920), film.

50. W. O. McGeehan, "In All Fairness," *New York Tribune*, April 12, 1920.

51. "A New Hero of the Great American Game at Close Range," *Current Opinion*, October 1920.

52. Mark Dyreson, "The Emergence of Consumer Culture and the Transformation of Physical Culture in American Sport in the 1920s," *Journal of Sport History* 16, no. 3 (1989): 261.

53. On celebrity culture during the 1920s, see Karen Sternheimer, *Celebrity Culture and the American Dream: Stardom and Social Mobility*, 50–71; Amy Henderson, "Media and the Rise of the Celebrity Culture," *OAH Magazine of American History* 6 (Spring 1992): 49–54; Charles Ponce de Leon, *Self-Exposure: Human-Interest Journalism and the Emergence of Celebrity in America, 1890–1940*. For a general survey, see Nathan Miller, *New World Coming: The 1920s and the Making of Modern America*.

54. "To Boost Yanks Visit," *New York Times*, January 9, 1920, 39.

55. W. J. MacBeth, "Babe Ruth Big Attraction at Way Stations in South," *New York Tribune*, March 1, 1920.

56. Rice, "Sportlight," *New York Tribune*, January 22, 1920.

57. Benjamin De Casseres, "Baseball Extra! Bat 'Em Out," *New York Times,* April 18, 1920.

58. W. J. MacBeth, "Mr. Mogridge Fans Famous Slugger Twice," *New York Tribune*, March 11, 1920.

59. "Babe Ruth's Muff Costs Yankee Opening Game with Athletics," *Evening World* (New York), April 15, 1920.

60. Robert Maxwell, "Babe Ruth Makes a Big Hit When He Takes a Joke," *Philadelphia Inquirer*, April 16, 1920; "Big Crowds Pay to See Ruth Fall Down," *Sporting News*, April 22, 1920.

61. McGeehan, "In All Fairness," *New York Tribune*, April 19, 1920.

62. W. O. McGeehan, "Ruth Will Be Out of Game for 10 Days, Says Physician," *New York Tribune*, April 24, 1920.

63. W. O. McGeehan, "Ruth's Presence Upsets Rivals in Last Inning," *New York Tribune*, April 22, 1920.

64. William B. Hanna, "Babe Slams Again for the Circuit," *The Sun* (New York), May 3, 1920.

65. Damon Runyon, "Honorable Ruth Is Rapidly Liquidating," *New York American*, May 3, 1920.

66. W. O. McGeehan, "Babe's Two Home Runs and Triple Barely Win for Yanks," *New York Tribune*, May 12, 1920.

67. Hugh Fullerton, "Baseball Returns to Old Slam Bang Style," *South Bend Tribune*, July 8, 1920. Veteran writer Fullerton argued that the "new" era of the lively ball actually represented a throwback to an earlier "system of play 25 years ago." Also see David Voigt, *American Baseball*, vol. 2, *From the Commissioners to Continental Expansion*, 150; and Montville, *Big Bam*, 111.

68. McGeehan, "In All Fairness," *New York Tribune*, May 31, 1920.

69. Sid Mercer, "The Modern Achilles," *Evening Journal* (New York), July 8, 1920.

70. Montville, *Big Bam*, 160.

71. Runyon, "Mornin's Mornin'," *New York American*, September 9, 1920.

72. W. O. McGeehan, "Did Babe Ruth Get Another Today," *New York Tribune*, August 22, 1920; On "autosuggestion," see Miller, *New World Coming*, 128.

73. "Babe Ruth Would Try for 55 Home Runs," *Daily News* (New York), September 14, 1920.

74. Allen Guttmann, *Sports: The First Five Millennia*, 5, 141.

75. "Ruth Hits 31st," *New York American*, July 20, 1920.

76. W.O. McGeehan, "Babe Ruth Home Run Record," *New York Tribune*, July 20, 1920.

77. Neil Sullivan, *The Diamond in the Bronx: Yankee Stadium and the Politics of New York*, 19.

78. Dan Daniel, "High Lights and Shadows in All Spheres of Sport," *The Sun* (New York), January 6, 1920.

79. W. O. McGeehan, "Champion Slugger Brings Toll to Thirty-One," *New York Tribune*, July 20, 1920.

80. Rice, "Sportlight," *New York Tribune*, August 11, 1920.

81. Damon Runyon, "Players Work Out on Links," March 3, 1920, in *Guys, Dolls, and Curveballs: Damon Runyon on Baseball*, ed. Jim Reisler, 299.

82. Babe Ruth, "Babe Ruth Earns B.B. Degree at Reform School," *Chicago Sunday Tribune*, August 8, 1920.

83. "Ruth Insists He Never Suffered with a Case of Ego," *Chicago Daily Tribune*, August 20, 1920.

84. "Sid Mercer's Close-Ups," *Evening World* (New York), July 10, 1920.

85. Edward Sparrow, "Heard Around the Horn," *The Sun* (Baltimore), August 15, 1920.

86. Grand Central Palace Shoes Advertisement, *New York American*, June 27, 1920.

87. "No Wonder She Smiles," *Ogden Standard Examiner*, June 12, 1920.

88. Sam Crane, "Hub Fans Greet Ruth Their Old Idol," *Evening Journal* (New York), May 27, 1920.

89. F. C. Lane, "How Babe Ruth Became the Home Run King," *Baseball Magazine*, April 1920, 656.

90. McGeehan, "Did Babe Ruth Get Another Today"; "Scribbled by Scribes," *Sporting News*, September 2, 1920.

91. George H. Ruth, *The "Home-Run King," or, How Pep Pindar Won His Title*, 4, 10.

92. Windom, *Headin' Home*.

93. "The Screen," *New York Times*, September 20, 1920.

94. Art Rust Jr., *Recollections of a Baseball Junkie*, 37–38. Also see Montville, *Big Bam*, 21, 365.

95. Fred Lieb, *Baseball as I Have Known It*, 164. Also see Tom Stanton, *Ty and the Babe: Baseball's Fiercest Rivals*.

96. David Steele, "The Babe Went to Bat for Black Players," *The Sun* (Baltimore), June 29, 2008; Bill Jenkinson, "Babe Ruth and the Issue of Race," last updated 2016, accessed October 15, 2016, http://www.baberuthcentral.com/the-humanitarian/babe-ruth-and-the-issue-of-race-bill-jenkinson/; Robert Kuhn McGregor, *A Calculus of Color: The Integration of Baseball's American League*, 83, 145.

97. "Babe Ruth Helps Church," *Chicago Defender*, October 20, 1923.

98. Bugs Baer, "Two and Three," *New York American*, January 6, 1920.

99. Louis Dougher, "Dougher Says Swatter Is Danger to Losing Out," *Washington Times*, May 25, 1925.

100. W. O. McGeehan, "Billy Evans Sad Manager after Splendid Start," *Wilmington Morning Star*, June 29, 1930.

101. "Campaign against Gamblers Started," *Sporting News*, May 27, 1920.

102. Robert Maxwell, "Babe Ruth Has Done More Than Help Yankees; He has Stimulated Interest in the Game Everywhere," *Public Ledger* (Philadelphia), July 30, 1920.

103. "Scribbled by Scribes," *Sporting News*, August 5, 1920.

104. "Ruth Is Hero Where Once Cobb Reigned," *Sporting News*, August 12, 1920.

105. "More Space to Ruth Than to Flag Race," *Sporting News*, September 16, 1920.

106. "Entitled to His Day," *Sporting News*, August 5, 1920.

107. Damon Runyon, "Pitched Ball in Yankee Game Fractures Chapman's Skull," August 17, 1920, in Reisler, *Guys, Dolls, and Curveballs*, 128.

108. "Babe's Swing Not Ball Is Guilty—U.S. Decides," *New York Tribune*, August 22, 1920.

109. McGeehan, "In All Fairness," *New York Tribune*, April 12, 1920.

110. McGeehan, "In All Fairness," *New York Tribune*, September 6, 1920.

111. "Ruth Injury Story a Gamblers Canard," *New York Times*, September 10, 1920.

112. "Yanks Lose; So Do Gamblers," *Daily News* (New York), September 10, 1920.

113. Rice, "Sportlight," *New York Tribune*, September 30, 1920.

114. Rice, "Sportlight," *New York Tribune*, October 3, 1920.

115. Photo of Ruth at Shibe Park, *Public Ledger* (Philadelphia), September 30, 1920.

116. "Ruth in a New Role," *Sporting News*, September 30, 1920.

117. W. O. McGeehan, "The Babe Breaks Through," October 2, 1927, in *Middle Innings: A Documentary History of Baseball, 1900–1948*, ed. Dean Sullivan, 127–28.

118. Montville, *Big Bam*, 124; Daniel Nathan, *Saying It's So: A Cultural History of the Black Sox Scandal*, 146; Tom Meany, *Babe Ruth: The Big Moments of the Big Fellow*, 51.

119. "The Dawn of Hope," *Daily News* (New York), September 17, 1920.

Chapter Three

1. Claire Ruth and Bill Slocum, *The Babe and I*, 61.

2. Edward Barrow to Kenesaw Mountain Landis, May 19, 1924, box 1, MSS 57, National Baseball Hall of Fame Library, Cooperstown, NY (hereafter NBL).

3. "Finds Baseball Generally Honest," *New York Times*, November 7, 1920.

4. "New Major League Might Result from Fight on Ban Johnson," *Milwaukee Sentinel*, November 17, 1919; Oscar Reichow, "Getting Out Not So Easy for Clubs of AL," *Sporting News*, October 28, 1920; "Sees Baseball War Lifting as Magnates Confer," *Brooklyn Daily Eagle*, November 8, 1920.

5. "Where the Players Come In," *Sporting News*, November 18, 1920.

6. "To End Ball Park Disorder," *New York Times*, September 3, 1920.

7. Alexander, *John McGraw*, 226–27.

8. David Voigt, *America through Baseball*, 75.

9. "Al Horwitz," in Holtzman, *No Cheering*, 192.

10. Oscar Reichow, "Reichow, the Original Landis Man, Pays Tribute to His Choice," *Sporting News*, November 18, 1920.

11. "Judge Landis Promises Hot Time for Crooks in Baseball," *New York Times*, January 31, 1921.

12. "Groh is Balking Again," *Pittsburgh Press*, June 12, 1921.

13. "Evers Says Landis Did Right Thing," *Miami Daily News*, June 30, 1921.

NOTES TO PAGES 69–75

14. "Babe Ruth Arrives in Shreveport Camp," *Daily News* (New York), March 7, 1921.

15. F. C. Lane, "Can Babe Ruth Repeat?" *Baseball Magazine*, May 1921, 555–57.

16. Hugh Fullerton, "Why Babe Ruth Is Greatest Home-Run Hitter," *Popular Science Monthly*, October 1921, 19–21.

17. Charleston A. Taylor, "Ruth Breaks Jail and Returns to Game," *New York Tribune*, June 9, 1921.

18. "Babe Ruth Plays after Day in Jail," *New York Times*, June 9, 1921.

19. "Topics of the Times," *New York Times*, June 10, 1921.

20. "Says Ruth Lost $35,000," *New York Times*, January 1, 1921.

21. F. Scott Fitzgerald, *This Side of Paradise* (New York: Charles Scribner's Sons, 1920), 195.

22. F. C. Lane, "Why Babe Ruth Has Become a National Idol," *Baseball Magazine*, October 1921, 519.

23. Heywood Broun, "Yanks Win Again and Odds Favor Big Series Here," *Evening World* (New York), September 27, 1921.

24. Grantland Rice, "The Sportlight," *New York Tribune*, January 3, 1922.

25. Thorton Fisher Cartoon, *Evening World* (New York), September 16, 1921.

26. Rice, "Sportlight," *New York Tribune*, October 5, 1921.

27. Martha Coman, "The World Series as a Woman Sees It," *Public Ledger* (Philadelphia), October 6, 1921.

28. "Ruth's Wife Takes Airview of Activities," *New York Tribune*, October 7, 1921.

29. Meany, *Babe Ruth*, 85.

30. Jack Lawrence, "How Ruth Gave Yankees a Start," *New York Tribune*, October 6, 1921.

31. Babe Ruth, "Ruth's Doctors Say He's Out of Series but Babe Says He Will Be Back," *New York American*, October 9, 1921.

32. Joe Vila, "Setting the Pace," *The Sun* (New York), 10 October 1921.

33. Montville, *Big Bam*, 141.

34. "Joseph Vila Dead," *New York Times*, April 28, 1934.

35. Grantland Rice, "Giants Even Series," *New York Tribune*, October 10, 1921.

36. Grantland Rice, "Giants Tie Series," *New York Tribune*, October 12, 1921.

37. Grantland Rice, "Giants World Champions," *New York Tribune*, October 14, 1921.

38. "Fultz Makes Protest," *Evening Star* (Washington, DC), October 24, 1916.

39. Fredrick Lieb, "Players Openly Defy Commission," *The Sun* (New York), November 26, 1919; "Three Home Runs for Ruth," *New York Herald*, October 4, 1920. Bill Francis, "At Home on the Road," accessed September 24, 2017, http://baseball-hall.org/barnstorming-tours. Starting in 1910, antibarnstorming language was included in all major league player contracts. The prohibition, however, was widely ignored. In February 1921, Section 8B of Article 4 was introduced into the Major League Code. The regulation prohibited recent World Series players from participating "as individuals or as a team in exhibition games during the year in which that world's championship was decided."

40. "Ruth Defies Landis, May Be Suspended," *New York Times*, October 17, 1921.

41. Montville, *Big Bam*, 143.

42. "Babe Ruth Declares He Is Fighting for a Principle," *Elmira Star-Gazette*, October 18, 1921.

43. Ruth and Considine, *Babe Ruth Story*, 104.

44. "Al Horwitz," in *No Cheering*, ed. Holtzman, 192.

45. W. J. MacBeth, "In All Fairness," *New York Tribune,* October 17, 1921.

46. "Organized Revolt behind Babe Ruth? Signs of It in Attitude of the Ball Players," October 14, 1921, clipping, Christy Walsh Scrapbooks, BA SCR 44, reel 2, NBL.

47. "Babe Ruth Talks Money End of Sport," *Chicago Eagle*, October 29, 1921.

48. T. L. Huston to Landis, October 26, 1921, MSS 57, NBL.

49. Ruth and Considine, *Babe Ruth Story*, 104.

50. "Ruth Defies Landis, May Be Suspended."

51. "Slugger Likely to Be Banished for 1922 Season," *New York Tribune*, October 26, 1921.

52. Ruth to Leslie O'Connor, November 15, 1921, MSS 57, NBL.

53. "Ruth Is Suspended, Fined Series Money," *New York Times*, December 6, 1921.

54. "Landis Action Wins Favor of Big Leagues," *Washington Times*, December 6, 1921.

55. "Colonels Not Disturbed," *New York Times*, December 6, 1921.

56. Westbrook Pegler, "Landis Stand in Ruth Case Backed by Owners," *Washington Herald*, October 18, 1921.

57. Dan Daniel, "Yankees Hit Hard by Landis Verdict," *New York Herald*, December 6, 1921.

58. Robert Crepeau, *Baseball: America's Diamond Mind, 1919–1941,* 50; "Oscar Reichow," *Sporting News*, July 19, 1950.

59. Oscar Reichow, "Ruth Lucky to Get Short Suspension," *Pittsburgh Press*, December 21, 1921.

60. Vila, "Setting the Pace," *The Sun* (New York), December 6, 1921.

61. W. J. MacBeth, "Ruth Makes Good Impression in His Debut as Thespian," *New York Tribune*, November 15, 1921.

62. "BR Sends New Year Promise from Post Radio," clipping, Christy Walsh Scrapbooks, BA SCR 44, reel 2, NBL.

63. Sid Mercer, "Ruth's Action to Cost Club $100,000 and May Kill Him as Attraction," *Washington Times*, December 7, 1921.

64. Louis A. Dougher, "Judge Landis Hands Out Stiff Sentence to Colonels," *Washington Times*, December 6, 1921.

65. Sam Crane, "Babe Ruth Foolish to Fight Landis," *Evening World* (New York), October 18, 1921.

66. "Babe Ruth Can Collect Fancy Sum from This Manager," *Washington Times*, October 17, 1921.

67. "Buck Weaver Gets Job," *Reading Eagle*, March 24, 1927.

68. "Says He Will Offer Babe Ruth $100,000, but Only Gets Laugh," *Chicago Daily Tribune*, April 12, 1922.

69. Barrow and Kahn, *Fifty Years in Baseball*, 135; Ruth and Considine, *Babe Ruth Story*, 111. In his memoirs, Ruth recounts much the same story, but has Landis calling him a "big baboon" and a "big ape." Also see Montville, *Big Bam*, 43–44.

70. Ruth and Slocum, *Babe and I*, 60.

71. "Roll of the Dice Swelled Babe Ruth's Pay by $10,000," *Evening Independent* (St. Petersburg, FL), February 5, 1924.

72. Ruth and Considine, *Babe Ruth Story*, 109.

73. "American League of Professional Baseball Clubs, Uniform Player's Contract," April 4, 1922, accessed March 30, 2015, goldinauctions.com.

74. "$500 Home Runs," *Evening World* (New York), March 7, 1922.

75. W. B. Hanna, "Notes of the Diamond," *New York Tribune*, April 10, 1922.

76. "Roll of the Dice Swelled Babe Ruth's Pay by $10,000."

77. "Babe Ruth Home Run Shoes," *New York Evening Post,* May 18, 1922.

78. "Bambino Smoking Tobacco," *The Sun* (Baltimore), May 1, 1922.

79. John Kieran, "Yankees Break Camp," *New York Tribune*, March 28, 1922.

80. Henry Farrell, "Clamor In Behalf of Babe Ruth," *Pittsburgh Press*, April 2, 1922.

81. John Kieran, "Commissioner Declines to Commute Sentences," *New York Tribune*, March 24, 1922.

82. Sid Mercer, "Sid Mercer's Close-Ups," *Washington Times*, April 11, 1922.

83. W. J. MacBeth, "Giants Oppose White Sox," *New York Tribune*, April 8, 1922.

84. "The Home Run King to Play First Base," *Evening World* (New York), March 11, 1922.

85. Bozeman Bulger, "Little Norman McMillan Fills Babe Ruth's Shoes," *Evening World* (New York), April 21, 1922.

86. John Kieran, "Homer by Ruth and Miller Help Yanks Beat Orioles," *New York Herald*, April 17, 1922.

87. Louis Dougher, "Weather and Absences of Star Players Cuts New York Attendance," *Washington Times*, April 22, 1922.

88. "The Exile of Babe Ruth," *New York Tribune*, April 14, 1922.

89. Babe Ruth, "Idleness Frets Ruth," *Washington Times*, April 16, 1922.

90. Babe Ruth, "Ruth Surprised That Griffmen Get Off to Such a Great Start," *Washington Times*, May 8, 1922.

91. W. O. McGeehan, "Down the Line," *New York Herald*, May 14, 1922.

92. Rice, "Sportlight," *New York Tribune*, May 20, 1922.

93. Damon Runyon, "Ruth to Play after 38-day 'Rest,'" *Washington Times*, May 20, 1922.

94. W. O. McGeehan, "Fans Storm Yankee Offices for Seats," *New York Herald*, May 19, 1922.

95. Heywood Broun, "38,000 Hail Ruth Back from Elba with a Puny Bat," *Evening World* (New York), May 21, 1922.

96. "Yanks Are Beaten as Ruth Returns," *New York Times*, May 21, 1922.

97. W. O. McGeehan, "40,000 Fans Welcome BR Back to Yankee Lineup," *New York Herald*, May 21, 1922.

98. "Babe Back Emulates Casey—Strikes Out," *New York Tribune*, May 21, 1922.

99. W. O. McGeehan "Babe's Bat Again Silent," *New York Herald*, May 25, 1922.

100. John Kieran, "Ruth First Home Run of Season," *New York Tribune*, May 23, 1922.

101. John Kieran, "Babe Ruth's Failure to Hit in Pinches Costs Hugman," *New York Tribune*, May 25, 1922.

102. Bozeman Bulger, "Senators Don't Fear Hugman," *Evening World* (New York), May 25, 1922.

103. "Ruth in Row with Umpire and Fan at Polo Grounds," *New York Times*, May 26, 1922.

104. "Ruth Is Chased by Umpire, Fan Is Chased by Ruth," *New York Tribune*, May 26, 1922.

105. "Bambino Starts Argument Which Hildebrand Ends," *Washington Herald*, May 26, 1922.

106. Babe Ruth, "Ruth Takes All Blame for His Bad Start This Season," *New York American*, May 28, 1922.

107. "The Razzing of Ruth," *New York Times*, May 27, 1922.

108. Steve Steinberg and Lyle Spatz, *The Colonel and Hug: The Partnership That Transformed the New York Yankees*, 104.

109. Creamer, *Babe*, 259.

110. "Ruth Fined $200 Loses Captaincy," *New York Times*, May 27, 1922.

111. W. O. McGeehan, "Between the Lines," *New York Herald*, May 28, 1922.

112. As quoted in Gary D. Best, *The Dollar Decade: Mammon and the Machine in 1920s America*, 11. On youth and the crisis of authority in the 1920s, see Paula Fass, *The Damned and the Beautiful: American Youth in the 1920s*; Lynn Dumenil, *The Modern Temper: American Culture and Society in the 1920s*, 149–59; Kathleen Drowne and Patrick Huber, *The 1920s*, 29–41.

113. "The Round-Up by the Staff," *New York Tribune*, June 26, 1922.

114. Davis Walsh, "Say It with Black Jacks, Owners Tell Huggins," *Washington Times*, June 28, 1922; "Uncle Robby to Be Yankee Manager Next Season," *Washington Times*, June 28, 1922.

115. Barrow and Kahn, *Fifty Years in Baseball*, 89.

116. "Landis Warns Players He'll be Roughish," *Washington Times*, June 29, 1922.

117. Louis Dougher, "Looking 'Em Over," *Washington Times*, July 22, 1922.

118. W. O. McGeehan "Yankees Pound Johnson and Regain League Lead," *New York Herald*, September 9, 1922.

119. Vila, "Setting the Pace," *The Sun* (New York), October 10, 1922.

120. "Marshall Hunt," in *No Cheering*, ed. Holtzman, 17.

121. James Crusinberry, "Ruth's 25th and 26th Homers Win Game for Yankees" *Daily News* (New York), August 21, 1922.

122. "Babe Ruth's Babe Makes Debut as Yankee Mascot," *Daily News* (New York), September 27, 1922.

123. George Daley (Monitor), "Rabid Fans Hurl Pop Bottles; Fielder Witt Knocked out as Yanks Beat St. Louis Team," clipping, Christy Walsh Scrapbooks, BA SCR 44,

reel 4, NBL; W. O. McGeehan, "Witt Knocked Unconscious by Bottle as Yankees Beat Browns, 2–1," *New York Herald*, September 17, 1922.

124. Ring Lardner, "Last Year It Was Mind Over Matter; This Year, Nothing's the Matter," *Boston Daily Globe*, October 4, 1922.

125. Jack Dempsey, "Confident Yanks Will Win Series," *New York American*, October 5, 1922.

126. Robert Boyd, "Huggins Thinks Babe Ruth Will Be Hero of World Series," *Evening World* (New York), October 2, 1922.

127. Babe Ruth, "Babe Ruth Admits He's the 'Big Bust' of the Series," *Washington Times*, October 10, 1922.

128. Grantland Rice, "Giants Win," *New York Tribune*, October 7, 1922.

129. "Giant-Yankee Game Is Likely Despite Mist," *Washington Times,* October 7, 1922.

130. "Some Thoughts on the Riot," *Sporting News*, October 12, 1922.

131. "Fans in an Uproar as Game Is Called," *New York Times*, October 6, 1922.

132. "Maybe They'll Do It Yet" *Sporting News*, October 19, 1922; Robert F. Burk, *Much More Than a Game: Players, Owners, and American Baseball Since 1921*, 6.

133. "Players Call on Landis to Discuss Division of Money," *New York Tribune*, October 7, 1922.

134. W. J. MacBeth, "Babe Ruth Roundly Hissed," *New York Tribune*, October 7, 1922.

135. Grantland Rice, "Giants Win Title," *New York Tribune*, October 9, 1922.

136. Vila, "Setting the Pace," *The Sun* (New York), October 2, 1922.

137. Frank O'Neil, "Yankees Hailed by Fans," *The Sun* (New York), October 2, 1922.

138. Paul Eaton, "Welcome Union if It Gives Fans Dope," *Sporting News*, October 26, 1922.

139. John Kieran, "New List Includes 21 Members of the World's Champions," *New York Tribune*, November 1, 1922.

140. "Ball Players Seek to Secure Reforms," *New York Times*, October 12, 1922.

141. "Heydler Sees No Need for Players' Union," *Evening World* (New York), August 17, 1922.

142. Sid Mercer, "New Union, Serious Topic," *Washington Times*, November 10, 1922.

143. Bryan Morse, "Off on Wrong Foot Is What Griff Thinks," *Washington Herald*, December 26, 1922.

144. Kieran, "New List Includes 21 Members."

145. "Union Ball Players May Go on Strike," *Lewiston Daily Sun*, October 12, 1922.

Chapter Four

Quotation in chapter title from "Babe Figures Flight Has Cost Him Million," *Sporting News*, March 15, 1923.

1. Grantland Rice, "The Sportlight," *South Bend Tribune*, May 14, 1926.

2. Joseph Campbell, *The Hero with a Thousand Faces*, 30–35.

3. Fred Lieb, *Baseball as I Have Known It*, 148.

4. "The Opening in New York," *Sporting News*, April 26, 1923.

5. "The Player Faces a Condition," *Sporting News*, February 15, 1922.

6. Christy Walsh, *Adios to Ghosts!*, 26.

7. "Bambino Edits All Sports Articles," *Boston Daily Advertiser*, Christy Walsh Scrapbooks, BA SCR 44, reel 2, NBL.

8. "Prize Contest for Boys," *Washington Times*, August 2, 1922.

9. Ruth and Considine, *Babe Ruth Story*, 105.

10. Walsh, *Adios to Ghosts!*, 32.

11. John M. Carroll, *Red Grange and the Rise of Modern Football*, 125.

12. Red Grange and Ira Morton, *The Red Grange Story*, 93.

13. "Ruppert Completes Deal for Yankees," *New York Times*, May 22, 1923.

14. "Barrow Denies $10,000 Ruth Fine," *Evening World* (New York), October 14, 1922.

15. "Critics Discuss What Is to Be Done about the Fallen Ruth," *Sporting News*, November 2, 1922.

16. Joe Vila, "Ruth Finds That Even in the Tank Towns He's a 'Bust,'" *Sporting News*, November 16, 1922.

17. "Ruth Knocks Out Two Homers," *New Ulm Review*, October 18, 1922.

18. "There's Plenty of Dope in Sight," *Sporting News*, November 2, 1922.

19. Babe Ruth, "Babe Comes Gallantly to the Defense of Gents He Once Tossed Sand at and Cussed," clipping, Christy Walsh Scrapbooks, BA SCR 44, reel 1, NBL.

20. Ruth and Slocum, *Babe and I*, 74.

21. Davis Walsh, "Babe Ruth Promises He Will Be Good in the Future," *Washington Times*, November 14, 1922.

22. "Babe Ruth Returns to Farm," *New York Times*, November 15, 1922; "Babe Ruth Climbs on the Water Wagon," *Washington Times*, November 14, 1922.

23. Montville, *Big Bam*, 158.

24. Paul Gallico, *Farewell to Sport*, 39.

25. Walsh, "Babe Ruth Promises."

26. Marshall Smelser, *The Life That Ruth Built*, 258; Campbell, *Hero with a Thousand Faces*, 246.

27. Ruth and Considine, *Babe Ruth Story*, 122.

28. "Swat King Digs In," *New York American*, November 15, 1922.

29. Joe Vila, "Vila Says Effort to Play up Babe Ruth Fell Flat," *Sporting News*, November 23, 1922.

30. "Babe Ruth Goes on the Wagon," *Daily News* (New York), November 15, 1922.

31. "Here's Farmer Babe," *Chicago Daily Tribune*, December 5, 1922.

32. "Babe Ruth Trains Up His Muscles for Coming Season," *Evening Independent* (St. Petersburg, FL), January 19, 1923.

33. "Ruth Loses Weight at Arkansas Camp," *New York Times*, February 21, 1923.

34. John Kieran, "Players Union Would Gain Favor," *New York Tribune*, December 23, 1922.

35. Burk, *Much More Than a Game*, 7.

36. "Reports Players of Major Leagues Form New Union," *Evening World* (New York), October 11, 1922.

37. John Kieran, "New List Includes 21 Members of the World's Champions," *New York Tribune*, November 1, 1922.

38. Joe Vila, "Players' Union Impossible Even if There Was Any Such," *Sporting News*, April 12, 1923.

39. "And Thus It Passes," *Sporting News*, February 1, 1923.

40. "R. J. Cannon Indicted," *New York Times*, February 4, 1923; Burk, *Much More Than a Game*, 6–7.

41. "Babe Figures Flight Has Cost Him Million," *Sporting News*, March 15, 1923.

42. "Yankees Deny They Have Cut Salaries," *New York Times*, February 10, 1923.

43. Arthur Robinson, "Fans Four Times but Yankees Win," *New York American*, April 11, 1923.

44. "How Wolves of the Underworld Entrap their Victims," *Pittsburgh Press*, August 5, 1923.

45. "Babe Takes Long Trip to Comfort Sick Lad," *New York Tribune*, April 6, 1923.

46. "Just Thinking about Babe Ruth," *Sporting News*, April 12, 1923.

47. Sullivan, *Diamond in the Bronx*, 2.

48. Heywood Broun, "Babe Did It Again for 74,000 Crowd," *Evening World* (New York), April 19, 1923.

49. Sullivan, *Diamond in the Bronx*, 2.

50. F. C. Lane, "Comparing the Two Big Leagues of 1922," *Baseball Magazine*, April 1923, 3.

51. Babe Ruth, "Babe Abandons Experiments in Quest of Home Run Record," *New York American*, April 18, 1923.

52. Joe Vila, "Everything Combines to Make Yankees' Opening Glorious," *Sporting News*, April 26, 1923.

53. Damon Runyon, "Ruth's HR Wins It for Yankees," *New York American*, April 19, 1923.

54. Grantland Rice, "74,000 See Ruth's Homer Beat Boston," *New York Tribune*, April 19, 1923.

55. Ibid.

56. Vila, "Everything Combines to Make Yankees' Opening Glorious."

57. Henry Farrell, "Ruth Thrills 74,000 Yankee Fans," *The Sun* (Baltimore), April 19, 1923.

58. Broun, "Babe Did It Again."

59. Babe Ruth, "I Wanted to Start Season Right and I Did," *New York American*, April 19, 1923.

60. Sullivan, *Diamond in the Bronx*, 7, 9.

61. "Bambino's Admirers Break Up Game, as Ruth Clouts Homer," *Chicago Daily Tribune*, April 30, 1923.

62. "Ruth Leads Attack," *New York Times*, April 21, 1923.

63. Frank J. Monaghan, "Secret of Ruth's Hitting Revealed," *New York American*, October 7, 1923. Monaghan, commissioner of health for New York City, examined

Ruth through "the courtesy of Arthur McGovern, physical trainer of many noted men," and later Ruth's personal trainer. McGovern also aided in the exam.

64. "Huggins Says Babe Ruth Now More Valuable Than Any Time in Career," *Brooklyn Daily Eagle*, June 3, 1923.

65. Babe Ruth, "Babe Tells How He Won High Honor," *New York American*, October 3, 1923.

66. Babe Ruth, "Ruth Gives up Chauffeur to Improve His Game," *New York American*, October 4, 1923.

67. "All Fair and Logical Enough," *Sporting News*, July 5, 1923; "Babe Ruth Unhurt, Reports to Yankees," *New York Times*, June 26, 1923.

68. Ken Sobol, *Babe Ruth & the American Dream*, 172.

69. "In the Wake of the News," *Chicago Daily Tribune*, September 28, 1923.

70. "Ruth Greatest Player in Game, Determined to Make Good," *Evening Journal* (New York), October 6, 1923.

71. W. O. McGeehan, "Down the Line," *New York Herald*, October 10, 1923.

72. Rice, "Sportlight," *New York Tribune*, October 9, 1923.

73. Ring Lardner, "Ring Lardner in a World Serious Mood," *New York Herald*, October 9, 1923.

74. Heywood Broun, "Ruth Comes into His Own with Two Homers," *Evening World* (New York), October 12, 1923.

75. Grantland Rice, "Ruth's Two Homers Give Victory to Yankees in Second Game," *New York Tribune*, October 12, 1923.

76. Ford Frick, "Pledge to Kids of Street Fulfilled Far beyond His Fondest Dreams," *Evening Journal* (New York), October 12, 1923.

77. Ruth and Slocum, *Babe and I*, 83.

78. Ibid., 27–28.

79. "Babe Ruth Day and Championship Flag Flying at Stadium," *New York Herald-Tribune*, May 14, 1924.

80. Landis to Ruth, May 23, 1924, MSS 57, NBL.

81. Barrow to Landis, May 19, 1924, MSS 57, NBL.

82. "Baseball Game in Detroit Ends in Riot," June 14, 1924, *New York Times*. Ruth to Ban Johnson, June 15, 1924, MSS 57, NBL. Ruth insisted to AL president Ban Johnson that he entered the fracas only "to prevent troubles."

83. John Kieran, "Bush, Always Effective, Misses Shut-Out on Error," *New York Herald-Tribune*, August 2, 1924.

84. Arthur Robinson, "My Friend Babe Ruth: An Intimate Story," *Collier's*, September 20, 1924, 7–8.

85. McGeehan, "Down the Line," *New York Herald-Tribune*, May 15, 1924.

Chapter Five

1. "Ruth in Spotlight after First Workout," *New York Times*, March 3, 1925.

2. "Babe Ruth Three Hour Drill," *New York Times*, March 4, 1925.

3. "Idle Babe Gains Fat, Worries Bosses," *Chicago Daily Tribune*, March 11, 1925.

4. "Babe Ruth Sued for Unpaid Bills," *New York Times*, March 7, 1925.

5. Barrow and Kahn, *Fifty Years in Baseball*, 126.

6. Leo Wise, "'Uncle' Wilbert Robinson Thinks Babe Ruth Biggest Asset of National Sports," *Daily News* (Miami), February 28, 1925.

7. Marshall Hunt, "Babe Ruth Wants to Manage Yanks," *Daily News* (New York), March 15, 1925.

8. Joe Vila, "Betting Policy Harmful to Ruth," *Sporting News*, March 19, 1925.

9. "Babe Ruth Race Bets Show Star Is Nearly Broke," *Reading Eagle*, March 11, 1925; Marshall Hunt, "Yanks Lose with Ruth in Lineup," *Daily News* (New York), March 17, 1925.

10. Marshall Hunt, "Babe Ruth Patterns Two Home Runs," *Daily News* (New York), April 1, 1925.

11. Paul Gallico, "Troubles of a Titan," *Daily News* (New York), April 7, 1925.

12. "Babe and the Breadbasket," *Sporting News*, April 16, 1925.

13. "279 Die in Chicago Grip Epidemic," *New York Times*, March 13, 1925.

14. "Baseball Casualty List Grows Hourly as Stars Suffer Ills and Injury," *St. Petersburg Times*, April 10, 1925.

15. John Kieran, "Ruth and Meusel Hit Two Home Runs," *New York Herald Tribune*, April 1, 1925.

16. "Babe Ruth Ill, Socks out Two Home Runs," *Chicago Daily Tribune*, April 6, 1925.

17. Grantland Rice, "The Sportlight," *South Bend Tribune*, April 11, 1925.

18. Will Wedge, "Babe Ruth Not Seriously Ill," *The Sun* (New York), April 8, 1925.

19. "Ruth Takes Seriously Ill," *Brooklyn Daily Eagle*, April 7, 1925.

20. Thomas S. Rice, "Babe Ruth Sacrificed Himself as Martyr to Baseball, Now Works for Team," *Brooklyn Daily Eagle*, April 8, 1925.

21. Robert Prew, "Big Hearted Babe Wins British Praise," *New York American*, April 10, 1925.

22. "London Press Interested," *New York Times*, April 10, 1925.

23. Paul Gallico, "Washington, Lincoln, and—," *Daily News* (New York), April 9, 1925.

24. Damon Runyon, "Ruth Victim of Ill Luck," *New York American*, April 10, 1925.

25. Paul Gallico, "Aw, Lay Off Charity," *Daily News* (New York), April 10, 1925.

26. "Runyon Says," *Chicago Herald and Examiner*, April 10, 1925.

27. "Ruth Improved and May Be out in a Few Days," *The Sun* (New York), April 10, 1925; "Babe Ruth Now out of Danger," *Evening Journal* (New York), April 10, 1925.

28. Gallico, *Farewell to Sport*, 35–36.

29. "Yank Star Improves," *New York Evening Post*, April 10, 1925.

30. "Ruth Is Restful," *Brooklyn Daily Eagle*, April 10, 1925.

31. Gallico, "Aw, Lay Off Charity."

32. Rice, "Sportlight," *South Bend Tribune*, April 13, 1925.

33. Montville, *Big Bam*, 203.

34. Ford Frick, "Frick's Comments," *Evening Journal* (New York), April 14, 1925.

35. Marshall Smelser, *Life That Ruth Built*, 312; Montville, *Big Bam*, 204.

36. W. O. McGeehan, "Down the Line," *New York Herald-Tribune*, April 14, 1925.

37. Joe Vila, "Ruth Will Go Away to Regain Strength," *Sporting News*, May 7, 1925.

38. Warren Susman, *Culture as History: The Transformation of American Society in the Twentieth Century*, 146.

39. Jack Ferrell, "Recovering Babe Sees Press and Makes Denial," *Daily News* (New York), May 3, 1925.

40. Fred Turbywill, "Babe Ruth Denies He Is a Big Eater," *Reading Eagle*, May 26, 1925.

41. McGeehan, "Down the Line," *New York Herald-Tribune*, April 14, 1925.

42. Ford C. Frick, "Yankees Not Hitting in the Pinches and Miss Ruth," *Evening Journal* (New York), April 20, 1925.

43. "Smith to Face Yankees First," *Cleveland Plain Dealer*, May 10, 1925.

44. "Babe Makes Game Try but Is Weak," *Cleveland Plain Dealer*, June 2, 1925.

45. Montville, *Big Bam*, 205.

46. James R. Harrison, "Ruth Back in Game but Yanks Lose," *New York Times*, June 2, 1925.

47. Joe Vila, "Giants Getting Full Reward at Gate," *Sporting News*, May 28, 1925.

48. Thomas Holmes, "Babe Ruth Comes Back and Plays through Six Innings on His Nerves," *Brooklyn Daily Eagle*, June 2, 1925.

49. Joe Vila, "Youngsters Instill New Sprit into Wavering Ranks of Yanks," *Sporting News*, June 18, 1925.

50. Joe Vila, "Ruth May Pay Heavy Penalty for Getting Back Too Quickly," *Sporting News*, July 2, 1925.

51. Babe Ruth, "Fans Stick by Ruth when Luck Deserts," *Cleveland Plain-Dealer*, July 1, 1925.

52. James Harrison, "Yankees Minus Babe Ruth Beat Senators," *New York Times*, June 25, 1925.

53. Paul Gallico, "Even John L. Failed," *Daily News* (New York), May 4, 1925.

54. "Huggins 'Broadway Butterflies' Charged with Mutiny in Gossip," *Sporting News*, June 11, 1925; Joe Vila, "Feeling Grows Yanks Conspire to 'Ride' Miller Huggins Out," *Sporting* News, July 23, 1925.

55. Joe Vila, "Yanks Beyond Control of 'Hug' according to Gotham Gossips," *Sporting News*, June 25, 1925.

56. "Will Not Fire Huggins Says Col. Ruppert," *Brooklyn Daily Eagle*, June 27, 1925.

57. Babe Ruth, "Predicts Yankees Will Be in Race," *Cleveland Plain Dealer*, June 7, 1925.

58. Francis C. Richter, "Casual Comment," *Sporting News*, July 9, 1925.

59. Ruth and Considine, *Babe Ruth Story*, 139–40.

60. Barrow and Kahn, *Fifty Years in Baseball*, 141; Meany, *Babe Ruth*, 68.

61. "Ruth Refuses to Play Again for Huggins," *New York American*, August 31, 1925; "If Huggins Stays, I Quit, Says Ruth," *New York Times*, August 31, 1925; Creamer, *Babe*, 293.

62. "If Huggins Stays, I Quit."

63. "Ruth Fined $5000, Costly Star Banned for Acts Off Field," *New York Times*, August 30, 1925.

64. "Ruth Refuses to Play Again for Huggins"; "If Huggins Stays, I Quit"; Creamer, *Babe*, 293.

65. "Ruth Fined $5,000 and Suspended," *New York American*, August 30, 1925.

66. Montville, *Big Bam*, 212.

67. Thomas Holmes, "The Day on the Circuit," *Brooklyn Daily Eagle*, September 1, 1925.

68. "Not Bigger Than Baseball," *Sporting News*, September 2, 1925.

69. Joe Vila, "Setting the Pace," *The Sun* (New York), August 31, 1925.

70. Alexander, *Ty Cobb*, 105–6.

71. "Ty Cobb Is Indefinitely Suspended for Arguing with Umpire Rowland," *Spartanburg Herald*, July 18, 1925.

72. "Two Heroes," *New York Times*, August 31, 1925.

73. "Spanking Baseball's Baby and Petting Its Paragon," *Literary Digest*, September 19, 1925, 58, 67.

74. "Ruth Fined $5000."

75. "Babe Ruth Unable to See Landis," *Brooklyn Daily Eagle*, August 31, 1925.

76. John Kieran, "Babe Outvoted by 3 to 1," *New York American*, September 1, 1925; John Kieran, *Not under Oath: Recollections and Reflections*, 35.

77. Vaughan Irving, "Babe Ruth Mad, Denies Orgies," *Chicago Daily Tribune*, August 31, 1925.

78. Holmes, "Day on the Circuit."

79. Creamer, *Babe*, 296.

80. Ibid., 298.

81. Ibid., 299.

82. "Dove Over the Stadium," *New York Times*, September 3, 1925.

83. Robert Zieger, Timothy Minchin, and Gilbert Gall, *American Workers, American Unions: The Twentieth and Early Twenty-First Centuries*, 4th ed., 42–50; also see Dumenil, *Modern Temper*, 58–71.

84. David Montgomery, *Workers' Control in America: Studies in the History of Work, Technology, and Labor Struggles*, 13–15; Alice Kessler-Harris, *Gendering Labor History*, 154–57.

85. "Ruth Sees Ruppert, Waves Olive Branch," *New York Times*, September 2, 1925.

86. "Review: The Week in Sports," *New York Times*, September 7, 1925.

87. Paul Gallico, "Yuh Made Muh What I Yam," *Daily News* (New York), September 1, 1925.

88. Damon Runyon, "Th' Mornin's Mornin'," *New York American*, September 3, 1925.

Chapter Six

1. Ruth and Considine, *Babe Ruth Story*, 142.

2. James Harrison, "Ruth Must Forego Hot Springs Trip," *New York Times*, December 18, 1925.

3. Ibid.

4. Will Wedge, "Babe Ruth Again in Uniform," *The Sun* (New York), September 8, 1925.

5. "Scribbled by Scribes," *Sporting News*, September 10, 1925.

6. Harry Cross, "Ruth Health Back, Plans New Record," *New York Times*, November 3, 1925.

7. Joe Winkworth, "I Have Been a Babe and Boob," *Collier's*, October 31, 1925, 15.

8. Richards Vidmer, "Jones Says Fault Was Not Bunnell's," *New York Times*, December 1, 1925.

9. Joe Vila, "Huggins Is Wearing His Spurs although It's Only December," *Sporting News*, December 10, 1925.

10. On slimming see Sternheimer, *Celebrity Culture and the American Dream*, 71–74; Lulu Hunt Peters, *Diet and Health, with Key to the Calories*.

11. "Gene Tunney Health Exercises on Orthophonic Victor Records," Victor, 1927, 78 rpm vinyl record.

12. Arthur A. McGovern, "If I Can Comeback, Anybody Can, Says Babe Ruth," *Collier's*, March 26, 1927, 12–14; Irving Crump, "The Power behind Babe Ruth's Big Bat," *Boy's Life*, June 1927, 10.

13. Cartoon, *New York American*, March 16, 1926.

14. James Harrison, "Ruth to Be First on Training Scene," *New York Times*, January 14, 1926.

15. James Harrison, "Ruth in Uniform Astounds Critics," *New York Times*, March 2, 1926.

16. Babe Ruth, "Babe Ruth Says He Is Sure He Will Have Great Season for the Yanks," *Evening World* (New York), March 14, 1926.

17. "My Stomach Is Where It Belongs, Says Ruth," *Evening World* (New York), March 12, 1926.

18. Grantland Rice, "The Sportlight," *South Bend Tribune*, April 14, 1926.

19. Westbrook Pegler, "Yankees Pretty Fair Ball Players, but Not Ball Team," *Chicago Sunday Tribune*, March 14, 1926.

20. Hugh Fullerton, "Can Babe Ruth Come Back?" *Liberty*, May 1, 1926, 56.

21. Steinberg and Spatz, *Colonel and Hug*, 249.

22. "St. Louis Lines Up on Park Expansion," *Sporting News*, October 29, 1925; "Col Ruppert Will Enlarge Yankee Stadium to Seat 80,000," *Sporting News*, November 19, 1925.

23. W. B. Hanna, "Yankee Batters Drive Walter Johnson from Mound," *New York Herald-Tribune*, April 21, 1926.

24. Marshall Hunt, "Babe Gets 12th As Yanks Crush Sox," *Daily News* (New York), May 16, 1926.

25. Marshall Hunt, "Big Swats Give Ruth New Mark as Yankees Win," *Daily News* (New York), May 20, 1926.

26. "Casual Comment," *Sporting News*, July 8, 1926; Irving Vaughan, "43,000 Watch Ruth, but Hose Do the Hitting," *Chicago Daily Tribune*, June 21, 1926.

27. Joe Vila, "Ruth's Ambition Is New Record, His Inspiration, New Contract," *Sporting News*, May 27, 1926.

28. Rice, "Sportlight," *South Bend Tribune*, June 11, 1926.

29. Paul Gallico, "Sultan of Swat Sings Saga of Sock," *Daily News* (New York), May 24, 1926. Ray Istorico, *Greatness in Waiting: An Illustrated History of the Early New York Yankees, 1903–1919*, 189. Newspaper cartoonist Robert Ripley—founder of "Ripley's Believe It or Not"—is credited with coining the term "Murderers' Row" in 1919.

30. "Babe Ruth Says: Home Runs Are Not the Biggest Thing in Baseball," *Evening World* (New York), May 19, 1926.

31. "In the Wake of the News," *Chicago Daily Tribune*, June 25, 1926.

32. James R. Harrison, "Record for Ruth Looms This Week," *New York Times*, May 17, 1926.

33. "Ruth Scouts Talk of $150,000 Salary," *New York Times*, October 12, 1926.

34. William Hennigan, "Babe and the Kids," *Evening World* (New York), August 22, 1926.

35. "Boys Greet Babe Ruth," *New York Times*, May 21, 1926.

36. "Babe Ruth to Aid Orphans," *New York Times*, June 14, 1926.

37. On advertising and consumption in the 1920s, see Roland Marchand, *Advertising the American Dream: Making Way for Modernity, 1920–1940*, 194–98; Gary Cross, "Origins of Modern Consumption: Advertising, New Goods, and a New Generation," in *The Routledge Companion to Advertising and Promotional Culture*, eds. Matthew McAllister and Emily West, 11–24.

38. Neal Patterson, "Babe's Promised Home Run Pulls Boy through Crisis," *Daily News* (New York), October 8, 1926.

39. Stanley Walker, *City Editor*, 250.

40. "Doc Ruth Cured Boy by Homers," *Daily News* (New York), October 7, 1926.

41. "Series Ball Aid Sick Boy," *New York Times*, October 7, 1926.

42. "Two Heroes," *New York Times*, August 31, 1925.

43. "The Baseball Hero," *New York Times*, October 8, 1926.

44. W. O. McGeehan, "Down the Line," *New York Herald-Tribune*, October 7, 1926.

45. Rice, "Sportlight," *New York Herald-Tribune*, October 7, 1926.

46. Paul Gallico, "Now Who's Raving," *Daily News* (New York), October 8, 1926.

47. Westbrook Pegler, "Finders Is Keepers When Babe Swings His Bat," *Chicago Daily Tribune*, October 7, 1926.

48. Heywood Broun, "It Seems to Me," *Evening World* (New York), October 7, 1926.

49. Babe Ruth, "Babe Ruth Says," *Evening World* (New York), October 6, 1926.

50. Thomas Rice, "Ruth's True Skill Isn't Appreciated," *Sporting News*, October 14, 1926.

51. "Broadway Hears Babe Will Ask $150,000," *Chicago Daily Tribune*, October 12, 1926.

52. Elenore Kellogg, "Who Wouldn't Be Sick in Johnny's Boots," *Daily News* (New York), October 12, 1926.

53. "Broadway Hears Babe Will Ask $150,000."

54. Montville, *Big Bam*, 239.

55. Lieb, *Baseball as I Have Known It*, 162.

56. Montville, *Big Bam*, 237.

57. "Broadway Hears Babe Will Ask $150,000."

58. "I Made My Comeback! So Can You!" *Chicago Herald-Examiner*, October 7, 1926.

Chapter Seven

1. William E. Leuchtenburg, *The Perils of Prosperity, 1914–1932*, 174.

2. "Broadway Hears Babe Will Ask $150,000," *Chicago Daily Tribune*, October 12, 1926.

3. Alfred McCoy, *Beer of Broadway Fame: The Piel Family and Their Brooklyn Brewery*, 46. On paternalism and labor in the 1920s, see Sanford Jacoby, *Modern Manors: Welfare Capitalism since the New Deal*, 25–31.

4. "Chart Shows How Babe Ruth Has Reduced since February 2," *New York Times*, March 4, 1927.

5. "Babe Ruth Considers Methods of Bolstering Financial Conditions," *Brooklyn Daily Eagle*, February 27, 1927.

6. "The Screen," *New York Times*, July 26, 1927. No copies of the film have survived.

7. Thomas Holmes, "Babe Ruth Indignant, Ed Barrow Smiles, and All Pro Bono Publicity," *Brooklyn Daily Eagle*, February 11, 1927; Westbrook Pegler, "Offer of $52,000 Not Intended as Insult," *Chicago Daily Tribune*, February 11, 1927.

8. "Babe Ruth Demands $207,000 Contract," *Chicago Sunday Tribune*, February 27, 1927.

9. Montville, *Big Bam*, 248; John Kieran, "Sports of the Times," *New York Times*, February 28, 1927.

10. "Ruppert Believes Ruth Will Relent," *New York Times*, February 28, 1927.

11. Marshall Hunt, "Moviedom Bids Bambino Farewell," *Daily News* (New York), February 27, 1927; "Babe Ruth Considers Methods of Bolstering Financial Conditions."

12. Marshall Hunt, "Babe Down to 220 for Ruppert," *Daily News* (New York), February 28, 1927.

13. Marshall Hunt, "Hands Up Col.!" *Daily News* (New York), March 2, 1927.

14. "Something Has Got to Happen, Says Ruth on His Way Here," *Brooklyn Daily Eagle*, March 1, 1927.

15. "Ruth Here Today, Will See Ruppert," *New York Times*, March 2, 1927.

16. James R. Harrison, "Ruth Due on March 2 for Salary Talk," *New York Times*, February 22, 1927.

17. Kieran, "Sports of the Times," *New York Times*, February 28, 1927.

18. "Something Has Got to Happen."

19. "Ruth Gets $210,000 For Three Years," *New York Times*, March 3, 1927.

20. "Ruth Right Handed Signing for $210,000," *New York Times*, March 5, 1927.

21. "Ruth Is on Route to Florida Camp," *New York Times*, March 6, 1927.

22. Westbrook Pegler, "$100,000 Offer to Mayor Gives Ruth Food for Thought," *Chicago Daily Tribune*, April 25, 1927.

23. Babe Ruth, "Babe Ruth Says," *Evening World* (New York), September 28, 1927.

24. Thomas Holmes, "Legal Means May Prevent Outlaws from Grabbing Ball Players," *Brooklyn Daily Eagle*, December 29, 1926.

25. "Stop, Look, Listen," *Sporting News*, September 2, 1926.

26. George Daley (Monitor), "Club Owners Only Directly Concerned in Any Gambling on Their Fields," *Miami News*, December 3, 1926; Wilbur Rodgers, "Landis War on Baseball Pools, Begun in 1922, Fails to End Big Lotteries," *Brooklyn Daily Eagle*, May 27, 1928.

27. "In the Wake of the News," *Chicago Daily Tribune*, May 2, 1926.

28. Ruth, "Babe Ruth Says," *Telegraph and Herald* (Dubuque, IA), June 5, 1927.

29. George Daley (Monitor), "Babe Ruth Has Changed Temper of Baseball Fans," June 27, 1926, Christy Walsh Scrapbooks, BA SCR 44, reel 3, NBL.

30. Grantland Rice, "The Sportlight," *New York Herald-Tribune*, October 1, 1927.

31. George Daley (Monitor), "Clout-Tying Mark Comes with Bases Filled; Crowd Wild," *Evening World* (New York), September 30, 1927.

32. Ford Frick, "Fan Called Turn for Ruth," *Evening Journal* (New York), October 1, 1927.

33. "Ruth Crashes 60th to Set New Record," *New York Times*, October 1, 1927.

34. W. B. Hanna, "Fandom Rooting for Ruth Hit 60th, with Two Games to Go," *New York Herald-Tribune*, September 30, 1927.

35. Paul Gallico, "And He Did It!" *Daily News* (New York), October 1, 1927. "Young Gehrig's part in Ruth's achievement should not be minimized, and the Babe would be the last one to do so. He is one of the most unselfish fellows in the world. The mechanics of Lou's assistance were these. He spurred Ruth on to greater effort than ever before and with his own devastating clouting he forced the pitchers to throw strikes at Ruth. To pass Ruth to get at Gehrig was public suicide."

36. Joe Vila, "Setting the Pace," *The Sun* (New York), October 1, 1927.

37. George Daley (Monitor), "Ruth Breaks Record with 60th Home Run," *Evening World* (New York), October 1, 1927.

38. "Ruth Wallops No. 60, Breaks Record," *Chicago Daily Tribune*, October 1, 1927; on the Cobb-Speaker scandal, see Roessner, *Inventing Baseball Heroes*, 159–60; Voigt, *American Baseball*, 2:145.

39. W. O. McGeehan, "Down the Line," *New York Herald-Tribune*, October 2, 1927.

40. Ring Lardner, "Lardner Has a Bright Idea," in *Yankees Century: 100 Years of New York Yankees Baseball*, ed. Glenn Stout and Richard Johnson, 124. On the 1927 World Series in general, see Harvey Frommer, *Five O'Clock Lightning: Babe Ruth, Lou Gehrig, and the Greatest Baseball Team in Baseball, the 1927 New York Yankees*.

41. Babe Ruth, "Yanks Can Beat Bucs," *Pittsburgh Press*, October 5, 1927.

42. Frommer, *Five O'Clock Lightning*, 167.

43. Steinberg and Spatz, *Colonel and Hug*, 264.

44. "McNamee Again at Radio Show," *Pittsburgh Press*, October 5, 1927.

45. Thomas Streissguth, *The Roaring Twenties*, 257.

46. Ted Patterson, "The Tenth Man: Baseball and Radio Broadcasting," in *Joy in Mudville: Essays on Baseball and American Life*, ed. John B. Wiseman, 79.

47. Eldon Ham, *Broadcasting Baseball: A History of the National Pastime on Radio and Television*, 43.

48. Thomas Holmes, "Ruth Well on the Way to Million Mark in Earnings," *Brooklyn Daily Eagle*, November 20, 1927.

49. Marshall Hunt, "Gehrig and Cobb in Fist Fight," *Daily News* (New York), May 9, 1926. According to Hunt, "Ruth became incensed [hearing of Gehrig-Cobb fight after game]. Why, this was awful to have Peaches Cobb always picking on the youthful Gehrig! And with the fire in his eye and only particularly robed, he made a break for the Detroit dressing room swinging his arms like flails. Well, the Detroit Tigers welcomed the Babe by practically tossing him out of the dressing room and slamming the door." See James Harrison, "Yankees Shower Hits on Tigers, but Lose," *New York Times*, May 9, 1926, for another version of the Cobb-Ruth-Gehrig melee.

50. Richards Vidmer, "Babe Ruth, Baseball Superman, Excels in Minor Sports Too," *New York Times*, June 10, 1928.

51. Lou Gehrig, "Following the Babe," *Pittsburgh Press*, September 23, 1927.

52. Lou Gehrig, "Veterans Generously Give Rookies Advice," *New York American*, September 27, 1927.

53. "The Babe Ruth of Columbia Is Now 'Columbia Lou' of the Yanks," *New York Times*, June 29, 1927.

54. "Best Player Award Goes to Lou Gehrig," *New York Times*, October 12, 1927.

55. "Ralph Davis Says," *Pittsburgh Press*, November 12, 1927.

56. Jonathan Eig, *Luckiest Man: The Life and Death of Lou Gehrig*, 195.

57. McGeehan, "Down the Line," *New York Herald-Tribune*, September 9, 1927.

58. On the Dempsey-Tunney relationship, see Eliott Gorn, "The Manassa Mauler and the Fighting Marine: An Interpretation of the Dempsey-Tunney Fights," *Journal of American Studies* 19, no. 1 (April 1985): 27–47.

59. Bugs Baer, "Yanks in Delirium Wreck Cardinals," *New York American*, October 10, 1928.

60. John B. Kennedy, "Innocents Abroad," *Collier's*, April 14, 1928, 44.

61. Ruth, "Babe Ruth Says: Rough Language Used by Fans in Bleachers Bad on the Kids," *Evening World* (New York), May 16, 1928.

62. Ruth, "Babe Ruth Says," *Evening World* (New York), August 29, 1927.

63. Ruth, "Babe Ruth Says," *Evening World* (New York), April 28, 1928.

64. Ruth, "Babe Ruth Says: Baseball Would Act as Cure for Crime Wave," *Evening World* (New York), July 9, 1928.

65. Richards Vidmer, "Babe Ruth, Baseball Superman, Excels, Too, in Minor Sports," *New York Times*, June 10, 1928.

66. Kennedy, "Innocents Abroad," 44.

67. George Barton Cutten, *The Threat of Leisure*, 123.

68. George Daley, "Sport Talk," *Evening World* (New York), April 30, 1928.

69. Carl Sandburg, "Carl Sandburg, Poet, Fans Babe Ruth with 750 Words," *St. Petersburg Times*, March 27, 1928.

70. Westbrook Pegler, "Poet Sandburg Lists Things for Babe to Ponder," *Chicago Daily Tribune*, March 16, 1928.

71. Ring Lardner, "Pluck and Luck or the Rise of a Home Run King," *Collier's*, March 16, 1929, 13.

72. Richards Vidmer, "Ruth Hits Two More," *New York Times*, May 16, 1928.

73. Irving Vaughan, "Too Much Yankees Epitomizes 1927 Baseball Drama," *Chicago Sunday Tribune*, January 1, 1928.

74. Photograph Caption, *New York American*, September 10, 1928.

75. Richards Vidmer, "Ruth Aims for Hits Not Home Run Mark," *New York Times*, September 1, 1928.

76. Richards Vidmer, "Ruth's Homer Puts Athletics to Rout," *New York Times*, September 12, 1928.

77. Marshall Hunt, "Ruth's 49th Gives Yanks 5–3 Victory," *Daily News* (New York), September 12, 1928.

78. Westbrook Pegler, "Yanks Machine Purrs as of Old as Ruth Finds Stride," *Chicago Daily Tribune*, October 5, 1928.

79. Marshall Hunt, "Ruth Clouts No 54," *Daily News* (New York), October 1, 1928.

80. James S. Collins, "Ruth Waddled to Right Like Turtle, But Ran Bases Like Scared Antelope," *Evening World* (New York), October 5, 1928.

81. Marshall Hunt, "Yankee Underdogs Bite," *Daily News* (New York), October 5, 1928.

82. Damon Runyon, "Th' Mornin's Mornin'," *Chicago Herald and Examiner*, October 5, 1928.

83. Westbrook Pegler, "Bambino's Convalescence Is Fact; Wallops 3 Home Runs," *Chicago Daily Tribune*, October 10, 1928.

84. Irving Vaughan, "Yankees Win 7–3; Ruth Gets 3 Home Runs," *Chicago Daily Tribune*, October 10, 1928.

85. "Babe Ruth's Record Breaking World Series," *Literary Digest*, October 27, 1928, 52.

86. James R. Harrison, "Yankees Win Series," *New York Times*, October 10, 1928.

87. Babe Ruth, "Babe Ruth Writes about Convention—Everything But," *Pittsburgh Press*, June 25, 1924; "Babe and Nick Call on Smith," *Southeast Missourian* (Cape Girardeau), June 24, 1924.

88. James O'Donnell Bennett, "Chummy Chat with Al on Hot Afternoon," *Chicago Daily Tribune*, July 4, 1928.

89. John Kieran, "Sport of the Times," *New York Times*, September 4, 1928. With baseball players lining up behind Smith, Kieran advised Hoover to seek "to swing the golf vote to Hoover."

90. Kieran, "Sport of the Times," *New York Times*, September 6, 1928.

91. William Hennigan, *Evening World* (New York), October 10, 1928.

92. Robert Slayton, *Empire Statesman: The Rise and Redemption of Al Smith*, 297–89.

93. "Babe Ruth on Radio in Support of Smith," *New York Times*, October 20, 1928.

94. "Al and Babe Meet," *Washington Reporter*, October 11, 1928.

95. "Babe Ruth King of Baseball Hits Homerun for Al Smith," *Telegraph-Herald and Times-Journal* (Dubuque, IA), October 21, 1928.

96. "Ex-Candidates on Stumping Tour," *Telegraph-Herald and Times-Journal* (Dubuque, IA), October 25, 1928.

97. "Babe Ruth's Record Breaking World Series," 60.

98. Smelser, *Life That Ruth Built,* 387. Ruth biographer Smelser dismisses the story of Ruth's offensive comments about Italians as a "legend." Also see Meany, *Babe Ruth*, 106–7. Smelser may have picked the story up from sportswriter Tom Meany, who tells it in his short 1948 biography of Ruth.

99. Montville, *Big Bam*, 279.

100. Walter LaFeber, *Michael Jordan and the New Global Capitalism*, 158.

101. Kennedy, "Innocents Abroad," 44.

Chapter Eight

1. Noel Busch, "Bambino Finds Handball Setup as He Melts Off Fat in Gymnasium," *Daily News* (New York), January 6, 1929.

2. "Walsh Denies Ruth Divorce," *New York American*, January 15, 1929.

3. "Babe Ruth to Wed Beauty," *New York American*, January 15, 1929.

4. "Sister-in-law Tells of Babe's Love Child," *Daily News* (New York), January 16, 1929.

5. "Mrs. Ruth's Fake Mate Surrenders for Inquiry," *Brooklyn Daily Eagle*, January 14, 1929; "Mrs. Ruth Murdered, Her Mother Declares," *Palm Beach Post*, January 15, 1929.

6. "Wife's Death Great Shock, Says Ruth," *Boston Globe*, January 14, 1929.

7. Ford Sawyer, "Ruth Overcome by Tragedy of Career," *Boston Globe*, January 15, 1929.

8. "Family of Dead Wife Proclaim Peace with Ruth," *Chicago Daily Tribune*, January 17, 1929.

9. "Mrs. Babe Ruth Dies in Fire," *New York American*, January 14, 1929.

10. "Babe Ruth Collapses at Wife's Casket," *Daily News* (New York), January 17, 1929.

11. Damon Runyon, "30,000 See Yankees Start with Victory," *New York American*, April 19, 1929.

12. "Wedding Bells and a Home Run to Left Field," *Literary Digest*, May 4, 1929, 66.

13. "Babe Ruth Says," *Evening World* (New York), April 19, 1929.

14. "Babe's Wife Clamps Down on Hot Dogs and Pop," *Pittsburgh Press*, August 15, 1930.

15. Herbert Barker, "Air of Uncertainty Hovers over Babe Ruth's Condition," *Miami Daily News*, June 8, 1929; "Ruth out of Game for Ten More Days," *New York Times,* June 8, 1929.

16. "Ruth Much Better Will Return Today," *New York Times*, June 16, 1929.

17. "What Babe Ruth Does with His Money," *Literary Digest*, October 5, 1929, 76–77.

18. Barrow and Kahn, *Fifty Years in Baseball*, 154.

19. "Taps for Huggins: A Great Little Bear Tamer," *Literary Digest*, October 12, 1929, 38.

20. John Drebinger, "Shawkey Named Yankee Manager," *New York Times*, October 18, 1929.

21. Barrow and Kahn, *Fifty Years in Baseball*, 154.

22. Ruth and Considine, *Babe Ruth Story*, 178.

23. "Ruth Not to Pilot Yankees, He States," *New York Times*, October 14, 1929; "Ruth Spurns Huggins' Job; Says He's Still a Player," *Chicago Daily Tribune*, October 14, 1929.

24. Drebinger, "Shawkey Named Yankee Manager."

25. Sobol, *Babe Ruth*, 172.

26. Joe Williams, "Babe Ruth Will Demand Salary Raise in 1930," *Pittsburgh Press*, February 6, 1929.

27. "Ruppert Says Nay to Ruth's $85,000 Offer," *Brooklyn Daily Eagle*, January 8, 1930.

28. Brian Bell, "On the Sidelines," *Lewiston Morning Tribune*, February 4, 1930.

29. Alan Gould, "Yankee Officials Feel More Than Generous with Babe," *Evening Independent* (St. Petersburg, FL), February 3, 1930.

30. "Yanks Stand Firm," *New York Times*, February 5, 1930.

31. "Ruth Independent Is Set to Hold Out," *New York Times*, February 4, 1930; "Babe Ruth Quits Baseball Unless Yanks Management Comes to Terms," *Lewiston Morning Tribune*, February 4, 1930.

32. John Kieran, "Sports of the Times," *New York Times*, February 5, 1930.

33. Harold C. Burr, "Ruth's Threat to Live on his Money Reacts as Boomerang on Yanks," *Brooklyn Daily Eagle*, February 4, 1930.

34. Westbrook Pegler, "Sport Salaries No Longer Incite Riots, Too Big," *Chicago Daily Tribune*, March 10, 1930.

35. Meany, *Babe Ruth*, 139.

36. "Ruth v. Ruppert," *Brooklyn Daily Eagle*, March 8, 1930.

37. Dan Daniel and Harry Salsinger, *The Real Babe Ruth*, 61–62; Ruth and Considine, *Babe Ruth Story*, 181. Presumably the sportswriters showed Ruth a newspaper other than the *New York American* whose headlines blared, "Cops Smash 20,000 Reds! Police Win Day against Communist Rioters," March 7, 1930, or *The Daily News* take on events headlined, "Police Rout Reds," March 7, 1930.

38. Daniel Levitt, *Ed Barrow: The Bulldog Who Built the Yankees*, 235.

39. Daniel and Salsinger, *Real Babe Ruth*, 62.

40. Ruth and Considine, *Babe Ruth Story*, 181–82.

41. Sobol, *Babe Ruth*, 172. Ruth 1930 Contract Addendum is dated March 10, 1930, accessed September 22, 2017, https://sports.ha.com/. Under the arrangement in 1930 and 1931, Ruth was entitled to 25 percent of gate receipts for exhibition games played during the regular season (not spring training).

42. Marshall Hunt, "Ruth Accepts Yank $80,000 Offer," *Daily News* (New York), March 9, 1930.

43. William Brandt, "Babe Ruth Accepts $160,000 for Two Years," *New York Times*, March 9, 1930.

44. "Ruth Signs, Gets $160,000 for Two Years," *Chicago Daily Tribune*, March 9, 1930.

45. "Ruth Accepts Two-Year Contract of $80,000: Wife Ordered Bambino to Take Offer Made by Col. Jacob Ruppert," *Brooklyn Daily Eagle*, March 9, 1930; Alan Gould, "Sports Slants," *Reading Eagle*, January 27, 1932.

46. "Edward Barrow Is Made to Apologize," *Gazette* (Montreal), June 28, 1930; Levitt, *Ed Barrow*, 251–52,

47. Ruth and Considine, *Babe Ruth Story*, 182–83.

48. Creamer, *Babe*, 351–52.

49. Barrow and Kahn, *Fifty Years in Baseball*, 157.

50. Richard Ben Cramer, *Joe DiMaggio: The Hero's Life*, 92.

51. Meany, *Babe Ruth*, 25.

52. Cramer, *Joe DiMaggio*, 93.

53. Barrow and Kahn, *Fifty Years in Baseball*, 167.

54. Westbrook Pegler, "If the Yanks Sign McCarthy It Might Be for One Year Only," *Chicago Daily Tribune*, October 10, 1930.

55. Harry T. Brundidge, "Babe Ruth Wants to Forget 'Bad Boy' Days," *Sporting News*, January 8, 1931.

56. John Kieran, "Sports of the Times," *New York Times,* September 2, 1930.

57. Steinberg and Spatz, *Colonel and Hug*, 304.

58. David Surdam, *Wins, Losses, and Empty Seats: How Baseball Outlasted the Great Depression*, 67–68.

59. "Ruth Refuses $10,000 Cut," *Reading Eagle*, January 14, 1932.

60. Surdam, *Wins, Losses, and Empty Seats*, 66.

61. Harold C. Burr, "Col. Ruppert Plays Ball with Other Magnates in Offer to Ruth," *Brooklyn Daily Eagle*, January 15, 1932.

62. Marshall Hunt, "Ho, Hum! Just another Ruth 'n' Ruppert Confab," *Daily News* (New York), March 15, 1932.

63. "In the Wake of the News," *Chicago Daily Tribune*, March 17, 1932.

64. Westbrook Pegler, "Some Ought to Tell Babe How Much $70,000 Really Is," *Chicago Daily Tribune*, March 16, 1932.

65. "Ruth, Ruppert, Talk 1/2 Hour, Score Still 0–0," *Chicago Daily Tribune*, March 15, 1932.

66. "Statement by Ruth, Ruppert after Babe Signed Contract," *New York Times*, March 17, 1932.

67. Charles Alexander, *Breaking the Slump: Baseball in the Depression Era*, 58.

68. Red Smith, "The Babe Was Always a Boy—One of Kind," *New York Times Magazine*, September 16, 1973.

69. Joe Williams, "Ruth Calls Shot as He Puts Homer No. 2 in Side Pocket," *New York World-Telegram*, October 1, 1932.

70. Paul Gallico, "Clown and Hero," *Daily News* (New York), October 3, 1932.

Chapter Nine

1. Rader, *Baseball*, 150.

2. Rader, *Baseball*, 152.

3. Harold C. Burr, "Babe Ruth's Clouting Scrapped Old Precepts of Strategy in Baseball," *Brooklyn Daily Eagle*, March 20, 1933.

4. "Hornsby to Gehrig," *Pittsburgh Press*, June 19, 1929.

5. John Drebinger, "Stage Now Set for Annual Drama Involving Ruth and Col. Ruppert," *New York Times*, January 4, 1933.

6. "In the Wake of the News," *Chicago Daily Tribune*, January 12, 1933; Steinberg and Spatz, *Colonel and Hug*, 303.

7. Haupert and Winter, "Pay Ball," 94.

8. "Pays $3,500,000 for Skyscraper," *New York Times*, January 6, 1932.

9. "Ruth Pins His Hopes of Big Salary on Beer," *New York Times*, December 23, 1932.

10. "Ruth Up for Manager of Red Sox Again," *Brooklyn Daily Eagle*, November 7, 1932.

11. "Babe Ruth May Quit Yankees before Season Is Open," *Pittsburgh Press*, March 8, 1933.

12. Jack Cuddy, "Call Ruth Cut Whip to Force Salaries Down," *Berkeley Daily Gazette*, January 18, 1933.

13. John Drebinger, "Ruth Says $50,000 Was Yank's Offer, *New York Times*, January 18, 1933.

14. James Dawson, "Ruth Unrelenting on $25,000 Slash," *New York Times*, March 6, 1933.

15. James Dawson, "Ruth Steals Show at Yankee Drill," *New York Times*, March 9, 1933.

16. "$50,000? Never! Ruth and the Yankee Owners Disagree," *Chicago Daily Tribune*, March 14, 1933.

17. James Dawson, "Ruth and Ruppert Clash on Salary," *New York Times*, March 14, 1933.

18. "Babe Ruth Signs for One Season, Will Get $52,000," *Chicago Daily Tribune*, March 23, 1933.

19. "Babe Ruth Signs for One Season."

20. Jeff Mashier, "Babe Ruth Ready to Join the Yankees," *Evening Independent* (St. Petersburg, FL), March 23, 1933; "Ruppert Realty Put at $30,000,000," *New York Times*, January 14, 1939.

21. Harold C. Burr, "Never Again $80,000 Ball Player Like Ruth," *Brooklyn Daily Eagle*, March 25, 1933.

22. Ed Hughes, "Mona Lisa For Sale!" *Brooklyn Daily Eagle*, October 20, 1933.

23. John Kieran, "Mr. Ruth, the Manager," *New York Times*, October 22, 1933.

24. "Babe Ruth May Manage Yanks after McCarthy," *Chicago Daily Tribune*, October 19, 1933.

25. Barrow and Kahn, *Fifty Years in Baseball*, 167.

26. Ed Hughes, "Ruth and the Red Sox," *Brooklyn Daily Eagle*, March 1, 1933.

27. "Ruth May Pilot Boston Red Sox," *Pittsburgh Press*, October 28, 1933; Harry Grayson, "Babe Ruth's Row with Ed Barrow Cost Him a Managerial Job," *Milwaukee Journal*, January 8, 1936.

28. Guy Butler, "Topics of the Tropics," *Miami Daily News*, May 6, 1933.

29. "Reds Tried to Get Ruth; Would Have Made Manager, but Ruppert Refused," *New York Times*, December 30, 1933; "MacPhail Goes after Bambino but Gets a 'No,'" *Milwaukee Journal*, December 30, 1933.

30. Ruth and Considine, *Babe Ruth Story*, 205–6.

31. "Babe Ruth Not Worrying Over 1934 Contract," *Brooklyn Daily Eagle*, December 22, 1933.

32. Hughes, "Mona Lisa for Sale!"

33. "Reds Tried to Get Ruth."

34. Meany, *Babe Ruth*, 143.

35. Harold C. Burr, "Babe Ruth Signs One-Year Contract with Yankees for $35,000," *Brooklyn Daily Eagle*, January 15, 1934; John Drebinger, "Ruppert Willing to Release Ruth," *New York Times*, October 27, 1934.

36. Frank Reil, "If Ruth Plays in 1935 He'll Be with the Yankees," *Brooklyn Daily Eagle*, December 12, 1934.

37. Ed Hughes, "A Boo to the Ball Fans Who Razz Ruth," *Brooklyn Daily Eagle*, May 17, 1934.

38. "Babe Ruth Says That He's Through," *Brooklyn Daily Eagle*, September 15, 1934.

39. Steinberg and Spatz, *Colonel and Hug*, 298.

40. Ruth and Considine, *Babe Ruth Story*, 205–7.

41. "Ruth Will Not Pilot Senators," *Brooklyn Daily Eagle*, October 28, 1934.

42. Joe Williams, "Babe Issues an Ultimatum to Manage Team," *New York World-Telegram*, October 8, 1934.

43. "Ruppert Is Satisfied," *Chicago Daily Tribune*, October 9, 1934.

44. "Managerial Alignment for 1935 Leaves Ruth's Future Speculative," *New York Times*, November 1, 1934.

45. "Ruth Must Have Manager's Job or He Will Quit," *Chicago Daily Tribune*, October 9, 1934.

46. Tommy Holmes, "Ruth Probably Knows Where '35 Job Will Be," *Brooklyn Daily Eagle*, October 25, 1934.

47. Creamer, *Babe*, 380; Meany, *Babe Ruth*, 161–62; Robert K. Fitts, *Banzai Babe Ruth: Baseball, Espionage, and Assassination during the 1934 Tour of Japan*, 78–79.

48. John Kieran, "Sports of the Times," in *We Saw It Happen: The News behind the News That's Fit to Print*, ed. Hanson W. Baldwin and Shepard Stone, 257.

49. Bill Jenkinson, "Babe Ruth and the Issue of Race," last updated 2016, accessed September 27, 2017, http://www.baberuthcentral.com/babe-ruth-and-the-issue-of-race-bill-jenkinson; Peter Kerasotis, "Home, at the Other House That Ruth Built: Babe Ruth's Daughter Returns to St. Petersburg, a City the Ex-Yankee Helped Make Famous," *New York Times*, March 11, 2014.

50. Ed Hughes, "Need a Manager?," *Brooklyn Daily Eagle*, December 12, 1934.

51. Tommy Holmes, "Dean Won't Hold Out Long," *Brooklyn Daily Eagle*, February 6, 1935.

52. Ruth and Considine, *Babe Ruth Story*, 208.

53. Harold Parrott, "I'll Never be a Bench Warmer," *Brooklyn Daily Eagle*, February 21, 1935. See also "Yanks Make Informal Offers," *New York Times*, January 18, 1935; Steinberg and Spatz, *Colonel and Hug*, 307.

54. "Plan Using Bat Star in Relief Role," *Milwaukee Sentinel*, December 14, 1934.

55. Harold Parrott, "Cost to the Nationals to Acquire Babe Exactly $47.50," *Brooklyn Daily Eagle*, February 27, 1935.

56. "Carrigan Sees Ruth Boosting Game at Hub," *Brooklyn Daily Eagle*, February 27, 1935.

57. Creamer, *Babe*, 391.

58. "3,500 Cheer Ruth in First Workout," *New York Times*, March 6, 1935.

59. "They 'Railroaded' Babe Says Hornsby," *Pittsburgh Press*, March 13, 1935.

60. "Ruth Denies He Plans to Quit May Take a Rest," *Chicago Daily Tribune*, May 17, 1935.

61. James Dawson, "Ruth Is Undecided on Future Plans," *New York Times*, June 4, 1935.

62. Smelser, *Life That Ruth Built*, 506.

63. "Western Trip May Decide Ruth's Future," *Brooklyn Daily Eagle*, May 16, 1935.

64. Harold Parrot, "Looks Like the Journey's End of Ruth," *Brooklyn Daily Eagle*, June 3, 1935.

65. "Babe Ruth Quits; So Boston Fires Him," *Chicago Daily Tribune*, June 3, 1935.

66. "McKechnie Puts Blame on Ruth for Team's Fall," *Chicago Daily Tribune*, June 4, 1935.

67. "Babe Ruth Quits; So Boston Fires Him."

68. Paul Gallico, "Exciting Truth," *Daily News* (New York), June 4, 1935.

69. Holtzman, *No Cheering*, 298.

70. "McKechnie Puts Blame on Ruth."

71. Frank Reil, "Ruth No Worry to McCarthy for Two Years," *Brooklyn Daily Eagle*, July 17, 1935.

72. Tommy Holmes, "Ruth's Retirement Matter of Conjecture," *Brooklyn Daily Eagle*, October 22, 1935.

73. Ibid.

74. Alan Gould, "Babe Ruth Steals Show at Annual Baseball Dinner," *The Day* (New London, CT), February 8, 1937.

75. Leo Durocher with Ed Linn, *Nice Guys Finish Last*, 55.

Chapter Ten

1. Meany, *Babe Ruth*, 59.

2. Red Smith, "The Babe Was Always a Boy—One of Kind," New York *Times Magazine*, September 16, 1973.

3. Ruth and Considine, *Babe Ruth Story*, 135.

4. Meany, *Babe Ruth*, 140.

5. Ibid., 9.

6. Ibid., 14.

7. Ibid., 99–119.

8. Waite Hoyt, *Babe Ruth as I Knew Him*, 11, 23.

9. Guernsey van Riper Jr., *Babe Ruth: Baseball Boy* (Indianapolis: Bobbs-Merrill, 1959).

10. Roger Kahn, *How the Weather Was*, xiii.

11. Roger Kahn, "The Real Babe Ruth," *Esquire*, August 1959, 27–30.

12. Gerald Holland, "The Babe Ruth Papers," *Sports Illustrated*, December 21, 1959, 111.

13. Ibid.

14. Leonard Shecter, *The Jocks*, 177.

15. Ibid., 119–21.

16. Roger Angell, "Still Getting the Ink," *New York Times*, October 13, 1974.

17. Creamer, *Babe*, 21.

18. Bruce Nash and Allan Zullo, *The Baseball Hall of Shame*, 155–57.

19. Roger Ebert, "The Babe," April 17, 1992, accessed July 17, 2015, http://www.rogerebert.com/reviews/the-babe-1992.

20. Dennis Lehane, *The Given Day*, 9, 15, 29.

21. Montville, *Big Bam*, 210–11.

22. Smith, "Babe Was Always a Boy."

23. Brad Snyder, *A Well-Paid Slave: Curt Flood's Fight for Free Agency in Professional Sports*.

24. Reggie Jackson and Kevin Baker, *Becoming Mr. October*, 30.

25. Ibid., 119.

26. Jonathan Mahler, *Ladies and Gentlemen, the Bronx Is Burning: 1977, Baseball, Politics, and the Battle for the Soul of a City*, 112.

27. John Kieran, "Sport of the Times," New York *Times*, February 12, 1930.

28. Grantland Rice, "The Sportlight," *Pittsburgh Press*, February 15, 1930.

29. "If Joe McCarthy Quits Babe Ruth Wants Job," *Chicago Daily Tribune*, July 26, 1945.

30. Damion L. Thomas, *Globetrotting: African-American Athletes and Cold War Politics*, 19.

31. "Babe Ruth Silent on Baseball Bias," *Pittsburgh Courier*, August 25, 1945.

BIBLIOGRAPHY

Bibliographical Note: In the absence of manuscript records that might have allowed for a fuller telling of this story, I relied heavily on newspaper accounts. The increasing availability of searchable newspaper databases allowed me to cast a remarkably wide net. Citing every newspaper and journal consulted for this study would present the reader with a long and unwieldy list. The major newspapers consulted were the *New York Times*, the *Daily Brooklyn Eagle*, the New York *Daily News*, and the *Chicago Tribune*. I supplemented this list with dozens of newspapers from throughout the country. Journals and magazines also proved helpful, in particular the *Literary Digest* and *Collier's* magazine. Additionally, the National Baseball Library houses a number of helpful collections, including some limited correspondence related to Ruth's relationship with the baseball establishment and a remarkable collection of Christy Walsh's scrapbooks relating to Ruth's career. What follows is a bibliography of major primary and secondary published works used in the preparation of this study.

PRIMARY SOURCES

Barrow, Edward and James Kahn. *My Fifty Years in Baseball*. New York: Coward-McCann, 1951.

Bent, Silas. *Ballyhoo: The Voice of the Press*. New York: Horace Liveright, 1927.

Cutten, George Barton. *The Threat of Leisure*. New Haven, CT: Yale University Press, 1926.

Daniel, Dan, and Harry Salsinger. *The Real Babe Ruth*. St. Louis: C. C. Spink and Sons, 1948.

Durocher, Leo, with Ed Linn. *Nice Guys Finish Last*. Chicago: University of Chicago Press, 1975.

Farrell, James T. *My Baseball Diary*. New York: A.S. Barnes, 1957. Reprinted, with new foreword by Joseph Durso. Carbondale: South Illinois University Press, 1998.

Gallico, Paul. *Farewell to Sport*. New York: Knopf, 1938.

Gilbert, Brother, CFX. *Young Babe Ruth: His Early Life and Baseball Career from the Memoirs of a Xaverian Brother*. Edited by Harry Rothgerber. Jefferson, NC: McFarland Press, 1999.

Grange, Red, and Ira Morton. *The Red Grange Story*. Urbana: Illini Books, 1993.

Guernsey, van Riper, Jr. *Babe Ruth: Baseball Boy*. Indianapolis: Bobbs-Merrill, 1959.

Holtzman, Jerome, ed. *No Cheering in the Press Box*. New York: Henry Holt, 1995.

Hoyt, Waite. *Babe Ruth as I Knew Him*. New York: Dell, 1948.

Jackson, Reggie, and Kevin Baker. *Becoming Mr. October*. New York: Doubleday, 2013.

Kahn, Roger. *How the Weather Was*. New York: Harper and Row, 1973.

Kieran, John. *Not under Oath: Recollections and Reflections*. Boston: Houghton Mifflin, 1964.

———. "Sports of the Times." In *We Saw It Happen: The News behind the News That's Fit to Print*, edited by Hanson W. Baldwin and Shepard Stone, 233–60. New York: Simon and Schuster, 1938.

Lardner, Ring. "Lardner Has a Bright Idea." In *Yankees Century: 100 Years of New York Yankees Baseball*, edited by Glenn Stout and Richard Johnson, 115–36. Boston: Houghton-Mifflin, 2002.

———. *Selected Stories*. Edited by Jonathan Yardley. New York: Penguin, 1997.

Lee, Ivy. *The Press Today: How the News Reaches the Public*. New York: Ivy Lee, 1920.

Lieb, Fred. *Baseball as I Have Known It*. Lincoln: University of Nebraska Press, 1996.

Mack, Connie. *Connie Mack's Baseball Book*. New York: Knopf, 1950.

Maulsby, William. *Getting the News*. New York: Harcourt, Brace, 1925.

Meany, Tom. *Babe Ruth: The Big Moments of the Big Fellow*. New York: A. S. Barnes, 1947.

Murphy, Lawrence W., ed. *Sport Writing of Today and Selections from the Best Sport Stories*. Champaign, IL: Service Press, 1925.

Peters, Lulu Hunt. *Diet and Health, with Key to the Calories*. Chicago: Reilly and Lee, 1918.

Rice, Grantland. *The Tumult and the Shouting: My Life in Sport*. New York: A. S. Barnes, 1954.

Runyon, Damon. *Guys, Dolls, and Curveballs: Damon Runyon on Baseball*. Edited by Jim Reisler. New York: Carroll and Graf, 2005.

Ruth, Claire, and Bill Slocum. *The Babe and I*. Englewood, NJ: Prentice Hall, 1959.

Ruth, George H. (Babe). *Babe Ruth's Own Book of Baseball*. New York: G. P. Putnam and Sons, 1928.Reprint, Lincoln: University of Nebraska Press, 1992.

———. *The "Home-Run King," or, How Pep Pindar Won His Title*. New York: A. L. Burt, 1920.

Ruth, George H. (Babe), and Bob Considine. *The Babe Ruth Story*. New York: E. P. Dutton, 1948.

Spalding, Albert G. *America's National Game*. New York: America's Sports Publishing, 1911.

Sullivan, Dean, ed. *Middle Innings: A Documentary History of Baseball, 1900–1948*. Lincoln: University of Nebraska, 1998.

Walker, Stanley. *City Editor*. New York: Fredrick A. Stokes, 1934.

Walsh, Christy. *Adios to Ghosts!* New York: Published by the author, 1937.

SECONDARY SOURCES

Abrams, Roger. *The Dark Side of the Diamond: Gambling, Violence, Drugs, and Alcoholism in the National Pastime*. Burlingame, MA: Rounder Books, 2007.

Alexander, Charles. *Breaking the Slump: Baseball in the Depression Era*. New York: Columbia University Press, 2002.

———. *John McGraw*. Lincoln: University of Nebraska Press, 1995.

———. *Ty Cobb*. New York: Oxford University Press, 1984.

Allen, Maury. *Where Have You Gone, Joe DiMaggio? The Story of America's Last Hero*. New York: Dutton, 1975.

Best, Gary D. *The Dollar Decade: Mammon and the Machine in 1920s America*. Westport, CT: Praeger, 2003.

Bryson, Bill. *One Summer: America, 1927*. New York: Anchor Books, 2013.

Burk, Robert F. *Much More than a Game: Players, Owners, and American Baseball since 1921*. Chapel Hill: University of North Carolina Press, 2001.

———. *Never Just a Game: Players, Owners, and American Baseball to 1920*. Chapel Hill: University of North Carolina Press, 1994.

Campbell, Joseph. *The Hero with a Thousand Faces*. Cleveland, OH: Meridian, 1942.

Carroll, John M. *Red Grange and the Rise of Modern Football*. Urbana: University of Illinois Press, 1999.

Cassuto, Leonard, and Stephen Partridge, eds. *The Cambridge Companion to Baseball*. New York: Cambridge University Press, 2011.

Cook, William. *The Louisville Grays Scandal of 1877*. Jefferson, NC: McFarland, 2005.

Cramer, Richard Ben. *Joe DiMaggio: The Hero's Life*. New York: Touchstone, 2000.

Creamer, Robert. *Babe: The Legend Comes to Life*. New York: Simon and Shuster, 1974.

Crepeau, Richard. *Baseball: America's Diamond Mind, 1919–1941*. Lincoln: University of Nebraska Press, 2000.

Cross, Gary. "Origins of Modern Consumption: Advertising, New Goods, and a New Generation." In *The Routledge Companion to Advertising and Promotional Culture*, edited by Matthew McAllister and Emily West, 11–24. New York: Routledge, 2015.

Di Salvatore, Bryan. *A Clever Base-Ballist: The Life and Times of John Montgomery Ward*. Baltimore: Johns Hopkins University Press, 2001.

Drowne, Kathleen, and Patrick Huber. *The 1920s*. Westport, CT: Greenwood Press, 2004.

Dumenil, Lynn. *The Modern Temper: American Culture and Society in the 1920s*. New York: Hill and Wang, 1995.

Dyreson, Mark. "The Emergence of Consumer Culture and the Transformation of Physical Culture: American Sport in the 1920s," *Journal of Sport History* 16, no. 3 (1989): 405–14.

Eig, Jonathan. *Luckiest Man: The Life and Death of Lou Gehrig*. New York: Simon and Shuster, 2010.

Emery, Michael, Edwin Emery, and Nancy L. Roberts. *The Press and America: An Interpretive History of the Mass Media*. 9th ed. Boston: Allyn and Bacon, 2000.

Fass, Paula. *The Damned and the Beautiful: American Youth in the 1920s.* New York: Oxford, 1977.

Fitts, Robert K. *Banzai Babe Ruth: Baseball, Espionage, and Assassination during the 1934 Tour of Japan.* Lincoln: University of Nebraska Press, 2013.

Frommer, Harvey. *Five O'Clock Lightning: Babe Ruth, Lou Gehrig, and the Greatest Team in Baseball, the 1927 New York Yankees.* New York: John Wiley and Sons, 2008.

Ginsburg, Daniel E. *The Fix Is In: A History of Baseball Gambling and Game Fixing Scandals.* Jefferson, NC: McFarland Press, 2004.

Gorn, Eliott. "The Manassa Mauler and the Fighting Marine: An Interpretation of the Dempsey-Tunney Fights." *Journal of American Studies* 19, no. 1 (April 1985): 27–47.

Guttmann, Allen. *Sports: The First Five Millennia.* Amherst: University of Massachusetts Press, 2004.

Halberstam, David. *The Summer of '49.* New York: Avon, 1989.

Ham, Eldon. *Broadcasting Baseball: A History of the National Pastime on Radio and Television.* Jefferson, NC: McFarland Press, 2011.

Harper, William. *How You Played the Game: The Life of Grantland Rice.* Columbia: University of Missouri Press, 1999.

Haupert, Michael, and Kenneth Winter. "Pay Ball: Estimating Profitability of the New York Yankees, 1915–1937." *Essays in Economics and Business History* 21 (2003): 89–101.

Henderson, Amy. "Media and the Rise of the Celebrity Culture." *OAH Magazine of American History* 6 (Spring 1992): 49–54.

Holmes, Dan. *Ty Cobb: A Biography.* Westport, CT: Greenwood Press, 2004.

Humphreys, Lesley. "Diamond Mines: Players Organize the Major Leagues Exhibit at the National Baseball Hall of Fame." *Labor's Heritage* 10 (Fall 1998): 5–21.

Inabinett, Mark. *Grantland Rice and His Heroes: The Sportswriter as Mythmaker in the 1920s.* Knoxville: University of Tennessee Press, 1994.

Istorico, Ray. *Greatness in Waiting: An Illustrated History of the Early New York Yankees, 1903–1919.* Jefferson, NC: McFarland Press, 2008.

Jacoby, Sanford. *Modern Manors: Welfare Capitalism Since the New Deal.* Princeton, NJ: Princeton University Press, 1998.

Kasson, John. *Amusing the Million: Coney Island at the Turn of the Century.* New York: Macmillan, 1978.

Kessler-Harris, Alice. *Gendering Labor History.* Urbana: University of Illinois Press, 2007.

LaFeber, Walter. *Michael Jordan and the New Global Capitalism.* New York: W. W. Norton, 1999.

Lanctot, Neil. "A General Understanding: Organized Baseball and Black Professional Baseball, 1900–1930." In *Sport and the Color Line: Black Athletes and Race Relations in Twentieth Century America*, edited by Patrick B. Miller and David K. Wiggins, 63–82. New York: Routledge, 2004.

Leerhsen, Charles. *Ty Cobb: A Terrible Beauty.* New York: Simon and Shuster, 2015.

Lehane, Dennis. *The Given Day*. New York: William Morrow, 2008.

Leuchtenburg, William E. *The Perils of Prosperity, 1914–1932*. Chicago: University of Chicago Press, 1958.

Levitt, Daniel R. *The Battle That Forged Modern Baseball: The Federal League Challenge and Its Legacy*. Chicago: Ivan Dee, 2012.

———. *Ed Barrow: The Bulldog Who Built the Yankees' First Dynasty*. Lincoln: University of Nebraska Press, 2008.

Lewis, Jerry. *Sports Fan Violence in North America*. New York: Rowman and Littlefield, 2007.

Lynch, Michael T. *Harry Frazee, Ban Johnson, and the Feud That Nearly Destroyed the American League*. Jefferson, NC: McFarland Press, 2008.

Macht, Norman. *Connie Mack: The Turbulent and Triumphant Years, 1915–1931*. Lincoln: University of Nebraska Press, 2012.

Mahler, Jonathan. *Ladies and Gentlemen, the Bronx Is Burning: 1977, Baseball, Politics, and the Battle for the Soul of a City*. New York: Farrar, Straus, and Giroux, 2005.

Mann, Leon. "Sports Crowds and Collective Behavior Perspectives." In *Sports, Games, and Play: Social and Psychological Viewpoints*, edited by Jeffrey Goldstein, 299–332. New York: Erlbaum, 1989.

Marchand, Roland. *Advertising the American Dream: Making Way for Modernity, 1920–1940*. Berkeley: University of California Press, 1985.

McCoy, Alfred. *Beer of Broadway Fame: The Piel Family and Their Brooklyn Brewery*. Albany: State University of New York Press, 2016.

McGregor, Robert Kuhn. *A Calculus of Color: The Integration of Baseball's American League*. Jefferson, NC: McFarland Press, 2015.

Miller, Nathan. *New World Coming: The 1920s and the Making of Modern America*. New York: DeCapo Press, 2004.

Montgomery, David. *Workers' Control in America: Studies in the History of Work, Technology, and Labor Struggles*. New York: Cambridge University Press, 1979.

Montville, Leigh. *The Big Bam: The Life and Times of Babe Ruth*. New York: Doubleday, 2006.

Murdock, Eugene C. *Ban Johnson: Czar of Baseball*. Westport, CT: Greenwood Press, 1982.

Nash, Bruce, and Allan Zullo. *The Baseball Hall of Shame*. New York: Pocket Books, 1985.

Nasaw, David. *The Chief: The Life of William Randolph Hearst*. New York: Houghton Mifflin, 2000.

Nathan, Daniel. *Saying It's So: A Cultural History of the Black Sox Scandal*. Urbana: University of Illinois Press, 2003.

Patterson, Ted. "The Tenth Man: Baseball and Radio Broadcasting." In *Joy in Mudville: Essays on Baseball and American Life*, edited by John B. Wiseman, 78–93. Jefferson, NC: McFarland Press, 2010.

Pilat, Oliver. *Pegler: Angry Man of the Press*. Boston: Beacon Press, 1963.

Ponce de Leon, Charles. *Self-Exposure: Human-Interest Journalism and the Emergence of Celebrity in America, 1890–1940.* Chapel Hill: University of North Carolina Press, 2002.

Rader, Benjamin. *Baseball: A History of America's Game.* 3rd ed. Urbana: University of Illinois Press, 2008.

Roessner, Amber. *Inventing Baseball Heroes: Ty Cobb, Christy Mathewson, and the Sporting Press in America.* Baton Rouge: Louisiana State University Press, 2014.

Rossi, John P. *The National Game: Baseball and American Culture.* Chicago: Ivan R. Dee, 1999.

Rust, Art, Jr. *Recollections of a Baseball Junkie.* New York: Morrow, 1985.

Seymour, Harold. *Baseball: The Golden Age.* New York: Oxford University Press, 1971.

Shecter, Leonard. *The Jocks.* Indianapolis: Bobbs-Merrill, 1969.

Slayton, Robert. *Empire Statesman: The Rise and Redemption of Al Smith.* New York: Free Press, 2001.

Smelser, Marshall. *The Life That Ruth Built.* New York: New York Times Books, 1975.

Smelser, Neil. *Theory of Collective Behavior.* London: Taylor and Francis, 1962.

Snyder, Brad. *A Well-Paid Slave: Curt Flood's Fight for Free Agency in Professional Sports.* New York: Penguin, 2006.

Sobol, Ken. *Babe Ruth & the American Dream.* New York: Random House, 1974.

Stanton, Tom. *Ty and the Babe: Baseball's Fiercest Rivals.* New York: St. Martin's Press, 2007.

Steinberg, Steve, and Lyle Spatz. *The Colonel and Hug: The Partnership that Transformed the New York Yankees.* Lincoln: University of Nebraska Press, 2015.

Sternheimer, Karen. *Celebrity Culture and the American Dream: Stardom and Social Mobility.* New York: Routledge, 2014.

Streissguth, Thomas. *The Roaring Twenties.* New York: Facts on File, 2007.

Sullivan, Neil. *The Diamond in the Bronx: Yankee Stadium and the Politics of New York.* New York: Oxford University Press, 2001.

Surdam, David. *Wins, Losses, and Empty Seats: How Baseball Outlasted the Great Depression.* Lincoln: University of Nebraska Press, 2011.

Susman, Warren. *Culture as History: The Transformation of American Society in the Twentieth Century.* New York: Pantheon, 1984.

Thomas, Damion L. *Globetrotting: African-American Athletes and Cold War Politics.* Urbana: University of Illinois Press, 2013.

Tunis, John R. "The Great Myth." In *A Literature of Sports,* edited by Tom Dodge, 207–14. Lexington, MA: DC Heath, 1980.

Voigt, David. *America through Baseball.* New York: Rowman and Littlefield, 1976.

———. *American Baseball.* Vol. 2, *From the Commissioners to Continental Expansion.* University Park: Pennsylvania State University Press, 1983.

White. G. Edward. *Creating the National Pastime: Baseball Transforms Itself 1903–1953.* Princeton, NJ: Princeton University Press, 1996.

Wiebe, Robert. *The Search for Order: 1877–1920.* New York: Hill and Wang, 1967.

Wood, Allan. *Babe Ruth and the 1918 Red Sox*. Lincoln, NE: Writers Club Press, 2000.

Zieger, Robert, Timothy Minchin, and Gilbert Gall. *American Workers, American Unions: The Twentieth and Early Twenty-First Centuries*. 4th ed. Baltimore: Johns Hopkins University Press, 2014.

INDEX

Note: Page numbers in italics indicate photographs.